Judas Iscariot

Judas Iscariot

Betrayal, Blasphemy, and Idolatry in
the Gospels and Acts

Richard Harvey

WIPF & STOCK · Eugene, Oregon

JUDAS ISCARIOT
Betrayal, Blasphemy, and Idolatry in the Gospels and Acts

Copyright © 2018 Richard Harvey. All rights reserved. Except for brief quotations in critical publications or reviews, no part of this book may be reproduced in any manner without prior written permission from the publisher. Write: Permissions, Wipf and Stock Publishers, 199 W. 8th Ave., Suite 3, Eugene, OR 97401.

Wipf & Stock
An Imprint of Wipf and Stock Publishers
199 W. 8th Ave., Suite 3
Eugene, OR 97401

www.wipfandstock.com

PAPERBACK ISBN: 978-1-5326-3955-5
HARDCOVER ISBN: 978-1-5326-3956-2
EBOOK ISBN: 978-1-5326-3957-9

Manufactured in the U.S.A.

Scripture quotations marked (NIV) are taken from the Holy Bible, New International Version®, NIV®. Copyright © 1973, 1978, 1984 by Biblica, Inc.™ Used by permission of Zondervan. All rights reserved worldwide.

I would like to dedicate this book to my loving and supportive wife Libby and our children David and Cassie. Without their active support, this thesis would never have been completed.

I also owe a great debt of gratitude to my excellent supervisor, the Reverend Dr. Fergus King, who has been a model of humility and scholarship as I worked through my first full-length thesis. Without his wisdom and willingness to challenge my reasoning, I am convinced that this thesis would have been much less valuable. I am also grateful to A/Prof Marguerite Johnson and Dr. Alan Libert for their very helpful suggestions.

Contents

Abbreviations | xiii
Preface | xvii

Section 1—Introduction, problem statement, methodology | 1
1.1. Perspectives on Judas Iscariot | 1
1.2. The figure of Judas Iscariot in historical perspective | 2
    1.2.1. The New Testament | 2
    1.2.2. The Ante-Nicene Fathers | 3
        1.2.2.1. Fragments of Papias | 3
        1.2.2.2. Irenaeus of Lyons | 3
        1.2.2.3. Tertullian | 4
        1.2.2.4. The Constitutions of the Holy Apostles | 4
        1.2.2.5. Summary of the Fathers | 5
1.3. Modern approaches | 5
    1.3.1. Karl Barth (1888–1968) | 6
    1.3.2. Hyam Maccoby (1924–2004) | 7
    1.3.3. Gary Greenberg (1943–present) | 8
    1.3.4. William Klassen (1930–present) | 9
    1.3.5. Hans-Josef Klauck (1946–present) | 11
    1.3.6. Anthony Cane (1961–present) | 14
1.4. The statement of the problem | 18
1.5. Methodology | 19
1.6. Conclusion | 20

Section 2—Greek terminology | 21
2.1. Introduction | 21
Polysemy | 22
2.2. Παραδίδωμι | 23

2.2.1. Handing over in Secular Greek | 23
2.2.2. Handing over in Flavius Josephus | 25
2.2.3. Handing over in the LXX | 28
   God hands the nations over to Israel: Appendix 2 | 29
   God hands Israel over to the nations: Appendix 3 | 31
   Someone will not be handed over: Appendix 4 | 33
   God hands the nations over to other nations: Appendix 5 | 35
   Some/One of God's people handed over: Appendix 6 | 35
   Other: Appendix 7 | 36
2.2.4. Handing over in the GNT: Appendix 8 | 36
   God the subject, etc. | 37
   Handing over an inanimate object | 39
   Jesus handed over for trial (Matt 26–27; Mark 14–15; Luke 22–23) | 40
   Followers of Jesus and John the Baptist handed over | 41
   Disobedient Christians, demons, handed over | 42
Conclusion | 43
2.3. Ἑταῖρος | 44
   2.3.1. Introduction | 44
   2.3.2. Ἑταῖρος in the LXX: Samson | 46
      Samson, his wife, and his father-in-law | 46
      Samson and Israel | 48
      Samson and Delilah | 49
      Patterns in Samson's life | 50
   2.3.3. Jonadab/Amnon | 53
   2.3.4. The dynamics between Hushai, David, and Joab | 55
      Hushai | 55
      Joab | 57
   2.3.5. Ahithophel | 59
   2.3.6. Summary of the LXX | 60
   2.3.7. "Friend" in Josephus | 61
      Gaius Julius Eurycles of Sparta | 61
      Noarus | 62
      Flavius Josephus ben Mattathias | 62
2.4. Conclusion for Section 2 | 65

Section 3—Rivals to God | 67
3.1. Introduction | 67
3.2. Human rivals to God | 68
Introduction | 68
    3.2.1. The nature of an idol | 68
    3.2.2. Human rivals to God | 70
        Adam and Eve | 70
        The king and the prince of Tyre | 73
    3.2.3. The New Testament | 78
        Simon Magus | 79
        Herod Agrippa | 81
        The "man of lawlessness" | 83
    3.2.4. Conclusion | 84
3.3. Supernatural rivals to God | 85
    3.3.1. Introduction | 85
    3.3.2. The "Opening the Mouth" ritual | 86
    3.3.3. Εἴδωλον words | 90
        Usage in secular Greek | 90
        Usage in Josephus | 91
        Usage in the LXX | 91
        Usage in the GNT | 94
    3.3.4. Δαιμόν words | 96
        Usage in secular Greek | 96
        Usage in Josephus | 97
        Usage in the LXX | 98
        Usage in the GNT | 100
    3.3.5. Beelzebul texts | 102
        Beelzebul in Mark 3:20–30 | 102
        Beelzebul in Matthew 12:22–37 | 104
        Beelzebul in Luke 11:14–26 | 105
    3.3.6. Conclusion | 106
3.4. Satan | 107
    3.4.1. Introduction | 107
    3.4.2. The demonic in God's presence: presumption to divinity | 107
    3.4.3. The desire of evil to harm God's people | 113
    3.4.4. Powerlessness: Satan irrevocably cast out | 115
    3.4.5. God's final judgment of evil | 124
    3.4.6. Conclusion | 128

3.5. Money: the material rival to God | 129
    3.5.1. Introduction | 129
Wealth in the Bible | 130
    3.5.2. The named, righteous rich | 130
    The New Testament | 134
    3.5.3. Πλοῦτος, πλουτέω, πλουτίζω | 138
    The New Testament | 141
    3.5.4. Δουλεύειν | 145
    The New Testament | 147
3.6. Conclusion to Section 3 | 152

Introduction to Section 4 | 153
Section 4—Judas in New Testament Narratives | 155
4.1. Introduction | 155
4.2. Narratives with Judas's presence at key points in Jesus' ministry | 156
    4.2.1. The call of the Twelve (Mark 3:13–19; Matt 10:1–4; Luke 6:12–16) | 157
        Mark | 159
        Matthew | 160
        Luke | 161
    Conclusions | 163
    4.2.2. Jesus teaching the Twelve: Insider Status (Mark 4:10–33; Matt 13:10–23; Luke 8:9–15) | 164
        Mark | 164
        Matthew | 165
        Luke | 166
    Conclusion | 166
    4.2.3. Jesus sends the Twelve out (Mark 6:6b–13; Matt 10:5–10; Luke 9:1–6) | 167
    Conclusion | 169
    4.2.4. Feeding the five thousand (Mark 6:30–44; Matt 14:13–21; Luke 9:10–17) | 170
        Mark and Matthew | 170
        Luke | 173
    Conclusion | 173
    4.2.5. Who is the greatest? (Mark 9:33–37; Matt 18:1–6; Luke 9:46–48) | 174
        Mark | 174

Matthew | 175
Luke | 176
Conclusion | 177
4.2.6. The third prediction of Jesus' death (Mark 10:32–34; Matt 20:17–19; Luke 18:31–33) | 177
Mark | 177
Matthew | 178
Luke | 180
Conclusion | 181
4.2.7. Conclusion | 181
4.3. Judas in the Passion Narratives | 182
4.3.1. Introduction | 182
4.3.2. The plot to betray Jesus (Mark 14:1–2; Matt 26:3–5; Luke 22:1–6) | 182
Mark | 183
Matthew | 186
Luke | 190
Conclusion | 191
4.3.3. Jesus anointed at Bethany (Mark 14:3–9; Matt 26:6–13; Luke 7:36–50; John 12:1–8) | 191
Mark | 193
Matthew | 194
John | 194
Conclusion | 196
4.3.4. The Last Supper (Mark 14:12–26; Matt 26:17–30; Luke 22:7–23) | 197
Mark | 198
Matthew | 198
Luke | 200
4.3.5. Judas's betrayal of Jesus (Mark 14:43–50; Matt 26:47–56; Luke 22:47–53) | 202
Mark | 202
Matthew | 205
Luke | 206
Blasphemy | 207
Arrest/Trial | 208
4.4. Judas after the betrayal (Matt 27:1–10; Acts 1:15–26) | 211
Matthew | 211
Acts | 215

4.5. Conclusion | 215

Section 5—Summary of Findings | 218
5.1. Παραδίδωμι and ἑταῖρος | 218
5.2. Rivals to God | 220
5.3. The identity of Judas Iscariot | 224
    5.3.1. A created being acting like God | 225
        5.3.1.1 Mîs-pî | 225
    5.3.2. Indwelt by evil | 228
        5.3.2.1. Parallels between Satan and Judas | 228
            The demonic in God's immediate presence | 228
            Tension toward God | 229
            Crisis and irrevocable casting out | 230
            God's punishment of Judas | 230
    5.3.3. Paid with money | 231
5.4. The Synoptic Gospels | 232
    5.4.1. Events during Jesus' ministry | 232
    5.4.2. Events in the week prior to Jesus' death | 234
    5.4.3. Events after the betrayal | 236
5.5. Conclusion | 237

Appendices | 239
Bibliography | 297
Author Index | 331
Index of Major Passages | 337

Abbreviations

A. General Abbreviations

CD	*Church Dogmatics*
GNT	Greek New Testament
LXX	Septuagint
MT	Masoretic text
NT	New Testament
OT	Old Testament
Q	Quelle ("Sayings" source in the Gospels)
UBS	The United Bible Societies' Greek Text

B. Abbreviations for Books of the Bible

OLD TESTAMENT

Gen	2 Kgs
Exod	1 Chr
Lev	2 Chr
Num	Ezra
Deut	Neh
Josh	Esth
Judg	Job
Ruth	Ps (Pss)
1 Sam	Prov
2 Sam	Eccl
1 Kgs	Song

Isa
Jer
Old Testament (*continued*)
Lam
Ezek
Dan
Hos
Joel
Amos

Obad
Jonah
Mic
Nah
Hab
Zeph
Hag
Zech
Mal

NEW TESTAMENT

Matt
Mark
Luke
John
Acts
Rom
1 Cor
2 Cor
Gal
Eph
Phil
Col
1 Thess
2 Thess

1 Tim
2 Tim
Titus
Phlm
Heb
Jas
1 Pet
2 Pet
1 John
2 John
3 John
Jude
Rev

C. Abbreviations of the Names of Pseudepigraphical and Early Patristic Books

Bib. Ant.	Ps.-Philo, Biblical Antiquities
Pss. Sol.	Psalms of Solomon
Adv. Haer.	Irenaeus, Against All Heresies
Adv. Marc.	Tertullian, Against Marcion

D. Abbreviations of Classical Literature

Jos.	Josephus
Ag. Ap.	Against Apion
Ant.	Jewish Antiquities
J. W.	*The Jewish Wars*
Life	*The Life of Josephus*
Xen.	Xenophon
Cyro.	Cyropedia
Mem.	Memorabilia
HG	*Historia Graeca*

E. Abbreviations of Orders and Tractates in Mishnaic and Related Literature

Sanh.	Sanhedrin

Preface

IN RECENT TIMES, SOME commentators from within mainstream Christianity such as Karl Barth, Hans-Josef Klauck, and William Klassen have attempted unsuccessfully to defend or exonerate Judas Iscariot. This thesis will assess the evidence for Judas's betrayal of Jesus. It has three main original contributions to knowledge.

Firstly, a thorough analysis of παραδίδωμι, the verb used for Judas's act of handing over Jesus, will show that it is consistent with betrayal, it is overwhelmingly a divine act, and it is normally coercive. Similarly, Matt's use of ἑταῖρος is a master stroke, continuing the pattern from the LXX and Josephus, where a previously close friend betrays. These two terms alone suffice to establish Judas's guilt.

Secondly, Judas is not only a traitor, as he uniquely encapsulates the three main rivals to God: human, demonic, and material. Like other human rivals to God, he is powerless, linked with evil, and directly judged by God. Satan enabling Judas to betray Jesus (Luke 22:3; John 13:2) shows Judas's betrayal in the worst light, but there is a deeper parallel. Both are named rebels, allowed to remain in God's presence until irrevocably cast out. The third rival is money: 'You cannot serve both God and money.' (Matt 6: 24; Luke 16: 13). Judas was paid to perform the divine like function of handing someone over to death. Although human, he displayed the essential features of an idol.

Mark's stark portrayal of Judas's guilt is only enhanced by Matthew and Luke. If Mark 3 casts Judas as an outsider, Luke 6 calls him προδότης. If Mark 14 links Judas with the chief priests in plotting against Jesus, Matt 23 inserts three παρουσία parables to show presumed disciples of Jesus being exposed in increasingly severe terms. Finally, Judas's disrespectful 'Rabbi' to Jesus in Gethsemane (Mark 14: 45), when he knew Jesus was so much more reflects the oral element of blasphemy in 1st CE Judaism. Abrogating to himself the divine privilege of handing over may fairly be called blasphemy by action.

In conclusion, there is sufficient evidence to show that Judas is a traitor and a blasphemer who has all the essential literary features of an idol. The electronic form of this thesis uses SBLHebrew and SBLGreek. Quotations in English are taken from the NIV, unless otherwise indicated. SBL abbreviations are used.

Section 1

Introduction, problem statement, methodology

1.1. Perspectives on Judas Iscariot

FOR MOST OF CHRISTIAN history, Judas has been seen as the consummate traitor who betrayed his Lord, the Son of God, to death. Few people are more reviled or so closely linked with betrayal. The names of few, if any, historical figures remain a term of deep abuse. Australian Federal Defence Minister Joel Fitzgibbon resigned on June 3, 2009, accusing "two or three Judases" of disloyalty.[1] Ex-Honduran President Manuel Zelaya referred to his opponents as Judases who kissed and betrayed him.[2]

We could assume that Judas has been universally condemned since his death. Until the late twentieth century, commentators in mainstream Christianity broadly condemned him, sometimes leading to anti-Semitism, while some commentators from other religions urged a more sympathetic view. This commenced with the Gnostic *Gospel of Judas*, to which Irenaeus referred in 180 CE.[3] In the twentieth century, the prior commitments of Karl Barth, William Klassen, Hans-Josef Klauck, and Anthony Cane from within Christianity, and the Jewish authors Hyam Maccoby and Gary Greenberg, precluded an objective examination of Judas. Works like the *Arabic Infancy Gospel*, Dante's *Divine Comedy*, *The Golden Legend* and the works by Timayenis, Monro, and Leloup can all be eliminated from serious discussion. They either diverge markedly from the gospel accounts or are so focused on one aspect that they lack balance. These texts are not meant to be exhaustive—only to illustrate general trends.

1. Snow and Pearlman, "Fitzgibbon," 4.
2. Australian Broadcasting Corporation 702 Radio News, July 5, 2009.
3. Irenaeus, "Against Heresies," 1.31.1; Maritz, "Testimony," 300.

1.2. The figure of Judas Iscariot in historical perspective

1.2.1. The New Testament

After praying all night (Luke 6:12), Jesus called twelve disciples, the apostles (Matt 10:2; Mark 3:14; Luke 6:13), by name to be with him and to preach (Mark 3:14), to heal and deliver (Matt 10:1; Mark 3:15). The order of names is largely uniform. They are in three groups of four, headed by Simon, Philip, and James, the son of Alphaeus. Identifying Thaddaeus and Judas the son of James is plausible.[4] Judas Iscariot is always last, and called he who "betrayed (or handed over) him (i.e. Jesus)/became a traitor."[5] The gospels show Judas associated negatively with money at Bethany (Matt 26:8; Mark 14:4; John 12:6).[6] Judas is the only one identified as complaining about the anointing, and Jesus answers similarly each time.

All the gospels say that Judas agreed to hand Jesus over to the temple authorities. Matthew 26:14 and Mark 14:10 have Judas taking the initiative, while Luke 22:3 and John 13:2 say Satan prompted him. They do not describe his motive, but their accounts all involve money (Matt 26:15; Mark 14:11; Luke 22:5). All agree that Jesus spoke of being handed over at the Last Supper (Matt 26:21; Mark 14:18; Luke 22:21; John 13:21). Luke 22:22 records Jesus' woe on the traitor. John 13:30 notes that Judas left the meal to finalize the deed, whereas the Synoptics imply it. All agree that Judas led the crowd which arrested Jesus (Matt 26:47; Mark 14:43; Luke 22:47; John 18:3).

Finally, Judas died ignominiously. Jesus reportedly said that Judas, the son of perdition, was the only apostle lost, and that fulfilled Scripture (John 17:2). Judas was remorseful, threw the money into the temple, and hanged himself. The chief priests used the money to buy the potter's field for gentile burials (Matt 27:3–7). Acts 1:18 states that Judas fell headlong in this field, his intestines spilled out, and he died. These accounts differ markedly, but both show an ignominious end. The infant church elected Matthias to replace Judas (Acts 1:16). It is hardly surprising that the early church condemned Judas.

---

4. Bauckham, *Eyewitnesses*, 108.

5. Maritz, "Judas Iscariot," 304.

6. See Section 4.3.3 (this form will be used henceforth). Luke 7:36–50 is arguably another incident.

1.2.2. The Ante-Nicene Fathers

1.2.2.1. Fragments of Papias

Fragment II explicitly calls Judas a traitor. Fragment III notes that Judas's body was so swollen that he could not pass where a chariot could. Judas's eyes could not see light, his body was covered with running sores, and he died in a lonely place, the stench still evident.[7] These fragments luridly embellish the gospels.[8]

1.2.2.2. Irenaeus of Lyons

Irenaeus[9] succeeded the martyred Pothinus as Bishop of Lyons in 177 CE. His few references accept Judas's treachery unquestionably: "the apostasy of Judas,"[10] "Judas the traitor,"[11] the Gospel of Judas being "fictitious history," and "the treachery of Judas."[12] Irenaeus's enthusiasm for opposing heresy sometimes overwhelms his work, but he never calls Judas anything positive. Secondly, in his eyes, there was little worse than Gnosticism, which linked Jesus, as the human part of Christ the twelfth eon, to the apostasy of the twelfth apostle Judas and Jesus' suffering in the twelfth month.[13] He asked how Judas, "the betrayer of Jesus," can be a type of the suffering twelfth eon, when it is clearly Jesus who suffered.[14] Judas "accomplished the mystery of the betrayal" and is linked with the Cainites in understanding secret knowledge.[15]

---

7. Kleist, *Didache*, 117, 119.

8. Papias, "Fragments of Papias," http://www.ccel.org/ccel/schaff/anf01.vii.ii.html.

9. He used logic and aesthetics to derive four principles of divine intellect (God, the source of all good, embraced all things), economy (salvation is discerned through Jesus), recapitulation (change is the norm for God and everything finds meaning in Jesus), and participation (God became human that we might become like God). He attacked the Gnosticism of Valentinus, who argued that the primal Bythos brought forth thirty eons in fifteen male-female pairs, called "syzygies," the most commonly cited pair being Jesus and Sophia (Osborn, *Tertullian*, 18–22, 265–70).

10. Irenaeus, "Against Heresies," 1.3.3; Rousseau and Doutreleau, *Irénée de Lyon*, 120.

11. Irenaeus, "Against Heresies," 2.20.4; Rousseau and Doutreleau, *Irénée de Lyon*, 207.

12. Irenaeus, "Against Heresies," 1.31.1; 2.20.2; Rousseau and Doutreleau, *Irénée de Lyon*, 201.

13. Irenaeus, "Against Heresies," 1.3.3; Rousseau and Doutreleau, *Irénée de Lyon*, 120.

14. Irenaeus, "Against Heresies," 2.20.2; Rousseau and Doutreleau, *Irénée de Lyon*, 203.

15. Irenaeus, "Against Heresies," 1.31.1; Irenaeus, "Against Heresies," http://www.ccel.org/ccel/schaff/anf01.ix.ii.html.

1.2.2.3. Tertullian

Tertullian's few references are telling. He rebukes Marcion for despising Yahweh's judgmental nature while wanting God to be just, an impossible contradiction.[16] Marcion overreaches when arguing that, had Yahweh foreknown Judas's treachery, he would not have chosen him, as this implied that Yahweh did not foreknow Judas's treachery, which is impossible for an all-knowing God. In 4.41, Tertullian cites Marcion's argument that such ignorance proves Yahweh's evil/inferior nature, but Tertullian notes the contradiction: it is Jesus, the son of (as Marcion admits) the good Heavenly Father, who chose Judas. Tertullian disputes Marcion's description of Yahweh's evil powers bringing Christ to the cross, as this denies the plain meaning of Scripture.[17] An evil Yahweh would have rewarded Judas for handing Jesus over. He further argues at 4.40 that Jesus might have been betrayed by a stranger but how then could Scripture be fulfilled? There was no need to betray him who "offered Himself to the people openly" and could easily have been captured.

Allowing for some overly enthusiastic expression, Tertullian has a uniformly severe view of Judas as "the traitor" (2.28), who committed "treachery" (3.23), and upon whom Christ's woe was justly pronounced (4.41). Moreover, Tertullian argues that only Marcion's evil demiurge would consider rewarding Judas (3.23). Given the thrust of "Against Marcion," it is hard to imagine a more damning case.[18]

1.2.2.4. The Constitutions of the Holy Apostles

The *Constitutions* link Simon Magus, who received "the seal of the Lord," with Judas, "one of us," in sin, and met death at God's hand.[19] Book Five recounts the Last Supper, arguing that it was Jesus' comment that it would have been better if Judas had not been born (the "birth woe") which

---

16. Marcion, *Adversus Marcionem*, 2.28.2. He said that the creator, Yahweh, was an evil demiurge, but that above him was a good and more powerful Father in Jesus. He founded a church which was a serious rival to the Catholic Church (whose streams of theology were recognized as valid and canonical at councils such as Nicea) into the third century. Marcion's arguments demanded a detailed response, which Tertullian did, as he expounded his central idea of the economy of salvation in Christ.

17. Marcion, *Adversus Marcionem*, 3.24.

18. Tertullian, "Five Books Against Marcion," http://www.ccel.org/ccel/schaff/anf03.v.iv.i.html.

19. "*Le sceau du Seigneur*" and "*qui était des nôtres*" (Metzger, *Constitutions*, 1:175).

INTRODUCTION, PROBLEM STATEMENT, METHODOLOGY   5

prompted him to go to the high priests.[20] Judas's "*baiser perfide*" is the proof of his treason.[21] Book Seven links Judas, and especially his theft, with that of Achan and of Ananias and Sapphira, who were killed for theft, and with Gehazi, whom God struck with leprosy.[22]

1.2.2.5. Summary of the Fathers

The *Fathers* is unanimous concerning Judas's treachery. He is either called a traitor or likened to some of the most heinous individuals in the Bible who professed some form of commitment to Jesus, such as Ananias and Sapphira and Simon Magus (Acts 5, 8). Irenaeus and Tertullian link him with heresies they are opposing—Gnosticism and Marcionism. His guilt is never diminished and his death is always understood as God's just punishment. While Papias embellishes, and Irenaeus and Tertullian use extravagant language, the core of their narratives reflects the gospels. Similar parallels could also be cited from Ignatius, Tatian, Clement, and Origen. None of the proto-orthodox suggested that Judas was anything other than a traitor.[23]

1.3. Modern approaches[24]

While many modern scholars view Judas as a traitor, some do not. I have chosen four scholars who attempt to exonerate Judas from within Christianity (Barth, Klassen, Klauck, and Cane) and two who write from within Judaism (Maccoby and Greenberg). They illustrate a modern trend where scholars, as opposed to more popular writers, attempt to highlight new perspectives on Judas.

---

20. Ibid., 2:251.
21. Ibid., 2:251.
22. Ibid., 3:31; Donaldson, "Constitutions of the Holy Apostles," http://www.ccel.org/ccel/schaff/anf07.ix.html.
23. Roberts and Donaldson, "Ante-Nicene Fathers," http://www.ccel.org/ccel/schaff/anf01.i.html.
24. While I referred to the *Golden Legend* (above), I will not use any other medieval or mystical texts, as their usefulness is (severely) limited by their anti-Semitism and composite nature. Paffenroth (*Images*, 17–57) has many examples of medieval anti-Semitic depictions of Judas as avaricious and generally evil.

1.3.1. Karl Barth (1888–1968)

If election is Barth's great contribution to theology,[25] then his Jesus Christ as "Electing and Elected" is perhaps his most original. Jesus as "elected man" is understood only in the light of his being simultaneously the "electing God."[26] Any divine decision included the Logos, who would then be bound as the incarnate Jesus.[27] This avoided speculation concerning a Logos who existed in and for himself alone before any decision for redemption, so that the incarnation added something new to his being and his death diminished his deity.[28] The identity of the immanent and economic Trinity is vital when discussing his view of Judas.

Judas is the test case of whether anyone is predestined to hell, as the loss of one so close to Jesus is a failure by God.[29] While conceding that we cannot know Judas's final state, Barth describes the relationship between Jesus and Judas as "the overwhelming power of grace and the weakness of human wickedness,"[30] so his betrayal does not finally undo his election. But he seems not to have applied consistently his belief in the Electing Jesus, for it is precisely this Jesus whom Judas betrayed. Judas's election sounds less like an act of a gracious Lord than an immutable decree, an idea which Barth was keen to criticize in Calvin.[31] This may show God's patience, but disregards Judas's free will.

Barth was accused of anti-Semitism when arguing that Judas represents Judaism in its rejection of Yahweh.[32] Yet he affirms that Christ became incarnate for all,[33] making this harder to understand. The idea that "[Judas] obviously represents the Jews,"[34] though argued by Maccoby and Greenberg, is unsupported. No NT text connects the similar names of Judas and Judah as representing Judaism.[35] It is difficult to convict Barth of anti-Semitism.[36]

---

25. McCormack, "Grace," 92.
26. *CD* II.1:99; II.2:109.
27. McCormack, "Grace," 94.
28. Ibid., 97–98.
29. *CD* II.2:475–76.
30. Ibid., 476–77.
31. McCormack, "Grace," 97.
32. *CD* II.2:464–65.
33. Gunton, "Salvation," 143.
34. *CD* II.2:464–65.
35. Maccoby, *Myth*, 28.

36. Was Barth anti-Semitic? Lindsay notes some unhelpful comments near the end of Barth's life, the difficulty in reading *CD* and his lack of genuine encounters with Jews (*Israel*, 19–24, 26). In Barth's defence, he noted his deep and mutual interaction with

Rather, his unfortunate comments show defects in his attempt to balance God's grace and human sin. God elected Israel, but a problem arose when Israel rejected the very same God.[37] He drops his opposition to universal salvation in a "final ... expansion of the circle of election."[38] While God elected that Jesus would die for all, people must still respond.

1.3.2. Hyam Maccoby (1924–2004)

Hyam Maccoby believes that, while the story of Judas is "almost entirely fictional," his betrayal coheres with the communal Jewish rejection of Jesus, and so Judas is used to justify anti-Semitism). The key weakness is, as he admits, that such a communal dimension is absent from the NT.[39]

Maccoby's argument rests on the unproven link between the name of Judas and the Jewish people. His apparent unfamiliarity with the Eucharist means that he argues that John 6 is a "denial of [its] efficacy," as Judas comes from Jesus' inner circle.[40] Asides like the "amazing co-operation between Jesus and Satan" in designating Judas at the Last Supper, defy belief.[41] Maccoby is so (rightly) insistent upon countering anti-Semitism that he proposes an extraordinary conspiracy, wherein the church vilified a good disciple in order to sustain a schism within the emerging church. Neither does he ask whether this demands a historical Judas, nor how this coheres with his "entirely fictional" approach. He fails to address two key points: the historical accuracy of a split between Paul and the Jerusalem church (Galatians 2 notwithstanding) and, even if that could be sustained, why Paul never mentions Judas in detailing any such split.

Jewish professors at Marburg, his sheltering of Jewish refugees, his public denunciation of anti-Semitism at Wipkingen, and his deep involvement in resistance efforts for the Jews, especially those in Hungary, before concluding that a couple of unfortunate comments should be seen against a lifetime of support for Jews, which exposed him to serious danger (Lindsay, *Israel*, 15, 27–29, 31–32, 33–35). Rabbi Taubes had no hesitation in approaching Barth for help (*Israel*, 34). We may conclude that he was not anti-Semitic.

37. Hunsinger, "Christology," 137. A similar situation existed between Jesus and Judas (s4.3.4).

38. *CD* II.2:417; Gockel, *Barth*, 188.

39. Maccoby, *Myth*, 2, 5, 28. So also Zwiep, "Judas and the Jews," 79.

40. Maccoby, *Myth*, 65.

41. Ibid., 73.

1.3.3. Gary Greenberg (1943–present)

Greenberg argued that the NT accounts of Judas are "historically implausible."[42] This approach permeates *The Judas Brief: Who Really Killed Jesus?*, where very little in the gospels happened the way they are narrated. Greenberg's use of secondary material is a real strength, but he fails to note his own findings on Pilate. He argues that Judas negotiated with the chief priests for Jesus to be arrested before Passover in order to prevent riots, but that Herod demanded Pilate execute him for claiming to be King of the Jews.[43] Post-Easter, tension between Jesus' disciples and other Jews led the evangelists to invent texts like Lazarus's raising and to malign the hitherto-respected and benevolent Judas.[44] The evangelists adapted their sources to decrease Pilate's culpability, but to increase that of the Jews. He adds to The Jesus Seminar's criteria, that the least hostile text is probably the earliest, failing to recognize that tensions between Jesus' followers and other sectarians likely emerged within his lifetime, not only after the first Easter (Mark 3:6).[45]

Greenberg's sources show Pilate's "cruelty, corruption," and love of extra-judicial executions.[46] He argued that Pilate would not have given in to a Jewish crowd, but fails to understand two things which he did fear: a riot or being reported unfavorably to Rome. These did sway Pilate (Matt 27:24; Mark 15:15; Luke 23:2; John 19:12). He could not afford another military standards affair, when thousands of Jews preferred death to the dishonoring of Jerusalem, or another Golden Shields affair, when Tiberius severely rebuked him.[47] Having misunderstood Pilate, Greenberg compounds his error with an argument which amounts to guilt by association when suggesting that, if the evangelists could not portray Pilate correctly, neither could they do so with Judas.[48]

---

42. Greenberg, *Myth*, 187.
43. Ibid., 187.
44. Ibid., 187, 147.
45. A brief but useful critique of the Seminar agrees with NT Wright, that Crossan's *Historical Jesus* (1991), which reduced Jesus to an illiterate "peasant Jewish Cynic" (421–22), is almost wholly wrong (Casey, *Jesus*, 18–21). Members voted on the authenticity of gospel texts, excluding any passage which was not attested twice, regardless of how well it fitted the context. Mark 1:16–38 was excluded, but the Gospel of Thomas was felt to have a higher proportion of original material than Mark (ibid., 19, 21).
46. Greenberg, *Myth*, 13.
47. Ibid., 94–100.
48. Ibid., 131.

Greenberg sees Judas as a trusted disciple, as he was treasurer.⁴⁹ He might have been more just if he was concerned for the poor, and Jesus only concerned about his looming funeral.⁵⁰ Judas's rebuke of Jesus was an occasion for the evangelists to blacken his name, and so John's charge that Judas was a thief can be dismissed.⁵¹ Despite his attempted source analysis, Greenberg's thesis is supposition with the gospels being little more than fabrication. Also, he is inconsistent in accepting what the gospels detail concerning Pilate, but not Judas. He does not explicate key terms like παραδίδωμι, and too readily accepts the connotations of Judas as treasurer.⁵² Jesus may have appointed Judas as treasurer to test him whom he foreknew would betray him. Greenberg's worst failure is not recognizing how vulnerable Pilate felt to the crowd's implied threat to report him to Rome.

1.3.4. William Klassen (1930–present)

William Klassen argues that Judas could not have betrayed Jesus, as παραδίδωμι is not translated "betray" in classical Greek, the LXX, or Josephus. Consequently, it cannot mean "betray" in the NT. Rather, προδοσία usually means "treachery." He cites Xenophon on Cyrus: "the garrisons . . . with . . . the terror inspired by Cyrus, were persuaded to surrender."⁵³ An object may be handed over (under coercion): "to receive his sword when he surrenders it."⁵⁴ He believes that betrayal is inappropriate for people handing over themselves or their weapons, but fails to note that each use of παραδίδωμι involves coercion. The NT narrative preserves this element which, with a person as the object of the verb, is an inalienable part of classical usage.

---

49. Ibid., 266.
50. Ibid., 147. Alternatively, the honor/shame culture of the time abhorred the lack of proper burial. Burial of the dead was a "universal duty," particularly by children for their parents (Allison, *Resurrecting*, 169–72). Jesus' comments about the dead burying their own dead and hating their father/mother (Luke 9:59–60; 14:26) are his way of saying that following him superseded all other duties (ibid., 170). Allison's discussion of 14:26 was complicated unnecessarily by omitting discussion of Jesus' climactic demand "even his own life," which shows that this is not just about superseding the Fourth Commandment.
51. Greenberg, *Myth*, 140.
52. Ibid., 132.
53. Klassen, *Betrayer or Friend*, 47–48; Cyro 5.4.51; Dindorfius, *Institutio*, 185.
54. Cyro 5.1.28; Dindorfius, *Institutio*, 185.

He argues that Josephus uses παραδίδωμι 293 times, but betrayal does not fit the contexts; rather, he uses προδίδωμι or προδοσία.[55] However, it is inconceivable that the "will of God" (*Ant.* 2.20), an office (*Ant.* 2.89), or a free self-offering (*Ant.* 2.137) could ever be "betrayed."[56] Nor does he engage with Josephus's use of προδότης at Yodefat, asserting rather than proving that Luke 6:16 provides no parallel.[57] Klassen does not examine this text which must call his thesis into question. He argues without support that "Luke deviates from his source by calling Judas the προδότης,"[58] surely a court of last appeal. He argues that no LXX example can be translated "betray," but he does not address all the data.[59] The verb occurs 194 times, with God usually the subject (Appendix 1). Sometimes, an object is handed over—e.g., land (Deut 1:8). Most uses show God's judicial wrath, when handing over the nations to Israel, as a penalty for sin, or the reverse (Num 21:3; Judg 6:1). Handing over is overwhelmingly a divine act, normally only in response to continual, unrepented sin. There are some exceptions—e.g., God hands over kingdoms to people (Dan 4:17).

Klassen argues that, as παραδίδωμι is not translated "betray" in classical Greek, the LXX, or Josephus, then it cannot be in the NT.[60] This lacks a clear logic, for it is difficult to argue that, say, ἀπόστολος should only be translated according to pre-NT usage. Secondly, the difficulties are compounded by his reliance on the work of others, and so his failure to note that God is mostly the subject of παραδίδωμι in the LXX (Appendix 1). For such a critical word, this is a serious omission. It is not just that παραδίδωμι is not translated "betray" in these cases, but rather that it could never be translated "betray." To whom would God betray anyone? He does not distinguish between voluntary and involuntary (coercive) handings-over, whether the object of the verb is personal or impersonal, or whether the act of handing over is for judgment or blessing.

There are frequent instances where Klassen has failed properly to evidence his claims. He asserts that Judas did "what Jesus asked him to do," yet provides no evidence.[61] He believes that Jesus could have escaped arrest, but ignores his agony in Gethsemane (Matt 26:39, 42) and his insistence that

---

55. Klassen, *Friend*, 49.
56. Ibid., 81, 86, 90.
57. Ibid., 116; s2.2.2.
58. Ibid., 117.
59. Ibid., 49.
60. Ibid., 47–49.
61. Ibid., 45. John 13:27 (uncited by Klassen) is a possibility, although this is better understood as Jesus bringing matters to a head, sensing that Judas will not repent.

INTRODUCTION, PROBLEM STATEMENT, METHODOLOGY   11

this is exactly what he would not do (Matt 26:53). He claims that the evangelists did not believe that "Judas did nothing until Jesus told him," and felt the need to "ascribe dark motives" to Judas.[62] This may be derived from John 13:27, but is absent from Matthew 26:14/Mark 14:9, where Jesus' anointing at Bethany seems to prompt Judas. Luke ascribes Judas's motivation to Satan (Luke 22:3). Saying that Jesus did not criticize Judas or imply that the impending betrayal was sinful is odd, given Jesus' "birth woe" on Judas (Matt 26:24; Mark 14:21).[63] Jesus did foreknow the betrayal (John 6:71), and highlighted this fact at the Last Supper in particularly solemn words. Ultimately, Jesus respected Judas's free will. Klassen has ignored the lexical fields which frequently give words their nuance, but his work nonetheless demands a reconsideration of the lexical evidence.

1.3.5. Hans-Josef Klauck (1946–present)

Klauck's *Judas, un disciple de Jésus: Exégèse et repercussions historiques* (2006) translates an earlier German work.[64] Disappointingly, it lacks the evidence to justify that "a rehabilitation of Judas is imperative."[65] Firstly, he argues that the data implicating Judas "only corresponds to a relatively narrow textual base."[66] Next, Judas "is not a demoniacal monster . . . but . . . is mistaken." Moreover, God has placed over the act of Judas "a veil of mystery which we cannot and do not wish to remove."[67] Lastly, "it will [only] be possible to render justice to Judas" when we have seen "our own traits" in Judas, as "we have transferred onto Judas . . . our desires of murder, our greed and our religious doubts."[68] The Judas texts are mainly a mirror to reflect ourselves rather than anything historical.

He divides the data into categories: "the personification of evil," "a figure symbolic of subversion," "representing the desire to assert oneself," "an innocent instrument," "a product of formation by legend," "a projection of the unconscious," and "a function of narrative structure."[69] Klauck's argument lacks a critical edge. He is rightly concerned not "to apply . . . to the

---

62. Ibid., 45.
63. Ibid., 45.
64. The work that he translated was *Judas—ein Jünger des Herrn*. It is unavailable in English. My translation is in the text.
65. Klauck, *Disciple*, 165.
66. Ibid., 12.
67. Ibid., 165.
68. Ibid., 165.
69. Ibid., 13, 16, 18, 21, 24, 26, 28.

Jewish people the . . . negative traits of Judas," yet even Maccoby notes that the NT never makes this connection.[70] Klauck argues that he is a joker who introduces "an aspect of contingency and uncertainty in which the narrative can unfold with a merciless necessity."[71] He does not explain how uncertainty coheres with necessity.

Klauck tries to argue that "the group of the 12 was only formed after Easter, as a response to the appearances of the risen one,"[72] and that another disciple who was not part of the Twelve betrayed Jesus. Judas's "treason" was "to leave the group of the 12 after Easter," at which point his name was "retro-projected" back onto the name of the actual traitor.[73] He provides no evidence whatsoever for this singular thesis.

Secondly, he argues that the relationship of παραδίδωμι with treason is "only . . . very marginal."[74] It is remiss not to study its pre-NT meaning, with its common thread of coercion (see section 2). He cites Barth approvingly: "Judas accomplished precisely what God wanted."[75] This is hard to reconcile with Jesus' clear anguish at the Last Supper, when pronouncing the "birth woe" (Luke 14:21). If Judas is "the particular agent . . . according to the design of God" and "*l'executor Novi Testamenti*," why the "birth woe"?[76] Arguing that Judas accomplished God's will, but not as God intended, does not recognize that Jesus rejected precisely this temptation from Satan (Matt 4; Luke 4).[77] For all his concerns about a simplistic good/bad dichotomy, no one says anything positive about Judas.

Any treachery in a relationship is problematic, which he admits in "the distance which separated them."[78] While recognizing that it is "tentative" to "absolve Judas of all fault," he believes that we can understand Judas's act as "something . . . historically understandable and plausible."[79] He reasons that Judas's act is between "divine election and the free decision of the human will."[80] But it is Judas's use of his free will that makes his act so heinous.

---

70. Ibid., 14; Maccoby, *Myth*, 28.

71. Klauck, *Disciple*, 28.

72. Ibid., 30. It is reasonable to see the Twelve existing during Jesus' lifetime (Meier, "Twelve," 671).

73. Ibid., 32.

74. Ibid., 45.

75. Ibid., 47.

76. Ibid., 47. *Particulier* in French means "special" or "distinctive," and highlights Judas's uniqueness.

77. Ibid., 47–48.

78. Ibid., 94.

79. Ibid., 165, 168.

80. Ibid., 168.

INTRODUCTION, PROBLEM STATEMENT, METHODOLOGY   13

Scripture foresaw the betrayal, but Jesus' anguish at the Last Supper shows that he did not want Judas to hand him over. It is difficult to imagine a more damning indictment than the "birth woe" (Mark 14:21).

Thirdly, "To consider avarice and greed as determining factors . . . blackens . . . Judas."[81] Rather, he was motivated by "messianic expectations."[82] While the NT never discusses his motivation, he is often associated with money and greed. Klauck rightly wants to disassociate anti-Semitism from connotations of greed, but cannot disprove the NT's association of Judas and greed. Contra Klauck, Judas does not appear simply mistaken, but mercenary.[83] If his only motivation was God's will, why accept the money offered or ask for it?

Fourthly, he says that the function of Judas's kiss "is not easy to determine," being "a legendary amplification of a more ancient report."[84] Judas's role in Jesus' arrest "is not possible to define" exactly.[85] There is nothing unclear about leading the arrest party (John 18:3). He does not help his case by using two OT examples of guilt: Joab and Esau.[86] Esau is not recorded as kissing anyone, and Joab's treachery will be considered in s2.3.4.

Lastly, Klauck notes the differences between Matthew and Luke on Judas's death. He says "If it is a historical fact," implying that Judas may not have died and may have "return[ed] to his own country, to live faithfully according to the traditions of his people."[87] Both Matthew (27:8, "why it has been called") and Luke (Acts 1:19, "Everyone in Jerusalem heard") report popular views about Judas's death, which need not agree.[88] Both describe an awful death: Matthew by suicide and Luke apparently by a sovereign act of God. Concluding that both are wrong when they agree on the awful nature of Judas's death requires more evidence than conflicting accounts. It is hard to see Luke implying God's sovereign slaying of someone who, according to Klauck, was simply mistaken.[89]

Klauck's points fail both individually and collectively. Judas was not caught in a deep contradiction or mistaken, but did what not even God

---

81. Ibid., 56.
82. Ibid., 164.
83. Ibid., 165.
84. Ibid., 68, 70.
85. Ibid., 71.
86. Ibid., 69–71.
87. Ibid., 137.
88. Zwiep, "Matthias," 108.
89. Ibid., 165.

did in handing over an innocent person (Matt 27:4).⁹⁰ Given Jesus' clear anguish at the Last Supper, it is difficult to acknowledge the degrees of guilt which Klauck allows, where he seeks not a pardon, but a plausible explanation.⁹¹ We cannot ascertain Judas's motivation, but this does not entitle him to an acquittal without compelling evidence. The motives of many Biblical characters are not explored in detail, but that does not entitle them to an acquittal. While some interpretations of Judas's actions have produced unfortunate results, this requires better exegesis, not arguing that "a rehabilitation of Judas is imperative."⁹² It is highly unusual, given Klauck's concern for sober exegesis, that his longest citation is from the *Golden Legend*.⁹³

1.3.6. Anthony Cane (1961–present)

Cane's *The Place of Judas Iscariot in Christology* argues that we should see Judas in "the tension between providence and tragedy."⁹⁴ He uses Barth to illustrate the allegedly providential role of Judas in salvation where "all things are directed and ordered by God."⁹⁵ In contrast, Cane uses MacKinnon's approach to tragedy: "those . . . intractable aspects of existence which expose the inadequacies of human ratiocination."⁹⁶ MacKinnon argues that attempts to resolve the Judas narrative show more of our need for answers than of the nature of reality.⁹⁷

Cane's handling of the Greek lacks rigor. He claims that παραδίδωμι is more neutral than the treacherous προδίδωμι, yet "'handing over' could be acceptable if done with due cause and proper authority," but he does not show this.⁹⁸ He then addresses fulfillment. How could Jesus go "as it is written," and yet it would have been better if Judas "had not been born" (Matt 26:20–25)? Moreover, is the loss of Judas a failure by Jesus? He concludes that, as the NT moves from Mark to John,⁹⁹ the portrayal of Judas becomes

---

90. Ibid., 176, 165. See s2.2.
91. Ibid., 168.
92. Ibid., 165.
93. Ibid., 160–62.
94. Cane, *Place*, 2.
95. Ibid., 5.
96. MacKinnon, *Borderlands*, 20.
97. Cane, *Place*, 6. More detailed arguments against Cane's position will appear in a future article.
98. Ibid., 17–19, 22.
99. This raises a number of questions about the relative datings and intertextuality of the gospel accounts, which he does not raise, let alone address. See s4.1.

more negative. Judas may have been chosen to fulfill a particular role, but once that has been completed, he disappears.[100] Based on Markan priority, I will show in s4 that Mark establishes Judas's guilt early on. His guilt is then not a later invention by the church.

Secondly, Cane argues that the loss of Judas is a defeat for Jesus, in whose company he spent three years, and he questions the effectiveness of Judas's (alleged) participation in the institution of communion and the footwashing.[101] He finds Jesus guilty as charged, and sees this as a necessary limitation of the incarnation.[102] This is odd, as Luke 6:12 states that Jesus spent all night praying to God and then called the Twelve. A better way to see if this is a result of the incarnation[103] is to ask if there is an OT parallel. Evil had continued access to God's presence—YHWH in the OT and Jesus in the NT (ss3.4; 5.3). The "heavenly assembly" included, for at least some time, beings in rebellion against/not submitted to God. As the same pattern happened in both the OT and the NT, it is not a limitation of the incarnation, but something inherent in God's nature. Therefore, Cane's argument must be assessed as problematic.

Thirdly, Cane asks if Judas repented by studying the word μεταμέλομαι. This is an odd choice, as μετάνοια would seem more appropriate. Cane disputes whether Judas is overcome by despair, but believes that "Judas is so repentant that he . . . hangs himself."[104] He notes Jesus' woe in Matthew 26:24 and the unfavorable comparison with Peter,[105] who wept bitterly after denying Jesus (Matt 26:75).[106] Lastly, for someone concerned with exploring tragedy, his solution is surprising. He argues that "it is Judas rather than Jesus who is truly lost . . . he is . . . necessary to the salvific death of Christ . . . and yet only finds condemnation."[107] Judas's role was unnecessary. Given the antipathy between the temple authorities and Jesus, he only had to walk alone into the temple to be arrested.[108] He had already stated his willingness to obey the Father in dying; e.g., Matthew 26:39, 42.

---

100. Ibid., 55.
101. Ibid., 89.
102. Ibid., 185.
103. And not say that Judas is a particularly poignant example of John 6:66.
104. Ibid., 48.
105. So also Oropeza, *Footsteps*, 1:75.
106. Cane, *Place*, 48–49.
107. Ibid., 155.
108. This obviates any need for Judas to hand Jesus over and hence any concern like Oropeza, *Footsteps*, 1:184 that Jesus could use Judas for such purposes fully knowing the perdition which awaited Judas.

Finally, he explores the descent into hell, but ignores the complexities of 1 Peter 3:18–19.[109] He argues that "if the saving power of Christ can extend even to the dead Judas,"[110] then all is resolved. Cane agrees with Nathanael Emmons, that God had the salvation of everyone else in mind when "effecting the eternal perdition of Judas."[111] Balthasar argues that Judas's fate must be seen against "the whole economy of salvation."[112] Although a follower of Christ, he is more akin to Judaism. Balthasar wants to avoid scapegoating the Jews, Judas, etc., and his solution is that God sent Jesus to save hell, not condemn it.[113] Cane simply follows Balthasar's reading of 1 Peter 3, ignoring the wider debate over the best meaning of the text.[114] Michaels argues that Jesus is announcing his victory to imprisoned, unclean spirits; Grudem that God preached through Noah to those who did not repent, later died, and are now in hell; and Kelly that he proclaimed defeat to the fallen angels.[115] There is no hint that Jesus was preaching to convert anyone. Cane's case is stated rather than argued.

Cane is heavily reliant on secondary literature, and does not display evidence of having considered key terms in the primary material. He fails to note the consistent element of coercion in παραδίδωμι in secular Greek, the LXX, and the GNT. Such a term allows evangelists to link together the various steps necessary for Jesus to be crucified, but allows Jesus to assign differing degrees of guilt to those involved (s4.3.5), something which Cane has not considered. The same criticism can be leveled at his analysis of Judas's alleged repentance and Christ's descent into hell.[116] He does not adequately critique his two poles of providence and tragedy. He fails to note that, despite Barth's concerns about anti-Semitism, even the Jewish scholar Maccoby notes that the NT never links Judas's name with Judaism.[117] Barth's singular view that Judas is indispensable for salvation is not supported by the NT or by common logic. If Judas was so indispensable, why did Jesus speak the "birth woe" (Mark 14:21)? Jesus did not need Judas's help to be

---

109. There are a number of NT passages on this theme (King, "Dead," 5, 7–10).
110. Cane, *Place*, 156.
111. Ibid., 156.
112. Ibid., 170.
113. Ibid., 176.
114. Carson, *1 Peter*, 1043.
115. Michaels, *1 Peter*, 3:18–19; Grudem, *1 Peter*, 203–39; Kelly, *Epistles*, 156.
116. Cane, *Place*, 155.
117. Maccoby, *Myth*, 28.

arrested himself.¹¹⁸ This undercuts MacKinnon's view that Judas is crucial to salvation, and so that his fate is ultimately God's responsibility.

Cane's belief that Judas is a defeat for Jesus due to an inherent limitation of the incarnation must be assessed as wrong on the basis of the clear, and even more telling, parallel of a sinful Satan's access to the heavenly council in the OT (s3.4.2).

The *Arabic Infancy Gospel*, Dante's *Divine Comedy*, *Jesus of Montreal*, *The Golden Legend* and the works of Timayenis, Leloup, and Monro are unworthy of serious study. They are obviously later texts driven by ideological concerns, and so of questionable reliability. The consciously theological treatments of Barth, Maccoby, Greenberg, Klassen, Klauck, and Cane deal with the original Greek and attempt some theological discussion. However, they are unconvincing due to prior theological commitments, such as Maccoby's and Greenberg's noteworthy desire to combat the anti-Semitism supposedly flowing from the link between Judas's name and Judaism. All else is subsumed under this desire. It is a red herring without scholarly support,

---

118. An allied point is whether Jesus had to die on the cross. To say that this was unnecessary ignores crucial data. First, Matt 26:54 argues that, otherwise, the Scriptures could not be fulfilled. To argue that necessity can be based in Scripture but not God's nature (Brondos, *Paul*, 54) severs the link between God's nature and its representation in Scripture. Second, arguing that God is not subject to any necessity, including his own nature, and could have forgiven however he chose, ignores the facts that God and his nature are not separate, and that in both testaments, his chosen method of forgiveness meant sacrifice (ibid., 30, 193).

Brondos's main argument is that Jesus' death is not the means of forgiveness by penal substitution, but as the culmination of his work to establish a new people of God (ibid., 50, 111). But Brondos has not shown that it cannot be understood as penal substitution. He has glossed over the idea of ransom (Mark 10:44–45) by arguing (correctly) that this does not imply that a price would be paid to someone, but failing to enquire in any sustained way why the evangelist would use such a graphic word (ibid., 43). Brondos argues that "no cost was involved for God" (ibid., 145) but this ignores the constant refrain that the Exodus, the OT salvation event, was accomplished by "God's mighty hand and outstretched arm" (Deut 5:15, etc.). Salvation involved a great cost to God: it was not just paid to anyone. Brondos disputes that forgiving sin required Jesus' death, arguing that Heb 9:22 is making an observation about purification under the old covenant (ibid., 54). It is not clear, however, that "without the shedding of blood there is no forgiveness" is limited to the OT, as this would presumably require a past tense. Finally, Brondos argues that forgiveness was facilitated by the prayer for repentance which accompanied the sacrifice, rather than the sacrifice itself (ibid., 130). The problem here is that the OT focuses on the mechanics of the sacrifice, and not on any accompanying prayer, and the closest that Brondos can get to this in the NT is to say that Jesus' death is "in effect" a prayer that God might forgive (ibid., 130). This is hardly convincing.

In essence, Brondos has separated God from his nature, and has not seen the consistent theme through the Bible that forgiveness and sacrifice are linked, but (not unnaturally) come to their sharpest focus in Jesus. He has not given due weight to momentous words like ransom. His thesis is unproven.

which must not intrude into a full examination of Judas. Maccoby has not shown that the early church split Judas into a good and bad Judas to safeguard its ministry to the poor. Greenberg does not grasp the import of his well-proven claim that even a tyrant like Pilate was vulnerable in two areas known to the crowd: the fear of another riot, and of being reported again to Rome.

Klassen's attempt to exonerate Judas is based on a misunderstanding. He believes that παραδίδωμι does not mean "betray" prior to the NT, but fails to note (due to heavy reliance on secondary data) that it always includes coercion. He does not address instances in the LXX and Josephus where παραδίδωμι not only can but must mean "betray." Klassen so focuses on Judas's innocence that he ignores data like Jesus' devastating "birth woe" (Mark 14:21). Barth uses Judas as the test case for his understanding of election. Barth so emphasizes the strength of God's grace that it is almost irresistible. He is then caught on the horns of a dilemma: is Judas saved because grace is strong and human sinfulness weak, or is he lost because he has handed over the Electing Jesus Christ? Barth claims that we cannot know, whereas more detailed consideration of cases like Eli (1 Sam 2) should have led him to conclude that God's election can be undone by serious, unrepented sin. Klauck fails to produce anything like enough evidence to merit Judas's rehabilitation. He repeats the errors of others by failing to research παραδίδωμι adequately. Lastly, Cane fails to show that Judas is somewhere between providence and tragedy by opting for providence where the risen Christ allegedly preaches salvation to the dead, including Judas. There is no single error which has led the writers to their various conclusions, but they frequently fail to work out the implications of their theories through all relevant texts.

1.4. The statement of the problem

It is apparent that attempts to exonerate Judas have hitherto failed for a number of reasons. Rather than approaching the text with this aim, a new direction may be appropriate. The main original contribution to knowledge of this thesis will be to examine whether Judas, although a human being, functions like an idol. Without prejudging the issue, there is prima facie evidence that this idea is worth pursuing. Idols are not just objects of stone or wood, but "the visible manifestations of the powers that oppose Yahweh" and his people.[119] This is primarily a Lukan feature, but echoes may be found in the other gospels. In the LXX, handing over is almost entirely God's pre-

---

119. Pao, *Acts*, 182.

rogative (Appendix 1). For Judas to hand over Jesus is therefore like a claim to divinity. He is empowered by Satan, the main demonic opponent to God and rewarded with money, which becomes in the NT for the first time, the main material rival to God ("You cannot serve both God and Mammon." Matt 6:24; Luke 16:13).[120] This thesis will examine the links between idolatry, evil and money. Judas thus potentially encapsulates within himself the three main types of opponents to God: human, demonic and material.

Crucial to this approach will be David Pao's, *Acts and the Isaianic New Exodus* (2000), which argued that Isaiah appropriated the Exodus traditions and reworked them to show the exiles as the true heirs of the Exodus, not those in Judea. Pao believes that Luke has reworked Second Isaiah in the light of Christ to argue that the church, not the synagogue, is Israel's true successor. The main themes in Isaiah 40:1–11 (the prologue to Isaiah 40–55) and Luke/Acts are the restoration of Israel, the power of the word of God, the anti-idol polemic (the most relevant theme) and the status of the Gentiles. Idols are not just stone or wood but "the visible manifestations of the powers that oppose Yahweh" and his people.[121] God's supremacy is shown over the nations, their rulers and deities but especially their idols.[122] Unlike Acts, there are no idols apparent in Luke and an area of investigation will be whether Judas, a human being, functions as Pao's missing idol. Other gospels and NT books will be studied to see if the same basic idea is present in them.

1.5. Methodology

This thesis will highlight polysemy, wherein a word has multiple meanings. To assume that παραδίδωμι, for example, has only one essential meaning so that its objects can be compared without further ado, will be shown to be hazardous. I will use semantic domains where words are "grouped into families" of similar usage.[123] Louw and Nida define semantic domains as consisting of shared features common to all elements in a set of lexical items with distinctive features differentiating the various meanings within that set and supplementary features which are relevant in certain contexts.[124] Their treatment of παραδίδωμι would have been considerably improved if they

---

120. ἕτερος shows the distinction between the two masters (Sandiyagu, "ΕΤΕΡΟΣ," 118).
121. Pao, *Acts*, 182.
122. Ibid., 181.
123. Grundmann, "μέγας," ix.
124. Louw and Nida, *Lexicon*, vi.

had noted that, when a person is the object of the verb, there is always coercion, but when an inanimate thing is the object, it is handed over for further use by the recipient.[125] Nonetheless, their lexicon is a valuable exposition of semantic domains.

1.6. Conclusion

Section 2 will investigate παραδίδωμι and ἑταῖρος. Considering both terms in their various lexical fields from secular sources, Flavius Josephus, the LXX, and the GNT, I attempt to show that individually and in combination they are consistent with betrayal.

Section 3 will address the main original contribution to knowledge of this thesis: to investigate whether Judas functions as an idol. I will examine the three types of rivals to God—human, demonic, and material, which coalesce in idolatry. I will again use secular sources, Flavius Josephus, the LXX, and the GNT. My aim is to investigate how closely Judas is linked with each of these rivals to God.

Section 4 will exegete narratives, largely from the Synoptics, where Judas can be shown to be present, either by name or as one of the Twelve. He will be shown as present at key points in Jesus' earthly ministry, but apparently did not take his teaching to heart. My conclusion in Section 5 will draw together the philological work on παραδίδωμι and ἑταῖρος, the work from the central section on the three main types of opponents to God, and finally the exegetical work, to determine if Judas can be legitimately described as both traitor and idol.

---

125. Ibid., 485.

Section 2

Greek terminology

2.1. Introduction

ALL COMMENTATORS HAVE NOTED the importance of παραδίδωμι, the verb for Judas handing Jesus to the Jewish authorities (Matt 26:25; Mark 14:44; Luke 22:48; John 18:5). Klassen studied its meaning in classical Greek via Liddell and Scott, as well as in the LXX, Josephus, and the GNT. He noted the different meanings of "hand over," "deliver," and "betray" before concluding, "This widespread variation in usage . . . underscores that we commit an error to translate . . . as 'betray.'"[1] This odd argument implies that, because we need not translate παραδίδωμι as betray, or the unjustified breach of an existing relationship for other than legal reasons, before the NT, then we must not in the NT. This is illogical: no one would argue that ἀπόστολος or ἀγάπη should only be translated according to pre-NT usage. Moreover, arguments from silence are always difficult, especially as Klassen did not acknowledge the element of coercion where people are the object of παραδίδωμι—e.g., Quintus Oppius.[2] Greenberg argued similarly that while "betray" is an appropriate secondary meaning, there is no clear reason why it is translated "betray" for Judas but nowhere else.[3] Greenberg is wrong, as there are instances where "betray" is the best translation (see below). Following Klassen, Greenberg argued that, originally, Judas handing over Jesus "was not considered . . . negative," but that, as his actions were seen "in a darker light," for reasons which are unexplained, the word took on "negative connotations."[4] Whilst possible, neither provide any evidence.

1. Klassen, *Friend*, 47.
2. Ibid., 48.
3. Greenberg, *Brief*, 132–33.
4. Klassen, *Friend*, 53; Greenberg, *Brief*, 134. Section 4 will show that Mark has

Polysemy

A key problem in Section 1 was that exegetes did not exercise sufficient care in working with παραδίδωμι by recognizing polysemy, where a word has at least two different related meanings.[5] For example, "let" may mean a prohibition "without let or hindrance" or permission "Let them eat cake."[6]

A second problem was first discussed over fifty years ago by James Barr, who argued that, while a dictionary offers substitutes for words,[7] Kittel's *Theological Dictionary of the New Testament* offered essays on related theological ideas. Barr wondered if a dictionary was the right place for this.[8] He suggested sorting "the words in groups, each representing a related semantic field."[9] Following Barr, Silva has critiqued other linguists who believe that studying relevant terminology completes their research.[10] Silva recommends studying how the GNT has adapted Greek words from the LXX and secular sources.[11] Most words have a stable semantic core, otherwise communication would be impossible, and studying synonyms can help establish the small areas of difference, which can provide nuances.[12]

The key in determining meaning is context which, depending on where one sits on the spectrum, either guides or virtually dictates meaning.[13] That this is not infallible is shown in his exegesis of Matthew 25:1–13, the parable of the bridesmaids, where he argues that oil means "good works." He cites the references to obedience (23:3; 25:45) and "the love of most will grow cold" (24:12) as a response to severe persecution, as supporting details.[14] It is not immediately clear how these ideas are linked. Silva has not considered

---

the harshest view of the disciples and this is ameliorated in Matt and Luke. There is no warrant for Klassen's or Greenberg's comments.

5. Leech, *Semantics*, 227; Goddard, *Analysis*, 18. A "strict demarcation" between the semantic weight of the word being defined and other words is "required to complete the meaning of the word group" (Roberts, "Review of BDAG," 58).

6. This is distinguished from homonymy, where two or more words share the same pronunciation and/or spelling, like "fare" and "fair" (Leech, *Semantics*, 237).

7. A formal equivalent or a gloss, where one word in English substitutes for a corresponding Greek word, differs from a (typically longer) definition (Roberts, "Review of BDAG," 54). Such substitutes "fully delimit . . . the word's semantic character" (Johnson, "Electronic Resources," 78).

8. Barr, *Language*, 233.

9. Ibid., 235.

10. Silva, *Meaning*, 22.

11. Ibid., 75.

12. Ibid., 103, 121.

13. Ibid., 137, 139.

14. Ibid., 156.

the documentary context of Matthew's use of Mark (s4.3.2), where the three παρουσία parables in Matthew 25 arguably show a serious breakdown in the relationship between would-be disciples and their Lord. The oil supports the picture of Jesus as the bridegroom by referring to the custom of the bridesmaids lighting the path of the groom to the brides' house. It is not just that the foolish bridesmaids have not done some good works, but that their lack of concern for the bridegroom shows that they never had an appropriate relationship with him, hence his "I don't know you" (Matt 25:12). Despite this, emphasizing the importance of context is sound.

While research cannot just be limited to a discussion of key terms, neither can it ignore them. No serious study of Judas should ignore παραδίδωμι or ἑταῖρος, but their meaning can only be understood by collecting examples into groups of similar meaning in appropriate linguistic and documentary contexts, and then attempting to interpret them. Provided this is done carefully and without the insuperable prior commitments which bedevilled many of the authors in Section 1, valid and useful results should emerge.

Secular Greek, Josephus, the LXX, and the GNT show that παραδίδωμι exhibits polysemy with only four distinct meanings (henceforth called such):[15]

1. the handing over of an object;
2. a self-offering;
3. the unjust handing over of a person; and
4. the handing over of a person under authority.

2.2. Παραδίδωμι

2.2.1. Handing over in Secular Greek

I will only study a small sample of the vast amount of data. Liddell and Scott give a number of meanings for παραδίδωμι.[16] Secular Greek has examples which contribute to the first meaning, the entrusting of inanimate objects

---

15. A great amount of work is necessary for valid results; for example, collecting examples into groups of similar meaning (Lee, *Lexicography*, 21–24). Lee argues that the 1988 publication of Louw and Nida's *Lexicon* was as significant as anything since 1514 as their adoption of semantic domains allowed discrimination between synonyms (ibid., 155). Lee criticizes them for things like definitions not being exact substitutions, not noticing changes in meaning in the NT compared with prior usages, and finding more synonyms than is warranted (ibid., 160–63). However, their basic structure of semantic domains, as "rules of thumb" rather than hard and fast categories, will form the basis of sections 2.2–3, to capture the nuances of παραδίδωμι and ἑταῖρος.

16. Liddell and Scott, *Lexicon*, 1308.

into someone's care. Demosthenes, at the trial of Charidemus before the Areopagus, said that he could tell many stories about it, some of which had been passed on to him.[17] An example from Herodotus has both the handing over of an object and coercion. Cimon, the father of the tenth Athenian general at Marathon, Miltiades,[18] won an Olympic chariot race, and repeated this victory in the next games, but gave the trophy to the tyrant Peisistratos, who then allowed him to return from exile.[19]

The second meaning is a self-offering. I can find no examples of this in secular Greek using παραδίδωμι.

The third meaning is an unjust act of handing over. Herodotus wrote that Astyages, the last king of the Medes, dreamt that his daughter had given birth to a new king, Cyrus. He told a general, Harpagus, to kill the child, who instead gave the boy to a herdsman whose wife had had a still birth.[20] He also noted that King Cyaxares gave some boys to the Scythians to learn their language, archery, etc.[21]

Herodotus records that the Persians emptied the city of Samos (with the infamous "sweeping the net") and gave it to Syloson.[22] Syloson had given a flame-colored cloak to Darius, then just a guardsman to Cambyses. On Darius's accession, Syloson had moved for recompense and was given Samos.[23] The citizens of Samos had no say in the matter.

The last meaning is where someone is handed over to justice. Andocides was charged with profaning the Mysteries, and was handed over for trial by Speusippus, a member of the Council. Andocides's elaborate arguments in defence show the seriousness of the charge.[24] Xenophon records the extraordinary aftermath of the Athenian naval victory at Arginusae in

17. Demosthenes, "Orations," http://www.perseus.tufts.edu/hopper/morph?l=paradedome%2Fna&la=greek&can=paradedome%2Fnao&prior=kala\&d=Perseus:text:1999.01.0073:speech=23:section=65&i=1.

18. Herodotus, *Historiae*, 6.103; Tritle, "Warfare," 209–23.

19. Neer, "Delphi," 231; Dewald, "Humour," 145–64; Herodotus, *Greek History*, 359, especially "παραδιδοῖ."

20. Herodotus, *Historiae*, 1.117. This shares certain themes with the story of Jesus and Judas in De Voragine, *Golden Legend*, http://www.fordham.edu/halsall/basis/goldenlegend/index.htm. Astyages's butchering, roasting, and serving the son to an unknowing Harpagus only accentuates the coercion involved in the word "παραδίδωμι."

21. Herodotus, *Historiae*, 1.73, especially "παρέδωκε." Cyaxares may have felt forced to act like this as the Scythian invasion forced him to stop besieging Nineveh and come to terms with the invaders (Vaggione, "Scythian," 523–30).

22. Herodotus, *Historiae*, 3.149; Asheri et al., *Herodotus*, 522, especially "παρέδοσαν."

23. van der Veen, "Syloson," 129–45; Baragwanath, *Motivation*, 121.

24. Jebb, *Orators*, 31–36; Calhoun, "Jurisprudence," 154–71, especially "παραδίδωσιν."

406 BC. Slaves were made citizens, but six victorious generals were handed over for trial for not picking up the shipwrecked and the dead.[25] The gravity of the charges shows coercion, in that none of the defendants agreed to trial.

These stories show a clear pattern when people are the object of παραδίδωμι: they have no choice.[26] When something is the object of the verb, it is entrusted by someone with the right to do so into someone else's care. Demosthenes seemed to take seriously the responsibility of safeguarding the various stories about the Council as a most significant Athenian institution and passing them on in turn. This element of entrusting differentiates the handing over of an object from that of a person. An object is handed over for further use by the recipient, but a person is handed over for trial.

While "hand over" would normally be appropriate, there are three cases where "betrayal," the unjustified breach of an existing relationship, is better in context. Astyages's plot to kill his rightful heir and grandson betrayed that relationship and his duty as monarch to uphold the law and ensure the succession.[27] Darius's sacking of Samos for a tiny debt betrayed the ideals of kingship. Antiope's handing over of Themiscyra for the love of an opposing general seems treacherous. The enormity of each case would justify a use of "betrayal," contra Klassen.[28] The trial and execution of the six victorious generals of Argusinae would be treacherous only if they were innocent.

2.2.2. Handing over in Flavius Josephus

Josephus's usage does not mesh precisely with these categories. His contribution to the first meaning, handing over an object, is seen in Gabinius committing (παραδοὺς) the care of the temple to John Hyrcanus.[29] He entrusted an object, the heart of the Jewish people and religion, to someone who was then responsible.

---

25. *HG* 1.7.3; Xenophon, *Opera Omnia*; Hunt, "Arginusae," 359–80; Van Wees, *Greek Warfare*, 234, especially "παραδοθῆναι."

26. I cannot find any examples of παραδίδωμι where the person has some say.

27. An earlier dream of Astyages had his daughter Mandane's urination flooding all Asia. A second dream clarifies the rather enigmatic first dream (urine symbolizes childbirth in Assyrian sources; Asheri et al., *Herodotus*, 157), to show that the child would reign in place of, and not succeed, Astyages. The urinary/genital thought is comparatively rare in Greek literature, according to Pelling, and suggests a darker interpretation than simple news of an heir ("Astyages," 71).

28. Klassen, *Friend*, 48.

29. Josephus *J.W.* 1:169; the Gabinius who had received the fortresses from Alexander, so Thoma, "Priesthood," 201.

His contribution to the second meaning, a self-offering, is seen in the handing over (παραδιδούς) of objects like fortresses and of the people of Hyrcanum, Machaerus, and Alexandrinium by Alexander, son of Salome Alexandra,[30] to Gabinius,[31] because they could no longer withstand the siege.[32] Similarly, those in Jerusalem handed themselves over (παρέδοσαν) to Pompey after a siege of three months.[33]

The third meaning is seen below in Josephus (*J.W.* 4.521–23) about Simon, son of Gioras. His contribution to the fourth meaning is seen in handing over under authority. A person may hand people over because they have authority over them, as when Caesar committed (παραδούς) two legions to Aristobulus and sent them to Syria.[34] People may be handed over for trial, as when Caesar sent (παραδοθῆναι) the Samaritan Celer bound to Jerusalem for torment and execution for provoking the Jews.[35] The procurator Cumanus had arrested Jews without justification and (bribed by Samaritans like his tribune Celer)[36] had not punished the Samaritan murderer of a Galilean sufficiently quickly, leaving Jerusalem in uproar.[37] Caesar exercised legal authority to punish the three main Samaritan offenders.[38] None of those handed over had any say.

Klassen claims that Josephus uses παραδίδωμι 293 times, "but not once can one legitimately translate it ... 'betray.'"[39] This is overstated. In many cases, it is not that παραδίδωμι was not translated "betray," but that it could never have been translated "betray." An inanimate object being handed to its own people to be cared for, the temple, was not "betrayed." The handing over of legions is simply a use of military authority. But a person being handed over normally has no choice in the matter. There are, however, a number of cases where betrayal is highly probable given the context.

Josephus has three cases, which include betrayal. Παραδίδωμι and προδίδωμι (usually meaning "betray") can refer to the same incident, showing that, to Josephus, they were not wholly distinct. In *J.W.* 4.521, Josephus

---

30. Sievers, "Women," 140.
31. Bellemore, "Josephus," 94–118.
32. Josephus, *J.W.* 1:167.
33. Josephus, *J.W.* 5:397; Titus reminded the inhabitants of Jerusalem of this in AD 66 (Seward, *Masada*, 226).
34. Josephus, *J.W.* 1:183.
35. Josephus, *J.W.* 2:246; Seward, *Masada*, 24.
36. Schwartz, *Judean Politics*, 82.
37. Loftus, "Revolts," 78–98.
38. Josephus, *J.W.* 2:246.
39. Klassen, *Friend*, 49.

used προδοσία, and παραδίδωμι for the same event in *J. W.* 4.523.⁴⁰ Just after Nero's death, Simon son of Gioras in Gerasa tried to subdue Idumea before attacking Jerusalem.⁴¹ However, an Idumean leader, Jacob, offered to betray (προδοσία) Idumea to Simon. He persuaded the Idumean commanders to give (παραδίδωμι) government to Simon. Then, Jacob invited Simon to invade Idumea.⁴² Josephus uses παραδίδωμι, but Jacob's actions (for personal gain) are treacherous.

In *Ant.* 5:131, both terms occur in the same paragraph about the same incident. The Ephraimites were besieging Bethel and caught an inhabitant. They promised that if he gave up the city, then they would spare him and his family. Josephus says that he was asked to "deliver up (παραδόντι) the city," and also that he "betrayed (προδοὺς) the city." In the context of siege and bargain, it would be appropriate to translate παραδόντι as "betray"; indeed, it is difficult to argue otherwise.⁴³

Secondly, Josephus used παραδίδωμι four times where the context implies betrayal. In *Ant.* 5:299, Josephus used παραδίδωμι, but the context implies betrayal, as Samson was delivered into the hands of his enemies by his supposed friends (Judg 15:11).⁴⁴ Coercion is shown by the Israelites bringing three thousand armed men to arrest Samson. Josephus highlights Samson's strength by arguing that his name means "strong," contrasting Samson's noble nature with that of the Israelites (*Ant.* 298).

In *Ant.* 6:277 and 280, the men of Ziph offer (παραδώσειν) David to Saul (1 Sam 23:19), not for justice but for a reward. The enormity of this offer was only heightened by Josephus's description of how David had just escaped from a similar fate in Keilah, and that David was falsely accused and unjustly sought after.

In *Ant.* 13.4, apostate Jews delivered up (παρέδοσαν) their former friends to Bacchides, Antiochus Epiphanes's friend. The enormity of this

---

40. Josephus, *New Complete Works*, 833.

41. Simon was a notoriously brutal man (Bartlett, *Jews*, 137). Matthias ben Boethus had opened the gates of Jerusalem to Simon, who repaid this by later executing Matthias and three of his four sons for sympathizing with Rome (Josephus, *J. W.* 4.574–75; 5.527–31; Schwartz, *Judean Politics*, 73). The fourth had fled to Titus (*J. W.* 5.530), so giving this some credence (Schwartz, *Judean Politics*, 80).

42. Seward, *Masada*, 139–40.

43. After this treachery, the Israelites neglected their duties to God (Schwartz, *Judean Politics*, 179).

44. Moore, *Judges*, 344. The Danite Samson had no claim to protection in Judah (ibid., 344). The text highlights the coercion of a crowd which came to arrest a man who had already decided to surrender (Soggin, *Judges*, 249–50). This is somewhat like Gethsemane. Also, rather than siding with the one who might have led them against the Philistines, they "disappear in silence" (ibid., 250). I will address Samson in s2.3.2.

is emphasized in *Ant* 13:17, 38–40, where Josephus records Bacchides imprisoning as hostages the sons of the chief men of Judea,[45] and rewarding whoever apostasized from Judaism. Jonathan had allied himself with Trypho, who feared him. He persuaded Jonathan not to fight, but to go to Ptolemais, where Trypho's troops killed him. In response, Simon strengthened the people and commanded those in Joppa not to deliver (παραδῶσίν) the city to Trypho (*Ant.* 13:202), who later murdered him.[46] Given Trypho's murderous duplicity, "deliver" should be "betray."

In each case, there is no valid exercise of authority or requirement of justice, but a breach of an existing relationship, fairly called betrayal. All are involuntary and most coercive. Most involve treachery with established enemies of Judaism like the Samaritans, Rome or Antiochus Epiphanes. Betrayal is an appropriate translation in each case.

It is also interesting to note Josephus's self-reference at Jotapata as προδότης (Luke's very term for Judas [6:12]) when surrounded, he prays that in surrendering, God will see him not as a traitor but as his minister. He persuaded most of his troops to commit suicide until only he and another remained alive (*J. W.* 3:388).[47]

Lastly, παραδίδωμι and προδίδωμι are variants in *Ant.* 9.63 and *Life* 129 so they were not wholly distinct in the copyists' minds.

Betrayal is appropriate at several points in Josephus. Coercion and compulsion occur in all cases involving people. Disappointingly, Klassen uses examples which could never mean betray but does not discuss cases where this could—indeed, should—be the translation.

2.2.3. Handing over in the LXX

The MT uses a number of words to mean "handing over," but the LXX translates them all by παραδίδωμι. They are מָגַן (magan), נָתַן (nathan), נָצַל (natsal), סָגַר (sagar), and פָּלַט (palat). נָתַן is by far the most prevalent, and is

---

45. Miller, "Cities," 453–67.
46. Schiffman, "King," 237–59; Seward, *Masada*, 95.
47. Josephus's main purpose in writing *J. W.* was rehabilitating his reputation, given the supposed inevitability of Roman conquest (Bellemore, "Josephus," 95). So also Kelley (*Josephus*, 257–74). His soldiers conceived the idea of the suicide pact, unwilling for a prize like Josephus to surrender to Rome, but Josephus, with characteristic wiliness, turned the tables on them (Seward, *Masada*, 96).

GREEK TERMINOLOGY

the only one to occur in all six categories described here.[48] Given the wide distribution of usage in the MT, it is unwise to base interpretation on this usage, but rather on how the LXX uses παραδίδωμι. I will divide the material up into semantic domains suggested by the text:

1. God hands the nations over to Israel.
2. God hands Israel over to the nations.
3. Someone will not be handed over.
4. God hands the nations over to other nations.
5. One of God's people is handed over.
6. Other.[49]

Number 6 contains some examples of objects being handed over which fall within meaning 1 (objects). There are no self-offerings (meaning 2). Number 3 may be taken as a group within meaning 3, where the handing over would be unjust if it proceeded. Numbers 1, 2, 4, 5 and the examples in number 6, with God as the subject, are done under authority and correspond to meaning 4 (done under authority). Appendix 1 provides a numerical summary, and appendices 2–7 give the breakup between the Torah, the Prophets, and the Writings.

God hands the nations over to Israel: Appendix 2

This group has seventy occurrences: twenty-four in the Torah and forty-six in the Prophets. God is explicitly the subject in sixty-eight instances. An exception is Deuteronomy 20:20, "the city at war with you falls," using the aorist passive subjunctive (παραδοθῇ). This is a divine passive, as the whole chapter consists of regulations, "a just war code" about dealing with people and plunder after God has given the city to Israel (Deut 20:13).[50] Christensen

48.

Appendix	2	3	4	5	6	7
מָנַן	Yes	No	No	No	No	No
נָהַן	Yes	Yes	Yes	Yes	Yes	Yes
נָצַל	Yes	Yes	Yes	No	No	No
סָגַר	Yes	No	Yes	No	Yes	No
פָּלַט	No	Yes	No	No	No	No

49. List different meanings with the most numerous meanings first (Newman, "Reflections," 93).

50. Niditch, *War*, 26. God is described as the ideal warrior who is with Israel and

notes the chiasm so that 20:1–20 is matched with 20:10–12 about sieges.[51] The second example is Deuteronomy 2:24–33, where God actively handed Sihon, the Amorite king, to Israel in Deuteronomy 2:24 (παραδέδωκα), 2:31 (παραδοῦναι), and 2:33 (παρέδωκεν). While 2:30 (παραδοθῇ) is passive, God is the ultimate cause: "the Lord your God had made his spirit stubborn . . . to give him into your hands." God demanded his "total destruction" as he refused Moses' reasonable request of right of passage.[52]

Handing over the nations is always a divine activity which is never delegated unlike, for instance, the handing over of an Israelite to justice (Deut 19:12). When Israel is obedient, the actions of God and Israel are parallel. While not exact, this is apparent in Josh 10:30: "The Lord . . . gave that city . . . into Israel's hand"; 10:32: "The Lord handed Lachish over to Israel"; and 10:35: "They captured it that same day," which the LXX prefaces with "and the Lord gave the city and its king into the hands of Israel."

There are two basic things which God hands over: people and their land. While not wholly distinct, Israel has different responsibilities in each case. The process of handing over reveals certain things about God.

Firstly, God keeps covenant by handing over people. Handing over the nations is not arbitrary, but fulfills a promise and allows God to punish sin directly. In 2 Chronicles 32:21, God sent an angel to destroy Sennacherib's army for equating the true God with idols: "the gods of the peoples . . . did not rescue [them] . . . so the god of Hezekiah will not rescue his people" (2 Chr 32:17). No one, least of all an idol, may take God's place. God may also express his wrath by his people, like when he waited until the sin of the Amorites was complete (Gen 15:16). In Deuteronomy 2:30, God hardened Sihon,[53] king of the Amorites, that he might give (παραδοθῇ) him to Israel. Christensen compares this with Yahweh's hardening of the pharaoh of the exodus.[54] The essential parallel of divine and sinful human hardening is shown in Exodus 8:32 and 9:12. God only hands over for good reason, summarized as serious, unrepented sin. It is never arbitrary.

God gave the nations to Israel,[55] but they still had to defeat them and take possession. Based on their knowledge of God, Israel could take the ini-

---

fights for them (Pierce, "War," 82). The element of proportionality is to prevent wanton destruction (Wright, "Warfare," 425).

51. Christensen, *Deuteronomy 1:1—21:9*, 20:9.

52. Niditch, *War*, 28, 65.

53. The Exodus was a warning to the Philistines not to harden themselves against God (1 Sam 6:6).

54. Christensen, *Deuteronomy 1:1—21:9*, 30.

55. Placing people under the ban illustrates its key feature, that the most valuable things, here captive people, are given over for God's use, not Israel's (Niditch, *War*, 35).

tiative, like when they "made a vow to the deity" to destroy Hormah (Num 21:2–3) if God handed it over.[56] While God may respond, he did not share his glory with anyone (Judg 7:7).[57]

Secondly, God is faithful in handing over land. The enduring nature of the gift of land to Israel is shown by the perfect tense; e.g., Deuteronomy 1:8 (παραδέδωκα) or 1:21 (παραδέδωκεν). Although unstated, it is based on Israel's obedience. A similar situation obtained with Eli (1 Sam 2:30).[58] Even an explicit and eternal promise by God to an individual was contingent on obedience and when that was not forthcoming, God revoked the high priesthood from Eli and severely judged his house. We may extrapolate from his dealings with sinful individuals to his dealing with the land of sinful peoples.

The land belongs to God even if its occupants do not acknowledge him. God handed over the land to fulfill his covenant with Abraham, Isaac and Jacob (Deut 1:8) but Israel was then responsible to God for the land and its inhabitants; e.g., a captive woman was to be treated respectfully (Deut 21:10).[59]

God handed people and land to Israel because of the nations' sin: it was never arbitrary. This handing over was always done by God and never delegated. It was a judgment on the nations and their idols so that no one would equate God with idols (2 Chr 32:17). Israel was responsible for non-combatants (Deut 21:10).[60]

God hands Israel over to the nations: Appendix 3

When Israel sinned, despite warnings from God, they in turn were handed to the nations.[61] There are fifty-four occurrences: three in the Torah, twenty-eight in the Prophets, and twenty-three in the Writings. There are

---

56. Niditch, *War*, 32.

57. Those who lapped showed fear and God's glory could shine more clearly through them than those who were braver (Soggin, *Judges*, 137, citing Josephus *Ant.* 5:217).

58. This is confirmed by a divine oath, "Far be it from me!" (Klein, *1 Samuel*, 2:30). Only rarely does God bind himself by an oath; e.g., Gen 15:18 (a covenant with Abram); 22:15 (the LORD swore by himself).

59. Baker, *Wealth*, 155; Niditch, *War*, 85.

60. Baker, *Wealth*, 155, 308.

61. Punishment is inflicted by those nations for whose religion Israel had forsaken their own (Moore, *Judges*, 71). An interesting parallel from a stele (a carved stone or wooden monument erected for particular purposes; eg., commemoration) by Mesha, king of Moab, ascribes Omri's oppression of Moab to the god Chemosh's anger with Moab (ibid., 91).

clear differences from Appendix 2. The passive tense is used more frequently (fourteen of the fifty-four), predominantly in the Prophets. In the covenant lawsuit of Micah 6,[62] the LXX has a passive future "will be given (παραδοθήσονται) to the sword," as though God is more circumspect about handing his own people over to the nations. Once again, parallel uses of passive and active forms show God as the ultimate cause. God said via Jeremiah that Jerusalem would be handed to Nebuchadnezzar (Jer 21:10[63] [παραδοθήσεται]; 39:28, 36, 43; 41:2; 45:3 passive) and Zedekiah would also be handed over (Jer 22:25; 24:8 active and 39:4; 44:17 passive). There is no essential difference in meaning.

God never delegates this to anyone, such as the Assyrians.[64] They are, at best, agents of God, never independent operators. Only God may hand his people over to their enemies. He always gave a reason for handing over such as the covenant lawsuit of Mic 6, which alleges dishonesty and violence. Smith also notes the charge in 6:16, that they had observed "all the practices of Ahab's house," which must at least include widespread Baalism (1 Kgs 18).[65] Judges 6:1 says, "the Israelites did evil in the eyes of the Lord," but a more compelling reason may be inferred from 6:10:[66] "do not worship the gods of the Amorites." If Israel wished to behave like the nations by worshiping idols, God would treat them as such. At this stage in their history, God would still respond to cries for help from Israel and in person (Judg 6).[67] Once Israel repented, they were restored, an option never offered to the nations.[68] It was a handing over for the purpose of discipline unlike the destruction of the nations. Moreover, although God helped Israel, they still had to fight for their

---

62. Smith, *Micah–Malachi*, 6:1.

63. This is contrasted with God's deliverance of Jerusalem during Hezekiah's reign (Baruchi-Unna, "Hezekiah," 293). God said that he would fight against Judah with "an outstretched hand and a mighty arm" (Jer 21:5), the same terms used by Moses in recounting the Exodus (Deut 4:34).

64. God did call Cyrus "His anointed" (Isa 45:1), with power "to subdue the nations," but the context makes clear that this is to rebuild Jerusalem, not just punish the nations.

65. Smith, *Micah–Malachi*, 6:16

66. In Judg 6:7-10, Midianite destruction of harvests is due to divine punishment (Baker, *Wealth*, 130). There is a prevalence of references to famine (Rogerson, *Ethics*, 128).

67. This is a theophany because of the parallel in Gen 22:15: "The angel of the LORD . . . said, "I swear by myself, declares the LORD" because of the identification of "angel of the LORD" and "LORD" (Moore, *Judges*, 183). A theophany is the most natural reading of Judg 6. Soggin (*Judges*, 115) supports this, saying that the niphal of "appeared" in 6:12 is a technical term for "the divine manifestation."

68. E.g., Jer 51:5: although Judas and Israel were "full of guilt," God would not forsake them like Babylon.

freedom. There is no recorded communication between God and the nations (except via Israel), even though God handed Israel to them. This contrasts with God's communication to Israel about the nations. The nations are God's enemies because of idolatry and general sinfulness; they are only being used by God for disciplinary purposes. God may limit Israel's penalty so that they will know that Yahweh is God. For instance, the Babylonian exile was limited to seventy years (Jer 25:11–12).[69] God then promised that he would punish Babylon by making it desolate forever.

Someone will not be handed over: Appendix 4

There are twenty-one occurrences. God is explicitly the subject nine times, and the divine passive is used four times. The Assyrian commander warns the Jerusalemites not to think, "The Lord will surely deliver us; this city will not be given into the hand of the king of Assyria." (2 Kgs 18:30). Similar warnings are in 2 Kings 19:10; Isaiah 36:15; 37:10. While the verb for Jerusalem being handed over is passive (παραδοθῇ), there is always a recognition of God's action, even if denied by the Assyrians.

While this group is defined by people not being handed over, a reason is given or implied to explain why the normal course of events is not happening. Firstly, God may not allow handing over when the person initiating it is evil. Balak, king of Moab, hired Balaam to curse Israel, but God would not listen and blessed Israel instead (Josh 24:10).[70] Numbers 22–23 has God's explicit commands to Balaam not to curse but to bless Israel. The Bible's verdict on Balaam was severe (Num 31:8; 2 Pet 2:15; Rev 2:14).[71] A reason for this when he seemingly only said what God wanted may be either greed[72] or idolatry by enticing Israel with the Baal of Peor (Num 31:16), despite his knowledge of the true God. Perhaps he was syncretistic for the pagan Balak sent for him (Num 22:4–5), but he also proclaimed "the Lord my God" (22:18).[73] As seen above in 2 Kings 18:30, while Jerusalem was ripe for judgment, God would not allow it through someone who equated God with idols.

---

69. Rogerson, *Ethics*, 119; Allen, *Jeremiah*. Interestingly, God warns Egypt that he will disperse them "among the nations" (as though Egypt is not part of the nations), but after forty years, God will return them to the land of Egypt so that both them and the Israelites will know that God is the LORD (Ezek 29:6, 12–13, 16).

70. Frankel, "Balaam," 34, 38.

71. Niditch, *War*, 79.

72. Carson, "2 Peter," 1056.

73. The angel of the LORD in Num 22:22 is Satan the opposer, because the angel is opposing Balaam (Aimers, *Devil*, 59). Such an apparently improbable exegesis requires more than mere assertion.

Secondly, David insisted that he would not kill Saul (1 Sam 24:11),[74] as although the Lord had given him into David's hands, he was still the Lord's anointed.[75] Saul had forfeited the kingship through disobedience (1 Sam 15),[76] but it was not until he consulted the witch at Endor[77] that God struck him through the Philistines (1 Sam 28).[78] Even so, Saul and his sons were not cast out of God's presence eternally (1 Sam 28:19). David, not knowing what would happen, still would not move against Saul by abrogating God's role to himself, an obvious contrast to Judas.

Next, there may be personal reasons why God is requested not to hand the person over. The person may be godly (LXX Ps 26:11, NIV 27:12). David asks not to be handed over because God is his light, salvation, and Savior (vv. 1, 9). The author is God's dove (LXX Ps 73:19, NIV 74:19), righteous and just (LXX 118:121, NIV 119:121). The psalmist distinguishes discipline from being handed over to death (LXX 117:18, NIV 118:18). A person in a right relationship with God may be disciplined, but not abandoned. Alternatively, he asks that the wicked not triumph through his downfall (LXX Pss 40:3, 139:9; NIV 41:2, 140:8). The individual is not identified in the anonymous LXX 118:121 (NIV 119:121) and LXX 117:18 (NIV 118:18), but they still describe specific events. Handing over must have regard for the person's whole situation, not just one incident.

Lastly, a wrongful handing over incurs a penalty, as in Proverbs 30:10, where it (παραδῷς) incurs a curse.[79] Someone who is about to be handed over may sometimes avoid the full penalty by obeying (Jer 38:20). Surrender may have mitigated some of Nebuchadnezzar's anger at a wayward vassal.[80]

---

74. There are few examples of blood vengeance within Israel (Baker, *Wealth*, 127). David must foreswear revenge on Nabal, just like Saul did for David (1 Sam 24, 26; Moyer, "Balaam," 179).

75. Weitzman, "David's Lament," 344.

76. The passage of Samuel's judgment on Saul reflects the ban (Niditch, *War*, 81, 61). Saul did not understand that the ban meant offering the best to God, which included the king and the animals.

77. σπεύδω (1 Sam 28:20–21) includes both dismay and haste, and so encapsulates the "fright/flight response" (Taylor, *Study*, 139–40).

78. Luck, *Magic*, 211.

79. This bears little relation to the context and may reflect Deut 23:16, which forbids returning a slave to an unjust master (Murphy, *Proverbs*, 30:10). Wisdom literature includes a number of references to the humane treatment of slaves (Baker, *Wealth*, 130).

80. Keown et al., *Jeremiah 26–52*, 38:20.

God hands the nations over to other nations: Appendix 5

There are fourteen occurrences. In eight of them, God does the handing over. Daniel 11:6 and 11 mention the kings of the North and South, but it is not immediately clear to whom they are referring.[81] While the data hints at coercion, there are two reasons why God would allow handing over. First, God may sovereignly punish an idolatrous nation (Isa 19:1–4; Jer 50:2 [LXX 27:2]) or God may punish a nation for enmity toward Israel (Isa 34:2, 5, 8).[82] As when God handed the nations over to Israel, there is no mention of repentance, as their guilt is so stark.

Some/One of God's people handed over: Appendix 6

This differs from Appendix 3, as none are for personal or corporate sin. One pattern is that, while God may actively hand over one of his people (Job 2:6),[83] this can also be shown by the divine passive (LXX Isa 38:12–13 twice). Here, God relents on his warning to Hezekiah that he will die, and adds fifteen years to his life.[84] In response, he wrote a poem which included these lines, so there is little doubt that he means God. A person may also actively hand over someone, such as the Israelites handing over Samson (Judg 15:12); however, no passive tense involves a human being handing over. This reflects previous results where God is usually the subject of the verb, and only God hands his own people over. Secondly, someone handed over is always restored and vindicated; e.g., Job 42.

Samson was handed to the Philistines to avenge those whom he killed. This may fairly be called betrayal, as the Israelites knew that God was still with Samson because of his victory over the Philistines, and that he would never receive a fair trial. It was only after his disclosure (Judg 16:17) that God's protection was withdrawn (16:20). Samson will be considered at greater length in s2.3.2.

---

81. They are generic terms for the occupants respectively of the Seleucid throne in Syria and the Ptolemaic throne in Egypt (Goldingay, *Daniel*, 11:6, 11). This is plausible, but regardless of human dealings, the angelic guide swore by "Him who lives forever," that all this would be accomplished (Dan 12:7). Only God ultimately hands over entire people groups.

82. Baker, *Wealth*, 126; Allen, *Jeremiah*.

83. "Job 2:6 resonates strongly with 1 Cor 5:5" due to the act of handing over to Satan (Smith, *Hand This Man*, 119). This is overstated, as the reasons are quite different: to show Job's integrity under trial versus discipline for the incestuous offender.

84. Baker, *Wealth*, 275.

Other: Appendix 7

This last group includes all other uses which do not fit any of the former parts. First, a person may be handed over under authority, such as a murderer being handed to the avenger of blood (Deut 19:12)[85] or women being given into the care of Hegai, the eunuch (Esth 2:3). We see the uniform principle that no one handed over has any say.

Secondly, God may hand over. God established cities of refuge for perpetrators of manslaughter (Exod 21:13). Παρέδωκεν εἰς τὰς χεῖρας implies that God allowed the non-judicial death for his purposes, as the text distinguishes intentional from unintentional death.[86] Another example of God working with or through a human agency is Proverbs 24:22, where "those two" mean "God and the king" (24:21), sending calamity on the evil man and the wicked. Proverbs 11:8 warns that the wicked will be handed over (παραδίδοται, passive) to trouble. This is almost certainly a divine passive.

Thirdly, God may hand over objects, like kingdoms, to people (Dan 4:17) or the shroud of death to destruction (Isa 25:7). Esau credited God with giving him success in hunting (Gen 27:12). God presumably lies behind the warning in Proverbs 27:24, that a crown is not secure, or given to the recipient's house, for all generations. Isaiah 33:6a uses a passive future (παραδοθήσονται) to indicate the handing over of knowledge, but 33:6b implies that God is the source, as "fear of the Lord is the key to this treasure."[87]

People may hand things or people over. People may offer sacrifices to the Lord (2 Chr 35:12). The women going to the harem could take whatever they wanted (Esth 2:13). People could provide surety to a neighbor (Prov 6:1) or kill a poor person (Job 24:14).

2.2.4. Handing over in the GNT: Appendix 8

The semantic domains of παραδίδωμι in the GNT are as follows:

1. God the subject of the verb/where the outcome is positive.
2. Judas handing over Jesus (held over until s4.3.5).
3. Handing over an inanimate object.
4. Jesus in the hands of Jewish or Roman authorities.

---

85. As opposed to vengeance inflicted by relatives of the deceased (ibid., 126).
86. Rogerson, *Ethics*, 63; Boyd-Taylor, "Linguistic," 160.
87. "[W]isdom," "knowledge," and "fear of Yahweh" have a striking cross-reference (Childs, *Isaiah*, 11:1–10).

5. Christians, etc., handed over.
6. Ungodly, evil angels, etc., handed over.

Number 1 corresponds to meaning 2 on self-offerings. Number 2 corresponds to meaning 3 on unjust handings-over. Number 3 corresponds to meaning 1. Numbers 4–6 correspond to meaning 4 on handings-over under authority.

God the subject, etc.

There are fourteen uses of the verb in this category: eight active and six passive. There are two important factors, explicit parallels between the Father/Son relationship and the Lord/disciple relationship, which are expressed firstly in the essential equivalence of active and passive verbal forms, and secondly in the sense of bearing burdens for the benefit of others. Jesus may be given over (παρεδόθη, Rom 4:25), or the Father may hand Jesus over (παρέδωκεν, Rom 8:32),[88] but in the thought world of Paul, who emphasizes both the unique relationship between Father and Son,[89] and Jesus' obedience in going to the cross,[90] there is little difference. Jesus balances these two emphases in "No one takes it [his life] from me, but I lay it down of my own accord.... This command I received from my Father" (John 10:18).[91]

Believers may be handed over by the church for ministry (παραδεδομένοι, Acts 14:26, passive[92]) or may hand over their own lives (παραδεδωκόσι, Acts 15:26). In Paul, they may be handed over for testing (παραδιδόμεθα, 2 Cor 4:11, passive). Given Paul's overt reliance on God's grace (2 Cor 1:10), presumably he believed that God had handed him over for testing,[93] but had sustained him through it. This accords with the LXX

---

88. Seifrid, "Romans," 634. It is to balance the threefold παρέδωκεν of Rom 1:24, 26, 28 so that 8:31–39 summarizes Paul's argument so far (Dunn, *Romans*, 8:31). Rom 8:32 parallels Gen 22:16 to Abraham: "you have not withheld your son, your only son" (ibid., 224). It is "the (probable) allusion" (Lee, *Lexicography*, 206).

89. Paul's use of the article puts Jesus' Sonship in a unique category; cf. other groups, like angels, who are also sons of God (Hurtado, "Son of God," 903). The unity of Father and Son is both functional ("whatever the Father does the Son also does," John 5:19) and organic ("I and the Father are one," John 10:30).

90. Rom 5:19 and Phil 2:5–9 mention obedience, and 2 Cor 8:9 mentions Jesus' grace in becoming poor "for your sakes" (Barclay, "Jesus and Paul," 499).

91. Keener, *John*, 820. I assume that the text fairly records the essence of Jesus' original words. Jesus uses covenantal language to relate his relationship with the disciples to God's relationship with Israel (Köstenberger, "John," 463).

92. They were handed over by the Holy Spirit (Johnson, *Acts*, 255).

93. Martin, *2 Corinthians*, 1:10. Kruse, *2 Corinthians*; Furnish, *II Corinthians*; and

pattern, where only God hands over his people. Moreover, 2 Corinthians 4:10 links the effects of the various handings over of Jesus and the apostles: "We always carry around in our body the death of Jesus, so that the life of Jesus may be revealed in our body." So, it is reasonable to parallel the nature of Jesus' handing-over by himself and also by the Father with that of the apostles by themselves and also by the Father.[94]

Secondly, the key theme here, with little if any echo in the LXX, is the lack of overt coercion and the great personal cost in being handed over, which leads to blessing for others. In the LXX, God's people were handed over for disciplinary purposes leading to repentance. However, as seen above, there is little practical difference in the NT between the Father actively handing Jesus over, Jesus consenting to this, and Jesus being handed over. The situation with the disciples is slightly more nuanced. As argued above, there is little difference between the church or God handing them over and a self-offering. But they are not in a vacuum—the self-offering has a Christological foundation: "Christ's love compels us" (2 Cor 5:14;[95] Gal 2:20). Paul had been freed by Jesus' death, but he then felt bound to obey Jesus to the point of death, "death to the jurisdiction of one's ego."[96] In the LXX, coercion was overt and external; in the NT, the compulsion to obey Christ is internal, as there were no external forces forcing Paul to follow Christ; quite the reverse. The compulsion which the disciples feel is analogous to the compulsion which Jesus felt to obey his Father, that "the Scriptures must be fulfilled" (Mark 14:49). The disciples thus mirror the self-giving devotion of Jesus (John 10:18).

The end result of the handing over is blessing for others. In Romans 4:25, Paul says of Jesus, "He was delivered (παραδόθη) over to death for our sins and was raised to life for our justification." Justification illustrates the benefit for his people, which Paul explains as "life for all" (Rom 5:18). Perhaps 2 Corinthians 4:11 best sums this up: Paul and his companions are constantly given over to death so that Jesus' risen life might be seen in their lives. Martin suggests that the use of παραδίδωμι means that this is Paul's

---

Hughes, *Second Epistle* do not express a clear view.

94. Contra Furnish (*II Corinthians*, 256). "Paul's intimate association of his apostleship with Jesus' death is a major theme of his ministerial life" (Martin, *2 Corinthians*, 4:10). Paul meant this concretely, as he faced persecution (Kruse, *2 Corinthians*, 107).

95. "Compels" means that, because of Christ's love for Paul (subjective genitive), he wants to become part of God's plan (Martin, *2 Corinthians*, 5:14). "his apostleship operates in response to and out of the love which God has bestowed in Christ" (Furnish, *II Corinthians*, 326). The parallel use of συνέχει in Phil 1:23 shows that Paul is torn between departing to be with Christ and serving the Philippians (Kruse, *2 Corinthians*, 121).

96. Longenecker, *Galatians*, 92.

fate as "decreed by God."⁹⁷ This is overstated, as Paul's compulsion would appear to be an internal response to the love of God shown in Christ, not the overt coercion of παραδίδωμι in the LXX. While not stated explicitly, in Philippians 3:7, Paul contrasts his former life in Judaism with his present life in Christ: he goes on to express a deep desire "to know Christ and the power of His resurrection" (Phil 3:10).⁹⁸ He treats as "refuse" everything which would prevent him reaching this goal.⁹⁹

In summary, the pattern of handing over for the blessing of others has no counterpart in the LXX, but is wholly new. Job's handing over to Satan eventually brought blessing for him when he saw God—"My ears had heard of you [God] but now my eyes have seen you" (42:5)—but there is no sense that Job's enhanced relationship would benefit others, except by praying for his friends' forgiveness (42:8).

Handing over an inanimate object

With some exceptions, this group shows one person with the authority to do so, entrusting something of value; e.g., the talents (Matt 25:14–30),¹⁰⁰ to another person who is then responsible for the gift (Matt 25:20). If faithful, they receive a large reward (Matt 25:21, 28).¹⁰¹ Other verses illustrate the benefits of adhering to godly teaching, which had been passed on to them (Luke 1:2; Acts 16:4; 1 Cor 15:3).

However, a person who does not act properly is penalized. The servant who had done nothing with his talent was rebuked for not investing the money and earning some interest (Matt 25:27). By doing nothing, he disobeyed the master, deprived others of the use of this gift, and learnt nothing in the process. His penalty is heavy: he is a worthless servant cast into darkness, where there is weeping and gnashing of teeth. Matthew uses the same terms for hell.¹⁰²

---

97. Martin, *2 Corinthians*, 4:11.

98. "One of the most profound articulations of the *transformation of value*" from the early church (Barton, "Money," 37).

99. Hawthorne, *Philippians*, 3:8.

100. Slaves could be entrusted with large amounts of money (Beavis, "Slavery," 40).

101. Possibly as his own or for further trading on his master's behalf.

102. Matt 8:12 (Garrett, *Temptations*, 44n49); 22:13 (Keener, *Matthew*, 601). Highlighting the slave's "physical punishment" (Glancy, "Slaves," 76, 89), which is precisely what he does not receive, minimizes the severity of the slave's punishment compared with the "darkness."

When someone's relationship with God is impaired or absent, they cannot successfully hand anything over. Jesus rebukes the Pharisees and teachers of the law for nullifying the word of God with human traditions which they "passed on" (παρέδωκατε Mark 7:13).[103] In Luke 4:6, Satan offers Jesus the kingdoms of the world in return for worship.[104] Jesus does not dispute Satan's right to do so, but rejects him.[105] Lastly, Paul knows that, even if he gives up (παραδῶ) everything but lacks love, showing an impaired relationship with God, he will gain nothing (1 Cor 13:3).

A person must accept responsibility for what they have received, and be in a right relationship with God to be rewarded. This is a clear difference from the LXX, where responsibility for what has been given is only implied; e.g., Isaiah 33:6a uses a passive future (παραδοθήσονται) to indicate the handing over of knowledge, but 33:6b implies that God is the source, as the "fear of the Lord is the key to this treasure." It is reasonable to imply that the person is then responsible to God for the use of this knowledge. A key idea here is that no one, neither the giver nor the receiver, is under coercion.

Jesus handed over for trial (Matt 26–27; Mark 14–15; Luke 22–23)

These passages show the Jews and Romans following a debased legal procedure. This is distinct because of Jesus' reaction. He never reproaches the Jewish or Roman authorities in the same way as Judas. It is clear that the procedure was debased. No capital trial should have been held at night (John 18:28[106]), there were no clear charges (John 18:30, "παρεδώκαμεν") and the chief priests were motivated by envy, not upholding the law (Mark 15:10, "παραδεδώκεισαν"; Matt 27:18, "παρέδωκαν").[107] While Jesus objects

---

103. The scribes have ruled the word of God "to be unlawful!" (France, *Mark*, 288). Dishonoring parents is like dishonoring God, so it is blasphemy (Watts, "Mark," 170).

104. Kuecker, "Other," 99. This assumes that they were Satan's to offer (Branden, *Conflict*, 43). While the divine Son of God rejects worshiping a creature, he does not dispute Satan's right to offer them. If Satan had no such right, Jesus could easily have said so. Job 1 supports the idea of Satan having some rights. When God asks Satan where he has been, he replies that he has been walking up and down on the earth, precisely what an owner/king would do. The source of his authority is never mentioned; perhaps it is idolatrous worship. Contra Fitzmyer (*Luke I-IX*, 516), who argues for a theological passive like Job 1. Comparing handing over a person for limited testing with all the kingdoms of the world sounds hazardous.

105. Bock, *Luke*, 376.

106. Cf. Brown, *John I-XII*, 358; the trial was probably held around 3–6 AM (Keener, *John*, 1098).

107. Best, *Soteriology*, 113.

to breaches of Judaic practice[108] like being struck (John 18:23),[109] he never disputes their right to try him, nor reproaches them, except for the unnecessary force of the arrest (Matt 26:55). In the Synoptics, the most severe rebuke is delivered to Caiaphas (Matt 26:64;[110] Mark 14:62[111]; Luke 22:68) "to assert his (Jesus') victory over his adversaries."[112]

While there is clear coercion, as Jesus is bound and taken from one trial to the next (Matt 27:2, παρέδωκαν; Luke 20:20, παραδοῦναι);[113] the constant theme is Jesus' innocence. The chief priests cannot sustain a charge against Jesus (Matt 26:59–60; Mark 14:57–59), whose innocence is affirmed by Pilate (Matt 27:23; Mark 15:14; Luke 23:4; John 18:38),[114] Pilate's wife (Matt 27:19), and even Judas (Matt 27:4).

Followers of Jesus and John the Baptist handed over[115]

These verses warn of what lies ahead: Jesus' disciples will be brought before synagogues, rulers, etc., "on account of my [Jesus'] name" (Luke 21:12, παραδιδόντες).[116] While there are warnings of persecution and death (Matt 24:9, παραδώσουσιν; Luke 21:16, παραδοθήσεσθε), there is also a consistent theme of witness by the persecuted believers to the authorities (Mark 13:9).[117] They were not to prepare a speech, because words would be given to them by the Holy Spirit (Mark 13:11). The best example is Paul, who (as Saul) had originally persecuted the infant church (Acts 8:3). Paul will be handed over by the Jews of Jerusalem to the Gentiles and ultimately sent to Rome as a witness for the gospel at the centre of the empire (Acts 21:11, παραδώσουσιν;[118] Acts 28:17, παρεδόθην).

---

108. Although not, interestingly enough, in the Synoptics.

109. δέρω, by this time, no longer means a "full beating" (Lee, *Lexicography*, 163).

110. Davies and Allison, *Matthew*, 3:531.

111. Only then will Jesus' opponents see his glory (Garrett, *Temptations*, 87). There is a significant movement from silence to speech: "the accusations deserved no response, but the question demands one" (ibid., 125). Jesus' opponents are Yahweh's enemies (Watts, "Mark," 234).

112. Fitzmyer, *Luke X–XXIV*, 1463.

113. Luke 22:54; John 18:13, and Luke 23:1; John 18:28 respectively use ἄγω for Jesus being taken to the high priest and Pilate. There is no real difference from παραδίδωμι.

114. Bond, *Pilate*, 157.

115. No real difference can be shown between passive and active tenses of the verb. The key parallel is the innocence of both John and Jesus.

116. Bovon, *Luke*, 112: "the persecution has only one honorable origin."

117. Beavis, *Mark*, 195.

118. This echoes Jesus' own passion predictions in Luke 9:44; 18:32 (Johnson, *Acts*, 370).

Even in these verses, Jesus seems to impute different degrees of culpability to those handing over. First, in Matt 10:19, Jesus talks in quite neutral terms about some anonymous people, "they," handing believers over, παραδῶσιν. But when he starts describing family members doing the same in 10:21, Jesus also includes children rebelling against parents, παραδώσει. Secondly, if the outcome of the more neutral handing over is an opportunity to witness, the outcome of the second is children having their parents put to death.[119] It may be appropriate to translate "hand over" in the former case, but to translate "betray" in the latter case due to the closer relationship and heightened emotion. This is not to equate heightened emotion with betrayal, for even the relatively neutral handing over of 10:19 would be accompanied by some emotion, but to recognize that all betrayal would be accompanied by a degree of emotion. It seems that the closer the relationship of the one handing over to the one being handed over, the greater the culpability and the more reasonable the translation "betray."

Disobedient Christians, demons, handed over

This last group consists of unrepentant people and sinful angels who have been handed over for punishment. God normally hands this group over so it reflects the LXX. The master in a parable on the kingdom of heaven may fairly be taken to be God, who hands over (παρέδωκεν) to the torturers the Christian who will not forgive a brother from the heart (Matt 18:34–35[120]).[121]

---

119. "the language is very strong" (Davies and Allison, *Matthew*, 2:186)

120. A massive debt and being sold to another is plausible, as slaves in royal households could access the master's wealth on his behalf (Glancy, "Slaves," 85). But the sheer size of the debt must argue against a literal reading. A better reading contrasts a person's overwhelming culpability to God with another's culpability to them. This is a communal warning: ὑμῖν (ibid., 83). Wright makes heavy going of a confronting parable: the king's (God's) attitude changes when the person will not forgive (Wright, "Debtors," 16–17).

121. Hagner, *Matthew 14–28*. The handing over is eschatological (ibid., 18:34; Sim, "Weeping," 135; and Davies and Allison, *Matthew*, 2:803). This is unlikely. First, Peter's question deals with forgiveness in the present and Jesus' preceding teaching on binding and loosing, the appropriate exercise of church discipline (Matt 18:15–20) must deal with present, not eschatological, discipline, as it is instruction for the church. Secondly, if the discipline is eschatological, then who are the jailers (a *hapax*)? For Hagner's scenario to be plausible, God would still have to be willing to hand sinful believers over to the power of spiritual evil, after its final overthrow. General judgment in Rev 20:12 only appears to happen after the final defeat of the devil, the beast, and the false prophet in Rev 20:10, which we may fairly take to represent evil. No godly creature is ever treated like this, and the nearest parallel is Paul's command to hand (παραδοῦναι) the incestuous offender over to Satan (1 Cor 5:5). Paul also handed Hymenaeus and Alexander

The language of handing over may explain what the NT writers view as improper behavior. Acts 7:42 records God handing a persistently sinful Israel over to idolatry, allowing them "to become captive to the consequences of their evil."[122] Romans 1:24, 26, 28 has God handing over (παρέδωκεν) persistent sinners to proscribed sexual activity. Finally, God handed over sinning angels to prison (2 Pet 2:4, παρέδωκεν). As in the LXX, where God hands Israel over to the nations, there is ample precedent for God to discipline his willfully sinful people. Occasionally, a person may hand themselves over to judgment by their persistent sin (Eph 4:19, παρέδωκαν). It is interesting to note that all the verbs are active. No one in this group is handed over (passive) for allegiance to Christ; rather, all are actively handed over for sin.

Conclusion

There is a remarkable similarity in usage across these four groups of sources, two of which—secular Greek and the LXX—predate the GNT, and the last (Josephus) is writing within recognizably the same thought world. A key idea in all texts dealing with people, is that the person handed over has no say in the matter. People may be handed over under authority, such as the accused murderer sent for trial (Deut 19:12), or be handed over coercively, such as Samson's arrest by three thousand armed Israelites (Judg 15:11). An object may be handed over by being entrusted into the hands of an accountable recipient, such as the talents in Matthew 25. A person may hand themselves over, but only when there is an external compulsion, like a siege (Niditch, *War*, 868), or under an internal compulsion to obey God (a new idea in the GNT) like Jesus in Mark 14:49.

The predominance of God as the subject of παραδίδωμι, or the divine passive, raises the possibility that a human handing over without reason might be guilty of blasphemy by abrogating God's activity. David's refusal to move against Saul when God had left him is a dramatic contrast to Judas handing over Jesus. David recognizes that he cannot act in place of God by acting against God's anointed. If abrogating to oneself a right held only

---

to Satan for blasphemy (1 Tim 1:20). While confronting, the most likely meaning is, when all else has failed, present discipline, so that the believer may not be lost eternally. First Cor 5:5 is similar "so that the sinful nature may be destroyed and his spirit saved on the day of the Lord." It addresses (present) discipline of an errant Christian (King, "Fencing," 10).

122. Johnson, *Acts*, 131.

by God is "an instance of blasphemy,"[123] and the same applies to acts done overwhelmingly by God, then David is clearly innocent of such blasphemy.

Each source has examples of betrayal, where a person breaches an existing relationship for personal gain and not for any requirement of justice. In each case, "betrayal" is an appropriate translation of παραδίδωμι. There is thus no evidence to support the basic thrust of Klassen's thesis, and many examples which refute it. Against Klassen, the evidence shows that "betrayal" may indeed be used of the act of handing over.

With this in mind, we turn our attention now to the meaning of Jesus calling Judas "friend." What can we determine from Jesus calling Judas "friend" when Judas hands him over to an armed mob?

2.3. Ἑταῖρος

2.3.1. Introduction

The language of friendship, and so the question of intimacy, clearly intrudes into the depiction of Judas and Jesus in the Synoptics. "Friend, do what you came for" (Ἑταῖρε, ἐφ' ὅ πάρει; Matt 26:50) could mean an agreement for Judas to hand Jesus over, or at least friendly relations.[124] Given that Matthew's other two uses of "friend" are the rebukes of 20:13, where the master, representing God, rebukes the laborers, and 22:12, where the inappropriately dressed wedding guest is cast out, one might think that such an interpretation is highly optimistic.[125] This interpretation is contradicted by uses of "friend" in both the LXX and Josephus. Maccoby believes that "Jesus's quiet acceptance" means that "the *treachery* is part of the divine plan."[126]

Ἑταῖρος has two opposite meanings. The first is in Liddell and Scott, where it is overwhelmingly positive.[127] No one called ἑταῖρος in secular

---

123. King, "Giants," 77.

124. Maccoby, *Myth*, 44. Matthew's other two instances show "an ungrateful action" of the addressee, but here it emphasizes "the relationship of trust," which supposedly existed between Jesus and Judas (Klassen, *Friend*, 103). Klassen gives no reason for this argument. "It sounds more like the speech between friends" (Maritz, "Judas Iscariot," 304). Maritz does not explain how this fits a scene of betrayal.

125. I will give more detail in s4.2.6.

126. Maccoby, *Myth*, 44; my emphasis.

127. Jesus and Judas; the human Priam and the divine Hermes can be (positively) ἑταῖροι (Stagakis, "Homer," 533). ἑταῖρος is contrasted with a social parasite (Corner, "Politics," 55). In the LXX, ἑταῖρα has negative notes in Judg 11:2, where Jephthah's brothers throw him out, as he is the son of a prostitute, and Prov 19:13 (LXX), where the offerings from a prostitute's wages are impure. In ancient Athens, ἑταῖρα was closer to "mistress" than "prostitute"; the latter was usually rendered by πόρνη (Cohen, *Nation*,

Greek ever betrays.¹²⁸ The LXX also contain examples of faithful friends; e.g., Hushai the Arkite is the "friend of David" (2 Sam 15:32, 37; 16:16; 1 Chr 27:33). The situation in the NT is very different. The only instances of ἑταῖρος are the three verses in Matthew, all negative.¹²⁹

The second part occupies the remainder of this section. It occurs only in the LXX and Josephus, and is the opposite in meaning.¹³⁰ Examples include most or all of the following: the explicit or implicit action of God, the use of ἑταῖρος or something similar, the use of παραδίδωμι or clear situational markers of betrayal, the betrayal of a superior by their inferior,¹³¹ a deteriorating situation and murder or other death(s).¹³² Far from indicating innocence, it heightens the enormity of the betrayal when a previously close friend betrays. In nearly all cases, the one betrayed had genuine power and authority. Using ἑταῖρος in such cases is a linguistic masterstroke, showing the breakdown in a once positive relationship to its denouement in treachery. This section does not describe the benefits of friendship, but shows that there is ample precedent in the LXX and Josephus for someone called "friend," or something similar, becoming a traitor.¹³³

156–57). In "Work," 95–99, Cohen argues that, while they cannot be precisely differentiated, πόρνη seems to be used in a more derogatory manner than ἑταίρα, although both involve the sale of sex. A negative note is in ἑταίρα for "unmarriageable woman" (Miller, "Kinship," 47). Unlike its Athenian use for male prostitution (Cohen, *Nation*, 157), nothing suggests that the GNT usages of ἑταῖρος are understood similarly.

128. ἑταῖρος is distinguished from the more intimate φίλοι (Konstan, "Friendship," 78). "Beloved companion" is a synonym (Grossman, "Death," 53).

129. Paul calls Philemon a friend using συνεργός. Paul uses συνεργός twelve times for his coworkers in the gospel: Rom 16:3, 9, 21; 1 Cor 3:9; 2 Cor 1:24; 8:23; Phil 2:25; 4:3; Col 4:11; 1 Thess 3:2; Phlm 1, 24; and it occurs once in 3 John 8. They are uniformly positive; he values them highly.

130. See the Appendix 9 grid for "friend."

131. King David and Josephus are the only two exceptions to this general rule.

132. A case of treachery which does not include either παραδίδωμι or ἑταῖρος is the murder of Gedaliah at Mizpah by Ishmael "while they were eating" (Jer 41:1), violating the Ancient Near East understanding of hospitality. This is like Ps 41:9: "he who shared my bread, has lifted up his heel against me."

133. To establish a "new sense of a given word incontrovertible examples . . . must be found" (Lee, "Matthew," 234, cited by Taylor, "Study," 141). This section has such incontrovertible examples.

2.3.2. Ἑταῖρος in the LXX: Samson

The Samson narratives are framed by παραδίδωμι (Judg 13:1; 16:23–24),[134] but driven by (false) friendship. Judges 14:11 has ἑταίρους τριάκοντα; 14:20 ἑταῖρος αὐτοῦ; and 15:2 συνεταίρῳ σου. His attempted reconciliation with his wife (Judg 15:1), while arguably naïve, shows that he thought the marriage was salvageable.[135] Her father's rebuff prompted Samson's revenge on the Philistines' crops, the main cause of his handing over. Samson is also betrayed by his own people and Delilah (Judg 15:12–13; 16).

Samson is in a very rare category where an armed mob betrays a fellow Israelite to a common enemy.[136] It is the closest OT parallel to Judas handing over Jesus. In the following pages, I will look at each betrayal of Samson before drawing conclusions.

Samson, his wife, and his father-in-law

Samson was called *in utero* to be a Nazirite, and an angel laid down strict conditions (Judg 13). Other stories about the pending births of heroes are similar: Sarah (Gen 18), Rebekah (Gen 25:21–28), and Rachel (Gen 29:31).[137] While most climax with giving the name, here Samson will be a Nazirite, holy to the Lord (Judg 6:1–21).[138] Yet, the following texts show his disregard for three key Nazirite requirements: abstention from alcohol, not touching corpses, and cutting the hair (16:17).[139]

---

134. There are recurrent themes of "women, sexuality, tricksterism and combat" (Niditch, *War*, 111). Dagon and his worshipers were humiliated by God, not finding protection in his own temple.

135. Especially at the fertile time of harvest (Niditch, *Judges*, 157).

136. Other examples are Judg 20:28, 2 Chr 13:16.

137. Niditch, *Judges*, 142. There are supposed textual allusions between the stories of Judah and Tamar in Gen 38 and the story of Amnon and Tamar in 2 Sam 13 based on the same name "Tamar," and the ill treatment of both by significant men (Rendsburg, "David," 438–46). Noble is very critical of this ("Allusions," 219–52).

138. Pressler, *Joshua*, 211.

139. The Nazirite vows may only have been for a fixed period; e.g., the pregnancy (Galpaz-Feller, *Samson*, 38). However, the threefold repetition (Judg 13:4, 7, 14) has no time limits. It is hard to imagine how the honey scooped from a lion's carcass by Samson (14:9) could not be unclean. Honey symbolizes fertility, and is therefore appropriate food in connection with a marriage (Niditch, *Judges*, 156). Moreover, being between liquid and solid, it is appropriate for Samson being between two cultures. My point does raise the issue of whether the Mosaic code was operative at this time. Given that the whole point of the Samson narratives turns on the meaning of the Nazirite vows, we may assume that the author(s) thought it was. The lion does not have a split hoof or chew the cud. Also, "Of all the animals that walk on all fours, those that walk

Samson's wife was his social inferior by age, gender, and status. While παραδίδωμι is not used here, his wife pressing him to divulge the riddle[140] is the first betrayal, as her loyalties should have been with him (14:16).[141]

The second betrayal occurred when Samson's father-in-law gave his wife to Samson's "friend," ἑταῖρος αὐτοῦ, after he had left (14:20). In that culture, his wife belonged to Samson, and was no longer at her father's disposal, despite being given to his "friend" (14:20).[142] A betrothed woman could not be given to a guest, to prevent more humiliation to the groom, but her father may have ignored such niceties.[143] The burning of his wife and father-in-law was not only "savage retaliation" (15:6), but wholly unjust.[144] However ill-advised the father was in giving her to Samson's "friend," so provoking him, it is highly unlikely that she had any say.

In that culture, Samson's father-in-law may have been socially superior to Samson by age, but God's hand had been on Samson *in utero*, a different kind of superiority. While not a strict inclusion, the notion of friendship frames and propels the narrative. As part of the ritual,[145] Samson was given thirty (probably pagan) friends ἑταίρους τριάκοντα (Judg 14:11), and thirty sets of garments (worth a large sum) were at stake in the riddle. While the friends doubtless did not intend it, their unwitting involvement inflames

---

on their paws are unclean for you; whoever touches their carcasses will be unclean till evening" (Lev 11:27). This includes lions (Hartley, *Leviticus*, 11:27). Honey is acceptable to offer to the Lord (Lev 2:12), but in general, unclean foods impart ritual uncleanness to hitherto clean foods and render them unfit for eating (Kelhoffer, "Locust," 308). Nevertheless, Samson is listed among the heroes of the faith (Heb 11:32). This must be considered when evaluating the Samson narratives (Gunn, *Judges*, 171).

140. Yadin, Samson's ḥîdâ, 407–26. The riddle was meant to smooth relationships between families and new in-laws (Niditch, *Judges*, 157). It is hard to imagine any riddle being less successful. In a wedding context, the most likely answers were "love" or "sex" (Pressler, *Joshua*, 216). It is unclear how either fits "out of the eater, something to eat."

141. Niditch, *Judges*, 157. It is a more neutral equation of his parents with his wife (Moore, *Judges*, 337).

142. "A grave insult" (Soggin, *Judges*, 242). Allowing for the Mycenean background of the Philistines, which required the groom unveiling the bride, the procession to the new home and then the consummation, the Timnite was not yet legally married to Samson, who had left in a rage (Yadin, *Samson*, 417). Samson's return in Judg 15:1 then becomes an attempt to finish the marriage formalities (ibid., 418). In response, the narrator believes that they are fully not partly married: "Samson ... went to visit his wife" (Judg 15:1).

143. Galpaz-Feller, *Samson*, 124.

144. Moore, *Judges*, 342.

145. The feast was normally at the bridegroom's home, but Samson gives the feast at his in-laws (ibid., 334). The mixed Hebrew-gentile nature of the marriage might have made eating difficult at Samson's parents' house. This may be the first time Samson breaches the Nazirite vows by eating (presumably) unclean food.

Samson at the wedding feast and when seeking to reclaim his bride. This led to intense hostilities between Samson and the Philistines, leading to the death of many Philistines and Samson's own death. The wedding was a positive relationship between Samson and his father-in-law, to his parents' obvious concern (14:3, 10).[146] If Judges 13:25 and 14:1 are connected, which seems reasonable, then the Spirit seems to lead him "into a liaison that violated Mosaic law."[147] "Feast" (14:10) includes excessive drinking, a breach of the angel's command on strong drink (13:4, 7).[148]

Samson and Israel

Samson's treatment by Israel is the third betrayal. The Israelites do not call him "friend" but he was a special figure (Judg 13:2, 13:25) and the Spirit of the Lord later helped him take the garments to satisfy the riddle (Judg 14:19).[149] The cause of his handing over by Israel was his anger in burning the Philistines' grain after his wife was given to his "friend," συνεταίρῳ σου (Judg 15:2).

The use of παραδίδωμι and the situational markers of betrayal occur in 15:12–13, when three thousand armed men from Judah come to hand Samson over (παραδοῦναι) to the Philistines. This illustrates the pattern previously established where no one who is handed over has any say. Samson extracted a vow that they would only hand him over (παραδώσομέν), not kill him.[150] In context, the reader knows that God's hand has been on Samson since before his birth and has not yet been withdrawn. Any doubts should have been dispelled by his actions under the power of the Spirit when he struck down many Philistines (Judg 15:14–15),[151] from whom Samson could never expect a fair trial. His handing over is an (attempted) betrayal by his own people,[152] "a strict piece of police work on behalf of their

---

146. So Soggin, *Judges*, 239; Moore, *Judges*, 327. Not just a foreigner, she was a Philistine, one of Israel's oppressors (Pressler, *Joshua*, 215).

147. Pressler, *Joshua*, 216.

148. Soggin, *Judges*, 236; Moore, *Judges*, 317.

149. The first of Samson's "fits of demonic rage" (ibid., 326). This is implausible without direct evidence, as Samson's rages always had at least some justification, however small.

150. Niditch, *Judges*, 159.

151. This would violate the Nazirite ban on touching corpses (Soggin, *Judges*, 250). He fails to account for the fact that it was done by "the Spirit of the LORD" (Judg 15:14).

152. The author did not see Judah's conduct "as pusillanimous," but only an opportunity for Samson to make "havoc amongst the uncircumcised." (Moore, *Judges*, 344) This is not shown by the text, with Samson attempting to make the best bargain with

enemies."[153] The angelophany (Judg 13:3, 13) and the effect of the Spirit (14:19; 15:14–15) show that he was superior to the ordinary Israelites of whom these things were not said. As expected, the narrative is held together by numerous references to God's presence (Judg 14:4, 6, 19; 15:14, 19).[154]

Samson and Delilah

If the Israelites had tried but failed to betray him to the Philistines, Delilah succeeded in the fourth and most serious betrayal.[155] Another woman coaxed him to divulge a secret, while protesting his love for her (Judg 16:5).[156]

Delilah is never called a friend of Samson, but he did fall in love with her (Judg 16:4), as shown by her presumably quoting his own words, "I love you," back to him (16:15). This is a deeper response than Samson expressed to anyone else. As a woman, she was socially inferior to Samson, quite apart from the marks of God's activity in his life. The narrator builds tension in the three attempted betrayals (16:8, 16:12,[157] 16:14[158]), with the same "Samson, the Philistines are upon you!" (16:9, 12, 14, 20). Delilah is the third woman with whom Samson has been linked—the others are his wife (ch. 14) and the prostitute in Gaza (Judg 16:1). Protesting his love for her, she brings him

---

three thousand armed Israelites. Such detail would be unnecessary for a story leading to Samson's triumph over the Philistines.

153. Soggin, *Judges*, 250.

154. This action of the Spirit is "divine rage" (Moore, *Judges*, 331). The problem is that the narrator does not mention any anger of God or Samson, unlike Judg 14:19, 15:3. The narrative reads like a provision of divine power for an essential life-preserving task, like his massacre of the Philistines (15:15). It joins his own anger with that of the Spirit (ibid., 338). This needs a better argument.

155. Delilah's name may mean "dedicated to deity X" from the Akkadian (Soggin, *Judges*, 253). Perhaps this shows that Delilah is pagan. It is unclear how one separated to God could consort with a prostitute without serious consequences. Samson, who followed the desires of his eyes, has them removed (16:21; ibid., 258), following the rabbinic Bab. Sotah 9b. An eloquent warning, perhaps.

156. Excepting Song of Songs, no woman in the Bible is ever said to love a man (Ackerman, "Personal," 437–58). While some relationships are clearly mutual—e.g., Rachel and Jacob—in most cases the socially superior party is described as loving the socially inferior party. This is why Hosea can slip so easily from Yahweh's covenantal love for Israel to his personal love for Gomer (Hos 14; ibid., 447).

157. One cannot decide whether the bindings were done in sport or while he slept (Moore, *Judges*, 352), but perhaps it did not matter, as Samson was conscious that he had not disclosed the source of his strength.

158. The hair was braided because "No razor may be used on his head" (Judg 13:5; Moore, *Judges*, 354). As a Nazirite, Samson's hair was the "symbol of his separation to God." (Num 6:7).

undone when he divulges the source of his strength (Judg 16:17),[159] and, contrary to Judges 13:5, is shorn.[160] This continues a pattern of disregarding the Nazirite requirements, and he pays with his life. Delilah's actions are treacherous,[161] as her motivation seemed to be the 1100 shekels promised by each Philistine lord (Judg 16:5).[162] In betraying someone close for money, she is somewhat like Judas.

The Philistines attributed Samson's capture to Dagon (παρέδωκεν) (Judg 16:23–24). God never let an action of his to be attributed to an idol, lest anyone doubt his uniqueness. This may explain why God answered the disobedient Samson's prayer in Dagon's temple.[163]

Patterns in Samson's life

Each of the preceding betrayals contains most of the elements referred to in s3.1. The final element, the deteriorating situation, can be seen as the narrative progresses. With each successive betrayal, Samson's condition worsens.

Firstly, seeing and perceiving correctly is a verbal thread. The angel of the Lord "sees" Samson's mother (Judg 13:3) and announces her pregnancy. The angel appears, or "sees," again in Judges 13:10.[164] In Judges 13:21–22, both see the angel ascend, but Manoah, afraid of being struck by God, does not perceive God's message correctly, though his wife does.[165] In the next four uses of seeing, Samson sees three unclean people/things: the pagan Timnite (Judg 14:1–2), the lion's carcass (Judg 14:8), and the prostitute

---

159. Niditch, *War*, 113.

160. Moore, *Judges*, 355. Monotheistic religions caused a rupture between ancient expressions of religion and sexuality because of "male" deities (Leeming, "Sexuality," 101). Women are now seen as dangerous, because they have been removed from the godhead. So, Leeming argues that Delilah deprived Samson of "his manhood by cutting off his hair" (ibid., 106). This does not pay careful attention to the text, where it is Samson's hair as a Nazirite, not as a man, which is the issue. He also does not address another possible interpretation: that women are not dangerous, but simply powerless, because of their alleged removal from the godhead.

161. Following the death of the Timnite, Delilah may have felt threatened, and did what was necessary to survive (Pressler, *Joshua*, 222).

162. It was over one hundred times more than Micah's priest's yearly stipend (Niditch, *Judges*, 169).

163. This is the first recorded time that Samson had to pray to exercise his strength (Judg 16:28); the mere regrowth of his hair was insufficient.

164. Galpaz-Feller, *Samson*, 21.

165. Cf. Gideon's sacrifice to the LORD in Judg 6:19–24, where Gideon, afraid that he had *seen* the LORD's angel, was comforted by the LORD; whereas here, Manoah's wife reassures him (Pressler, *Joshua*, 213).

(Judg 16:1). In each case, Samson sees but does not perceive the danger to a Nazirite. The angel of the Lord said three times in Judges 13:4, 7, and 14 that the mother should eat nothing unclean, but honey from the lion's carcass would have been unclean.[166] The final group of seeing verbs relate to pagans, who see but do not perceive. In Judges 16:5, the Philistine lords asked Delilah to find the source of his strength, which she "saw" in Judges 16:18. In Judges 16:24, when the Philistines "saw" the captive Samson, they praised Dagon. While they saw outwardly, they did not perceive correctly, because, unlike Samson's mother, they did not perceive the hand of God. Ironically, Samson only saw his reliance on God and the need for prayer (Judg 16:28) on being blinded.[167]

Secondly, Samson's relationships with women display a similar deterioration. Marriage to the Timnite was a recognized relationship, but inappropriate for an Israelite, especially a Nazirite. She is unnamed, and her dialogue with Samson is telling, accusing him of not loving her by not revealing the riddle (Judg 14:16). His response is dismissive, but he later unsuccessfully attempts a reconciliation (Judg 15:1). She betrays Samson, and both she and her father pay with their lives (Judg 15:6). Samson's second "relationship" is with a prostitute (Judg 16:1). She is also unnamed, and no dialogue is recorded,[168] but at least there are no deaths. Such a casual relationship is worse than marriage.[169] Samson's last and worst relationship is with Delilah, presumably pagan, as it is hard to imagine a faithful Israelite woman in league with the Philistines. Samson seemed to love Delilah, who coaxed him into revealing his secret. The Timnite's coaxing led to the deaths of herself and her father (Judg 14:15; 15:6), whereas Delilah's coaxing led to the deaths of over three thousand Philistines and Samson himself.

Lastly, as the story progresses, there is an increasing number of deaths. While God used the events to punish the Philistines, Samson's decisions cost the lives of his wife, her father, thirty men from Ashkelon, many Philistines

---

166. Lev 11:3, 8: "You may eat any animal that has a split hoof completely divided and that chews the cud . . . You must not eat their meat or touch their carcasses; they are unclean." A lion does not chew the cud, so it was unclean. Contact with its carcass made Samson unclean.

Samson's marriage with a pagan unfortunately reflected the earlier situation of Esau (Gen 36:2), who had similarly made his parents' lives bitter (Gen 26:35). Samson appeared to have forgotten Joshua's dire warning in 23:12–13: "if you intermarry with them . . . they will become snares and traps for you . . . until you perish from this good land, which the LORD your God has given you."

167. The best example of "everyone doing what was right in their own eyes" (Galpaz-Feller, *Samson*, 280).

168. In her muteness, she functions as a mirror to Samson (ibid., 143).

169. It "contributes to his portrayal as a womanizer" (Niditch, *Judges*, 167).

at Lehi, three thousand Philistines at the temple of Dagon, and Samson himself (Judg 14:19; 15:6, 15; 16:30). The Spirit is linked with all deaths except the Timnite and her father. It is ironic that the Philistines gathered to sacrifice to Dagon (Judg 16:23), only to become a sacrifice (16:30). "Gideon pulled down the altar of Baal; Samson . . . the entire temple of Dagon."[170]

In summary, Samson's life is a parable of the danger of false friendship. A lonely figure, he was betrayed by the two women to whom he was closest: his wife and Delilah. His one-sided love for Delilah[171] blinded him to what was happening, but his own lack of concern for the Nazirite vows proved his undoing. Had he been more careful here, he may have escaped, as in the past. However, for all his faults, God never abandoned him, and used him to win a significant victory over the Philistines, particularly where it mattered most: the temple of the idol Dagon.[172]

Samson's handing over is a very rare event where one part of Israel hands another part to a common enemy without reason, like Jesus. Despite Samson's open disobedience, God's presence was not finally withdrawn until he was shorn. It was inconceivable that Samson could have received a fair trial, given Philistine antipathy, just as Jesus could never have received a fair trial from the temple authorities, who were actively seeking evidence for a capital charge (Luke 22:2). Both also died: Samson in Dagon's temple (Judg 16:30), and Jesus on the cross (Luke 24:46). A crucial difference was Samson's increasing disdain for the Nazirite requirements, against Jesus' resolute obedience to the point of death. Finally, the terms παραδίδωμι and ἑταῖρος, which are essential in interpreting the act of Judas, are arguably the most critical terms in the Samson narratives.

170. Pressler, *Joshua*, 223.
171. Galpaz-Feller, *Samson*, 165.
172. There is another element in the verb "saw"; *b*, with the infinitive of *ra'a*, means looking at an enemy in Prov 29:16; Obad 13; and Ps 91:8 (Emerton, "Looking," 195). He regards its use in Judg 16:27 as "ambiguous," as it is not clear that "the verse is saying more than that the crowd came to watch . . . Samson" (ibid., 190). It is hard to imagine the Philistines not gloating at their former tormentor, blinded and grinding in the temple of their god, Dagon. Further evidence is found in Lemos, "Shame," 225–41. Mutilation is caused "by an external agent or force," and shame relates to lacking honor in the eyes of "an observing other" (ibid., 227–28). Apart from giving eloquent testimony to a power differential, mutilation struck at the heart of the Israelites' equation of beauty with symmetry and freedom from blemishes, enabling participation in the cult (ibid., 231); e.g., 2 Sam 5:8. See s2.3.4 for an understanding that disability repulsed David. The Ammonite humiliation of David's envoys in 1 Sam 10, "damaging their beauty," shows that this understanding was not restricted to the Israelites (Avioz, "Beauty," 345). What makes mutilation shameful is its public nature (Judg 16; Emerton, "Shame," 239). Samson had been blinded, bound, and reduced to a woman's work of grinding (Judg 16:21). None of this needed to be public, but shame can only be public, and so they summoned Samson to play before them (Judg 16:25), which led to their deaths.

2.3.3. Jonadab/Amnon

The incident with Amnon[173] and Jonadab, after David's murder of Uriah, is an outworking of God's judgment (2 Sam 12:10).[174] Amnon was a son of David, and Jonadab a son of David's brother Shimeah, so they were cousins (2 Sam 13:1, 3).[175] Jonadab was called τῷ Ἀμνων ἑταῖρος (2 Sam 13:3). Amnon was in line to the throne as a son of David, and so superior to Jonadab. He was σοφὸς σφόδρα (LXX), "shrewd" or "exceedingly wise."[176] The ungodly nature of his wisdom became clearer as he advised Amnon on raping the object of his desire,[177] his cousin Tamar (2 Sam 13:5).[178] Tamar was asked to cook special food[179] to entice her into Amnon's room.

Jonadab's advice was the first betrayal as he ignored his responsibilities to uphold the law by protecting female members of the court. He also betrayed his friendship with Amnon, as his advice led to Amnon's murder by Absalom's men (2 Sam 13:29),[180] Tamar being Absalom's sister (2 Sam 13:1).[181]

173. "Amnon" (ironically) means faithful (Anderson, 2 *Samuel*, 13:1).

174. David's crime was bloodshed, and his house will suffer similar violence (ibid.). Nathan's speech breaks the flow and prefigures Markan sandwiches (Edwards, "Markan Sandwiches," 202). The whole saga is integral to the Succession Narrative, foreshadowing the trouble to affect David (Blenkinsopp, "Succession," 38).

175. Anderson, 2 *Samuel*, 13:3.

176. Wesselius's belief that the narrator's view of Jonadab "is on the whole not unfavorable" is extraordinary ("Joab's Death," 350). Jonadab's advice means the rape/desolation of Tamar, Amnon's death, and (arguably) sets in motion Adonijah's rebellion. The narrator views none of this favorably. This is heightened by 2 Sam 21:21: "Jonathan son of Shimeah, David's brother"; and 2 Sam 13:3: "Jonadab son of Shimeah, David's brother," so they were brothers. He argues (without proof) that, besides Uriah, a number of other "servants of the king" were killed (2 Sam 11:17, 24; ibid., 351), which may have included Jonathan. Jonadab's advice to Amnon was a desire to punish David. Punishing David by having his granddaughter raped is completely at odds with a "not unfavorable" assessment by the narrator, and secondly, the text provides no evidence at all of this as his motivation. He wisely concludes (ibid., 351): "All this must remain speculative, of course."

177. The threefold repetition of Amnon's love for Tamar (vv. 1, 4, 15) so jars our sensibilities that some translate the word as desire or lust, but Ackerman argues that the word carries its normal Biblical pattern of the feelings (debased here, of course) of a superior for an inferior (Ackerman, "Personal," 453).

178. Tamar, being unmarried, may have been confined to the women's quarters, and hence inaccessible to Amnon (Anderson, 2 *Samuel*, 13:2).

179. "Make" can also mean (sexually) "arouse," to indicate what lies ahead (Anderson, 2 *Samuel*, 13:6).

180. Absalom had probably decided that conventional legal methods offered little prospect of justice, and decided on direct action like "Simeon and Levi (Gen. 34:30–31)." (ibid., 13:20). "David thought that this would be an acceptable step towards a termination of the affair" (Daube, "Absalom," 320).

181. This may have whetted Absalom's appetite for the throne (Wesselius, "Joab's

This may be an outworking of God's judgment. Leviticus 20:17 bans a man from intercourse with his sister. David and Abigail are both children of Jesse (1 Chr 2:13–16), so David breached Leviticus 20:17 (1 Sam 25:39),[182] if she is the same Abigail. "He ... will be held responsible" means divine punishment, not a human court (Num 5:31).[183] The marriage and the rape seem linked: "disgrace" is common (2 Sam 13:13; 1 Sam 25:39). In Hebrew, Tamar's "wicked fools" resonates with Nabal, Abigail's late husband, and her "will not keep me" resonates with Amnon's name and the words spoken by David and Abigail to each other (1 Sam 25:26).[184] Yet again, David's disregard for the law has its own penalty.

More evidence about Amnon's nature is shown by צנה, normally translated "rape," which means the victim's debasement, not the act itself. Where a man has intercourse with a woman betrothed to another, there is no force, as the woman was punished for not calling for help (Deut 22:23–24). The crime is the woman's debasement, not rape.[185] When the act happens in the country, only the man dies, as forcing down the woman is like forcing down and killing a man (Deut 22:25–27). Amnon desires to sleep with Tamar who, while protesting, offers a solution: asking David for her as his wife (2 Sam 13:13). But he will not listen and rapes her. Tamar's protest at her expulsion shows his true desire: to rape and humiliate, implying that not even a rapist would marry her.[186]

David's indifference to Tamar is a second betrayal. He is not called a "friend" of Tamar, but her rape occurs because of Jonadab's betrayal of Amnon. As she was the sister of his son, he should have brought Amnon to justice, quite apart from his role as king. It is a very rare case of a superior betraying an inferior. It also showed, for the first (but not the last) time, David as a "weak father."[187] He did not bring Amnon or Absalom to justice (2 Sam 13:21). David is "guiltier ... than Amnon: he has the last say ... social death."[188] He may have felt that Amnon's crime was all too similar to his crime against Uriah.[189]

Death," 346).

182. Hepner, "Marriage," 153.

183. Ibid., 154.

184. Ibid., 153.

185. Van Wolde, "Analysis," 536.

186. Anderson, *2 Samuel*, 13:12–14; Van Wolde, "Analysis," 540.

187. Sweeney, "Solomon," 618. David was the same with Adonijah, not rebuking his behavior (1 Kgs 1:6).

188. Daube, "Absalom," 317.

189. Wesselius, "Joab's Death," 345; Avioz, "Beauty," 350.

2.3.4. The dynamics between Hushai, David, and Joab

Hushai

The narrator prepares the ground for the enormity of Joab's betrayal of David by implicitly contrasting him with two others whose loyalty to David is questioned, but who remain loyal: Hushai, and to a lesser extent Mephibosheth. Who is his true friend: Hushai, who is described with variations of Χουσι ὁ ἑταῖρος Δαυιδ (2 Sam 15:32, 37; 16:16) and as πρῶτος φίλος τοῦ βασιλέως (1 Chr 27:33),[190] or Joab who is called ὁ ἀρχιστράτηγος ἑταῖρος (of David) in Solomon's outburst[191] to Bathsheba (1 Kgs 2:22)?[192] The narrator views Hushai favorably, helping David when it was unclear whether he would succeed. However, Joab is viewed unfavorably: to Solomon, he is linked with Abiathar, whom he removed as priest, "fulfilling the word the Lord had spoken . . . about the house of Eli" (1 Kgs 2:27).

The true nature of Hushai's friendship is shown in agreeing to a dangerous request to be David's spy in Absalom's camp. Even Absalom is taken aback by Hushai's apparent rapid change of allegiance from his "friend" (2 Sam 16:16-17),[193] but Hushai replies in words like David's, and is accepted. He did not notice that Hushai was apparently plotting the death of the king he had been serving so recently. Hushai's protestations that he would serve the one chosen by the Lord (2 Sam 16:18) was a masterful sleight of hand.

The narrator compares the behavior of Mephibosheth toward David with that of Hushai toward Absalom, as both are asked "Why did you not go?" (2 Sam 19:25, 16:17).[194] There is no doubt about Hushai's loyalty, but Mephibosheth compares David to "an angel of God" used by the Tekoite when deceiving him (2 Sam 19:27; 14:20).[195] His relief at David's return may be no more than, with Shimei's pardoning (2 Sam 19:23), him not

---

190. This shows that ἑταῖρος and φίλος can apply to the same person, but their usage in Samson's case (s2.3.2) shows that they are not identical.

191. He is like "a typical oriental potentate" (Blenkinsopp, "Succession," 44).

192. David, being the brother of Joab's mother Zeruiah, was his uncle (1 Chr 2:16). After Joab killed Abner, David rebuked him and Abishai as "sons of Zeruiah" (2 Sam 3:39). By not using the normal patronymic, he may have been reminding them of their familial relationship to him, and so stressing their disloyalty. This may be an important royal office, as Zabud is listed with other high officials as "the king's friend" (1 Kgs 4:5; Anderson, *2 Samuel*, 15:37). It also makes better sense of 2 Sam 16:18, where a royal official could serve any king, rather than just those for whom he felt some personal attachment.

193. Schipper, "Mephibosheth," 344-51.

194. Ibid., 349.

195. Ibid., 350.

eliminating enemies.[196] Schipper argues that both Mephibosheth and Hushai are only pretending to be loyal to David and Absalom respectively, but neither are. Is there a traitor near David?

In 2 Samuel 9, Mephibosheth is called to David. His servant, Ziba, will only use his patronymic "son of Jonathan," adding that "he is crippled in both feet" (2 Sam 9:3). All Jonathan's property went to Mephibosheth due to "kindness" (הֶסֶד or covenantal faithfulness), which links this passage (2 Sam 9:1, 3, 7) and David's departure from Jonathan (1 Sam 20:8, 14–15).[197] Schipper fails to note Ziba's attitude (who lies to David in 2 Sam 16). When asked why Mephibosheth was not with him, Ziba said, "He is staying in Jerusalem, because . . . 'Today the house of Israel will give me back my grandfather's kingdom.'" (16:3). This was a treasonous accusation and a betrayal. Ziba had taken the very asses which the lame Mephibosheth needed and claimed improbably that he was a contender for the throne. David said to Ziba, without even questioning Mephibosheth, "All that belonged to Mephibosheth is now yours" (16:4).[198] Why?

Vargon analyzes "the blind and the lame" (2 Sam 4:4, 9; 5:6–9; 9:27) to argue that David had a genuine distaste for the disabled. It shows David's "cruel . . . vengeful" nature, like when he executed Moabite prisoners of war (2 Sam 8).[199] Niditch also notes that the Chronicler removed the reference to the blind and lame (1 Chr 11) to avoid David's difficult response.[200] It is easier to imagine this deletion from an earlier account in 2 Samuel 5, compared with adding it for no clear reason. The narratives of those destined for greatness frequently show them triumphing over adversity, like David killing Goliath (1 Sam 17). But Vargon argues that David's contempt for the Jebusites, "the lame and the blind" (2 Sam 5:8), reveals an internal struggle. Perhaps Ziba knew this.

As requested by David, Hushai rebuts Ahithophel's good advice, advising Absalom first to gather overwhelming force (2 Sam 17:11). Hushai stressed David's well-known fighting skills and his smaller but battle-hardened army.[201] The hand of God is seen twice: to fulfill the punishment that the sword would never depart from David's house (2 Sam 12:10) and to bring disaster on Absalom (2 Sam 17:14),[202] presumably for rebellion

196. Ibid., 351.
197. Vargon, "Blind," 504.
198. Ibid., 506.
199. Niditch, *War*, 130.
200. Ibid., 133.
201. Anderson, *2 Samuel*, 17:5–11. David and his men are men of valor (Niditch, *War*, 91)
202. Janzen, *Ethics*, 131.

against David. As expected, one of the main players died when Joab killed Absalom (2 Sam 18:14). Although Hushai pretended to serve Absalom, at great potential cost he served David. Like Jonathan previously interceding for David with Saul (1 Sam 20:32), Hushai showed his true, loyal nature.

Even at Mephibosheth's restoration (2 Sam 19), David almost cuts him off, and orders him and Ziba to divide the fields, only giving back half. If Hushai pretended to betray David but was loyal, Mephibosheth was also loyal, but treated like a traitor/opportunist, arguably because of David's dislike of the disabled; Ziba clearly fitted both descriptions. Mephibosheth's loyalty to David, with much to lose personally, heightens the enormity of Joab's later betrayal of David, who had received much from David, and also reveals an unpleasant character flaw in him.

Joab

The narrator would want us to see Joab, ὁ ἀρχίστράτηγος ἑταῖρος (of David; 1 Kgs 2:22), very differently. Joab, as army chief, is listed first amongst David's officials (2 Sam 8:16), but was inferior to David. Joab is never the subject of παραδίδωμι, but there are many situational markers of betrayal as this "friend" betrays David four times.[203]

---

203. But Biddle argues cogently (although confusing Saul and Solomon): "Although in some instances Joab and other members of David's circle apparently act from their own motives (the ambush of Abner, for example), in every case they accomplish something for David he cannot or will not do for himself (the assassination of Ishbaal and the execution of Abner, for example). In at least one instance, the reality of David's motive underlying his apparent innocence is laid bare, namely, Joab's betrayal of Uriah. David's deathbed recommendation to Saul concerning Joab confirms the notion that David kept Joab around largely because Joab's violent propensities benefited the king" ("Motifs," 617–38).

Their relationship was "mainly . . . utilitarian" (Wesselius, "Joab's Death," 336–37) as David felt unable to resist Joab and Abishai when they killed Abner, whose correct spelling is "Abiner," based on 4QSama (Freedman, "Abiner," 125; 2 Sam 3:39). However, David insisted that they undertake public mourning to show that "David did not intend the death of Abner," even though the presumption "is that the king is responsible for the actions of . . . his men." The people approved of David's grief for Abner (Weitzman, "David's Lament," 354). Joab led the attack on the Jebusites, and became commander-in-chief as David promised (1 Chr 11:6). The Chronicler portrays Joab positively versus 2 Sam 5:8, which says nothing of David's offer or Joab's achievement. Kalimi regards the Chronicles account as historically weak ("Jerusalem," 66–79). The death of Abner is the first of four cases where a man's passion for a woman led to his death or that of her husband—the others being David, Amnon, and Adonijah (Von Seters, "Love," 121).

Joab and Abishai murdered Abner[204] *hors de combat*, as he had killed their brother Asahel in battle (2 Sam 3:27; 2:23).[205] Abner had left David "in peace" (2 Sam 3:23) to bring Israel over to him. Ironically, Joab accused Abner of treason toward David in 3:25: "Abner . . . came to deceive you."[206] He also killed Amasa (2 Sam 20:10),[207] possibly jealous that David had asked him, not Joab, to summon Israel. David advised execution for these two deaths in particular (1 Kgs 2:5–6).[208]

In the next betrayal, he obeyed David, so that Uriah the Hittite died (2 Sam 11:14).[209] It is extraordinary that Joab did this. Why not fake his death? Joab betrayed his responsibilities to Uriah, as well as his responsibility to resist David's criminal orders. If he had resisted, he may have been more successful in resisting David's disastrous census (2 Sam 24:3).[210]

Thirdly, Joab, against David's explicit orders, killed Absalom *hors de combat* (2 Sam 18:15), betraying his duties to David and the army. It is reasonable to see this as an outworking of God's judgment on Absalom (and David), but Joab must be accountable for Absalom's death.[211] Also, "Joab . . . has been as much a father to Absalom as has the king."[212] Joab sensed David's grief for Absalom, and asked the Tekoite to give this judgment: "the king has not brought back his banished son" (2 Sam 14:14).[213] David thinks first of Joab when discerning her motive. Having been restored, but forbid-

---

204. It "may have been . . . personal revenge and not a legally justifiable act" (Anderson, *2 Samuel*, 3:27) is too mild. The narrator gives no justification. Joab is "odious" (Blenkinsopp, "Succession," 40).

205. Niditch, *War*, 96.

206. Anderson, *2 Samuel*, 3:25.

207. "Joab may have wished to prolong his suffering, and therefore deliberately did not administer the *coup de grâce*." (Anderson, *2 Samuel*, 20:11). Blenkinsopp calls it "treacherous" ("Succession," 42).

208. David's request is unfair and based "in his own feelings of guilt" for his rebellious son Absalom (Niditch, *War*, 136). Whatever his feelings, he had a duty as king to uphold the law, so perhaps this should be seen as better late than never. This shows how far David has fallen since 2 Sam 3—his grief is now improper and socially isolating (Weitzman, "David's Lament," 354).

209. Ironically, Uriah carried his own death warrant (Anderson, *2 Samuel*, 11:14). He also argues that the murder was pointless, as it was hardly likely that any Israelite court would convict the king of adultery, and if so, what penalty could they possibly impose? Uriah was one of the Thirty Heroes (2 Sam 23:39; Daube, "Absalom," 320). It was "an utterly revolting deed and a grave offence" (Wesselius, "Joab's Death," 345).

210. "For once Joab is presented as the voice of good sense" (Anderson, *2 Samuel*, 24:3)

211. Abner's prior slaying of Asahel is Joab's pretext (Von Seters, "Love," 122).

212. Abramson, "Drama," 63–82.

213. Niditch, *War*, 36.

den to see David, Absalom turned on Joab by, unusually, burning his fields (14:30). None of this prevented Joab from killing Absalom the next time he saw him (2 Sam 18:14).

Lastly, in the worst betrayal, Joab supported Adonijah as king (1 Kgs 1:7)[214] to capitalize on David's infirmity. He attended the feast, but then fled, and Benaiah killed him on Solomon's orders (1 Kgs 2:34).[215] Bathsheba did not leave this entirely to providence, asking David to appoint Solomon as king else, "I and ... Solomon will be treated as criminals." (1 Kgs 1:21). Solomon pardoned Adonijah, but when he later requested Abishag, Bathsheba omitted his acknowledgement of Solomon's kingship (1 Kgs 2:15) when asking publicly, "making the ... elimination of Adonijah and Joab, Adonijah's most dangerous partisan, almost inevitable."[216] She caused the death of Adonijah, and of Joab, who had killed her first husband Uriah.[217]

Joab's treachery in supporting Adonijah is the true measure of the one who had been a friend of the king. All the deadly turmoil in David's house was a result of God's punishment, but no one, not the narrator or any of the characters—least of all David—saw this as excusing Joab. He, like Judas, is truly a trusted servant who turned on his master.

2.3.5. Ahithophel[218]

Ahithophel is never called the ἑταῖρος or φίλος of David, but he may have been even more important. Hushai was called πρῶτος φίλος τοῦ βασιλέως, but Ahithophel was σύμβουλος τοῦ βασιλέως (1 Chr 27:33). The key difference is that David and Absalom regarded his advice as like God's (2 Sam 16:23), something not said of Hushai. So, it is appropriate to consider him amongst other former friends who turned traitor.

---

214. Adonijah controlled the army, compared with Benaiah's smaller palace guard (DeVries, *1 Kings*, 1:7).

215. David's advice to Solomon was based on Joab's killing of Abner and Amasa without warning, as well as his support for Adonijah's accession, so that Solomon could be Joab's next target. Executing Joab would remove the bloodguilt for two innocent men from David's—and Solomon's—house (Janzen, "Joab," 265).

216. Wesselius, "Joab's Death," 348.

217. Ibid., 348.

218. Ahithophel was Bathsheba's maternal grandfather; see 2 Sam 11:3: "Bathsheba, the daughter of Eliam"; and 23:34: "Eliam son of Ahithophel the Gilonite." Bathsheba betrayed her husband to be with David. God's judgment set in motion the circumstances which lead to Ahithophel's betrayal of David to Absalom (Daube, "Absalom," 321). So also Hertzberg, *I & II Samuel*, 310.

It is remarkable how quickly Ahithophel changes camps.[219] Called David's counselor (2 Sam 15:12), very soon (and without explanation) he was "among the conspirators with Absalom" (15:31). Joab had a history of murder and wilfulness by the time he betrayed David, perhaps to ensure his position in the incoming administration, but the narrator provides no reason for Ahithophel's switch.

If Joab betrayed David the most, only Ahithophel counseled how David might be killed, and so he is worse. His advice for Absalom to lie with David's concubines is puzzling, for this was no additional warrant for the throne, but may have had him acting as though David was dead.[220] This fulfilled David's punishment from God, that what he had done secretly would happen in broad daylight (2 Sam 12:12).[221] While this would irritate David, Joab's advice to fight the king immediately was potentially lethal, and shows the extent of his treachery.[222] God was again working to punish Absalom by defeating Ahithophel's wise advice (2 Sam 17:14).[223] Absalom's obsession with his appearance—"there was no blemish in him" (2 Sam 14:25)—may have been crucial. He preferred Hushai's flattery to the plainspoken Ahithophel.[224] In context, there is a real contrast between Hushai, who pretends to betray David but is faithful, and Ahithophel, who makes clear where his sympathies lie. Again, as expected, the traitors died: Ahithophel by suicide (2 Sam 17:23) and Absalom by Joab (2 Sam 18:15).

2.3.6. Summary of the LXX

The data shows a friend, or one of whom friendly relations can be presumed because of the trust placed in them, turning on their master, who is usually in a position of social superiority. While God is always shown as achieving his purposes through the treachery, nowhere is the traitor thereby absolved. God would never reward Jonadab for advising Amon on raping Tamar, or Joab for his murders *hors de combat*, or Ahithophel for counselling how David might

---

219. The loss of being the king's counselor was too much (Zwiep, "Matthias," 68).

220. Anderson, *2 Samuel*, 16:21.

221. Unlike other Ancient Near East countries, Israel's king was subject to the law of God (Baker, *Wealth*, 200).

222. Anderson, *2 Samuel*, 17:2–3.

223. Carasik, "Limits," 221–32: "the only instance of direct divine intervention in the Succession" (Wesselius, "Joab's Death," 349).

224. Ackerman, "Good," 41–60. While Absalom is attractive (2 Sam 14), he lacks the internal moral beauty which was felt to accompany physical beauty (Avioz, "Beauty," 352).

be killed (2 Sam 13:5; 3:27; 17:2). The traitor usually dies, and in a gruesome manner (Joab in 1 Kgs 2:34; Ahithophel in 2 Sam 17:23), although others may also die. Hushai places himself at great personal risk to support David, his friend, as Jonathan had done many years previously (2 Sam 15:34).

2.3.7. "Friend" in Josephus

Josephus is another ancient writer who discusses treacherous friends, using both ἑταῖρος and φίλος. The following three narratives all include some of the following: someone called a "friend" is appointed to a position of trust, they consciously abuse that trust for base reasons, and death results. In context, all three would appear to be traitors.

Gaius Julius Eurycles of Sparta

Eurycles was not appointed to an office, but Josephus recorded that he became one of Herod's "most intimate friends" because of his skill in manipulating Herod and his regard for Sparta (φίλος; *J.W.* 1:515).[225] He had two strategies: he gave Herod "splendid gifts," but also "perceived Herod's blind side . . . and did everything that might please him" (*J.W.* 1:515). He also perceived the weaknesses of the sons Antipater, Aristobulus, and Alexander. While lodging with Antipater, he moved to work on the others. He "falsely claimed to be an old acquaintance (φιλίᾳ) of Archelaus" (*J.W.* 1:516), which disarmed them. He pretended friendship toward Alexander, but drew out his negative view of Antipater.

He then led Aristobulus to say similar things, and induced both brothers to complain about Herod (*J.W.* 1:516). He "undertook the work of bringing Alexander and Aristobulus to their graves" (*J.W.* 1:520) and presented to Herod serious accusations against them. While "Herod found the proofs too weak," Herod still called him "his savior and benefactor" and imprisoned his sons (*J.W.* 1:530). Caesar later banished him for his many crimes, not least of which the attempt on the lives of Alexander and Aristobulus.

No one died immediately because of Eurycles, but only because Herod found the proofs unconvincing, not through Eurycles's lack of effort. Though a friend, he betrayed Herod for money. Later, however, Diophantes died for forgery (*J.W.* 1:529), Alexander and Aristobulus died in Sebaste

---

225. Herod "always had Greeks about him," so Eurycles's access was not unusual (Gilbert, "Jews," 520–40).

(*J.W.* 1:551), as well as their allies. Eurycles was a traitor as he engineered these deaths for his own advantage.

Noarus

When Agrippa went to Antioch, he left a "friend" (τῶν ἑταίρων) in charge: Noarus[226] (*J.W.* 2:481), a relative of King Sohaemus, son of Sampsigeramus.[227] Philip Ben Jakimos fell ill and, fleeing to Gamala in Galilee, sent a letter to Agrippa via Noarus,[228] who felt threatened and killed the messengers.[229] Seventy men came from Batanea asking for protection. Instead, he sent a palace guard to kill them, despite them being "his own countrymen," and later killed twelve men on a peace mission from Caesarea.[230] Josephus gives no motive beyond calling Noarus "a lover of money." When Agrippa was told, he did not have him executed, "out of regard to Sohemus," but immediately ended his procuratorship.[231] By killing, without any reason whatsoever, the countrymen of King Agrippa, who appointed him, Noarus can fairly be called a traitor.

Flavius Josephus ben Mattathias

The greatest concentration of "friend," "hand over," and "traitor" is in Josephus's speech at Jotapata. He was the Jewish general in Galilee (*J.W.* 2:360; 2:568), possibly the son of a priest and one himself (*J.W.* 2:352). He had unrivaled positional and personal authority. The terms in Josephus's speech show that he was acutely aware of being labeled a traitor by his soldiers, whom he calls ἑταῖροι in *J.W.* 3:362 and 3:379.

---

226. Josephus mistakenly called Varus "Noarus" (Ilan and Price, "Onomastic," 189–208). Price ("Enigma," 80, 89) and Jones ("Ituraean," 265–75) agree.
227. Barrett, "Sohaemus," 154.
228. Price, "Enigma," 80.
229. Ibid., 80.
230. Ibid., 80.
231. Ibid., 80.

GREEK TERMINOLOGY

J.W.	Term	Implication
3.354	Traitor	Prayer that he might not be seen as a traitor when surrendering to the Romans.
3.360	Traitor	Soldiers threaten to kill him if, having led so many Jews to death, he now surrenders.
3.361	Treachery	Would he betray his responsibilities to God if he died before the Jews were set free?
3.362	Friends	Seeking a hearing from his soldiers.
3.370	Plot against	Secretly taking life is treachery.
3.379	Friends	As for 3.362.
3.381	Traitor	He will not surrender.

The key question of whether Josephus was a traitor is complicated by his well-known ability to present himself in the best light,[232] and also that he is the only witness to some of the events described. While one other soldier emerged from the cave with Josephus, only he could describe the silent prayer (*J.W.* 3:354).[233] However, we have no choice but to engage with Josephus.

Josephus considered surrender to Rome for two reasons. First, God allowed him the allegedly prophetic task of interpreting dreams (*J.W.* 3:351).[234] His prayer that he hoped to go not "as a deserter of the Jews, but as a minister from Thee" is a request to God to fulfill this ministry (*J.W.* 3:354). Second, he adapted the prophetic view of history to explain how God was on the side of Rome to punish Jewish sin, because of Roman reverence for the temple and because all of Israel's good fortune had gone over to Rome (*J.W.* 5:378; 6:123; 3:354).[235]

---

232. Kelley, "Josephus," 258.

233. Josephus's silent prayer was not the norm in pagan societies, to avoid accusations of witchcraft (van der Horst, "Prayer," 1), where the prayer could then be counteracted by more powerful opponents. While audible prayer was normal in Judaism, van der Horst argues that the silent but effective prayer of Hannah in 1 Sam 1 initiated a change in Judaism, and later in Christianity, so that it became acceptable (ibid., 1). Hannah probably prayed silently so that her rival Peninnah would not provoke her more, but it is clear that both Josephus and Hannah were in desperate straits. This is confirmed by Josephus's use of ἀνάγκη to frame his speech in 3.361 and 3.385. Whatever the motivation, God answered Hannah and, doubtless, Josephus hoped for a similar response (ibid., 13). It is notable that Josephus even feels the need to record a prayer for which he is the only witness, and shows that he understands προδότης negatively, which is confirmed by his soldiers' reaction (Josephus, *J.W.* 3:360).

234. Kelley, "Josephus," 271.

235. Kelley, "Josephus," 262.

The speech's structure shows the pressure which Josephus felt. The symmetry is not perfect, as προδοσία precedes ἀνάγκη in 3.361. He feels threatened and appeals for calm from his troops, while trying to extricate himself from a potentially lethal situation.

    3.361: προδοσιαν

        3.361: ἀνάγκη

            3.362: ἑταῖροι

            3.379: ἑταῖροι

        3.381: προδότης

    3.385: ἀνάγκη

Josephus prayed, and then tried to accept the Roman offer, but his troops intervened and accused him of treachery. This was not the first time that Josephus had been so accused, for some young men of Dabarita had ambushed and robbed Agrippa's steward, and brought the money and goods to Josephus (*J.W.* 2:595–607). He put the money into safekeeping, intending to return it, but was put on trial for his life, only to talk his way out. He uses ἐνεδρεύω both times for treachery (*J.W.* 2:595; 3:370).

The soldiers advanced on him, and he became concerned that he would betray God if he died before they were delivered (*J.W.* 3:361). This is difficult to understand, given his later conduct, where he persuaded all but one to commit murder by lot. In the meantime, Josephus reasoned with them, much like at Dabarita, that surrender to the Romans may be appropriate, but suicide never is. This was well within current Jewish thinking.[236] Suicide was seen as a viable option during the Jewish War,[237] but Josephus and his troops differed. Josephus (conflicted due to a prophetic call) argued that surrender and slavery were preferable to an immoral suicide.[238] However, his troops were only too aware that, while slavery may have been offered, the Romans were more likely to crucify. When Josephus could not persuade

---

236. Many intertestamental texts show a lively debate on the relationship between voluntary death or martyrdom and divine reward (Shepkaru, "Afterlife," 2). He gives examples of Jews committing suicide to avoid Hellenization (1 Macc 3:17; 1:63); of the aged Eleazar going to the rack rather than submit to King Antiochus IV Epiphanes (2 Macc 6:18–30) and the examples given by Josephus: the mass suicide at Masada (*J.W.* 7.337) and Jews preferring death to effigies in the temple (*Ant.* 18.55; Shepkaru, "Afterlife," 5, 2, 9, 7). In no case was there an expectation of resurrection, just an honorable posterity. Olyan argues that Pseudo-Philo Liber Antiq. Bib. may be dated from the Jewish War, because of its debate on suicide versus fighting versus slavery ("Debate," 81). He shows that Josephus does report individual and mass suicides at Gamala, at the temple and at Masada (*J.W.* 4.79–80; 6.280; 7.389–406).

237. Olyan, "Debate," 90.

238. Ibid., 90.

them, he offered murder/suicide by lot, and they accepted. When only he and one other were left, he explained this as providence and persuaded him "to live as well as himself" (*J. W.* 3:391).

Did he betray his men? At one level, the answer must be yes. As a Jewish general in Galilee, he was responsible for all his men, and should not have had them killed unnecessarily like Joab and Uriah (2 Sam 11:14). They had all freely accepted possible death by fighting Rome, but none would have envisaged this at the hands of their comrades. He was obligated to lead his men against the Romans, not to encourage suicide *hors de combat*. Had he done so, the outcome could not have been any worse for the men who died, and they would also not be guilty of murder. If Josephus had felt called to be a prophet, he still had to do his duty to his men and leave the outcome to God. It is hard to imagine his troops not agreeing to such a proposal, especially as they all essentially agreed to suicide. While Josephus was severely pressured, his duty to his men was clear and he failed. It is reasonable to see his behavior as treacherous. Finally, like David betraying Tamar (s2.3.3), this is another example of the rare case of a superior betraying their inferiors.

2.4. Conclusion for Section 2

Secular Greek, the LXX, Josephus, and the GNT are remarkably consistent when a person is the subject of παραδίδωμι. Almost always, the handing over is coercive, like the accused murderer sent for trial (Deut 19:12) or Samson's arrest by three thousand armed Israelites (Judg 15:11). A self-offering only occurs under an external compulsion, like a siege (*J. W.* 868) or an internal compulsion to obey God (a new idea in the GNT) like Jesus in Mark 14:49. By contrast, an object is given to an accountable recipient for future use, e.g., the talents (Matt 25). An object cannot be betrayed; a person can.

God's predominance as the subject of παραδίδωμι suggests that a human handing over might be abrogating God's activity. David's refusal to kill Saul when God had left him is a dramatic contrast to Judas handing over Jesus. If abrogating to oneself a right held only by God is "an instance of blasphemy,"[239] and the same applies to acts done overwhelmingly by God, then Judas is not only a traitor but also a blasphemer.

The LXX and Josephus give examples of a "friend" who betrays a close relationship, normally with a superior, and frequently ends up paying with their own life. This breach of an existing relationship defines betrayal, and calling the traitor "friend" is a literary masterstroke which neatly

---

239. King, "Giants," 77.

encapsulates this uniquely distressing element of betrayal. As the Psalmist said, "Even my friend in whom I trusted, one who ate my bread, has lifted up his heel against me" (41:9; LXX Ps 40:10). Alternatively, a friend like Hushai can pretend to betray, but remains faithful at great potential cost.

A lack of attention by Klassen to these nuances has led him to exegete them in ways quite foreign to the LXX and Josephus. Such usages provide powerful lexical support for Judas as traitor. A key parallel is Samson, who like Jesus was called *in utero* and empowered by the Holy Spirit before (unlike Jesus) his own sin led to his undoing. Like Jesus, he was also betrayed by fellow Israelites to a common enemy for ill-treatment, if not death. There are many other examples which refute Klassen's basic thesis. Having considered the key philological terms, we now address themes which are used in the depiction of Judas.

Section 3

Rivals to God

3.1. Introduction

SECTION 2 SHOWED THAT παραδίδωμι and ἑταῖρος are consistent with betrayal. When a person is the object of παραδίδωμι, they have no say. If there is no legal or military requirement, it is always coercive. Classical and Hellenistic Greek appear to have no depiction of betrayal by a friend, which uses ἑταῖρος and παραδίδωμι, whereas Josephus does. Appendix 1 showed that God is the subject of παραδίδωμι almost 90 percent of the time. So, an improper use of παραδίδωμι may be a false claim to divinity. To avoid circularity, I will consider Judas later in the thesis, but there is nothing inherently improbable in describing a traitor by these terms.

Section 3 will try to establish whether Judas functions like an idol.[1]

To answer this, I will study the three main rivals to God: human (s3.2), demonic (s3.3–4), and material (s3.5), which coalesce in idolatry. Human and demonic rivals to God have the following four features (and material rivals to a lesser extent):

- An ascription by others or presumption by the person of divinity.
- A malicious nature or an association with evil.
- A strange powerlessness.
- A final judgment by God.

An idol is a created thing which is treated like God, is empowered by evil, and served with money. Judas is a human being who acts and is treated (wrongly) like God by the temple authorities. There are unique, profound

---

1. Pao's references deal with Luke and Acts, but further study is needed to find this pattern in the other gospels.

parallels between Judas and Satan. Lastly, Judas is rewarded with money, the NT material rival to God. Parallels between Judas and these rivals to God will be shown in s5.3.

3.2. Human rivals to God

Introduction

This section will examine the key characteristics of idols and human rivals to God, to determine if Judas has similar features and is Pao's missing idol (s1.4).

3.2.1. The nature of an idol

Idols are not just material objects, but "the visual manifestation of the powers that oppose Yahweh" and his people.[2] Yahweh's supremacy is shown over the nations, their rulers, and deities, but idols (and their makers) are especially mocked.[3] Contrasting the creativity and power of God and the idolators is relevant to the interaction between Jesus and Judas, if (as I will show) he is a NT idol.

Isaiah 40:18–20 contrasts Yahweh's claims to deity with the idolators, who are the subject of four verbs which are elsewhere used of God:[4] "spread out" (40:19; 42:5), "test" (40:19; 48:10), "select" (40:20; 41:8), and "set up" (40:20; 45:18).[5] The first two are usually used for God's creative acts, and the last two for his redemptive acts.[6] The idolators are not just making an idol—they are presuming divinity, ironically by making something which they then revere as divine. God created the heavens and the earth, but just as importantly gave life to its inhabitants (Isa 42:5; 45:18). The idolators created an idol from precious metals (Isa 40:19; 44:12; 46:6). As people are less significant than Yahweh, so are their creative efforts.[7] By misusing their limited, but still real, creative power, the idolators have forfeited that power and incurred serious consequences.

---

2. Pao, *Acts*, 182.
3. Watts, *Isaiah 34–66*, 101.
4. God's utter incomparability (Childs, *Isaiah*).
5. Holter, *Idol-Fabrication*, 54–59.
6. Ibid., 58.
7. Rudman, "Jeremiah," 66; Holter, *Idol-Fabrication*, 105.

RIVALS TO GOD

In a trial scene, Isaiah 41:4–7 mocks the idol-makers' impotence as they encourage each other.[8] The idols cannot encourage them, and they have forsaken Yahweh's encouragement, given only to his people.[9] Isaiah 41:8–10 recalls Jacob's status as chosen of the Lord, and Abraham as the one called by God to show his ongoing faithfulness.[10] Both idols and their makers will be shamed, the makers becoming (worthless) like their idols (Isa 44:9–11, 18–20).[11] The condemnation of idols is directly related to God's sovereignty over all things, especially his people. The whole nature of Second Isaiah shows that his willingness to save is not to be presumed upon. The God who judged the nations and idols also sent Israel into exile for serving those same idols.[12]

Next, Isaiah 40–55 stresses Yahweh's power and his opponents' impotence;[13] only he is God and there is no one beside him (Isa 45:21–22).[14] Yahweh is sovereign on behalf of an obedient Israel against the powerless nations and idols.[15] He reassures exiled Israel that he will deliver them when he is ready, and no one will stop him.[16] Yahweh recalls his judgment on "all the gods of Egypt"[17] in the Exodus to reassure his people that he can and will act again. Paul's speech at the Areopagus takes up this anti-idol message.[18]

---

8. Watts, *Isaiah 34–66*, 101; Walsh, "Summons," 369.

9. Childs, *Isaiah*, 41:8–10.

10. Walsh, "Summons," 362–63.

11. So also 2 Kgs 17:15: "They pursued worthless idols and became worthless themselves" (Holter, *Idol-Fabrication*, 135). It is not so much the idol which rivals God, but the smith who makes the idol (Rudman, "Jeremiah," 66). Idolators will become as lifeless as the idols they serve (Beale, "Idolatry," 272).

12. Walsh, "Summons," 358. Israel worshiped Babylonian idols, so God used Babylonians to punish them (Beale, "Idolatry," 275). The anti-idol passages heighten the contrast between Israel and Babylon (Franke, "Lament," 418).

13. They only pretended to create life (Rudman, "Jeremiah," 68).

14. Rather than a judgment, God issues a call to salvation (Childs, *Isaiah*).

15. Pao, *Acts*, 190.

16. Laato, "Isaiah," 214.

17. The only reference to "the gods of Egypt" is in the law instituting the Passover. Apart from this, the gods are not mentioned; the Egyptians do not pray to them (Patrick, "Pentateuch," 114). Another reference in Num 33:4 stresses the idols' impotence: "the LORD executed judgment against their gods," with specific reference to the deaths of the Egyptians' firstborn.

18. δεισιδαιμονεστέρους (17:22) can be understood either positively or negatively, but its cognate noun is used derogatively in 25:19, so at most, Paul may be trying not to offend his audience while expressing what he really "thought of their religion" (Williams, *Acts*, 304). Luke's Paul characterizes his audience negatively as the stock characters of busybodies, so their curiosity is not commendable (Acts 17:22; Gray, "Athenian," 113). After a speech which includes Stoic ideas on God, Paul introduces the Christian

Seven of the nine canonical uses of "made by human hands"[19] in the LXX are in Isaiah, and Paul uses this word in Acts 17:24, which reflects Isaiah 42:5.[20] Both verses stress God's uniqueness as creator of the heavens and the earth, so God differentiates himself from idols (Isa 42:8). Paul attacks idols as gold, silver, and stone (Acts 17:29).[21] In Isaiah, the anti-idol polemic shows God's sovereignty over the nations, like Paul in Acts 17:30–31,[22] predicting God's judgment of the world. Finally, passages in the OT and intertestamental Judaism link gods, idols, and evil.[23]

3.2.2. Human rivals to God[24]

Human rivals to God are likened to God, associated with evil, powerless, and usually receiving God's direct judgment. Idols also share several common features with people who consciously or unconsciously function as rivals to God.

Adam and Eve

Adam and Eve are likened to God in four ways. Schneider and Seelenfreund cite Rabbinic sources that originally Adam and Eve were clothed in God's glory, the "supernal radiance," so they looked like God. The אוֹר of the "garments of light" was replaced by the צוֹר of the "garments of skin," after they sinned.[25]

Second, at three crucial points in Genesis—creation (1:26–27), expulsion from Eden (3:22), and at Babel (11:7)—God proposes action related to

---

resurrection, and they lose interest, Gray believes, for two reasons. Paul's call for introspection is uncomfortable for those used to examining others' sins, and as Ἀνάστασις is not a consort of Jesus, there are no salacious details. They are (implicitly) mocked as much as Isaiah's idolators.

19. Χειροποίητος Lev 26:1, 30; Isa 2:18; 10:11; 16:12; 19:1; 21:9; 31:7; 46:6; Mark 14:58; Acts 7:48; 17:24; Eph 2:11; Heb 9:11, 24.

20. So Williams (*Acts*, 305) and Marshall (*Luke*, 286). The divine-human likeness in Acts 17:29 (from Gen 1:26) "does not extend to creating gods in the image of humans." (Nasrallah, "Acts," 563).

21. Williams, *Acts*, 308.

22. Pao, *Acts*, 194–96; Johnson, *Acts*, 317.

23. So Deut 32:16–17; 1 En. 19:1, 99:7 (Rosner, "Temple," 344). The link between evil, idols, and sin is clear in the NT: Goulder, "2 Cor 6:14—7:1," 47–57.

24. See s5.3 for the application to Judas.

25. Schneider and Seelenfreund, "Kotnot," 118; "a tender maternal moment." God clothes them before banishing them (May, *Grace*, 111).

humans with the plural "us."[26] Who does "us" refer to? Eslinger argues that 1:26–27 means "unidentified heavenly peers,"[27] but there are problems. The only other beings described as created in Genesis 1 were animals, birds, etc. God's presumed creation of angelic beings is not mentioned and it is difficult to see them as his peers.[28] "Our image" would then include both God and angels, but humans are never described as in the image of angels. Gen 1:27 links humans exclusively to God's image. A hypothetical parallel like Isa 6:8 "who will go for us" is problematical as God is never said to send people on behalf of angels.[29]

If the plural "us" means a plurality in God, then this would make better sense of an intriguing grammatical feature of Genesis 1, with plural subjects like אֱלֹהִים,[30] but singular verbs like בָּרָא (Gen 1:1). There is much to commend this, as it avoids the difficulties associated with interpreting "us" as including the created but unfallen host of heaven. The importance of this for understanding the text is that God describes Adam and Eve as being very like him, in his image. Moreover, on behalf of this plural God, Adam and Eve (and presumably their descendants) are given the divine-like task of ruling over all other creatures (1:26). While not an ascription of divinity, it is rare, if not unique.[31]

Thirdly, Moberly argues that "knowledge of good and evil" (3:5) is moral autonomy, with Adam and Eve presuming to decide right and wrong for themselves),[32] an "autonomous wilfulness";[33] like the snake recasting and then refuting God's words. The fourth similarity is that Adam was given the God-like task of tending the garden, but after his sin and expulsion from Eden, this was given to the cherubim (3:24).[34] The link with evil is

26. Eslinger, "Plurals," 171.

27. Ibid., 171. So also Wenham, *Genesis 1–15*, 1:26. His argument is weakened by not addressing the obvious difficulties below. He believes that a reference to the Logos could well be the *sensus plenior*.

28. The "we" statements mark the human-divine boundary given a new occurrence like creation (Eslinger, "Plurals," 173). However, he never convincingly shows why the plural is necessary in such situations.

29. The plurality evidences Israel's supposed "second God," the Great Angel (Barker, *Angel*, 206). She fails to address the fact that humans are never described as in the image of, or sent by, angels.

30. "Plural in form but singular in meaning" (Wenham, *Genesis 1–15*, 1:1).

31. Perhaps the only parallel is John 10:34–35: "Is it not written in your law 'I have said you are gods'?"

32. Moberly, "Serpent," 24.

33. May, *Grace*, 110

34. Bovell, "History," 364n19.

shown by the snake deceiving Eve,[35] the continuity between the way it is described, and the way Satan is later described.[36] Genesis 3 does not identify the snake as Satan, but a talking snake is highly unusual, indicating "a higher intelligence."[37]

---

35. The gnostic *Testimony of Truth* portrayed the serpent as a teacher of divine wisdom who tried to open Adam and Eve's eyes to God's supposedly despicable nature (Pagels, *Adam*, 69).

Snakes symbolized both good and evil across the Ancient Near East, and Gen 3 does not equate the serpent with Satan or call it evil (Charlesworth, *Serpent*, 18, 21, 23). Despite the mass of data which he adduces, he has not proven his case. He produces much evidence to show that people from the Early Bronze Age to Greek and Roman culture saw many admirable qualities in snakes like energy, power, beauty, etc., as well as obviously negative qualities like its lethal bite (ibid., 225, 227, 198). These points are well-taken, but he has not shown that ancient Israel or the early church saw snakes positively. The sole possible exception is Num 21, although it is a bronze serpent, not an actual snake. I concede that there are positive elements to God undoing the effects of judgment, but being an (inanimate) agent of healing is not inherent in being a snake, whereas the qualities like energy and power, which the ancients valued in snakes, are.

As I showed in discussing ἑταῖρος (s2.3), Biblical writers can take a word from secular Greek and give it a new meaning. Charlesworth's study of the serpent in Gen 3 is instructive but finally unconvincing. He notes correctly that the serpent calls God "God" (3:1), not the covenantal "Lord God," indicating that the serpent is outside a "caring relationship with Yahweh God" (ibid., 303). He believes that the serpent has "the features of a god" (ibid., 314) without explaining exactly what this would mean in a monotheistic environment, or why an apparently divine being would give advice so disruptive of relationships. While he admits that the serpent spoke the truth but not the whole truth (ibid., 308, 315), he relativizes this by saying (ambitiously) that God failed "to speak the full truth," as Adam and Eve did not die on the same day they ate the fruit (ibid., 316). This data shows that the writer of Genesis considered the serpent to be evil, while the NT makes this explicit (Rom 16:20). In no fair way can the serpent be considered a positive influence on Adam and Eve, much less superior to the Lord God. He is, rather, a competitor with God.

36. Page, *Powers*, 16. In the wider Biblical canon, after starting the narrative of the woman and the dragon by referring to the dragon, for no apparent reason John introduces the serpent, and in Rev 12:9 explicitly identifies the serpent, the dragon, and the devil as the same individual. In Gen 3:13, Eve said that the serpent deceived her, ἠπάτησέν, and John said that the serpent was deceiving (ὁ πλανῶν) the world.

In classical Greek, δράκων usually means snake, and is frequently interchangeable with ὄφις (Eynikel and Hauspie, "δράκων," 126). Δράκων is often a symbol of evil, usually with the body of a snake. The MT has five words which refer either to mythological or evil creatures. The LXX translates them all by δράκων to mean the "symbol of evil forces" (ibid., 135), arguably preparing the way for these titles to coalesce in Satan. They also note that Gen 1:26 is the only place where חנין is not translated in the LXX by δράκων. If it were, it would imply that Adam and Eve were to have dominion over the evil symbolized by δράκων (ibid., 130).

37. Kelly, "Adam," 14; Page, *Powers*, 13.

RIVALS TO GOD

Adam and Eve's powerlessness is shown by nakedness, implying innocence,[38] and their expulsion. There is a play on similar words: "crafty," "naked," and "cursed."[39] The snake also acts like God by arbitrating what is good, namely, to disobey and seek to be like God by having their eyes opened to know good and evil.[40] It may also be significant, in showing tension between the snake and God, that the snake calls him "God," not the covenantal "Lord God."[41]

The penalty is condign: pain in childbearing increases and work becomes oppressive. It is also gracious: they are banished from Eden's tree of life (3:22) that they might not "gain sufficient divine qualities" and so compete with God.[42] While the serpent's words are strictly true, as they did not die at once,[43] they became mortal and later died. Adam and Eve were like God, being in his image, but sinned when they wanted to rival God in the knowledge of good and evil.

The king and the prince of Tyre

The second example is the king/prince of Tyre (Ezek 28). There are two important questions. First, who is the king of Tyre,[44] and is he distinct from the prince (28:2)? This addresses claims to divinity and the association with evil. Secondly, what relationship, if any, does the "holy mount of God" bear

---

38. Levine, "Curse," 192; cf., the snake's shrewdness.
39. Page, *Powers*, 16; Moberly, "Serpent," 24.
40. It is unclear, apart from knowledge of their nakedness, how Adam and Eve became more knowing (ibid., 21). Nonetheless, knowledge of good and evil characterizes maturity (Deut 1:39).
41. Page, *Powers*, 17; Charlesworth, *Serpent*, 303.
42. May, *Grace*, 12, 111.
43. Page, *Powers*, 18.
44. There have been some unlikely suggestions about the king's identity. Some identified the king as Adam, taking Eden literally, as in Gen 2–3. The writer uses Uzziah as a model for Adam due to a proud heart (Anderson, "Garden," 145). References to Eden, cherubim, and arrogance could mean "some form of correspondence" with Gen 2–3 (Williams, "Mythological," 50). The king was either the human king of Tyre or an "independent supernatural being" who accompanied the king of Tyre in Eden, equating the two locations (Launderville, "Cherub," 169; Patmore, "Masoretes," 246). No text implies such a presence in Eden before Adam's expulsion. It would require the king to be "the model of perfection" (Ezek 28:12), which is unlikely. Importing a "with" into 28:14, so that the expulsion is directed at a companion of the guardian cherub, is less likely than the cherub itself being expelled (Barr, "Thou," 219). Page attempts a singular exegesis by arguing that, while the MT supports equating the ruler and the king, following the pattern of the LXX (*Powers*, 41), many modern exegetes support a revocalization of the MT (surely a last resort) to include the cherub "with the king."

to "Eden, the garden of God" (28:13–14)? This addresses powerlessness and God's judgment. This section will conclude that the prince and king are related[45] but separate, with the king, Satan, empowering the prince, the human ruler of Tyre, and that God judges both.

Three crucial pieces of information help establish the king's identity. Firstly, there is an inconsistent use of gendered pronouns. Secondly, the king and the prince are linked but not identical. Lastly, God's reaction of grief is unparalleled.

Arbel argues that the king/cherub (28:14) is Eve, due to linked themes in Ezekiel 28 and Genesis 2–3.[46] The primal human in Gen. Rab. 18.1 has an indeterminate gender, the text using masculine and feminine pronouns.[47] "Settings" (Ezek 28:13) is usually translated "timbrels," which are associated with women, whose Hebrew word comes from "timbrels."[48] Arbel has not considered that the mixed use of gendered pronouns may imply someone above such distinctions.[49]

Secondly, Arbel's study of gendered pronouns is important, but she has not analyzed all the data. In the MT, the being was called a prince (נָגִיד) (Ezek 28:2) who claimed deity, but a king (מֶלֶךְ) (Ezek 28:12)[50] who was the model of perfection.[51] The LXX calls both ἄρχων, while the NIV restores the MT distinction with "ruler" (28:2) and "king" (28:12). Contra Bertoluci, who suggests that prince/ruler and king are "interchangeable," it is more accurate to say that, while a king can also be called a ruler—e.g., David in 2 Sam 6:21—a ruler who has not been anointed by a prophet cannot be called king.[52] If the oracles refer to the same person, then we have the incredible situation of a violent prince who grasped at deity, becoming a perfect king.

However, there are strong structural and thematic links between 28:1–10 and 28:11–19. Both include the rare words "traffic, merchandise," and

---

45. They can be confused, calling the king a "human who has come to think he is a god," when it is the prince/ruler who is accused of this (28:2; Barr, "Thou," 213).

46. Arbel, "Eve," 641, 645.

47. Ibid., 643. So Barr, "Thou," 215.

48. Arbel, "Eve," 647, 649.

49. The Enoch/Metatron narrative's redactors had so absorbed Ezek 28 that they based the narrative on Ezek 28's implied primal human (Arbel, "Seal," 134), due to the shared themes of an obedient human exalted to heaven who then grasped at divinity and was demoted (ibid., 128, 136). So also Bock, *Blasphemy*, 127, 177. But she never identifies the king of Tyre.

50. Wilson, "Tyre," 211. The arrogant claims of Dan 11:36–37 mirror the boasting of the king of Tyre (Garrett, *Demise*, 144).

51. Goering, "Word," 489; Wilson, "Tyre," 211.

52. They are "different personages" with a distinction between them (Bertoluci, "Guardian Cherub," 250, 280).

"splendor" (28:5, 16, 8; 28:7, 17).[53] Both are charged with hubris by either claiming deity or wealth (28:2, 15–16). Wisdom and beauty are imputed to both (28:3, 12; 27:7, 12) and both are defiled and cast down (28:7, 16). A key structural marker, "you ... will be no more" (26:21; 27:36; 28:19), binds them together, contra Wilson's "apparent lack of unity."[54] Goering's solution is that distinct units were combined in the final text.[55] While possible, this is barely credible, as it posits a redactor who skillfully selects and melds narratives together but ignores the most obvious difference: the addressees.[56]

Lastly, assuming that the prince and the king are the same does not account for God's reaction. To the "ruler" who claimed deity, God ordained a terrible death by ruthless foreigners to show his mortality (28:9). God's reaction to the king of Tyre is only paralleled by his reaction to Pharaoh (Ezek 32:2), where Ezekiel must lament over a deposed ruler. Normally, the reason for a lament is clear. God did not have to command David to lament over Saul and Jonathan (2 Sam 1:17). Joel commanded drunkards to weep (1:5) because invaders had stolen their wine (Stuart, *Hosea*, 1:5). God may command a lament if the judgment is unknown on earth. At the time of writing, it may not have been obvious that the princes of Israel would be deported to Babylon (Ezek 19:9), that Tyre would fall (28:2), or that Pharaoh would be deposed (32:2). The lament signals God's irrevocable judgment, shown in a dirge.[57]

God's reaction (28:12–19)[58] sounds like grief, as he contrasts the perfection of the king of Tyre with his expulsion. God tells Ezekiel to "lament concerning the king of Tyre" (28:12) with phrases which are inappropriate for a human: "the model of perfection," who lived in "Eden, the garden of God," a "guardian cherub" who was "blameless ... till wickedness was found in you." Arguing that the lament's sole object is the human king of Tyre must justify this extravagant language applying to a deeply sinful human. God could have said something similar about the expulsion of the hitherto-perfect Adam and Eve, but did not.

---

53. Goering, "Word," 499. The combination of these verses probably means that the prince's skill in trading (28:5) was inspired by Satan (28:16), who had no personal need for money.

54. Wilson, "Tyre," 211.

55. Goering, "Word," 499.

56. They were "lumped together in their general theological impact" (Barr, "Thou," 221).

57. Goering, "Word," 492.

58. The break at 27:12 shows heightened emotion, even heartfelt sadness (Tonstad, *Saving*, 101).

God is grieved about the king of Tyre, but taunts the king of Babylon (Isa 14:4).[59] The other laments in the OT have no similar language (Saul, 2 Sam 1:17; Abner, 2 Sam 3:33; the princes of Israel, Ezek 19:1; and Pharaoh, Ezek 32:2). This could be genuine grief from God about the fall of the most perfect being which he had created. The lament starts with God's anger against the human ruler of Tyre (28:1–10), but then shifts to grief against a fallen angelic figure (vv. 11–17),[60] before returning to language more suitable to a human (vv. 18–19). It is not a classic inclusion, but the language needs to be addressed in order to argue that this only applies to a human.[61] One could argue that God is being ironic about the fall of the king, but the intensity of the grief argues against this.

Next, the powerlessness of the king and prince is shown by their looming judgment, expressed by "Eden." Some assume that the "holy mount of God" is the Eden of Genesis 2–3.[62] Havrelock says "paradisical themes from Genesis 1–2 and Ezekiel 28 coalesce."[63] Carr argues that Genesis 2–3 and Ezekiel 28 drew on a common theme of expulsion.[64] Williams believes that Ezekiel 28 is a more mythical version of Genesis 2–3, which the Yahwist redactor modified for Genesis 2–3.[65] Allen concludes that the garden of God is Eden, and that the text is about Adam: "it credits the first man with wisdom and adorns him in bejeweled clothing and apparently leaves him dead."[66] This is unsatisfactory as it contradicts much of Genesis 3, as he admits. Also, Allen must then say that the cherub is the agent of removal (like Genesis 3:24, where cherubim prevent Adam and Eve returning), rather than interpret Ezekiel 28:16 as the cherub being the one removed.

Newsom argued that Ezekiel 28 has little to do with Genesis 2–3,[67] but rather the Jerusalem temple, due to the precious stones (Ezekiel 28:13),

---

59. Luke reworked Isa 14 to describe Satan's expulsion from heaven in Luke 10 (Garrett, *Demise*, 50).

60. "Ultimately . . . a heavenly being" (Tonstad, *Saving*, 93). "The fall of the highest of angels" (Grabiner, *Cosmic*, 55), citing Cooper (*Ezekiel*, 266–67). "Unlikely that a strictly human . . . is in view" (Grabiner, *Cosmic*, 56).

61. Taking seriously the MT distinction between prince and king obviates the need for textual surgery like Wilson ("Tyre," 212), who excises the precious stones, the wisdom, and the defiling of the sanctuary. While the king seems to exercise authority over the prince (hence his superior title), both are guilty, but for different reasons. Contra Homsher ("Combat," 86), both are humans likened to ancient rebellious deities.

62. Craigie, *Ezekiel*, 207.

63. Havrelock, "Maps," 654.

64. Carr, "Eden," 581.

65. Williams, "Mythological," 49.

66. Allen, *Ezekiel 20–48*, 28:11–14.

67 Newsom, "Oracles," 161.

some of which were on the high priest's shoulder piece, and the presence of a cherub.[68] Bunta believes that these stones adorned a statue of Yahweh standing in the temple,[69] but provides no evidence. Havrelock argues that the temple was to recreate the ambience of Eden.[70] These scholars have not addressed the serious difficulties in identifying "holy mount of God" with either the Eden of Genesis 2–3 or the temple. These are so great that one wonders if anyone would have made the connection in the absence of "Eden" in Ezekiel 28:13. Eden is better understood as a type than a location.

Even a cursory comparison of Ezekiel 28 and Genesis 2–3 shows striking differences.[71] Unlike the king, Adam was never described as "full of wisdom and perfect in beauty" (28:12).[72] Adam and Eve clothed themselves in leaves, and God later clothed them with skin (Gen 3:7, 21) not precious jewels and gold (28:13). While God banished Adam and Eve from Eden and placed cherubim (plural) to prevent them from accessing the tree of life in their fallen condition (Gen 3:24),[73] in Ezekiel 28 the king of Tyre is called a cherub (singular). No identifiable human is called "cherub" in the Bible. Adam's sin was to eat the forbidden fruit contrary to God's instructions, whereas the king of Tyre was corrupted because of his beauty and splendor and thrown to the ground before kings (28:17), things never said of Adam. Finally, Genesis 2–3 records no lament by God, but rather concern at their disobedience, while Ezekiel 28 has God commanding a lament from Ezekiel.

Given the chasm between Ezekiel 28 and Genesis 2–3, it is better to see Eden as a type and determine its function. While Patmore is correct that Ezekiel refers to Eden more than any other book bar Genesis, his argument that Eden is a place of fertility is unsupported by the text.[74] The key passages in Ezekiel referring to Eden all show God judging the king of Tyre (28:13), Pharaoh (31:9), and Pharaoh's allies (31:16, 18). Pharaoh is the only other person for whom Ezekiel is commanded to lament (Ezek 32:2). Given the insuperable difficulties reconciling Ezekiel 28 and Genesis 2–3, it is better to see Eden in Ezekiel 28 as a type, showing when God banished creatures,

---

68. Anderson, "Garden," 143; Newsom, "Oracles," 162.

69. Bunta, "Statue," 238.

70. Havrelock, "Maps," 653.

71. It is very optimistic to claim "scholars find the passage obscure but they *know* it is about the story of Eden" (my emphasis), but Barr later admits that the Ezek 28 version of the Eden myth is "certainly . . . considerably different from . . . our present Genesis 2–3" (Barr, "Thou," 222).

72. Ibid., 220.

73. Their banishment is gracious, to protect humanity's freedom, not God's power (May, *Grace*, 111).

74. Patmore, "Masoretes," 246.

some of whom were hitherto perfect,[75] namely, Adam and Eve from Eden and the king from "the holy mount of God."

The LXX parallels the mortal human ruler of Tyre (28:2) with the fallen angelic figure (28:12) by a common ἄρχων. This would indicate that, behind the human ruler of Tyre, lay a malevolent, fallen being. The MT, and modern translations like the NIV, highlight the superiority of this being by calling him "king," but the human ruler of Tyre is only called a prince, despite being a king.[76] The most likely candidate is Satan. Similarly, an angel told Daniel (10:13) that "the prince of the Persian kingdom" withstood him for three weeks, so that he needed the archangel Michael's help. No human could withstand an angel for three weeks, so ἄρχων should mean a fallen, angelic being. Page, by default, acknowledges something similar in Psalm 82, saying that the "gods" are suprahuman beings who are judged by God. He concludes: "the psalmist may well have believed that the celestial 'gods' exercized their influence on earth through terrestrial rulers."[77] Page should allow this principle in Ezekiel 28 also as it leads to the best understanding of the text. The human prince of Tyre and the demonic king of Tyre, Satan, are linked by their sin but distinguished by God's reaction to their looming judgment, showing their impotence.

Ezekiel 28 illustrates all facets of a human rival to God. The human prince of Tyre claimed divinity, but God said he would expose his powerlessness through an enemy (28:2, 7, 9). The king is probably Satan, who was described in divine-like terms as "perfection" and "blameless," but who sinned and was judged by God (28:12, 15–16). The mingling of the titles shows Satan as the real power behind the human king of Tyre.

3.2.3. The New Testament

Two passages in Acts show similar combinations of false ascription (by others) or presumption (by the person) to deity, an association with evil (except for Herod), powerlessness, and death. They show the dangers of inappropriate relationships with various combinations of the three NT rivals to God.

---

75. It is partly right to see Eden as "symbolic of humanity's rightful relationship with God's grace" as we "rely upon grace as our ultimate security" (May, *Grace*, 119). But the total meaning is more complex, and includes the examples above, where people rejected God's grace and were removed from his presence.

76. Identified as Hyram by Rabbinic tradition (Patmore, "Masoretes," 256), as Ithobaal II (Page, *Powers*, 40), and Ethbaal III (Launderville, "Cherub," 169; Bertoluci, "Guardian Cherub," 247). "Prince" may rebuke his pride (28:2), reminding him that real power lay with the "king."

77. Page, *Powers*, 58.

Simon Magus was like a human rival to God, doing miracles, and addressed with divine-like titles such as "Great," but whose power arguably came from evil. He was rebuked by Peter for offering money in exchange for being able to give the Holy Spirit. Herod Agrippa was acclaimed as a god, but was struck down by an angel for not glorifying God. "The man of lawlessness" (2 Thess 2) will make the most complete claim to deity before being killed by Jesus at his παρουσία. There is a broad consistency among the attributes of these human rivals to God.

Simon Magus

In Acts 8:4–24, Simon Magus tried to buy the ability to give the Holy Spirit. Simon claimed to be great, and others also believed this (Acts 8:9–10).[78] Greatness is a title which can be claimed for an idol, but Fossum claims it is a Samaritan name for Yahweh.[79] Grundmann argues that it shows Simon as embodying "divine power."[80] No one else in the NT is called the "Great Power."[81] "Great" as a NT title is only applied either to God (Matt 5:35; Titus 2:13)[82] or to idols/competitors with God, like Artemis of the Ephesians (Acts 19:28, 34) or Babylon (Rev 14:8; 17:5). A theologically significant title, it is never used for anyone in a right relationship with God.[83] The act of the crowd calling Simon the Great Power sounds like worship. Eventually, the Samaritans and even Simon converted to Christianity (Acts 8:12–13), although this may have reflected his desire to repeat the apostolic signs.[84] Miracles based in magic had to be distinguished from those done by God's power.[85]

Simon's association with evil is latent, but still present. Μαγεύω (Acts 8:9) is a *hapax* like μαγεία (Acts 8:11), but its cognate μάγος is in Daniel 1:20; 2:2, 10, 27; 4:7; 5:7, 11, 15; and Acts 13:6, 8 about Elymas, whom Paul calls υἱὲ διαβόλου (13:10).[86] While his miraculous powers are not explic-

---

78. Calling Simon a θεῖος ἀνήρ in a neutral sense (Wink, *Naming*, 161) is wrong, as the passage is clear that Simon is not right with God (8:20–23). Simon was great "in his own mind" (Parsons, *Acts*, 8:9).

79. Wink, "Name," 162–91; Parsons, *Acts*.

80. Grundmann, "μέγας," 575.

81. Early Christian texts called Simon the Great Power; e.g., Justin Martyr (Dickerson, "Samaria," 218, 220).

82. Marshall, "Acts," 156.

83. It was beyond what was due to a human being (Garrett, *Demise*, 65).

84. Marshall, "Acts," 156; Fernando, *Acts*, 272.

85. McCabe, "Words," 173.

86. The μάγ words cover a number of potential identifications from sage to quack. This emphasizes that this is really a battle between good and evil (Parsons, *Acts*,

itly called evil, that is a reasonable assumption, as they show a key feature of such powers as less powerful than God's. This can also be seen in the Chaldean astrologers' protest to the king that he was asking the impossible (Dan 2:10, 27).[87] Significantly, Simon was dubbed Magus in post-apostolic writings to highlight the source of his powers.[88] No one in Luke/Acts in a right relationship with God is ever called μάγος,[89] and the relative weakness of their power is usually seen publicly. The exception in the wider NT is the μάγοι in Matt 2.

Simon's powerlessness[90] is shown in four ways. First, he was amazed at the σημεῖα καὶ δυνάμεις μεγάλας done in Jesus' name, implicitly[91] admitting the inferiority of his own (Acts 8:13).[92] Next, Simon must ask for this ability, whereas the pre-Easter Jesus claimed this for himself (Luke 24:49). Thirdly, Simon offers money, whose corrupting influence is already noted in Luke/Acts.[93] Lastly, Jesus came to set people free from what Simon is still bound by, being "full of bitterness and captive to sin" (Acts 8:23).[94] Peter warned him of the dire consequences if he did not repent:[95] he and his money would

---

13:9–10). Paul was blinded by a great light and turned to Jesus (Acts 9:3, 18) but Elymas has been blinded by and remains in darkness (Acts 13:11). His use of magic appears to have led to his corruption of the straight paths of the Lord (McCabe, "Words," 181).

87. It is a pointless test because the dream had hidden itself (Goldingay, *Daniel*, 2:24–30). We might also add the contest between Pharaoh's magicians and Moses and Aaron prior to the Exodus.

88. Fernando, *Acts*, 272. "The father of all heretics" (Spät, "Mani," 6). So also Ferreiro, "Simon Magus," 54.

89. It was a common accusation to label someone negatively (Parsons, *Acts*, 8:9).

90. The *Acta Petri* has Simon flying over Rome, but Peter asks God to remove the demons holding Simon up, who then promptly plummets to the ground, dies, and is damned (Ferreiro, "Simon Magus," 57; assuming they are the same Simon: Bruce, *Acts*, 195).

91. Ironically: Williams, *Acts*, 155.

92. Garrett, *Demise*, 69.

93. Gagnon, "Motives," 143. While Philip's and Simon's miracles may appear outwardly similar, their very different behaviors imply quite different sources of power (Parsons, *Acts*, 8:9).

94. Pao, *Acts*, 198. This reflects the anti-idolatry language of Deut 29 (Parsons, *Acts*). Its background is Prov 5:4 (going after loose women) and Deut 29:17 (idolatry; Johnson, *Acts*, 149).

95. Simon never really repented, so his baptism was "a sham" (Garrett, *Demise*, 74). "Peter views Simon as still . . . unregenerate" (Fernando, *Acts*, 274). Simon wanted to dispense the Spirit without having received the Spirit himself (8:16; Dickerson, "Samaria," 227). Whilst not ascribing Simon's motivation to Satan (cf. Acts 5), Peter places him "in the damning space of excommunication" (McCabe, "Words," 175).

go to ἀπώλειαν.⁹⁶ If εἰς is like ὡς, "as," then if Simon did not repent, he would be a root of bitterness in the early church.⁹⁷ It is a transaction (rebuffed) of silver between a leader and a spiritually immature member of God's people who presumed to act as though divine. The common elements of money and deceitfulness form a parallel with Ananias and Sapphira (Acts 5). The key difference with Simon Magus is that his fate is not recorded.⁹⁸ In short, Simon is like an idol, performing (counterfeit) miracles and acclaimed in divine terms, but ultimately powerless.

Herod Agrippa

Next, the death⁹⁹ of Herod Agrippa occurs in Acts 12:20–23.¹⁰⁰ There are a few ways in which Herod appears or presumes to be divine. Firstly, Herod had just been persecuting the church and had had James executed, and Peter imprisoned (Acts 12:1–3). By handing people over to death, Herod was doing something normally reserved for God or his appointed representatives under strict conditions (s2.2).

Secondly, Herod acted like God by giving the people of Tyre and Sidon peace and food, normally the preserve of God. In the LXX, αἰτέω can mean either a request to another person, such as the Israelites requesting gold, silver, etc., from the Egyptians (Exod 3:22), or in twenty-four of seventy occurrences, it can mean prayer to God for either a specific or general request.¹⁰¹ It is not a command—the person being asked can refuse. The NT usage is similar, with two differences. A higher proportion (thirty-one of sixty-seven)¹⁰² of uses concern prayer, and there are promises about answers to prayer in Jesus' name (John 14:13). While αἰτέω alone does not show Herod functioning as a god, it is not inconsistent with such a scenario, given his handing over of the apostles and not disavowing the crowd's acclamation.

---

96. Marshall, "Acts," 159; Bruce, *Acts*, 184.
97. Williams, *Acts*, 158; Fernando, *Acts*, 274.
98. Garrett, *Demise*, 72.
99. Josephus, *Ant.* 19.343–50.
100. Agrippa 1, so Kraemer, "Herodias," 333.
101. Deut 18:16; 1 Sam 1:17, 20, 27; 12:17, 19; 1 Kgs 3:5, 10–11, 13; 19:4; Ps 2:8; 21:4; 27:4; 78:18; 105:40; Prov 30:7; Zech 10:1; Isa 7:11–12; 58:2; Dan 6:8, 13–14.
102. Matt 6:8; 7:7–8, 11; 18:19; 20:22; 21:22; Mark 10:35; 11:24; Luke 10:13; 11:9; John 4:10; 11:22; 14:13–14; 15:7, 16; 16:23–24, 26; Acts 7:46; 13:21; 1 Cor 11:22; Col 1:9; Jas 1:5–6; 4:2–3; 1 John 3:22; 5:14–15.

Thirdly, the immediate cause of Herod's death[103] was that the crowd acclaimed him a god.[104] He did not deny this—he was struck by an angel of the Lord, dying in agony five days later. Josephus records the shining garment he wore that day, which doubtless contributed to the acclamation.[105] He is like the king of Babylon, who also made claims to deity and was struck by God (Isa 14:12–14).[106] Whilst this could be seen simply as an idolatrous act, it may resonate with Luke's earlier description of Satan demanding that Jesus worship him (Luke 4:7).

Herod's powerlessness is portrayed starkly: presuming to act like God in handing people over for trial and then dispensing food and peace, he is acclaimed as a god, but then struck down and killed by an angel of the same Lord who had just rescued Peter (Acts 12:7).[107] Like Ananias and Sapphira, Judas (arguably), and "the man of lawlessness," he is one of the very few killed directly by God's action in the NT. Herod[108] is drawn into the deaths of both Jesus and John the Baptist; but while they are buried in tombs, Herod is struck down by an angel, the persecutor becoming a victim.[109] Herod is like an idol, embodying some key features shown previously: he is likened to God, he is an object of ridicule, and much more powerless than he appears.

By contrast, when the over-excited crowds at Lystra acclaimed Paul and Barnabas as gods because they had healed the crippled man, they affirmed their mortality but, unlike Herod, rejected the acclamation of deity (Acts 14:15).[110] Herod did no recorded miracles, but presumed to act like God; Paul and Barnabas acted like (or better, in the name of) God by heal-

---

103. It was possibly chronic kidney disease exacerbated by gangrene (Trivedi, "Death").

104. Duling, "Swear," 308. The imperfect ἐπεφώνει makes the crowd's reaction more like a chant (Williams, *Acts*, 218). This reverses Luke/Acts' theme of God being praised for his mighty works (Cosgrove, "Providence," 188).

105. *Ant.* 19.344.

106. Garrett, *Demise*, 50. Luke's account of Satan's ejection from heaven in Luke 10 is "modelled" on Isa 14. Herod is "eaten by worms" (σκωληκόβρωτος; Acts 12:23), but the king of Babylon is covered with worms (σκώληξ).

107. The angel who πατάξας to wake Peter, did the same to kill Herod (Johnson, *Acts*, 212, 215). It "is typically used of God 'smiting' his enemies" (Parsons, *Acts*, 12:23); cf. Exod 2:12; Judg 1:5; Pss 3:8 LXX; 77:66 LXX; also Luke 22:49–50; Acts 7:24.

108. King has analyzed the role of Herod as part of a wider narrative involving Jesus and John the Baptist, showing that he is compared unfavorably to both. Herod acquiesces to Herodias about John the Baptist's death, making him an object of ridicule in the Ancient Near East honor-shame culture ("John the Baptist," 174).

109. Ibid., 176.

110. Johnson, *Acts*, 249. Paul is offended in both Lystra and Athens by people who cannot draw proper lines between deity and humanity (Nasrallah, "Acts," 562).

ing the man, but refused to be treated as gods. The language of idolatry is a boundary-marker between God's people and others.[111] Idols are a snare for God's people, and are also the visible manifestations of the powers opposing God. They are powerless and ultimately under God's control.

The "man of lawlessness"

In 2 Thessalonians 2:4, Paul foretells the destruction of the "man of lawlessness."[112] Paul was addressing an eschatological problem at Thessalonica, where some had stopped working, as they thought Jesus' return was imminent or had actually happened.[113] Paul argued that Jesus' παρουσία could not yet have happened, as he would destroy "the man of lawlessness" when he appeared.[114]

He is seen as rivaling God in three ways. First, he will have his own παρουσία, like Jesus (2 Thess 2:1), so he is like a rival Messiah.[115] Each παρουσία will have a very different outcome,[116] with Jesus killing him. Next, he exalts himself over every god and "sets himself up in God's temple." Such overt assertions of divinity mirror "the way Antiochus IV is depicted in Dan 11:36–37."[117] He would set himself up in the holiest part of the Jerusalem temple, τὸν ναὸν, where the true God was felt to live.[118] Thirdly, he proclaims "himself to be God," either mirroring the words/attitude of the prince of Tyre (Ezek 28:2) or like Herod, allowing himself to be addressed as divine (Acts 12:21–23).[119] It is difficult to find a more direct assertion of false divinity in the Bible.

---

111. Pao, *Acts*, 208.

112. Klassen's use of 2 Thess 2:3 is puzzling, as 2:4 says that "he sets himself up in God's temple, proclaiming himself to be God." (Klassen, *Friend*, 153). There is no evidence that Judas did anything like this. 2 Thess 2:6 says, "And now you know what is holding him back, so that he may be revealed at the proper time." This implies that something was restraining him at the time of writing, clearly after Jesus' earthly ministry, but that he would be revealed at "the proper time," or after the time of writing. This cannot apply to Judas, who would have been long dead.

113. Bruce, *1 & 2 Thessalonians*, xxxvii.

114. Kaye, "Ethics," 53.

115. Bruce, *1 & 2 Thessalonians*, 167.

116. Kerkeslager, "Apollo," 121.

117. Bruce, *1 & 2 Thessalonians*, 168; Aus, "Plan," 541; Goldingay, *Daniel*, 11:36–37; Weima, "Thessalonians," 887.

118. Bruce, *1 & 2 Thessalonians*, 168–69.

119. Ibid., 169; Parsons, *Acts*; Fernando, *Acts*, 363.

There are clear links with evil. He is called ὁ ἀντικείμενος, "the adversary."[120] It is used for Satan accusing Joshua the high priest before being rebuked by the Lord (Zech 3:1).[121] Ἀντικείμενος is used for Rezon as Israel's adversary (1 Kgs 11:25).[122] In the NT, ἀντίκειμαι is used for serious opposition to the work of the gospel. Sometimes, evil is explicitly mentioned (Luke 13:16–17). Paul foretells that those who oppose the Philippian church will be destroyed (1:28), describes how lawbreakers and rebels oppose sound doctrine, and how some widows have left to follow Satan, τῷ ἀντικειμένῳ (1 Tim 1:10, 5:14). While the consequences are serious for those opposed, such as betrayal (Luke 21:15), they are more serious for those opposing, and include destruction (Phil 1:28) or following evil. Lastly, Satan is said to empower the man's counterfeit miracles (2 Thess 2:9).[123]

His powerlessness is shown twice. Satan, not the man, empowers his miracles (2 Thess 2:9). Secondly, his powerlessness is clear as he is one of the very few in the NT who are killed by God's direct action. He will be destroyed by Jesus himself at his advent. Both the "man of lawlessness" and Judas are called "the one doomed to destruction" (2 Thess 2:3; John 17:12[124]).[125]

3.2.4. Conclusion

Human rivals to God are few but consistent. Adam and Eve were likened to God by God himself (Gen 1:26), but were deceived into wanting to be "like God" (Gen 3:5) by Satan (Rom 16:20),[126] and were doomed to mortality (Gen 5:5). The most complete example of a sinful human, evil, and money is the prince/king of Tyre in Ezek 28. Behind the human prince of Tyre lay Satan as the king. The prince claimed divinity, and the king dwelt in God's immediate presence (Ezek 28:2, 13). Both were associated with wealth (28:4, 16) and pride (28:5, 17). Both suffered God's direct judgment (28:7, 18).

In Acts, two people show ascription/presumption of deity and powerlessness. Simon Magus was treated as divine for his miracles and claimed something similar for himself, but was negatively associated with money (Acts 8:9–10, 20). His fate is unrecorded. Herod was asked for food and security

---

120. Satan, the adversary, and God cooperate to energize disbelief amongst unbelievers (Kelly, *Satan*, 120). No evidence is provided for this odd suggestion.

121. Aus, "Plan," 539.

122. Bruce, *1 & 2 Thessalonians*, 168.

123. Aus, "Plan," 539.

124. This insinuates that Judas is damned (Maritz, "Judas Iscariot," 307).

125. Bruce, *1 & 2 Thessalonians*, 167; Garrett, *Demise*, 146n44.

126. Martin, *2 Corinthians*, 11:3.

and acclaimed as a god, but was struck and died (Acts 12:20, 22). While evil is not mentioned, worship is also what Satan wanted (Luke 4:7). Lastly, the "man of lawlessness" proclaimed himself God, and his miracles were empowered by Satan, but he will be killed directly by Jesus at his παρουσία (2 Thess 2:4, 8–9). In most cases, evil is present either overtly or covertly.

Sections 3.3–5 will show that the negative features of evil and money are intensified beyond anything we might expect from the OT. S3.3 uses the "Opening the Mouth" ritual from Babylon to illustrate the close connection between an idol and an animating power of evil. A close examination of the εἴδωλον and the δαιμόν word groups shows a clear pattern. In secular Greek and Josephus, these word groups can have positive meanings, something which never happens in the LXX or the GNT. As the reader moves from the LXX to the GNT, the descriptions of evil are both more prevalent and more graphic. S3.4 lays the groundwork to illustrate four unique parallels between Judas and Satan: both are named rebels, allowed to remain in God's presence until irrevocably cast out; they then face a final judgment by God. S3.5 will show how the Biblical view of money changes dramatically from the OT to the NT.

3.3. Supernatural rivals to God

3.3.1. Introduction

When considering the Biblical data concerning Satan, there is clearly a wide range of views. Brown has detailed the history of interpreting Biblical references to Satan from detailed descriptions to denial of existence, highlighting Bartsch's quote from Bultmann: "It is impossible . . . to [use] modern medical . . . discoveries, and [also] to believe in the New Testament world of daemons and spirits."[127] Such a bold statement fails to explain why he believed that technology invalidated the fallen parts of the spiritual realm, but not the godly, or why people believe in the existence of both. Brown notes that scholarly interest in the demonic increased after the discovery of the Dead Sea Scrolls, which showed a deep interest in the topic.[128] Pagels thinks that "satan" reflects how people see themselves vis-à-vis "others" in order to malign them,[129] like the intertestamental Jews, who saw themselves as faithful, maligning and demonizing fellow Jews, whom they saw as collaborating

---

127. Bultmann, "Mythology," 5, in Brown, "Devil," 201.
128. Ibid., 201.
129. Pagels, *Origin*, xviii.

with Antiochus Epiphanes.[130] Pagels has not said if she thinks that Satan is an ontological or a psychological reality. Nürnberger argued, "The decisive question is not whether they 'exist' and in what form, but what they stand for and *what they do* to us."[131] This thesis will only attempt to determine Satan's role in the texts.

It is proposed that Satan, Judas and idols form an ungodly trio, with significant common features. We will study the Babylonian ritual of "Opening the Mouth," where the god was invited to indwell and enliven its image, to establish that evil could inhabit and enliven idols. Given the Bible's constant refrain against idolatry (e.g., Deuteronomy 13), it is inconceivable that God would so act. I will then study the various uses of εἴδωλον and δαιμον, and the Beelzebul passages (Matt 12; Mark 3; Luke 11).

3.3.2. The "Opening the Mouth" ritual

The Babylonian ritual of "Opening the Mouth" (*mîs-pî*) is reflected in Second Isaiah and forms a key part of its anti-idol polemic. I will show that, while Luke lacks an overt anti-idol polemic, traces of the *mîs-pî* ritual which are in Luke via his adoption of material from Second Isaiah are relevant for studying the NT role of evil. Second Isaiah's critique of the process of making an idol and the subsequent idolatry is so thorough and caustic that one wonders how anyone, no matter how unsophisticated, could use some parts of a tree for fuel and other parts for an idol which they worshiped, saying, "save me; you are my god" (Isa 44:16–17). They knew that both pieces of wood came from the same tree; how could they worship a god which they had made?[132] Dick quoted Thorkild Jacobsen's "The Graven Image": must we conclude that "the ancient Mesopotamians, a highly intelligent and civilized people, . . . would fall down to a block of wood"?[133]

The ritual may provide an explanation, as it was meant to let the god indwell the image which represented it.[134] While this may sound odd, a similar idea is reflected in both testaments. The "good news" of the deaths

---

130. Pagels, "Preliminary," 108; "Part Three," 491.

131. Nürnberger, *Living God*, 107 (their emphasis).

132. "Nobody would claim (to worship) . . . wood or stone; it always stands for something else" (Janowitz, "Idolatry," 239–52).

133. Dick, "Image," 1–44.

134. Greenspahn, "Syncretism," 480–94. Ezek 16:63 means that Israel will no longer have the opening of the mouth from pagan idols, and Ezek 29:21 means that the Lord will give Ezekiel the opening of the mouth by the Lord, thus allowing him to speak the Lord's words (Kennedy, "Hebrew," 233).

of Saul and his sons at Gilboa was proclaimed firstly τοῖς εἰδώλοις, and only then to the people (1 Chr 10:9–10). In some sense, the Philistines expected the idols to share in the news as much as the people. This is confirmed by the description of the temple where Saul's head was hung as the "temple of Dagon," not the "temple of Dagon's statue." In an earlier battle against the Philistines, Israel had raised such a shout when the ark was brought into their camp that the Philistines said that a god, not just its image, had arrived, and this greatly troubled them (1 Sam 4:7–9).[135] After their victory, they revised this to "the ark of the god of Israel" (1 Sam 5:7), but as expected, God did not allow the victory to be attributed to Dagon, who was found prostrate before the ark, without head or hands. Crucially, the narrator said that Dagon, not his statue, was prostrate before the ark, so identifying the thing signified, Dagon, with its image.[136]

Such beliefs appear at least to inform understandings of inappropriate worship in the NT period. In Revelation 13:15, a beast who came out of the earth "was given power to give breath to the image of the first beast (who was killed with the sword but lived), so that it could speak and cause all who refused to worship the image to be killed." It is not said explicitly that the first beast indwelt the image, but the result was the same: people worshiped its image.[137] The main purpose of animating statues was to give oracles,[138] and the command to kill non-worshipers is like an oracle from the god to the people.[139]

A full description and analysis of "Opening the Mouth" is beyond the scope of this thesis, but the salient point is that the creation of a god was "a supreme act of synergy between heaven and earth," which could only happen as the gods allowed.[140] The completed image was taken from the temple workshops in procession, back to the forest whence the tree came. The craftsmen ritually swore that they had not created it, their hands being symbolically cut with tamarisk knives to symbolize this.[141] Symbolically reborn free of human interference, it awaited the dawn to receive its divinity.[142] The rite used the language of gestation and birth to recreate the statue as

---

135. The Philistines' expectations about the battle, based on the Exodus, were wrong even though they clearly expected Israel's god(s) to fight for them (Klein, *1 Samuel*). "Hebrew" is mostly an insult hurled at Israel by the Philistines (Lowery, *Sabbath*, 27).

136. Dick, "Image," 31.

137. Pagels, "Part Three," 493.

138. Aune, *Revelation 6–16*, 13:15.

139. Macaskill, "Rome," 245.

140. Dick, "Image," 38–39.

141. Ibid., 40.

142. Walker and Dick, "Ritual," 17.

the god.¹⁴³ The priests washed the mouth of the idol with liquids to prepare it for contact with the divine, and then by the ritual of "Opening the Mouth," invited the god to indwell it.¹⁴⁴ The consecrated image was regarded as the god's actual presence, and while offerings were made to the statue of the king, offerings were always made to the actual god, not just its image.¹⁴⁵ Egyptians believed that the god's divine force resided within the image and had to be sustained through offerings.¹⁴⁶

It is important to show that the ritual lay behind the relevant passages, not just that similar ideas were present in both texts, potentially allowing a common textual ancestor. Firstly, the order of certain events in Second Isaiah is nonsensical in ordinary terms, but mirrors the ritual accurately. Scholars have noted the puzzling nature of some events in Second Isaiah. In Isaiah 44:12–14, the order of events is exactly the reverse of normal. Holter says that, if the author intended to present the stages "as a logical progression, . . . this verse . . . is a failure."¹⁴⁷ The smith fashions the image on a bed of coals (v. 12), then the carpenter fashions the inner wooden core (v. 13), before finally going to the forest to choose a tree from among a list which is reflected in the Babylonian ritual.¹⁴⁸ While, as Dick notes, a parody does not have to be strictly correct,¹⁴⁹ it is noteworthy that this is the exact order of the ritual, where the image was first worked on in the temple workshops, before being returned to the place where the tree was felled, so that human craftsmanship could be ritually denied, before the statue was reborn at the behest of the gods. Without this ritual, the image was felt to be just wood, as per Deut 4:28: "man-made gods of wood and stone, which cannot see or hear or eat or smell."

Secondly, both the ritual and some Biblical texts have the same emphasis: the deity is identified with but distinct from its image. The Babylonians asked how they could construct gods, and decided that it was only possible if the gods guided the process.¹⁵⁰ The Bible denies that this was even possible, but it is hard to see why the writers would argue this unless

---

143. Boden, "Mesopotamian," 29.
144. Walker and Dick, "Ritual," 12.
145. Ibid., 6.
146. Lorton, "Cult Statues," 123–210.
147. Holter, *Idol-Fabrication*, 170. Holter's preferred solution, that the deliberate juxtaposition of scenes is a literary technique, is lacking, as he fails to provide a convincing reason why (ibid., 205).
148. Dick, "Image," 28–29.
149. Ibid., 40.
150. Boden, "Mesopotamian," 107.

at least some people thought it possible. The ritual intended indwelling,[151] with the statue manifesting the deity it represented. The man in Isaiah 44:17 addresses not just the idol, but the god which it represents: "Save me; you are my god";[152] Micah, angry at the loss of the idol, said "You took the gods I made" (Judg 18:24). In 1 Samuel 5:1–5, the writer records that the god Dagon, not just his image, fell before the Ark.[153] From Isaiah's viewpoint, the criticisms of the god are heightened but similar criticisms of the idol: neither can move (Isa 46:7; 40:20), nor answer (Isa 46:7; 44:17), nor save (Isa 46:7; 45:20).[154] This criticism of gods/idols reaches its climax when Bel and Nebo, the main deities of Babylon,[155] the place of Judah's exile (1 Chr 9:1; 2 Chr 36:20), are named. Not only are Bel and Nebo named, they are also mocked when carried into exile.[156] The exile is the most likely place when this novel thought entered Israelite understanding: an idol could manifest a god. The long list of woods and the setting of the orchard show a clear debt "to a Babylonian lexicon."[157]

The final point is that evil was associated with idols. Compared with the NT, there are fewer references to evil on earth in the OT. Nonetheless, some passages in the OT and intertestamental Judaism link gods, idols, and evil.[158] Moses rebuked Israel for provoking God "with foreign gods" and sacrificing to "demons, not God" (Deut 32:16–17).[159] Rosner cites 1 Enoch 19:1—"And Uriel said to me: 'Here shall stand the angels who . . . shall lead them (people) astray into sacrificing to demons as gods'"—and 99:7—"[They shall] worship impure spirits and demons, and all kinds of idols not according to knowledge."[160] Whether other supernatural entities are identified as "gods" or "demons," they are in every respect inferior to the true God.

---

151. Walker and Dick, "Ritual," 12.

152. Holter, *Idol-Fabrication*, 179, 203; Childs, *Isaiah*.

153. Dick, "Image," 31.

154. Holter, *Idol-Fabrication*, 219.

155. Ibid., 225.

156. Franke, "Lament," 414.

157. Dick, "Image," 43. Sherwin disputes this, but it is only a minor part of the argument ("Trees," 514–29).

158. The NT link between evil, idols, and sin is clear: Goulder, "2 Cor 6:14—7:1," 47–57; e.g., 1 Cor 10:20–21.

159. Rosner, "Temple," 344.

160. Ibid., 344. The Essenes expected that they and fellow sons of light would be evenly matched in an eschatological war with Satan, and their armies would only win with God's help (Vermes, *Dead Sea Scrolls*, 58–59).

The *mîs-pî* ritual is the most likely background for the anti-idol passages in Second Isaiah, as it illustrates the otherwise inexplicable: someone, no matter how uneducated, could actually believe that a god inhabited an idol which they had made. Boden has carefully researched the ritual in Babylon, and while she uses a sixth-century BC version, there are versions dated to the ninth century.[161] Whatever the idolators thought, Second Isaiah argues that idols and their related deities are non-existent: why serve nothing? This process, although having different names and forms in different cultures, was prevalent across the entire Ancient Near East, including monotheistic Israel. Ancient peoples believed that the supernatural could reside in the natural.

3.3.3. Εἴδωλον words

This section will show the close links between idolatry and evil, of which Satan is increasingly seen as prince. Secular Greek and Josephus have a neutral, even favorable, opinion in marked contrast with the LXX and the GNT.

Usage in Secular Greek

Εἴδωλον occurs rarely in ancient Greek. Herodotus describes a statue as "a female figure."[162] Aeschylus in *Agamemnon* stresses its insubstantial nature with "phantom of a shadow."[163] Finally, Plato writes that "the bodily corpses are images of the dead."[164] All usages are either insubstantial, like false friendship, or someone or thing which is not alive, like a dead person or a statue. The εἴδωλον has no independent life of its own, but is never spoken of negatively or linked with evil. This mirrors the Ancient Near East understanding that the deity indwelt and animated the idol, which itself had no life.[165] These features are in marked contrast to its usage in the LXX, Josephus, and the GNT.

---

161. Boden, "Mesopotamian," 28–29. The idea of a god indwelling an idol predates 2000 BC (Vanstiphout in Porter, *Deity*, 15–40).
162. Herodotus, *Historiae*, 1.51, especially εἴδωλον.
163. Aeschylus, *Agamemnon*, 839–40, especially εἴδωλον.
164. Plato, *Laws*, vol 2:532, especially εἴδωλα.
165. Comfort, "Idolatry," 424; Greenspahn, "Syncretism," 483.

Usage in Josephus

Of all the words in the group, Josephus only uses εἴδωλον, and that only ten times, but in two different ways. He castigates Jehoram for compelling idolatry; Jeroboam,[166] who was "very wicked in worshipping idols"; and Ahaz, who sacrificed "his own son" (*Ant.* 5.98; 9.205; 9.243). By contrast, he praises Hezekiah, who "cleansed the city of . . . idols," and Josiah, who persuaded those in Jerusalem to renounce idolatry (*Ant.* 9.273; 10.65–66).[167] His other uses include using εἴδωλα of young men dying of famine in a siege, and the spirits of Catullus's victims, who kept on reappearing to him (*J.W.* 5.513; 7.452). These two uses reflect the secular use of εἴδωλον as something insubstantial or related to death, as in Aeschylus and Plato. They are more like the Graeco-Roman usage, and explicable by Josephus's straddling of both cultures, but with the added feature from the LXX usage of personal or corporate sin being linked to εἴδωλον. Unlike the LXX, Josephus never links idols with evil by such words as δαιμόνιον.

Usage in the LXX

Firstly, God forbids idolatry and promises restoration when Israel repents.[168] Secondly, pagans may have been idolatrous.[169] Lastly, some in Israel may have worshiped idols.[170]

There are four points of interest. Firstly, polytheism, henotheism,[171] and idolatry were explicitly banned (Exod 20:2–6; Deut 5:8) based on the

---

166. Jeroboam exemplifies a key trope of Josephus: a good father has a bad son (Mason, "Historical," 127).

167. Josephus: the hereditary priesthood is the proper Judean ruling elite (Mason, "Pharisees," 210).

168. Exod 20:4; Lev 19:4; Num 33:52; Deut 5:8, 29:16; 2 Kgs 23:24; 2 Chr 14:4; 15:16; 17:3; 23:17; 34:7; Zech 13:2; Isa 27:9; 30:22; Ezek 36:25; 37:23; Dan 3:12, 18.

169. 1 Sam 31:9; 1 Chr 10:9; 16:26; Pss 97:6; 115:4; 134:15; Isa 10:11; 37:19; Dan 5:4, 23.

170. Gen 31:19, 34–35; Lev 26:30; Num 25:2; Deut 32:21; 1 Kgs 11:2, 5, 7, 33; 2 Kgs 17:12; 21:11, 21; 2 Chr 11:15; 24:18; 28:2; 33:22; Hos 4:17; 8:4; 13:2; 14:9; Mic 1:7; Hab 2:18; Isa 1:29; 41:28; 48:5; 57:5; Jer 9:14; 14:22; 16:19; Ezek 6:4, 6, 13; 8:10; 16:16; 18:12; 23:39; 36:17; 44:12.

171. Henotheism serves one god while not denying the existence of other gods. "Those sections in the Hebrew Scriptures that appear to propagate the purist's notion of religious monotheism and its consequent cultural separatism have to be read in a different light" (Gruenwald, "Myth," 432). There is much debate as to whether polytheism or monotheism came first, but by the time the Hebrew Scriptures began to be written, it was clear that idolatry of any sort was deeply and personally offensive to God.

Exodus, the OT salvation event,[172] which was judgment on all the gods of Egypt (Exod 12:12).[173] It is hard to imagine a surer basis in the OT for commanding obedience. Israel had seen both the power of Yahweh, who spoke to them by Moses and Aaron, and the impotence of Egypt's gods, whom the Egyptians never address.[174] God gave another reason for obedience, that he was a jealous God who would inflict generational punishment (Exod 20:5b-6). All Pentateuchal references to God's jealousy concern idols.[175]

Winiarski expends much effort in establishing adultery and idolatry as mutually reinforcing metaphors, which show God's emotional investment in the covenant, and also that adultery is both a figure of and a possible cause of idolatry.[176] These points are well made, but she overstates her case by not recognizing that God's jealousy is not that of a cuckolded husband, but he has deeper concerns for those who reject the living God for lifeless idols. Her discussion of Deuteronomy 24, where a man must not remarry a former wife who remarried another man after divorcing him and then divorces again, does not see that the essential problem is not the divorce, but the second marriage.[177] If adultery and idolatry are figures, then the second marriage corresponds to a commitment to another god, arguably rendering a renewed commitment to Yahweh very difficult, if not impossible.[178] An example is the Baal of Peor, where Israel "ate the sacrificial meal and bowed down before these gods" (Num 25:2).[179] The immorality was bad enough, but idolatry endangered the very relationship with God, hence his

---

172. Durham, *Exodus*, 20:2. Moses, an Egyptian priest, led his fellow Egyptians out so that they could worship the true God (which is very different from the Biblical account), who could not be "conceived or worshipped through images" (Gruen ["Exodus," 95] cites Strabo 16.2.34–39).

173. Judaism recast Egyptian legends to shape Jews as former rulers of Egypt, thus allowing an easier reentry back into Egypt when it was judged necessary (ibid., 113). This is farfetched, as Yahweh is never seen as just one of the Egyptian pantheon, but as the only true God, in contrast to Egypt's idols. It also makes the commands in Jeremiah (2:18, 36, etc.) not to return to Egypt harder to understand.

174. Goldingay and Wright, "Yahweh," 55; Patrick, "Pentateuch," 114.

175. Rosner, "No Other Gods," 159.

176. Winiarski, "Adultery," 41, 43, 48.

177. By remarrying her first husband, the situation is like adultery, with the woman living with one man, then another, and then her first husband (Craigie, *Deuteronomy*, 305; Christensen, *Deuteronomy 21:10—34:12*, 24:4).

178. A possible NT parallel is Heb 6:4–6.

179. These issues appear again in the Corinthian "food offered to idols" situation.

strong response.[180] Winiarski's concerns over Jeremiah 13 are then not so confronting.[181]

Secondly, there was no compromise, a corollary of the adultery/idolatry metaphor. While idolators were dispossessed, lest they be a "constant snare and hindrance to Israel,"[182] the idols and high places were destroyed (Num 33:52).[183] Israel had already experienced the episode of the Baal of Peor (Num 25),[184] and were told that if they allowed the conquered people to remain, God would do to them what he had planned for the idolators (Num 33:56). So great was God's offence at idolatry that both forms of the Decalogue included graphic penalties to the third and fourth generations (Exod 20:4–6; Deut 5:8–10).[185]

Thirdly, restoration of godly behavior in Israel was invariably linked with iconoclasty. God commended kings Joash, Josiah, Asa, and Jehoshaphat for destroying idols (2 Kgs 11; 23:24–25; 2 Chr 14:5; 17:6), although some of them later fell into sin (2 Chr 35:22; 20:35–37). No reform seemed to have happened in Israel without the destruction of idols. While Israel was expected to obey the law, God alone could do certain things when Israel repented. Only God's direct action, conditional on repentance, could atone for "Jacob's guilt" (Isa 27:9), cleanse Israel from idolatry (Ezek 36:25), or remove false prophets and the spirit of impurity (Zech 13:2).

---

180. Phinehas ignored judicial process and received an eternal covenant of peace (Feldman, "Phinehas," 323). He notes Josephus's problems with Phinehas, who did exactly that for which Josephus condemned the Zealots: extrajudicial executions (ibid., 327). This was only heightened by many rabbis approving of his zeal (ibid., 319). Josephus's solution is an extra-biblical attack by Zimri on Moses' tyranny (ibid., 330), and Zimri is then killed by Phinehas for insolence. Given the antipathy between Rome and the Zealots when he was writing, Josephus did not call Phinehas a zealot (ibid., 344).

181. Winiarski, "Adultery," 50–51.

182. Budd, *Numbers*, 33:52.

183. Gruen, "Exodus," 108.

184. Hahn and Bergsma, "Laws," 204.

185. It is difficult for a law attributed to God to be changed, so another way around this commandment had to be found (Levinson, "Canon," 23). Ezek 18's individual responsibility seems to contradict the Decalogue's transgenerational responsibility, which reflects legal wording in Esarhaddon's treaties (ibid., 27). However, there are three issues which he does not seem to have noticed. First, Ezek 18 talks of death, while Exod 20 talks (less severely) of punishment. Second, he has not explained why the Pentateuchal writers slavishly followed surrounding cultures in adopting Esarhaddon's wording and could not express things differently. Finally, if Deut was written in the late seventh century BC as a trigger for Josiah's reforms by emphasizing cultic centrality (Weitzman, "Lessons," 382), why include transgenerational responsibility?

Finally, refusing to worship idols in some circumstances could mean martyrdom for a faithful Israelite (Dan 3:12, 18).[186] In summary, idolatry was forbidden on the most serious grounds of conflicting with the exodus, by which God made Israel a nation. Pagans were to be dispossessed and their temples destroyed,[187] but guilty Israelites were executed. Finally, both Israel and Judah were exiled for idolatry. There was no compromise possible on idolatry. Moreover, all of this was in stark contrast with how other Ancient Near East peoples saw idols as a way of accessing a god.

Usage in the GNT

First, while the above sources use only a small number of terms, the GNT uses five, all of which appear in 1 Corinthians 8–10: εἰδώλιον (1 Cor 8:10), εἰδωλόθυτος (Acts 15:29; 21:25; 1 Cor 8:1, 4, 7, 10; 10:19; Rev 2:14, 20), εἰδωλολατρία (1 Cor 10:14; Gal 5:20; Col 3:5; 1 Pet 4:3), εἰδωλολάτρης (1 Cor 5:10–11; 6:9; 10:7; Eph 5:5; Rev 21:8), and εἴδωλον (Acts 7:41; 15:20; Rom 2:22; 1 Cor 8:4, 7; 10:19; 12:2; 2 Cor 6:16; 1 Thess 1:9; 1 John 5:21; Rev 9:20). 1 Corinthians 8–10 intensifies an existing negative impression.

Secondly, unlike secular Greek and Josephus, but in full continuity with the LXX, there is no compromise with idolatry or Christian idolators, as there is no agreement between God and idols (2 Cor 6:16).[188] While 1 John 5:21 warns readers to keep themselves from idols, 1 Corinthians 10:14 counsels the more active idea of fleeing from idolatry. First Corinthians 5:10–11 warns the Corinthians to shun Christians who are also idolators, as idolatry is specifically linked to participation in the cultic life of the pagan gods in Corinth.

Thirdly, idolatry is linked with things which are forbidden in the LXX, but where the parallel warnings in the NT are more severe. The Decalogue forbids adultery (Exod 20:14), and the Baal of Peor incident eloquently condemns fornication (Num 25). When Revelation addresses εἰδωλόθυτος, the

---

186. Goldingay and Wright, "Yahweh," 60.

187. In later second-century CE thought, rabbis addressed the status of idols, but did so less severely than the LXX. Rather than calling for idols to be smashed, they instructed their followers to deface the idol by removing the tip of its ear or nose (Furstenberg, "Idolatry," 337). This reflected the prevailing Ancient Near East view that the deity actually resided in the idol, and that damaging the idol could impinge negatively on the god's standing. In a further concession, they limited the effect of idols to their effect on the idolators (ibid., 340). This is a major change compared to the LXX's demand to smash all idols.

188. Balla, "2 Corinthians," 770–71.

text refers to Satan's presence in Pergamum (Rev 2:13)[189] and the threat of Jesus himself fighting against his unrepentant people. In the letter to Thyatira, Jezebel's teaching of εἰδωλόθυτος and immorality are "Satan's so-called deep secrets" (Rev 2:24).[190] These texts reflect Deuteronomy 32's identification of idolatry and the demonic, as well as Numbers chapter 25's association of idolatry (εἰδωλόθυτος) and immorality, but strengthen the punishment. It is no longer a Moses or a Phinehas who inflicts punishment on God's behalf, but Jesus himself (Rev 2:16, 23).

While the LXX condemns greed (Prov 28:8), the NT equates it with εἰδωλολατρία (Col 3:5) and εἰδωλολάτρης (Eph 5:5).[191] This has no parallel in the OT, as greed is the only sin in the NT equated with idolatry, which is further compelling evidence of money's uniquely negative status in the NT, where it is the only physical object portrayed as a rival object of worship to God (Matt 6:24). The link with evil is seen in Galatians 5:20, where εἰδωλολατρεία is linked with φαρμακεία,[192] and Revelation 21:8, where εἰδωλολάτραις are consigned to the lake of burning sulphur along with the devil, the beast, and the false prophet (20:10). Εἰδώλιον is explicitly linked with evil, where pagan sacrifices are offered to demons (1 Cor 10:20), and where worshiping demons and idols is equated (Rev 9:20). The penalty for εἰδωλολάτρης is losing eternal life (1 Cor 6:9; Eph 5:5; Rev 21:8).

1 Corinthians 8–10 warns against eating εἰδωλόθυτος in certain circumstances, while linking idolatry and evil (1 Cor 10:20). Greed and immorality were part of the feasts involving εἰδωλόθυτος. Dining out in Corinth could be a clearly religious affair, like dinner at the Asklepeion to celebrate the host's birthday, or to thank a god for healing; but even dinner in a private home could be religious, with diners placing food before statues to encourage fellowship with the gods.[193] Nonattendance at sacrificial meals could cause problems for the Corinthian Christian given the importance of patronage.[194] Paul's resolution of this problem shows much about his thinking on the relationship between idolatry and the demonic, and also a person's ultimate loyalty.

The topic of εἰδωλόθυτος was apparently known to both Paul and the Corinthians, as shown by Περὶ δέ.[195] Paul affirmed that an idol is nothing

---

189. It is an evil power (Wink, *Naming*, 19).

190. Ladd, *Revelation*, 53.

191. Comfort, "Idolatry," 426.

192. Ibid., 426. It is using drugs in sorcery (Longenecker, *Galatians*, 255). Rev 9:21 and 18:23 also link sorcery and evil.

193. Fotopoulos, *Food*, 39, 69.

194. Smit, "Idolaters," 42; Fotopoulos, *Food*, 252.

195. Ibid., 193.

(1 Cor 8:4),[196] but that if knowledgeable Christians who understood that were seen eating in a temple, their weaker fellow believers might recall the idolatry behind the meal and be offended—or worse, assume that worship was being offered. Paul asks stronger Christians not to use their right to eat such meat, just as he had forsaken some of his apostolic rights (1 Cor 9).[197] First Corinthians 10 seems different, with Paul using examples of people from Israel's past who sinned and were judged.[198] While believing that idols are nothing, he knew that demonic influences are behind idols and sacrifices, so the idols become significant when treated as divine,[199] as eating actualizes the fellowship between guests and demons (1 Cor 10:20),[200] so compromising the believer's relationship with God. The crucial admission which rendered eating impossible for the Christian was that the meat had been sacrificed, with all that this implied about idolatry (1 Cor 10:28). Other problems associated with sacrificial meals were the implied greed in being more concerned about being seen at the right meals than God's glory, and the immorality offered by the quaintly named "flute girls."[201]

3.3.4. Δαιμόν words

Like εἴδωλον, the δαιμόν group of words are used favorably by Greek secular writers, with a darker edge by Josephus but reaching full condemnation in the LXX and the GNT.

Usage in secular Greek

The δαιμόν words can apply to human beings, like an Achaean chieftain,[202] or Xenophon's "encomiastic description" of Socrates's humanity.[203] It can mean something divine, like divine involvement in Lycomedes's death,[204] or

---

196. Page, *Powers*, 225; Smit, "Idolaters," 47.
197. Still, "Aims," 337; Fotopoulos, *Food*, 223.
198. Smit, "Idolaters," 51.
199. Fotopoulos, *Food*, 235.
200. Willis, *Meat*, 189; Page, *Powers*, 225; Smit, "Idolaters," 52; Wink, *Unmasking*, 113.
201. Fotopoulos, *Food*, 171, 248.
202. Homer, *Iliad*, ii.2.190; Homer, *Opera*, 1920, especially δαιμόνι.
203. Mason, "Essenes," 251–52; Xenophon, *Mem*. 1.3.5; Xenophon, *Opera Omnia*, vol 2, especially δαιμόνιον.
204. *Hist Graec* 7.4.3., especially "δαιμονιω."

Socrates's divinities.²⁰⁵ Herodotus wrote that the Athenians attributed their defeat to "divine power."²⁰⁶ None of the usages have any hint of evil; rather, the δαιμόν beings are sought for guidance (Socrates), or intervene to ensure justice (Herodotus). Rather than being rejected, people cultivate their influence, especially as illuminators of wrongdoing.²⁰⁷

Usage in Josephus

Josephus has three words in this group: δαιμονίον (also in the GNT), δαιμονίος, and δαίμων. Unlike the LXX, where all uses are negative, he uses these words respectively for spiritual beings, whether good or evil, a providential visitation by a spiritual being, and the incorporeal aspect of someone who has died.

Josephus uses δαιμονίον for God telling John Hyrcanus that his sons would be less successful in government (*J.W.* 1.69)²⁰⁸ and holding Aristobulus guilty for the murder of Alexander (*J.W.* 1.84)²⁰⁹ when Israel was obedient.²¹⁰ Mimicking Xenophon (*Mem.* 1.1.2), Josephus claimed that Socrates was guided by a δαιμονίον (*Ag. Ap.* 2.263), or God, apparently.²¹¹ By contrast, he also uses δαιμονίον to mean evil spirits which cause "distempers," but which could be exorcized with Solomonic rites (Ant 8:45–48).²¹² No other Biblical word means both God and an unclean spirit.

The second word is δαιμονίος, a providential act/visitation by God or another spiritual being. God holding Aristobulus accountable for Alexander's murder was shown by a servant providentially spilling some of

205. Xenophon, *Opera Omnia*, vol 1; Xenophon, *Mem.* 1.1.2., especially δαιμόνια. Reece cites Kierkegaard, that Socrates's divinity represents a questioning of the state's power and authority, cf. the expected obedience (Reece, *Irony*, 14). This explains Socrates's trial and execution for leading Athenian youth astray.

206. Herodotus, *Historiae*, 5.87.2; Herodotus, *Greek History*, 231, especially δαιμόνιου.

207. Flint, *Magic*, 284. Brenk traces the uses of δαιμόν through Plutarch to conclude that, while he opens up a range of possibilities, Plutarch does not finally state whether they are malevolent or not ("Daimon").

208. Mason, "Irony," 169.

209. Bond, *Pilate*, 64.

210. Mason, "Essenes," 258.

211. Since Homer, δαιμονίον and δαιμον meant "divine being." The distinction between these terms and θεός was not always clear until the later Hellenistic period when the former terms were used for lower spiritual beings and θεός for higher ones. However, Socrates believed that his δαιμονίον gave him moral guidance and could not simply be called evil (Luck, *Magic*, 207).

212. Mason, "Essenes," 272

his blood on the spot where he killed Alexander (*J.W.* 1.82). He said that God guided (the presumably pagan) Vespasian and then his son Titus (*J.W.* 4.501, 622), possibly to ingratiate himself, as he also claimed that God enriched Vespasian, who built a pagan temple with the proceeds, "celebrating victory" over the Jews (*J.W.* 7.159).[213] He also used δαιμόνιος for a "divine fury" which came upon the Roman troops to enable them to rout the Jewish army, build a wall, or burn the temple (*J.W.* 3.485, 5.502, 6.252). While he does not discuss the nature of the δαιμόνιος, it always seems obedient to God; e.g., Josephus uses δαιμόνιος for the demons which oppressed Saul under God's providence (*Ant.* 6.214).

The final word is δαίμων, meaning either an expression of God's providence in guiding events or the spirits of those who have died, particularly in their desire for justice. Even when the demons were evil, like those which tormented Saul or which Solomon learnt to expel (*Ant.* 6.168, 8.45), they are still under God's control. Titus assured his troops that those who died in battle would become good δαίμονες (*J.W.* 6.47).[214] Herod said that his son Alexander had a δαιμόνων ἀγαθῶν to guide him (*Ant.* 16.210). Finally, the spirits of people like John Hyrcanus, Mariamne, and Alexander appear, wanting justice (*J.W.* 1.521, 599), although in *Jewish Antiquities* 13.415, Alexander's spirit is a "fatal demon," which could exact revenge.

The key idea linking these different terms is that they are overwhelmingly positive. Δαιμόν words mean either God's providence, or other spiritual beings guiding the living or ensuring justice for the dead, even when described in unflattering terms. In some sense, they are like the lying spirit in 1 Kings 22—under God's control, but still malevolent. There is nothing like the uniformly negative picture of the GNT.

Usage in the LXX

The link between sin, evil, and idols in the OT is clear in Deuteronomy 32:17, where Moses lamented that Israel had sacrificed to the δαιμονίοις, gods which their fathers had not known.[215] The writer of Deuteronomy knew of other gods (32:12, 17, 21, 31, 37)[216] which are linked to demons and idols (32:17, 21).[217] Deuteronomy 32:17 and Psalm 106:37 say that Is-

213. Mason, "Audience," 66.

214. Mason, "Essenes," 266.

215. This may allude to the Golden Calf, to which the Israelites sacrificed (Exod 32:6).

216. Fotopoulos, *Food*, 235.

217. Joosten, "Note," 553; Willis, *Meat*, 191; Page, *Powers*, 66–68. Some have tried

rael sacrificed their children to the שֵׁדִים.²¹⁸ In LXX Psalm 90:6, trusting in God gives protection from δαιμόνιου μεσημβρινοῦ. Demons are linked with idols in Psalm 96:5, and arguably in Isaiah (13:21; 34:14; 65:3).²¹⁹ Every OT use of δαιμονίον involves idolatry or God's judgment. God "rejected them" and "abhorred his inheritance" (Deut 32:19; Ps 106:40). If they acted like Canaanites, God would use them to punish Israel.²²⁰

In his oracle of judgment, Isaiah lists iniquity and pride as reasons why Babylon will be so ruined that only animals and δαιμόνια will inhabit it (13:11, 21). A similar fate awaited Edom, whose cities would also be populated by δαιμόνια.²²¹ God is exasperated with those who burn incense τοῖς δαιμονίοις, possibly meaning necromancy (Isa 65:3).²²² Isaiah 65:11 describes those who have forsaken the Lord as preparing a cultic meal for Fortune and Destiny, but the LXX said that they prepared a table τῷ δαίμονι. Hosea 4:12 describes those consulting a wooden idol as led astray by a πνεύματι πορνείας.²²³ Adams argues that this is not sacred prostitution, as the sexualized language is better interpreted as non-sexual religious apostasy, because metaphors are more about how two images differ, than any similarities.²²⁴ Covenant is a marriage, and so the language of prostitution

---

to define the nature of Deut 32. Weitzman suggests a lawsuit with an indictment or wisdom (32:15–18; "Lessons," 377), but concludes that it is in the "last words" tradition of the fifth-century BCE *Words of Ahiqar*, where a dying teacher both instructs and rebukes his followers (ibid., 380–82). But Miller ("Psalms"), Page (*Powers,* 67), and Hahn and Bergsma ("Laws") note the close parallels with Ps 106. Deut stresses Israel's distinctiveness and gives reasons to obey, like God's jealousy (so Willis, *Meat,* 214, 280) and release from slavery. Psalms record Israelite prayers to this God (Miller, "Psalms," 9–10).

Ps 106:28—"they offered sacrifices to lifeless gods"—could mean sacrifices to dead ancestors (Lewis, "Estate," 602). Despite his best efforts, this is an unlikely reading of the Baal of Peor incident (Num 25), the defining sin of the second wilderness generation (Hahn and Bergsma, "Laws," 204). Relations between Israelite men and Moabite women led to Israel bowing before Baal (25:2; Klawans, "Impurity," 290–91). Linking adultery/fornication and idolatry was common in Jewish religious polemic (Willis, *Meat,* 150).

218. Christensen, *Deuteronomy 21:10—34:12,* 32:17; Willis, *Meat,* 191.

219. Page, *Powers,* 70.

220. Allen, *Psalms 101–150,* 106:40.

221. Watts, *Isaiah 34–66,* 34:14.

222. Ibid., 65:3.

223. Hos 4:12 is "not an independent spirit-being, but a powerful, habituating devotion to heterodoxy" (Stuart, *Hosea*), but Stuart provides no reason for spirit not to take its usual meaning. Page (*Powers,* 77) is similar.

224. Adams, "Hosea," 295, 297.

allows the wronged husband, Yahweh, to vent his anger fully at Israel's apostasy.[225]

But Miller argues that the verb means extramarital sexual relationships, regardless of payment, and does double duty, describing literal fornication with the Moabite women and metaphorical fornication with Baal.[226] While both have strengths, Adams's approach better reflects God's anger at apostasy and allows another stringent critique of idolatry. The same πνεύματι πορνείας prevents them acknowledging the Lord (Hos 5:4), but equally importantly, this spirit is "in their heart," the first reference to evil inside a person. Finally, Zechariah 13:2[227] links God cutting off idols with the departure of (LXX "false") prophets and τὸ πνεῦμα τὸ ἀκάθαρτον. I covered Rosner's examples of intertestamental literature linking demons, idols, and sin in s3.3.2.

The above verses paint a consistent picture where idolatry and sacrifices (including children) are offered to demons, not God. Nothing positive is said about idolatry, demons or sin, quite the reverse. Rather, these ungodly things are linked. God's judgment is to abandon his people and hand them over to the nations. With the exception of Hosea 5:4, the OT texts lack the NT's concern with the spirits indwelling people.

Usage in the GNT

The GNT uses three words: δαιμονίζομαι, δαιμόνιον, and δαιμονιώδης. The contrast with secular Greek and Josephus could hardly be greater, as they mean evil spiritual beings who oppose God's people. The GNT preserves the LXX's emphasis of demons as spiritual evil linked with sin like idolatry, but intensifies matters by having Jesus converse directly with evil, and by demons affecting people internally.

Firstly, different terms can mean the same being. The boy in Mark 9:17 was afflicted by a πνεῦμα ἄλαλον, but when Matthew relates this incident, he calls it τὸ δαιμόνιον (17:18). Luke 9:42 calls it both τὸ δαιμόνιον and τῷ πνεύματι τῷ ἀκαθάρτῳ.

Secondly, evil is always inimical to people. The demonized are linked with those suffering various diseases or severe pain, as needing Jesus' ministry (Matt 4:24). The Gerasene demoniac was isolated from all human

---

225. Ibid., 299–300.

226. Miller, "Response," 505

227. Raabe compares this with Ps 16:4: "I will not pour out libations of blood to such gods or take up their names on my lips" ("Ambiguity," 219).

company amongst the tombs and cut himself (Mark 5:5;[228] Luke 8:29).[229] The demon correctly called Jesus "Son of the Most High God," and obeyed. Matthew 8:28 has a similar healing of two demoniacs. No GNT texts resemble secular Greek and Josephus, where the δαιμόνιος can substitute for God; rather, this is done by Jesus, who resolutely opposes evil. Also, the idea in secular Greek and Josephus, that δαιμον words mean spiritual beings who are God's instruments for justice or guidance, is nearly absent from the GNT. There was no such indication when Jesus expelled the demon (Matt 17:18). The one exception is 1 Corinthians 5:5, where the incestuous offender is "παραδοῦναι . . . τῷ Σατανᾷ." The NT never has a δαιμόνιον doing anything unambiguously good; at best, they are instruments of God's discipline for his people.[230]

Thirdly, the demoniacs always addressed Jesus correctly and knelt before him (Mark 3:11). They could not have known Jesus' true identity, so the demons were recognizing his deity, as they never knelt before any other human. Jesus sometimes talks to the demons, like when he asked the demoniac his name, but the demons answered (Mark 5:9). The demons always respond immediately to Jesus' authority, the only possible exception being their request to Jesus at Gerasa not to be sent to the abyss (Luke 8:31). This is unparalleled in any of the three sources listed above.

Fourthly, unlike any prophet in the OT or Socrates,[231] Jesus was accused of being demonized himself. While Socrates's alleged guidance by the deity perturbed his contemporaries, it differs from the biting accusations of Jesus' enemies.

---

228. Horsley argues that as the demon was called "Legion," the cause of the man's distress was the Roman army (*Magic*, 145–46). This does not acknowledge the reason given by the demons: "we are many" (Mark 5:10), or explain how the Roman army could possess him. In so doing, Horsley falls into the trap which he accuses others of: an anachronistic reading based primarily on the social and political.

229. Bock, *Luke*, 773; his "tragic isolation."

230. Paul intends suffering at Satan's hands for discipline, but nowhere else uses destruction of the flesh to mean death (Fee, *1 Corinthians*, 210–14). Charlesworth should have noted a key feature of this text—that a being can be an instrument of God's judgment without having any positive features. He argues that the serpent has "positive and negative meanings" in the NT (*Serpent*, 353). His work here is quite simply unconvincing. He argues that the reference to Num 21 in 1 Cor 10:9 has a positive meaning of "one who carries out God's intentions" (ibid., 354), although it is arguably closer to his negative image of the serpent as "death-giver" (ibid., 198). Neither Satan nor the serpents are portrayed positively.

231. Xenophon, *Mem.* 1.1.2.

3.3.5. Beelzebul texts[232]

All the synoptics record an incident where Jesus was accused of being possessed or helped by Beelzebul, the prince of demons (Matt 12:24; Mark 3:22; Luke 11:15). This incident will be used to summarize the general pattern of usage of the δαιμόν group, particularly in reference to Satan.

Beelzebul in Mark 3:20–30

Mark 3:9—4:11 has a marked insider/outsider contrast where Jesus' family, who would normally be insiders, are outsiders. Ahearne-Kroll notes the frame (3:22, 30) about Jesus allegedly being demonized, but should also note the outer frame of Jesus' family (3:21, 31).[233] The most relevant question is if οἱ γραμματεῖς from Jerusalem are insiders or outsiders. The data shows that they are outsiders and linked with Satan, whom Jesus has already bettered.[234] The scribes and Jesus' family are not contrasts, but two different forms of outsider. In s4.2.1, this will be studied in more detail.

Οἱ γραμματεῖς have been distinguished so far in Mark by having an inferior authority to Jesus (1:22), charging him with the capital offense of blasphemy (2:7),[235] and the ritually unlawful action of eating with tax collectors and sinners (2:16).[236] In their next appearance, they accuse Jesus of colluding with Beelzebul, or Satan, in exorcism (3:22).[237] These are serious charges, and Jesus responds by calling them, using προσκαλέομαι.[238] Jesus

---

232. It means "lord of the flies/filth" (Luck, *Magic*, 208). These terms do not stand scrutiny, and it may have been coined for the occasion to link Jesus with evil (Guelich, *Mark*, 3:22; citing Gaston, "Beelzebul," 523). Its derivation is unclear, but Mark uses it as a synonym for Satan; e.g., 3:23 (France, *Mark*, 170).

233. Ahearne-Kroll, "Family," 11. The role of Jesus' family is completely different and has no demonic dimension. Myers's identification of Satan's realm with the scribal establishment is unconvincing (*Binding*, 164–66).

234. Mark does not explicitly say that Jesus defeated Satan, but Matt 4:11 and Luke 4:13 are clear. Horsley (*Magic*, 156) disputes, due to the paucity of references, that there is an "apocalyptic dualism," where people hoped that God would overthrow Satan, who controlled the world, history, etc. This is overstated, as I will show in s3.4.5; the references to evil in the NT are more numerous and more immediate than in the OT, as the main arena of conflict between good and evil is now on earth.

235. Page, *Powers*, 101. Mark 2:7 and 3:29 establish a "battle of the blasphemies" between Jesus and his opponents, with each side claiming that the other side offends God in their evaluation of Jesus (Bock, *Blasphemy*, 188).

236. France, *Mark*, 134.

237. Page, *Powers*, 100. Whatever the prior relationship between "Beelzebul" and "satan," Mark 3:22 equates/conflates them.

238. Jesus is calling his disciples because of the use of προσκαλέομαι (Busch,

uses this verb to call the Twelve and the disciples (6:7; 8:1), his actual followers, and the crowd (7:14), who are potential followers. Will they follow Jesus?

Jesus must first address the source of his power in exorcism, which they declare is Satan. Jesus responds that this would be self-defeating. Busch argues that, if Satan authorized Jesus' exorcisms, then his house would fall, and since that is not happening, then Satan is not allowing them.[239] This is illogical, as although Satan's kingdom has not fallen,[240] it is under sustained attack. Jesus defeated Satan in the wilderness, and no demon has been able to resist Jesus;[241] the most that Legion, demonic but not necessarily Satan, could do was bargain with Jesus about their destination (5:12). To say that "Jesus is a demonic party"[242] in the conflict is unsupported by the text, as the key question is not whether Satan's kingdom has fallen, but regarding the source of the attacks against it, namely Jesus. Anyone aligned with Satan is then opposed to Jesus.

Jesus speaks to the scribes using the phrase "ἐν παραβολαῖς," its first use in Mark. Insiders are addressed in plain speech (4:11).[243] Jesus is creating a gap between the scribes and himself, which they can cross, if they will obey him. Their attitude toward Jesus hitherto does not engender any such confidence. The imperfect ἔλεγεν implies "sustained... vilification."[244] Like his family, the scribes make unsupported allegations,[245] but face a harsher judgment. First, Jesus establishes his power, contrasting the relative weakness of the strong man. Satan is a "strong" demon.[246] Binding[247] a

---

"Questioning," 479), but the disciples are already inside (Mark 3:20), and it is the scribes who accuse Jesus, not his disciples. It is better to see that Jesus is calling the scribes to test their response.

239. Busch, "Questioning," 483.

240. I take this from the use of aorist passives in the text. If the evangelist wanted to say that Satan's kingdom was permanently divided, perfect passive forms would be more appropriate.

241. France, *Mark*, 168. Jesus closely associates Satan and the demons (Page, *Powers*, 103). An attack on the least demon is an attack on Satan himself (France, *Mark*, 171).

242. Busch, "Questioning," 484.

243. Guelich, *Mark*, 175.

244. France, *Mark*, 169.

245. Ahearne-Kroll, "Family," 13.

246. Busch, "Questioning," 484; Page, *Powers*, 106; France, *Mark*, 172.

247. Guelich quotes several authors who argue that Jesus' defeat of Satan in the desert was the binding (*Mark*, 176–77). What are we then to make of Jesus entering Satan's house? I will argue that the expulsion of Satan and his angels from heaven (s3.4.4) was his binding, or defeat, and Jesus' later victory over Satan in the desert actualized on earth the prior victory in heaven. In Mark, only after the (very brief) account of his

strong man needs someone stronger,²⁴⁸ and John the Baptist called Jesus "ὁ ἰσχυρότερός" (1:7).²⁴⁹ Jesus has shown his greater strength by defeating Satan in the wilderness²⁵⁰ and his repeated exorcisms. Far from accepting the accusation of blasphemy (2:7), Jesus warns them that they could blaspheme by ascribing evil to the Holy Spirit (3:29) and pay an eternal price.

Jesus portrays the scribes as outsiders, whose accusation that Jesus is aided by Satan is illogical, as Satan would hardly help Jesus destroy his kingdom. The exorcisms show that Jesus is indeed ὁ ἰσχυρότερός, who can restrain Satan and plunder his kingdom, and that any allegations that Jesus and Satan are colluding could have eternal consequences.²⁵¹

Beelzebul in Matthew 12:22–37

Matthew explained that Jesus healing the ill (12:15) fulfills the prophecies of the Servant of the Lord (Isa 42). His command of silence may have been to forestall what happened when he healed the demoniac, prompting people to ask if he might be the Son of David (12:23), one way by which Second Temple Judaism referred to the Messiah (Pss. Sol. 17:21).²⁵² This prompts the Pharisaic accusation of collusion with Beelzebul,²⁵³ or Satan (Matt 12:24). Matthew's Jesus repeats Mark's argument that this is illogical, but adds two new points: the Pharisees' followers also drive out demons. Exorcism by the Spirit of God, the only other possibility, shows the presence of the kingdom of God. Either the Pharisees' followers are in league with Satan, or Jesus is similarly empowered by God.²⁵⁴ If the Pharisees do not admit Jesus' God-given powers, they too are in league with Satan.

---

temptation (1:13), does Jesus do any exorcisms, which could then be the plundering of Satan.

248. France, *Mark*, 169.

249. Watts, "Mark," 145.

250. Calling Jesus' defeat of Satan an actualization on earth of Satan's prior defeat in heaven has the benefit of being a single event, a binding, as opposed to multiple exorcisms. It also recognizes that, in some sense, Jesus has entered Satan's territory, as shown in him offering Jesus "all the kingdoms of the world" (Matt 4:8; Luke 4:5) and Jesus not disputing his right to do so (Kelly, *Satan*, 87, 91).

251. It may be that describing Judas's treachery in handing over Jesus as godly could be the opposite error to this verse, attributing to God what is manifestly evil. Similarly, Isaiah 5:20: "Woe to those . . . evil good."

252. Hagner, *Matthew 1–13*, 12:22.

253. Davies and Allison, *Matthew*, 2:335.

254. Branden, *Conflict*, 58.

Healings and exorcisms are enough evidence for people to express faith in Jesus,[255] so requests for a sign when they had heard what Jesus had done (12:38, 24)[256] is more evidence of their attitude (12:34). Those in Matthew are arguably more culpable than those in Mark, due to the healing of the blind and mute demoniac, which πάντες οἱ ὄχλοι saw. Judas also saw many miracles which validated Jesus' identity, but called him (merely) "Rabbi" in Gethsemane (Mark 14:45), a potential insult (s4.3.5).

Beelzebul in Luke 11:14–26

Again, Luke has the same basic details as Mark about the source of Jesus' power (11:15), but with some differences. First, it is not just the scribes and Pharisees who accuse Jesus of being demonized or colluding with Beelzebul[257] and then want a sign, but the very general "τινὲς . . . ἐξ αὐτῶν" and ἕτεροι (11:15–16).[258] Opposition to or suspicion of Jesus may be more widespread.[259]

Secondly, the presence and nature of evil in various forms may link the surrounding texts. Jesus concludes the teaching after the Lord's Prayer by calling the disciples πονηροὶ (11:13),[260] before Luke describes the exorcism of a δαιμόνιον (11:14). Jesus then gives an extended riposte to the accusation of being demonized, showing the implacable hostility between God and Satan.[261] He then describes the return of τὸ ἀκάθαρτον πνεῦμα, along with seven other worse spirits (11:24, 26).[262] After an interlude on the nature of blessedness, Jesus castigates those asking for a sign as a γενεὰ πονηρά (11:29). While Matthew has similar passages, Luke has widened their reach considerably by replacing Pharisees and the like with "τινὲς . . . ἐξ αὐτῶν" and ἕτεροι (11:15–16) and "Τῶν . . . ὄχλων" (11:29), suggesting that many more are in danger, and that evil is more prevalent—not to mention more insidious—than the people seem to believe.

255. Keener, *Matthew*, 367.

256. A repetition of a Pharisaic similar accusation (Matt 9:34).

257. Page, *Powers*, 100.

258. ἕτεροι: they differ from those accusing Jesus of siding with Beelzebul (Sandiyagu, "ΕΤΕΡΟΣ," 113).

259. Nolland, *Luke 9:21—18:34*, 11:15–16.

260. Nolland argues (surprisingly) that being called "evil" is not a criticism (ibid., 11:13).

261. Such a clear attack against evil is not morally ambiguous (ibid., 11:16).

262. Nolland's belief that the unclean spirit has simply chosen to leave of its own free will and wander in waterless places before returning with seven other demons (ibid., 11:26) suffers from the fatal flaw that he gives no Biblical parallels, where by contrast, all unclean spirits are commanded to leave.

3.3.6. Conclusion

In the Babylonian exile, Judah arguably saw something novel: idolatrous priests would construct an idol before taking it to where the wood came from, and then perform certain rituals so that at the following dawn, the idol could receive its divinity from the gods. This is the best explanation for the anti-idolatry polemic in Second Isaiah which mirrors the ritual accurately, as it would be difficult to understand such polemic if no one in Israel believed such indwelling was possible. Given the sustained anti-idol polemic throughout the OT, it is inconceivable that the Holy Spirit or any godly being would inhabit an idol, so the indwelling spirit must have been evil.

We then examined two groups of words, based on εἴδωλον and δαιμόν, to show a pattern. Secular Greek writers use such terms positively for beings who are to be sought for guidance or to ensure justice for the dead. Josephus has a slightly darker edge, where the terms can mean insubstantial beings or things associated with the dead, or spiritual beings who can be approached for guidance, respectively. However, he also uses them to highlight past Israelite sin, or vengeful beings who can be instruments of God's justice. In a clear contrast, the LXX uses both terms uniformly negatively. Εἴδωλον is linked with one of the darkest episodes of the wilderness generation, the Baal of Peor incident (Num 25), and Deuteronomy 32:17 links idols and demons.

The GNT intensifies these negative features. In continuity with the LXX, there is no compromise with idolatry or Christian idolators, as there is no agreement between God and idols (2 Cor 6:16). Idolatry is linked with things which are forbidden in the LXX, but where the parallel warnings in the NT are more severe; e.g., Jesus himself will punish his idolatrous people (Rev 2:16, 23). First Corinthians 8–10 eloquently condemns all aspects of idolatry. For the first time, Satan's presence is explicitly associated with idolatry in Pergamum (Rev 2:13). The Beelzebul texts clearly associate Satan with the demonic, especially its harmful aspects, in a controversy after an exorcism by Jesus. These passages culminate in Jesus' graphic teaching that God and evil are implacably opposed, and that being on the wrong side of this division can have eternal, negative consequences. Blaspheming the Holy Spirit will not be forgiven (Matt 12:30–32; Mark 3:29; Luke 11:23).

Idols, demons, and Satan form an unholy alliance. There is no compromise possible between these things and God or God's people, and Jesus will oppose those of his people who are involved. While Judas is the only person explicitly described in the Bible as being entered or indwelt by Satan, the relationship between them goes deeper. S3.4 will show the evidence that Satan is a named rebel, allowed to remain in God's presence until he is irrevocably cast out, and who will then face a final judgment by God. The same headings will be used in s5.3 for Judas to show how profound are the parallels between Satan and Judas. This must cast the gravest shadow over Judas's actions.

3.4. Satan

3.4.1. Introduction

In s3.3, I showed the implacable opposition between God and evil, and also the increasing intensity in that opposition as we move from the LXX to the GNT. God's people must side with Jesus against evil if they are to be saved. If not, Jesus himself will discipline them (Rev 2:13). In these circumstances, it is no light matter to be indwelt by Satan, the prince of evil, when betraying Jesus (Luke 22:3; John 13:2, 27). Moreover, there are four important parallels between Satan and Judas:

- The demonic in God's presence; presumption to divinity;
- The desire of evil to harm God's people;
- Powerlessness; evil irrevocably cast out of heaven;
- God's final judgment of evil.

These headings will be used in s3.4 for Satan and in s5.3 for Judas.

3.4.2. The demonic in God's presence: presumption to divinity

The OT "heavenly assembly" included, for at least a time, Satan, who was in rebellion against/not submitted to God. Brown[263] approvingly quotes Day's *An Adversary in Heaven: sātān in the Hebrew Bible*, arguing that, as Satan can be understood as either an opponent or prosecutor,[264] then there "is not one celestial śāṭān in the Hebrew Bible, but rather the potential for many."[265] While respecting his wish not to read in a later, more developed demonology, this is too subtle, ignoring the consistent themes in all passages which

---

263. Brown, "Devil," 203.
264. Brant is conflicted: he is "a prosecuting attorney or the lying spirit" (*Drama*, 221). He cannot be both.
265. Day, *Adversary*, 15. Kelly commits the opposite error, where all "satans," regardless of what they are doing or who they are, are essentially the same, thus equating the satans in Num 22, Job 1–2, and Zech 3 (Kelly, *Satan*, 15). He believes that Satan is like a prosecutor, but fails to explain why he neither acts like nor is treated like one (ibid., 2).

mention Satan or evil. They have direct access to God, but are still under his authority; they are personal, but either accuse and/or seek to harm people. We will study the different texts on Satan, to see if a metanarrative emerges which does justice to its constituent texts. We study them simply to identify what they say about Satan; other issues are beyond the scope of this thesis.

In 1 Chronicles 21, the Chronicler may have adapted[266] an earlier account from 2 Samuel 24[267] on David's sin in the census of the army,[268] to replace the Lord as the agent of the incitement with Satan.[269] Second Samuel 24:1 may imply unrepented sin: "*Again* [my emphasis] the anger of the Lord burned against Israel."[270]

---

266. While we cannot be sure on literary dependency, it seems that the Chronicler has adapted an earlier account from 2 Sam, or a common source. While challenging to interpret, there is evidence in Job 1–2 that Satan could operate (malevolently) within God's permission, but no evidence that God would take up a plan devised by Satan, as would be the case if 1 Chr 21 was the earlier text. Even in 1 Kgs 22, God proposes a definite course of action and asks for a volunteer. The lying spirit does nothing until God gives permission. 1 Sam 16:14 describes the evil spirit which tormented the disobedient Saul as "from the Lord."

The question is why the Chronicler amended the source to have Satan, not God, opposing Israel. Exegeses which have God one step removed from allowing evil (Braun, *1 Chronicles*, 21:11) are inadequate, as God is still the ultimate cause (Stokes, "David," 100; Page, *Powers*, 76; Braun, *1 Chronicles*, 21:1). It is difficult to see how replacing LORD in 2 Sam 24 with Satan in 1 Chr 21 creates any appreciable distance (contra Kelly, *Satan*, 20). It is most likely consistent with other OT references to Satan, that a sovereign God may allow Satan to oppress his sinful people. This pattern arguably continues in the NT with the incestuous offender (1 Cor 5:5). As seen below, when Satan oppressed upright Job, Job's integrity shone through; but when Satan rose up against Israel, the outcome was disastrous because of David's lesser integrity. Job's integrity survived Satanic testing; David's arguably did not, and after Joshua's sin (representative of wider Israel [Page, *Powers*, 31]) is taken away, he was promised a bright future if obedient (Zech 3).

267. The Succession Narrative makes better sense in the early years of Solomon's reign by showing that he was David's legitimate heir, as opposed to a Saulide (Anderson, *2 Samuel*, Introduction). Braun dates 1 Chr much later, in 515 BC (*1 Chronicles*, Purpose and Date).

268. David's sin may have been in proposing the census himself, rather than seeking God's guidance on the matter, as Num 1:3 has the Lord commanding Moses to number those "able to serve in the army."

269. Some have been too quick, in my opinion, to find favor of Joab in opposing the census; e.g., Braun (*1 Chronicles*, 21:1): "For once Joab is . . . the voice of good sense" (Anderson, *2 Samuel*, 24:1). No one betrays David more than Joab (s2.3.4). His reluctance may not have been because of his theologically correct reason, but a lack of respect for David. Correct theology or David's wishes did not seem to matter to Joab when conspiring with Adonijah against Solomon, David's chosen successor (1 Kgs 2).

Wink is possibly inconsistent. He questions Satan's existence by remarking, "If Satan has any reality" (*Unmasking*, 25), but Wink still wants him as God's *agent provocateur*.

270. Anderson, *2 Samuel*, 24:1; Page, *Powers*, 36.

There are some points to be considered. Firstly, is Satan human or an unspecified member of the heavenly council?[271] Stokes concludes that Satan is not human because "less pleasant" tasks are delegated to superhuman beings (Num 22), no human is mentioned in 2 Samuel 24 (the source of 1 Chronicles 21), and identifying Satan as human leaves much unresolved, not least his identity.[272] We may conclude that he is not human.

Secondly, there are parallel passages where Satan opposes God's people. Both Job 2:3 and 1 Chronicles 21:1 use "incite" with Satan as the subject.[273] Both Zechariah 3:1 and 1 Chronicles 21:1 have Satan rising up against Israel.[274] Satan not only accuses God's people but "incites them to evil."[275] Stokes found five parallels between Balaam in Numbers 22 and 1 Chronicles 21, such as an anarthrous satan, the angel of the Lord in Numbers 22:22 and Satan in 1 Chronicles 21, to argue that Satan is "a superhuman agent of divine punishment," an emissary of Israel's God but not his archenemy.[276] This is unconvincing, as other OT texts on Satan show him at odds with God or his people, something never said of the angel of the Lord.[277] Nonetheless, God can oppose his sinful people by an intermediary. In conclusion, 1 Chronicles 21 shows a malevolent, supernatural Satan who is opposed to God's people, but still subject to God.

In Job 1, Satan may still appear before God with the angels, but his attitude to God is unbearably insolent and wrong for a creature.[278] Perhaps this is why the Lord[279] questions him. Satan replies that he has been walking up and down the earth,[280] acting like the owner, God. His insolence shows that

---

271. Stokes ("David") reviewed Day (*Adversary*) and Japhet ("Ideology"), who argued that Satan could be a military or any human opponent because anarthrous Satan could be an ordinary human.

272. Stokes, "David," 97–99.

273. Page, *Powers*, 34; Stokes, "David," 95.

274. Page, *Powers*, 35.

275. Braun, *1 Chronicles*, 21:1.

276. Stokes, "David," 101–4, 106

277. Pagels ("Social Three," 491) and Branden (*Conflict*, 17) fail to note this.

278. Satan "advises extreme measures" and Satan's "consultation with God" (Kelly, *Satan*, 26, 168) are too weak, as Satan is very malicious.

279. Job 1 shows the Lord as (merely) one of the sons of El Elyon, the supreme God (Barker, *Angel*, 5). This is unlikely, as while the "sons of God" are clearly inferior to the Lord, there is no hint that there is anyone superior to the Lord.

280. MacMullen attempts to parallel Satan and those patrolling the earth in Zech 1:8–11 (*Paganism*, 275). This is unlikely, as Satan is not said to patrol the earth, only to walk on it, and secondly, his insolent attitude to God is completely unlike the attitude of the horsemen to the angel of the Lord.

he is not the Lord's royal spy,[281] reporting back to him.[282] God does not treat Satan as such by asking for reports of sin.[283] He also does not function like a forensic prosecutor, or even a wandering one. Fleming makes the valuable point that, by default, Satan's main accusations are against God, not Job, accusing God of being worshiped not for himself, but for the wealth given to worshipers.[284] Satan's "You" is emphatic.[285] Moreover, if Satan is not evil, why does he twice reproach God for protecting Job (1:9, 2:4)?[286] If Satan was on God's side (neutrality presumably not being an option), would not Satan have wanted God to protect Job?[287]

It is highly unlikely that Satan is God's spy, but some argue that he is a prosecutor, exposing human sin,[288] due to being titled "the" Satan, meaning "the adversary."[289] There are difficulties, as he does not act like a prosecutor.[290] First, Page argues that the arthrous lying spirit in 1 Kings 22:21 is a "generic definite," or "a spirit."[291] This sounds like special pleading. Secondly, the accuser should present evidence against the accused and allow them to respond, but here, God the judge provides a character reference for Job, at

281. Contra Malina (*Insights*) and Wink (*Unmasking*, 23).

282. Contra Habel, *Job*, 89. This seems to elude Clines entirely, who sees this rudeness as (almost) principled: "What he [Satan] must question—and what *must* be questioned (there is nothing 'satanic' about the question)—is what the link between Job's godliness and his prosperity is" (*Job 1–20*, 1:9), as though God would not know this.

283. Habel, *Job*, 90.

284. "Tale," 471. Also, "[accusing] . . . God's government/God" (Grabiner, *Cosmic*, 43, 53).

285. Habel, *Job*, 90.

286. Sherlock argues that, while Satan "is not presented as evil," he nonetheless approvingly quotes Ling (*Significance*, 5–6), that "the accuser's prosecution of Job is unjust." (Sherlock, *Satan*, 5). Given the OT's uniform picture of Satan as inimical to people, one wonders how this could not be evil. This is unexplained. Satan "advises" God to test Job (Kelly, *Satan*, 21). This ignores Satan's insolence.

287. Page argues (correctly, in my opinion) that due to Satan's malicious pleasure in afflicting people, "it hardly seems appropriate to regard the Joban Satan as one of God's dutiful servants." (Page, *Powers*, 27)

288. Page, *Powers*, 25; Stokes, "David," 95; Wink, *Unmasking*, 13. Habel is supremely optimistic to deny any malice by Satan toward Job by word or action (*Job*, 89).

289. Page, *Powers*, 23. In the OT, "satan" always has the definite article, except 1 Chr 21:1, so nothing much can be derived from its presence here (Smith, *Micah–Malachi*, Zech 3:1), contra Kelly, *Satan*, 3, 29.

290. It is anachronistic to describe Satan as a prosecutor, a creation of Roman and later Western law, as no such office existed in Israel. Rather, judges were appointed to decide between competing claims. The most that could be claimed for Satan is (not unnaturally) that he is accusing Job, but God declares Job innocent before hearing any of Satan's "evidence."

291. Page, *Powers*, 79.

which point Satan accuses God. Satan agrees with God's assessment of Job's behavior, but impugns his motives.[292] Lastly, all such scenarios rely on the accused knowing the charges against them, with the impartial judge only hearing the evidence in court. However, Job is wholly ignorant of why these things have happened, and God declares his innocence before Satan speaks.[293] Stokes describes Job as "innocent" and "exemplary"; Rodd, "utter sincerity."[294]

Aimers (approvingly) cites sources with Satan as a wandering prosecutor who tests "hapless people" but argues that Satan is more righteous than God by indicating sins which God would rather hide. He argues that Job's wealth must have been earned unjustly.[295] This ignores the fact that God, not Satan, raised Job's piety, not his sin. Satan cannot impugn Job's deeds, only his supposed motivation (1:9; 2:4). His supposed resolution that "Job's repentance allows . . . restoration" misses the clear meaning of the text that Job repented of ignorance (42:3), not sin, the key point of the Lord's speeches.[296]

The key is Job's integrity (2:3, 9; 27:5). Both narratives end with Job innocent of sin (1:22; 2:10b). Satan has charged that God bought Job's affections (1:9–11; 2:4–5), and God must respond to protect the reputation of his obedient servant.[297] Satan can test Job within limits set by God (1:12), and

292. Ibid., 27.

293. Morriston, "Answer," 342.

294. Stokes, "David," 95; Rodd, *Glimpses*, 213. God is not omnipotent, and the "firework" of the divine discourse in Job 38–41 shows flaws in "the created universe" (Lacocque, "Job," 83–84). Lacocque argues that God creates "weal and woe," and asks if God needs his sense of security boosted by winning a bet with Satan (ibid., 88, 93). The universe is permeated with evil, obstructing its original purpose, and God needs Job as his viceroy (ibid., 96). He believes that if Job discovers God's weakness, he may not persevere (ibid., 94). Lacocque's odd exegesis comes from not seeing that God did not create Job's woe, but allowed it so that Job's integrity could be seen under trial. Responding to Lacocque, Guillaume argues that God needs Job's help to counter God's folly, not his weakness ("Dismantling," 499). God's supposed informant-in-chief accuses Job, but things go wrong, and God "swallows Job for naught" (ibid., 499). This fails to take seriously Job's integrity.

295. Aimers ("Devil," 60, 65) contra Clines, *Job 1–20*, 1:2

296. Aimers, "Devil," 65. For an alternate view, see Pelham, "Crisis."

297. Again, something which has escaped Clines (*Job 1–20*, 1:12) who only sees a zero-sum game: "Affirm that the Lord is infinitely omniscient, and you assert that Job's suffering serves only to prove God right in the eyes of one of his subordinates. Affirm that the Lord knows that Job will not waver, and you cannot explain why the Lord takes the slightest notice of the Satan's questions or why h e does not dismiss them out of hand from superior knowledge." Clines seems to not understand that Job's integrity will be seen as real when he stands firm under trial. The apparent mystery of evil happening to someone so devout is illuminated by the conversation between God and Satan. In another odd comment, Barker says "the other sons of God" taunted Yahweh so that he

returns to God's presence (2:1), clearly rebellious[298] after this fails, to ask for more authority, which he receives (2:6). None of this would have happened if he had not accused Job. Satan is not an impartial prosecutor, as he wants to destroy Job (and his family),[299] not just accuse him.

Steinmann has studied the speeches to conclude that, while we expect a threefold pattern because of the three friends, there is a fourfold pattern of Job replying to the friends, forcing the reader to reassess. God speaks four times to Job, alternating short and long speeches.[300] God restores Job and calls him to leave his desire to control everything[301] by offering sacrifices for the possible sin of his children, and return to trusting God.[302] The picture of Satan which emerges is not that of God's spy or an impartial prosecutor, but an accuser who wants to harm Job and his family. Exegeses which fail to note the importance of God defending Job's integrity are deficient. This unjust, accusatory air is also seen in Zechariah 3,[303] where Satan is set to accuse the high priest Joshua, who is somehow present, although the Lord cuts him off.[304] This could be blasphemy by action, as it would seem God's prerogative to judge his high priest.

Perhaps the most thorough attempt to see Satan positively is that of Aimers, who aims for a "deliberate bias towards the satan." He notes the

---

agreed to test Job (*Angel*, 30). She provides no evidence at all.

298. Another parallel between Judas and Satan is their insolence to God. Satan argues with God about Job, and Judas argues with Jesus about Mary's use of nard on his feet. Neither Satan nor Judas have any genuine concern about Job or the nard respectively; Satan's treatment of Job is cruel, and Judas is a thief (John 12:6). Satan does not appear again in Job, and Jesus rebukes Judas: "Leave her alone" (John 12:7). Satan may have killed Job, except God forbade him (Smith, *Hand This Man*, 149).

299. Contra Wink (*Unmasking*, 14) that Satan is merely "overzealous."

300. Steinmann, "Structure," 94, 91–92.

301. Clines, *Job 1–20*, 1:5.

302. Janzen, *Ethics*, 129; Steinmann, "Structure," 99.

303. There are many parallels between Job 1–2 and Zech 3 (Smith, *Micah–Malachi*).

304. Sherlock does not pursue the difficulty for his argument of Satan apparently not being "opposed to the Lord," but nonetheless attempting to accuse the high priest before being rebuked by the Lord (*Satan*, 5). If he is not opposed to the Lord, why will the Lord not even hear Satan's evidence? Klassen claims, "satan's concern would appear to be for the integrity of the divine service" (*Friend*, 14), a rather forced reading. Apparently, Satan also sought to promote "God's holiness and justice" (ibid., 144). These are extraordinary statements for which Klassen has no evidence or argument. If Satan was so concerned for the integrity of divine service, he should have said so, instead of accusing Joshua. Moreover, God would then have commended instead of rebuked him. Grabiner does not see that the Lord's attitude to Satan must raise serious doubts about him having a formal role as accuser (*Cosmic*, 54). Satan's evidence is not so much rejected, but rather, Joshua's sins have been absolved (Kelly, *Satan*, 25). The text says nothing like this.

core meaning of Satan as adversary, and that he is "even rebuked" for opposing Joshua without exploring the difficulties which this presents for his thesis.³⁰⁵ While Satan may be like the accuser in Psalm 109:6, the fact that God restores Joshua without even hearing Satan's evidence shows that he is working against God.³⁰⁶ This eludes Smith, who believes that the similarities with Job 1–2 strengthen the image of Satan as prosecutor.³⁰⁷ Once more, there is real tension between God and Satan, and Satan is rebuked, an accuser who cannot win a case. Joshua's filthy clothes represent either his own sin, or that of Israel.³⁰⁸ The Lord rebukes Satan in similar words to Michael (Zech 3:2/Jude 9),³⁰⁹ and promises Joshua a bright future if he is obedient. These passages consistently picture Satan's nature.³¹⁰

In summary, these texts are consistent. Satan may still attend the heavenly council, but there is always tension between him and God. Either God forbids Satan from presenting evidence (Zech 3), or he intervenes on behalf of the absent accused (Job 1–2). Satan cannot be a royal spy, as God does not ask him for evidence or an accuser/prosecutor because God consistently opposes him. Only a few verses in the OT mention evil, but they frequently show Satan or an unclean spirit in God's immediate presence. There are many more NT references to evil, but none of them show Satan in any capacity in God's immediate presence. I will argue that Satan has been removed permanently from God's presence (s3.4.4). While still a major factor in the life of the early church, he can no longer accuse God's people to God.

3.4.3. *The desire of evil to harm God's people*

1 Kings 22:20 does not mention Satan, and there is no tension between the evil spirit and God—quite the contrary, as God proposes a course of action and asks for volunteers. The Lord muses as to how he will entice Ahab to fall on Gilboa, due to serious sin (1 Kgs 16:30; 20:42; 21:29; Naboth's vineyard).³¹¹ The Lord sits and the host of heaven stand: there is no dualism (22:19).³¹² A

---

305. Aimers, "Devil," 59.
306. Page, *Powers*, 32–33.
307. Smith, *Micah–Malachi*, Zech 3:1.
308. Page, *Powers*, 31.
309. Carson, "Jude," 1075.
310. Contra Wink, who believes that Satan is a "prosecuting attorney" (*Unmasking*, 12–13), but cannot explain why God prevents Satan from giving any evidence or why God needs him to do so anyway.
311. Rogerson, *Ethics*, 83; Rodd, *Glimpses*, 298.
312. "There was only one member of any divine council, the Lord" (Sherlock, *Satan*,

lying spirit presents before the Lord and offers to deceive Ahab by his prophets.[313] DeVries's belief that this is the Holy Spirit, due to some supposed OT parallels (Jer 20:7, 10; Ezek 14:9), is unlikely.[314] He argues that God entices the prophet in Jeremiah 20, and Ezekiel 14:9 describes the enticement, but not how it happens. This is irrelevant, as God told Jeremiah that people would oppose him (1:19), and the enticement in Ezekiel 14 occurs when an idolator also seeks the Lord. The LXX uses of ἀπατάω are unsupportive. In Genesis 3:13, the serpent (called Satan in Romans 16:20, citing Genesis 3:15)[315] deceives Eve, and she and Adam are expelled from Eden (Gen 3:23). A man deceived a virgin (Exod 22:16) and Delilah deceived Samson (Judg 14:15; 16:5). The Spirit of God could not be party to this, as no sin or moral failure is ever imputed to any divine person.

Secondly, the Spirit of God is always described in the OT with divine features like "the Spirit of God/the Lord" (Gen 1:2; 2 Sam 23:2), or moral characteristics like "the Holy Spirit" (Ps 51:11). The Holy Spirit is never just a spirit, as the term means "God's own life."[316] The lying spirit[317] apparently came forward from the host of heaven,[318] which is inappropriate for the divine Spirit of God.

Next, the text clearly distinguishes between the spirit which inspired Ahab's prophets and the spirit which inspired Micaiah,[319] as his altercation with Zedekiah shows (1 Kgs 22:24–25).[320] Jehoshaphat thought that something was awry, asking for confirmation by a prophet of the Lord despite the unanimity of Ahab's four hundred prophets (22:6). Micaiah's prophecy came true, not that of the four hundred.[321] The spirit is fallen, but still has

---

5). Barker (*Angel*, 29) says (oddly) that "Yahweh is the Holy One of Israel,... *one heavenly being among many*" (her emphasis). This fails to recognize that Yahweh is never shown as just equal, much less subservient, to anyone else.

313. MacMullen, *Paganism*, 209. 1 Kgs 22 is an example of a passage showing the idea of "democratic rule" from Israel's pagan neighbors (Sherlock, *Inside*, 230n). This is difficult, as God asks for ideas, and the lying spirit still needs God's permission to act. This is not so much democratic rule as monotheism in action.

314. DeVries, *1 Kings*, 22:20.

315. Page, *Powers*, 197.

316. Sherlock, *Inside*, 94–95.

317. MacMullen contrasts El's helpless gods with a member of God's court, who proposes action (*Paganism*, 206).

318. The spirit is not specifically identified as Satan (Page, *Powers*, 79).

319. Israelite prophets received prophecies "in being caught up to" Yahweh's court (Horsley, *Magic*, 160).

320. Page, *Powers*, 79. Micaiah's approach forces Ahab to choose between truth and a lie (Bodner, "Locutions," 538).

321. The vision authenticated Micaiah's prophecy (Barker, *Angel*, 35). It is at least as

access to God. It desires harm for Ahab, but can only function with God's permission, and it imitates the modus operandi of the Spirit of God. In summary, the term "lying spirit" implies that, at this time, spirit(s) who were not aligned with God were in God's presence.

3.4.4. Powerlessness: Satan irrevocably cast out

If the OT hints at the expulsion of Satan from God's presence, the NT makes it explicit. The pattern of Satan as accuser also occurs in Revelation 12:10: "the accuser of our brothers." However, an uncritical approach can hide relevant facts. No NT text has Satan in heaven, like Job 1–2 or Zechariah 3, despite Revelation's many scenes of heaven.[322] It is likely that Satan and his angels were expelled at the Massacre of the Innocents (Matt 2; Rev 12:9),[323] so the main reference of Revelation 12 is Mary giving birth[324] to Jesus, and only secondarily to the NT church. Revelation 12:1–6 seems to describe Jesus' birth with the dragon, Satan,[325] keen to kill the boy who would rule the nations with a rod of iron. The reference to the Messianic Psalm 2:9[326]

---

possible that Micaiah's correct prophetic prediction authenticated his claim "I saw the LORD" (1 Kgs 22:19).

322. Contra Kelly: Satan is still exercising an alleged prosecutorial role (*Satan*, 154).

323. Luke 10:17–18: "I saw Satan fall" is not necessarily linked with the mission, as though it caused the fall. While not denying the fall, Jesus is refocusing the seventy-two on what really matters: their names are written in heaven. The aorist participle means a final fall from heaven (Nolland, *Luke 9:21—18:34*, 10:17), which I argue actualizes, on earth, evil's prior defeat in heaven. This is the end of Satan's (alleged) prosecutorial role in heaven (Fitzmyer, *Luke X–XXIV*, 862), although when this will happen is unstated. Pao and Schnabel say that it is based on Isa 14 ("Luke," 318), but Fitzmyer points out that the King has exalted himself, and Satan is not mentioned. There is no literary relationship between Isa 14 and Rev 12 (Fekkes, "Prophetic Traditions," 192). If Isa 14 refers to Satan, it could mean a primeval fall, whereas Rev 12 seems to be Satan's final exclusion from heaven.

I am not arguing that Revelation is in any way dependent on Matthew, only that two different authors can describe the same event in different ways.

324. "Whom the readers would identify as Jesus" (Collins, *Apocalypse*, 81); "the details of the birth do not match [those] of Jesus' birth . . . in the Gospels" (King, *Scroll*, 103). But Rev 12 gives almost no details. It is a stretch to use John 19:27 to say that the woman is the community of the faithful awaiting the Messiah, as this is not linked in any way with pregnancy/birth (ibid., 103). The words could mean "literal childbirth," but he prefers a symbolic meaning (ibid., 104). This is unlikely for the reasons given here.

325. Aune, *Revelation 6–16*, 12:3.

326. Ibid., 12:5. "The child prefigures Christ"; as if the child is Christ, the text moves too quickly from birth to exaltation (Grabiner, *Cosmic*, 146) but this ignores the NT use of ἁρπάζω.

also identifies Jesus (Rev 19:15).[327] The attempt to kill Jesus and Satan's consequent expulsion would then correspond to the Massacre (Matt 2:16–18).[328]

Not all agree, but they often fail to address key terms. The verb for giving birth, τίκτω, occurs four times (Rev 12:2, 4–5, 13). Its 208 LXX uses only have two meanings: the birth of a live human/animal (95 percent of uses) or metaphors strictly referencing pregnancy/birth for inanimate objects; e.g., being "pregnant" with evil gives "birth to" trouble/deceit (Ps 7:14). A possible exception is Isaiah 66:7–8, with four uses. In 66:7, "she" (Zion) gives birth (ἔτεκεν) to "a male," and in 66:8 gives birth (ἔτεκεν) to "her children." While 66:7 could be an actual birth,[329] the Lord's comments that it is highly unusual, happening before labor (cf. Rev 12:2),[330] that the woman is explicitly called "Zion" and that "son" and Zion's children are metaphors for Israel (or at least its obedient members), means that it must be metaphorical. It is God's promise of Jerusalem's rebirth.[331] Fekkes has noted parallels in themes and words, but not given due weight to the manifest differences.[332] As Isaiah 66 is clearly symbolic, but the circumstances of the birth are so different from Revelation 12, it cannot be used to show that Revelation 12 is symbolic. Despite its apparent attractiveness as a background, it has no stars or threatening dragon. While "son" can refer to Israel, there is no similar usage of "male son" or "the male" (12:5, 13). Nobody has established that Isaiah 66's setting applies to Revelation 12.

Similarly, in the GNT, at least eleven of the seventeen uses are human birth.[333] The others are metaphors for crops (Heb 6:7) and sin (Jas 1:25). Revelation 12:2, 4–5, and 13 refer to actual birth, as metaphorical uses do not entail a live birth.[334] The birth of a "male son" does not fit a metaphorical

---

327. Rev 2:27's use of Ps 2:9 is not another example, as the promise is to anyone at Thyatira who "overcomes and does My [Jesus'] will" (2:26). In Rev 19:15, it identifies Jesus alone (Sim, "Weeping," 99).

328. Josephus's lack of references to the Massacre argues against its historicity, but more importantly, Matt narrates it as an actual historical event (Park, "Herod," 473–74). Davies and Allison (*Matthew*, 1:265) argue that if the Massacre is accepted as historical, then so must the Magi. This guilt by association is not worthy of an academic argument. The text more than likely "preserves a historical core" (Keener, *Matthew*, 98), but focuses on its theology, as does Matt. "Herod" is actually Herod Archelaus, not Herod the Great (Smith, "Quirinius," 286).

329. Fekkes, "Prophetic Traditions," 190.

330. Unnoticed by Siew, *Beasts*, 153.

331. Watts, *Isaiah 34–66*, 363.

332. Fekkes, "Prophetic Traditions," 188.

333. Matt 1:21, 23, 25; 2:2; Luke 1:31, 57; 2:6–7, 11; John 16:21; Gal 4:27.

334. "Physical pregnancy cannot here be excluded" (Tavo, *Woman*, 263).

use (Rev 12:4).³³⁵ No use of τίκτω supports Beasley-Murray, who states that the text is "prophetic symbolism of Jerusalem as mother" of God's people, or Grabiner, who argues that the woman could be the church throughout history, or God's OT people, as no OT text has a collective Israel giving birth to an individual messiah.³³⁶

Secondly, Blevins says that she is "obviously mother Israel,"³³⁷ and Collins says "heavenly Israel" or "the Queen of Heaven,"³³⁸ without asking if it is Mary. The OT does have Israel in labor,³³⁹ and Beasley-Murray argues that she is not Mary, because 12:17 describes her children as the church,³⁴⁰ which Satan opposed. But it is hard to see why national Israel would be led into the desert by God to escape persecution by Satan because of the birth of the messiah,³⁴¹ or how they could hold fast "their testimony about Jesus" (Rev 12:17). Resseguie argues that the woman is "an image of the church," with her birth pangs a metaphor for the church's distress.³⁴² However, he does not

---

335. Rev 13 is based on myths from the imperial cult and concerns emperor worship (Friesen, "Resistance," 303). While some such allusion is nearly certain, he has not addressed the fact that the dragon in Rev 13 must be the same as in 12:9, Satan. The uses of δράκων and βάλλω ensure the unity of chapters 12–13 (Siew, *Beasts*, 73). Satan is the real enemy, not "elite families" from Asia Minor (Friesen, "Resistance," 310).

The curses of Gen 3:15–20 dominate Rev 12, as they are executed and finally reversed (Minear, "Curse," 71). He rightly notes the references to labor pain (Gen 3:16; Rev 12:2), but fails to apply this consistently. If this is so, then it is more evidence that this text concerns childbirth, as John's use of τίκτω suggests, not (following Caird) the cross (ibid., 73). He tries to parallel the role of the earth in Gen 3 and Rev 12 (ibid., 74), but does not note that, in Gen 3, the earth conceals a murder, while in Rev 12, it prevents one. While admitting that the role of the earth is "opposite" (ibid., 75) in Rev 12, he argues that the serpent spews out "rivers of deceit," which is absent from the text.

336. Beasley-Murray, *Revelation*, 198; Grabiner, *Cosmic*, 145; Tavo, *Woman*, 289. He has not addressed the fact that τίκτω overwhelmingly means normal birth.

337. Blevins, *Revelation*, 58. He states that the woman's flight is persecuted Christians fleeing Jerusalem after the death of Stephen (Acts 8; Barker, *Revelation*, 222), but fails to note that the dragon only wants to kill the boy. The woman is Israel because of the parallel in Isa, a woman crying out in birth (Pagels, "Part Three," 487). Biguzzi ("Figurative," 392) has no opinion.

338. Collins, *Myth*, 134; Collins, *Apocalypse*, 85.

339. Morris, *Revelation*, 152; Mounce, *Revelation*, 237; Ladd, *Revelation*, 168.

340. Beasley-Murray, *Revelation*, 198. So also Grabiner, *Cosmic*, 145.

341. It is the flight of Christians to Pella (Sowers, "Pella," 315), but Sowers still wants to interpret the woman as Israel, not Mary, without explaining why national Israel would need to flee to the desert. Herod's attempted killing of the infant Jesus shows that national Israel, or at least its leaders, were persecuting, not suffering persecution. Tavo does not address the difficulty of Israel needing to flee (Tavo, *Woman*, 266).

342. Resseguie, *Revelation*, 171. John 16:20–22 links the grief of the persecuted community to birth pangs (Pataki, "Myth," 261) but Rev 12 says nothing of a community. He has not shown that the woman is a community cf. an individual.

see that symbolic uses of τίκτω are closely tied to pregnancy/birth, or try to establish the identity of the baby. Beale and McDonough argue that the woman is "God's people," particularly Israel, giving birth to the Messiah,[343] but none of the texts cited mention the twelve stars; only one mentions a son (Isa 66:7–9), and they use a variety of references for the woman. Most are clearly symbolic. Isaiah 26:17–18 and Micah 4:9–10 use labor pains as images of pain, but neither have an actual birth.[344]

Siew argues that the stars cast down represent "an attack on Israel" or that they are saints who "suffer martyrdom"[345] but Revelation 12:4 is clear that the stars are cast down from heaven to earth by the dragon. There is no hint that they are persecuted on earth; rather, Aune recognizes that stars can mean evil angels.[346] Micah 5:3 seems to mean actual birth, and is widely regarded as Messianic,[347] but does not mention the stars or the dragon. These texts fail individually and collectively as a background for Revelation 12 for the reasons given. Blevins concluded too quickly that the mother is Israel based on the twelve stars,[348] but the greatest usage of "twelve" in Revelation is chapter 21's image of the new Jerusalem. The unity of God's OT and NT peoples is seen in the twelve gates named for Israel's tribes and the twelve foundations named for the apostles. It may be best to see the woman as the faithful Israelite Mary[349] giving birth to Jesus, who then needed protection in the flight to Egypt. The twelve stars would then signify Mary as Jesus' mother, as the crucial intersection between the twelve OT tribes and the twelve NT apostles.

Thirdly, the baby is υἱὸν ἄρσεν, which is redundantly male.[350] Beasley-Murray does not exegete it.[351] Others deny that the son ruling the nations with a rod of iron is Jesus. Ladd says it "does not refer to the birth of Jesus in

343. Beale and McDonough, "Revelation," 1122.

344. Morris's identification of Israel as the travailing woman based on Isa 26 does not give due weight to the fact that Isa 26 has no birth, no stars, and no dragon (*Revelation*, 152–53).

345. Siew, *Beasts*, 154.

346. Aune, *Revelation 17–22*.

347. Smith, *Micah–Malachi*.

348. Blevins, *Revelation*, 59.

349. Barnett, *Apocalypse*, 102.

350. Mounce, *Revelation*, 238; Morris, *Revelation*, 154. The "refugee gives birth to those... faithful to the testimony of Jesus" (Humphrey, "Apocalypse," 89), but this ignores the specifically male gender of the baby: ἄρσεν is redundant, as all sons are male. Aghiorgoussis cites a St. Methodios of Olympos, who said that Rev 12:5 had the church as mother bringing its children to birth in baptism ("Baptism," 34). Again, this does not allow for the unique maleness.

351. Beasley-Murray, *Revelation*, 200.

Bethlehem." He gives no reason, protesting that John should have referred to the cross, seemingly "the triumph of the powers of darkness."[352] John does not have to include all parts of the gospel in each passage, but may concentrate on one thing at a time.[353] Morris (12:4)[354] and Barnett identify the child as Jesus[355] and the intended death as the Massacre, and this seems the most likely meaning. Morris further argues that "The 'war in heaven' (v. 7) appears to be an attempt to destroy the Man Child," whom he previously identified as Jesus.[356]

Next, the use of ἁρπάζω. In the LXX, it usually means oppression (e.g., Ezek 18:12), or the snatching away of something or judgment by God (e.g., Hos 6:1). Some take "caught up to God" as the ascension;[357] however, Jesus ascended as a man,[358] not as a baby.[359] Also, the purpose of being "caught up" is to protect his life, so the closest parallel is the flight to Egypt, which immediately precedes the Massacre. Ladd is closer when saying that this could not be the ascension, which "did not have the purpose of escaping Satan's hostility."[360] In the GNT, it can mean Satan seizing things (Matt 12:29; 13:19), but over half of its usages mean being taken to/by God and/or away from evil: John 10:29–30; Acts 8:39; 23:10; 2 Corinthians 12:2, 4; 1 Thessalonians 4:17; Jude 23. Tavo calls it removal by the power of God.[361] It is not improbable that Revelation 12:5 reflects the NT meaning, as opposed

---

352. Ladd, *Revelation*, 169.

353. Morris, *Revelation*, 155.

354. Ibid., 154. Morris is not entirely consistent. He argues on page 155 of *Revelation* that "John omits everything between [Jesus'] birth and the ascension," but still maintains that the references to the Lamb looking slain (pp. 95, 97–98, 165) are to Jesus' death, which clearly happened between these milestones. Further, the natural meaning of his quoted words above is that 12:5 does mean the ascension, but he professes ignorance of the actual timing on page 154, while asserting that it is the Father protecting Jesus from Satan, even though Ladd (*Revelation*, 170) shows clearly that this was not the ascension's purpose.

355. Barnett, *Apocalypse*, 102–3. As does Tonstad (*Saving*, 65, 81), who says nothing about the Massacre.

356. Morris, *Revelation*, 158, 154.

357. Beasley-Murray, *Revelation*, 200; Aune, *Revelation 6–16*, 12:5.

358. Tavo argues (unconvincingly) that 12:5 is the entire Christ-event (*Woman*, 273) but the snatching away seems to happen immediately when the child is born, and the whole point of the Christ-event was for Christ to defeat evil, not simply escape from it. Minear (unconvincingly) talks of the "actual enthronement of the male child" ("Curse," 73), when Jesus ascended and was enthroned as a grown man.

359. Collins, *Myth*, 101.

360. Ladd, *Revelation*, 170.

361. Tavo, *Woman*, 273.

to that of the OT, and is heaven's perspective on God protecting the infant Jesus from harm.

Taking the identifications of Jesus using the phrase "rod of iron" (Rev 12:5; 19:15),[362] the cue for Satan's expulsion from heaven (and evil more generally) was his attempt to kill the infant Jesus via Herod.[363] Evidence for this is that, unlike the OT, the only recorded arena for interaction between divinity and evil is now on earth.[364] In verses such as Mark 3:11, demonized individuals cry out to Jesus that he is the Son of God,[365] at the demons' behest. They address him correctly, the only beings apart from God to do so before the centurion (Mark 15:39), as "they knew who he was" (Mark 1:34).[366] "Son of God" is more "christologically loaded" than the "Holy One of God" (Mark 1:24), but is elaborated further in the final demonic confession: "Son of the Most High God" (Mark 5:7).[367] Despite the NT's far greater number of references to evil (twenty-five of twenty-seven books) and to heaven, all recorded interactions between divinity and evil are on earth, starting with the attempt on the infant Jesus' life.

Siew states that the "majority of scholars"[368] hold that Revelation 12:5 refers to Jesus' birth, but argues that it means the church from different viewpoints: the woman as the church in its heavenly aspect, the male son as the church's ultimate security in God, and the woman's other offspring as the persecuted church on earth.[369] He argues that, since all the references in Revelation 12 are symbolic, the son cannot be literal, because the snatching up of the child to God does not fit the details of Jesus' birth. Despite his

362. Rev 12:5 is evil's attempt on Jesus' life, and 19:15 is Jesus leading the armies of heaven against evil.

363. Contra Page, who thinks this may mean Satan's fall in the temptation of Jesus in the wilderness (*Powers*, 110).

364. I do not suggest a one-to-one correspondence between actions in heaven and results on earth, but the idea that actions in heaven affect things on earth is supported by any reference to prayer, and also by the seals, trumpets, and bowls (Rev 6, 8–9, 16); so time and eternity are not unrelated. Those who claim that evil still has access to heaven must explain why no NT passage places evil in heaven like the OT. This eludes Minear, who argues that Jesus' ascension "triggered the serpent's eviction from heaven" ("Curse," 73).

365. It is difficult to see "son of God" as simply recognizing a godly man (Sherlock, *Inside*, 49), as Mark 3:11 shows the demonic reaction: Whenever they saw Jesus, "they fell down before him," as did the Gerasene demoniac (5:7). No other passage in the Bible records demons kneeling before humans, much less acclaiming them "son of God."

366. Guelich, *Mark*, 1:34.

367. France, *Mark*, 155.

368. Siew, *Beasts*, 157. He does not identify them, and may be implying that the majority are pre-critical.

369. Ibid., 164, 281.

strong feelings ("A sign in Rev 12 is not to be taken literally"[370]), he has failed to consider all the data, and even points which he has made himself.

Firstly, the book of Revelation is highly symbolic, but that does not preclude an event having a literal interpretation as well as or in place of a symbolic one: "signs are symbols . . . to depict heavenly *(and earthly) realities* beyond the literalness of signs."[371] Also, "whatever happens on earth corresponds to, and . . . is determined by what happens in heaven."[372] Apart from Revelation 12:1, 3; other uses of σημεῖον either clearly occur on earth (Rev 13:13–14; 16:14; 19:20) or in heaven, with an intentional effect on earth (15:1).[373] That a real event (Jesus did die) can be referenced symbolically is shown by references to a Lamb looking slain (Rev 5:6, 9, 12; 13:8).[374] The cognate, σημαίνω, refers explicitly to Jesus' death (John 12:33; 18:32). Siew's insistence against the literalness of signs contradicts his own work and the usages in John and Revelation. Every use of "sign" has a heavenly and an earthly aspect. Collins sees the vision as the prototype of Jesus' birth.[375]

Secondly, Siew has not properly investigated τίκτω, which means either a literal birth or a symbolic use; e.g., the ground gives birth to crops (Heb 6:7). His approval of Tan's guilt by association that because some things in Revelation 12 are symbolic, then all must be, is inadequate.[376] A live birth distinguishes the literal from the symbolic. If this birth is symbolic, Siew should explain why it differs so markedly from established usage.

Thirdly, his alleged OT references simply cannot carry the weight he assigns. His bold claim that the woman "clearly alludes" to Genesis 37[377] is unsustainable, as it has eleven stars,[378] no dragon, and no birth. Also, in Genesis 37, the eleven stars show Joseph's (future) superiority, while in Revelation 12, the twelve stars show the woman's status. Fekkes argues the woman "function[s] mainly as a corporate image," and Siew that she is "Jerusalem."[379] The parallels from Isaiah are unconvincing. The pain in

370. Ibid., 158.
371. Ibid., 158. My emphasis.
372. Ibid., 77.
373. Ibid., 124.
374. Ibid., 203, 273.
375. Collins, *Myth*, 135.
376. Siew, *Beasts*, 159.
377. Ibid., 150.
378. A hypothetical argument that Joseph is the twelfth star is unlikely, as the "sun" (Jacob) and the "moon" (Rebekah), as well as the eleven stars (his brothers) bow down to Joseph, who seems superior to them all.
379. Fekkes, "Prophetic Traditions," 185; Siew, *Beasts*, 151.

Isaiah 26 is a metaphor for sinners in God's presence, as there was no birth. I previously addressed the shortcomings of Isaiah 66.

Finally, Siew correctly sees that ἁρπάζω has the connotation of "rescue from attack,"[380] so Revelation 12 cannot mean Jesus' ascension. This does not fit the church, which was rescued through (not from) persecution. It is more appropriate for the flight to Egypt of Joseph, Mary, and Jesus.

In short, Siew has not fairly evaluated key terms like τίκτω and ἁρπάζω. Despite acknowledging that signs can portray both heavenly and earthly realities, he has not applied this consistently. His OT references simply do not support his reading of Revelation 12.

It may be quite reasonably objected that there is no mention of Satan prompting Herod to order the Massacre of the Innocents (Matt 2:16–18) to kill the infant Jesus.[381] I concede this, but note that the absence of evidence of Satan's activity is by no means evidence of its absence.[382] The uniform picture of Satan in both testaments is of murderous malice. Nothing positive is ever said about him. Prompting Herod[383] like this would seem entirely in character, like inciting David to take a census (1 Chr 21:1), which also led to many Israelite deaths. The dragon warring against the woman's offspring (12:17) may fit the ascension better, but no timeframe is given. Secondly, the demons' reaction to Jesus' incarnation must be given appropriate weight. The OT shows that evil once had access to God's immediate presence, but there is nothing similar in the NT. The most logical explanation is that evil was expelled from heaven prior to this. I contend that my exegesis produces better results than that of those scholars listed above, many of whom do not even attempt to say when or why Satan was expelled.

Homsher argues that the Hebrew writers were mythopoeic, forming Biblical texts from extant traditions, particularly the so-called combat myth, a premundane war for supremacy between good and evil.[384] The council of gods could not find a suitable champion, and turned to a junior deity who, after suffering a temporary reversal, finally defeats evil, creates the cosmos, and is acclaimed.[385] The myth is used to explain the presence of good and evil

---

380. Ibid., 161.

381. Pataki bravely argues that Satan has nothing to do with the cross ("Myth," 268), despite John 13:2, 27. Herod is merely a pawn in a process foreordained by God (Sim, "Weeping," 83), but gives no evidence.

382. Branden (*Conflict*) makes no such finding, but this is not unexpected, as he focuses on Matt, not Rev.

383. Herod hardly needed much prompting. Park portrays him as capable of doing whatever was necessary to eliminate a perceived threat ("Herod," 477).

384. Collins, *Myth*, 29; Collins, *Apocalypse*, 86.

385. Homsher, "Combat," 4–5

in the world, and to provide a cosmogony and propaganda for the chief god.³⁸⁶ Grabiner argues that it is "the conceptual framework" of Revelation 12.³⁸⁷

While there seems significant common ground between the myth and the Bible, this is more apparent than real, and moreover, the Biblical texts lack the *raison d'être* of the myth, that there was chaos *ab initio*, which required defeating. If we assume that the Hebrew writers employed these myths, we cannot assume that they were bound by them.

Contrary to the myth, there was no initial chaos;³⁸⁸ rather, Genesis 1–2 portrays purposeful creation by God, who is pleased with the results. In the Babylonian version, Baal is the hero; hardly an option in the Bible, given its widespread condemnation of Baalism; e.g., 1 Kings 18. Michael, not a junior deity, defeats the dragon (Rev 12).³⁸⁹ Grabiner's efforts to explain Michael as an angelomorphic description of Jesus are unconvincing. Next, the Bible has no parallel (and could never have one) to the deity's initial defeat.³⁹⁰ Finally, the Bible has little detail on the actual combat.³⁹¹

Homsher argues that the Hebrew writers do not reproduce the myth, as they assume readers were familiar with it. This argument from silence ignores the fact that, not only are there profound differences between the myth and the Bible, but the Bible lacks the myth's cosmology. Contrary to the cosmos being created from the defeated enemy, Gen 1–2 assume creation *ex nihilo*, and the first reference to what we might call evil in Genesis 3 (the serpent) is post-creation. John so abominated paganism that it is highly unlikely that he would use such references as sources.³⁹² If John did, it is more plausible that he did so to disparage them.

Moreover, assuming—like Grabiner—that the myth underlies Revelation 12 can skew exegesis.³⁹³ First, Grabiner argues that ἄρτι (Rev 12:10) implies a specific time for Satan's downfall, which he assumes is the cross. But this implies that Satan could access heaven during the thirty-three years of Jesus' earthly life. This is an argument from silence, as no NT text has Satan in heaven, unlike the OT. Secondly, he argues that, if Jesus is the child in Revelation 12:5, then it is too abrupt to move from his birth to his exaltation.³⁹⁴ This ignores the NT meaning of ἁρπάζω, which means being

386. Redding, "Myth," 3; Homsher, "Combat," 119–20.
387. Grabiner, *Cosmic*, 141.
388. Contra Homsher, "Combat," 44
389. Contra ibid., 5.
390. Ibid., 36, 117.
391. Redding, "Myth," 14.
392. Morris, *Revelation*, 151.
393. Grabiner, *Cosmic*, 141.
394. Ibid., 146.

taken to/by God and/or away from evil. Next, having Michael as an angelomorphic image of Jesus shows Jesus as the true victor over Satan, like the junior deity's destruction of evil.³⁹⁵ However, he has not seen that Michael's victory removed Satan from heaven to earth, where he would still cause trouble (Rev 12:12) before his final defeat in Revelation 20. Lastly, he argues that Satan's deceptions must be exposed, not simply overpowered.³⁹⁶ The problem here is seeing an either/or situation. The Exodus, the OT's main salvation event and precursor to the cross, shows the Egyptian gods' powerlessness (Exod 12:12) and God using force against Egypt. Given the tenuous links between the myth and Biblical texts and the exegetical issues caused by undue reliance on the myth, it is better to assume that the myth does not impact markedly on the Biblical texts when exegeting.

In summary, the use of τίκτω, which overwhelmingly means actual human birth, the grave difficulties with interpreting the woman as Israel or the church and the redundantly precise description of the newborn as υἱὸν ἄρσεν on balance show that Revelation 12 is primarily about Mary giving birth to Jesus and evil's expulsion from heaven. Mary as mother of Jesus becomes a sort of mother of the NT church, or "those who keep the commandments of God and hold fast the testimony of Jesus" (Rev 12:17), things which could not both be said collectively of God's OT people.

3.4.5. God's final judgment of evil

Images of evil being defeated in battle and then confined in the lake of fire forever (Rev 20:10)³⁹⁷ seem to indicate a final punishment of evil. This part is the longest, as it includes extensive criticism of Charles Sherlock's thesis that what seem to be final battles³⁹⁸ with evil in Revelation are, following Caird, heaven's view of the cross.³⁹⁹

395. Ibid., 153.
396. Ibid., 244.
397. It is "the final destruction of the ultimate root of evil" (Ladd, *Revelation*, 270); "There is no intermission and no end" (Morris, *Revelation*, 233) and "a place of torment" (Resseguie, *Revelation*, 249). Satan will be tormented in God's presence forever (Wink, *Unmasking*, 40).
398. Cosmic conflict is the controlling image, but Satan the deceiver must be unmasked rather than controlled by force (Tonstad, *Saving*, "Preface"). However, he does not see that being bound for one thousand years and confined in the lake of fire are expressions of force (Rev 20:2, 10).
399. Sherlock, *War*, 366. I summarize my reasons later, but more extensive reasons will appear in a future article. I am, of course, not disputing that the cross is a major defeat for evil; in Kovacs's words, "the locus of a cosmic battle, in which Jesus achieves a decisive victory over Satan" ("Ruler," 246). She examined John 12's apparent use of

Sherlock traces the idea of God as warrior from the Exodus/conquest through settlement to exile, and then into the NT, particularly via the ban.[400] He makes the valuable point that Yahweh is not Israel's battle-god, but Lord of all, including the nations and warfare.[401] He concludes that Christ's death as the supreme victory over sin and death means that might is not right.[402] I believe that he has not made out his case sufficiently. He has not exercised sufficient care in his discussion of God allegedly being on both sides of various conflicts; God fighting for Israel; the existence and role of the "heavenly council"; the person of Satan; and whether his ultimate conclusion, that might is not right, is supported in the Bible. I will critique his thesis and show that he has discounted elements which are more Biblically based and coherent.

Firstly, Sherlock claims that "God acts on both sides of many conflicts, . . . as defender . . . [and] adversary" and "Yahweh . . . stood on both sides of the [Exodus]."[403] While it is admirable for people not to claim that God is theirs alone, Yahweh was not on both sides in analogous ways, as he was never said to act for Pharaoh or Egypt.

His second point is that the conquest was God's initiative to give Israel the land and to punish Amorite sin (Gen 15:16). God would send the hornet (Exod 23:28), and Sherlock notes the required responses of destroying idols and serving Yahweh,[404] but omits the equally important need to fight. This is especially puzzling in light of Judges 3:1–2, which describes the armed conquest as God's deliberate action to teach the wilderness generation how to fight.

Thirdly, he has a puzzling attitude toward the "heavenly council": "Elijah had access to the word of Yahweh in the divine assembly"; "the heavenly council idea has been employed . . . without syncretism"; "Joshua . . . arraigned before it";[405] "[B]iblical narratives are accepted as broadly corresponding to historical reality;" but "the use of mythological concepts

---

apocalyptic literature, particularly as it focused on the heavenly warrior, to show that God won a decisive victory over evil on the cross, which was in fact Jesus' throne. I am simply disputing that this is the final defeat of evil. King (*Scroll*, 104) argues that it is not helpful to see Rev 12, 19 as a war. However, πόλεμος always means war, never a court case. The final issue is how exegetes envisage post-Easter, that evil will finally be defeated. Will it simply just give up, or is further effort involved?

400. This means "killing all humans" (Niditch, *War*, 20). "God is wholly loving, wholly just, and all-knowing, which allows him the unique ability to judge the Canaanites" (Pierce, *War*, 83).

401. Sherlock, *War*, 388.

402. Ibid., 396.

403. Ibid., 1, 13.

404. Ibid., 36.

405. Ibid., 135, 147, 226.

... repudiated ... any idea that the heavenly council had some literal existence."[406] These are contradictory: the last implies that, because Israel's idea of the heavenly council had some commonality with Phoenician/Caananite[407] concepts, then its very existence was questionable. The differences are deeper than any similarities.

Fourthly, problems occur in his analysis of Satan. He wants "a more moderate view of Satan,"[408] but cannot substantiate it. For example, he explains Satan's role in the parable of the seeds as "taking away ... the word of salvation, consistent with an accusatory role."[409] An accuser should bring evidence before a judge to decide, not obstruct salvation. The best way to understand Satan in the OT is as a parallel with the nations. Despite claiming that "No contrast is drawn between God and Satan ... in (OT) texts,"[410] just like the nations, God and Satan are always at odds, and Satan is always opposed to/desiring to harm God's people (2 Sam 24/1 Chr 21; Job 1–2; Zech 3).

These problems have serious consequences. If Satan makes no successful accusations in the OT and none in the NT, it is difficult to see how Christ's death removes Satan's either ineffective or non-existent ability to accuse. It is better to argue that it addresses God's wrath at sin, unaided by Satan. Next, the reason that Satan cannot accuse God's people to God is not Christ's death,[411] but because he and his angels have been expelled from heaven, thus losing the access to God's presence, which they had in the OT.

Reasoning (against the data) that "Christ's victory ... on the cross is ... the means by which Satan's power to accuse is taken"[412] entails more errors. Firstly, if Satan has been defeated on the cross, it is unclear why evil remains a problem.[413] He argues that Satan is defeated, but this has not yet been revealed openly, without explaining why this matters.

The second consequence is that, while Sherlock has many eloquent arguments that the cross perfectly illustrates that might is not right and is also the means of overcoming evil, he then must conclude that what seem to be battles in Revelation are actually heaven's perspective on the cross. But

---

406. Ibid., 4, 241.

407. Israel's theophany language was largely drawn from the cult of Baal (Cross, *Canaanite*, 156–57).

408. Sherlock, *War*, 245. Exegetes should try to find what relevant texts say, not look for a particular slant.

409. Ibid., 273.

410. Ibid., 382.

411. Contra Humphrey ("Apocalypse," 86).

412. Sherlock, *War*, 368.

413. Tavo also falls into this trap (*Woman*, 277).

there are examples in the Bible where God's explicit action is expressed by the use of force, as opposed to a legal procedure; e.g., the Exodus.

He then argues that the powers which bind human beings are "expressions of the will of God," without explaining why they then need to be defeated.[414] He argues that, if these battles are real, then they call into question the finality of the cross[415] and legitimate triumphalism. This is difficult as, for example, Matthew has Jesus using a perfect ἤγγικεν[416] to announce the kingdom's inauguration, but still commands us to pray "Your kingdom come" (Matt 4:17; 6:10).[417] To pray this is not to dispute Jesus' words, but to see the already/not yet pattern in the NT. The kingdom was inaugurated in Jesus' ministry, but will not be fulfilled until his return. The cross was the most important victory over evil, but the Lord's Prayer—"deliver us from the evil one"[418]—recognizes its ongoing activity. Sherlock recognizes the reality of evil, but not as the NT does: a defeated enemy still capable of inflicting serious harm. The central problem is an over-realized eschatology.

Sherlock has made a thorough, but unsuccessful, attempt to trace the image of Yahweh as a warrior throughout the Bible. While admitting that might could be right,[419] he has not seen the consequences. If might was right in the major salvation event of the OT, the Exodus, it could be right again. His understanding of Satan is also deficient, focusing on his ability to accuse, which the evidence showed is either ineffective or absent. To argue that the cross removed this ability is, simply, unsupported.

Once he believed that the cross was the final actual defeat of evil, he was left with little choice but to explain away the battles in Revelation. He did not explain why the cross needed fuller revelation to defeat evil, or how this might happen. A final battle with evil is not triumphalism, but recognizes that, while evil has suffered a great defeat on the cross, it has not yet been finally vanquished, as every repetition of the Lord's Prayer emphasizes. There is ample precedent, as Sherlock admits, for God to use might against evil, and as unsettling as it might be, this remains the most probable reading of the admittedly difficult texts in Revelation, with the fewest complications.

---

414. Sherlock, *War*, 344.

415. Ibid., 364. So also Ladd (*Revelation*, 171).

416. Hagner, *Matthew 1–13*, 3:2.

417. A parallel is Jesus' defeat of sickness on the cross, hence Matt 8:17's quote of Isa 53:4, "He . . . carried our diseases," in the context of both healing and exorcising. No one claims that Jesus' victory over illness is complete, but Matt seems to claim that Jesus' death brought an initial victory, which will be consummated in heaven. Each evangelist includes examples of both healing and exorcism as a proof of this victory.

418. Ibid., 6:13.

419. Sherlock, *War*, 45, 225.

I will conclude with three quotes of contradictory themes, which (to my mind, at least) have not been fully worked through. Sherlock says "Jesus' work [was] patterned on ... the exodus/conquest," of which he said "godly might ... was exercized to see right prevail," but that "[Jesus'] power consisted in his refusal to go the way of power."[420] Godly might was central to the Exodus, and so anything patterned on it, such as God's final defeat of evil, may (and, in my belief, does) contain might as part of the solution. God may combine might with right, but we rarely do.

In summary, we can conclude that God's defeat of evil follows the NT's standard already/not yet model. Evil has suffered a catastrophic, but not final, defeat on the cross. It has already been cast out of God's immediate presence,[421] but is still active, as every repetition of the Lord's Prayer emphasizes. Its final defeat lies in the future.[422]

3.4.6. Conclusion

In the OT, most of the texts about Satan show him or an evil spirit with direct access to God, with God allowing evil to test his people for faithfulness or expose their sin. Sometimes, the canon makes the role of evil more apparent. In 2 Samuel 24, the author has God inciting David to conduct a census of Israel. The reason is not made clear, but God appears to have allowed this to judge unrepented sin. First Chronicles 21 appears to have adapted this earlier account from 2 Samuel 24, to have Satan inciting David to number the army. The reason for this being the most likely order of events is that passages like 1 Kings 22 show evil operating within God's permission to discipline God's unfaithful people but no passage shows God acting on a suggestion by evil.

God let Satan test Job's integrity under trial to demonstrate that his devotion to God was not simply for the material benefits which God provided. God is not simply responding to Satan's suggestion, as God had previously raised Job's piety (Job 1:8). Evil always wants to harm God's people, and there is increasing tension between Satan and God, particularly Zechariah 3, where God cuts Satan off before he can accuse Joshua, the high priest. In the NT, there are many more references to evil, but none of them show

---

420. Ibid., 260.

421. Tonstad is concerned that, though Michael leads the war, Christ is praised for the victory (Rev 12:7, 10; *Saving,* 83–85). A similar situation is in Josh 10. Michael and his angels expelled evil from heaven but Jesus and the armies of heaven will defeat all the kings of earth and their armies, a far bigger victory (Rev 19).

422. Sim, "Weeping," 74.

Satan having direct access to God. The most likely reason is the expulsion of all evil from heaven, showing its powerlessness, around the time of the Massacre of the Innocents (Matt 2:16–18; Rev 12). The final destruction of evil will be led by Jesus himself (Rev 19–20).

Satan, idols, and human rivals to God are very similar, given their different states of being. While the humans claimed divinity, or idols have it ascribed to them, Satan argued with God as though his equal. While the prince of Tyre was greedy and violent, Satan wanted to destroy Job and his family completely. While Simon Magus was forced to acknowledge the inferiority of his powers, and idols are derided as powerless, Satan was expelled from heaven. While Herod died after five days, possibly allowing repentance, Satan will be in hell forever. In each case, and not unnaturally, while the human rivals show certain aspects of Satan's character, none of them are as evil as Satan himself.

The next subsection considers the third and final rival to God—the material rival of money. For the first time in the NT, money becomes the main material rival to God ("You cannot serve both God and Mammon" Matt 6:24; Luke 16:13).

3.5. Money: the material rival to God

3.5.1. Introduction

If idolatry offers rivals to God, so does money, which, as shall be seen later, also figures prominently in the accounts about Judas. Thus, it is worth considering how money operates as a rival to God by examining the named, righteous rich; πλοῦτος and its cognates, and δουλεύειν. As we move from the OT to the NT within each strand, there are three important changes. There are no named, righteous rich in the NT; the negative descriptions of wealth and the wealthy are intensified from the OT to the NT, and money is deified as an alternate object of service to God. This will illuminate the πτωχός, about whom Judas was said not to care (John 12:6), and the thirty pieces of silver. Money will be shown in an increasingly negative light from the OT to the NT as the material rival to God.[423]

---

423. The four items in s3.1, "Introduction," are not as relevant for inanimate money, which is not specifically described as animated by Satan, but parallels will be footnoted.

Wealth in the Bible

3.5.2. The named, righteous rich

Each testament has unrighteous rich; e.g., ungodly kings like Jeroboam (1 Kgs 14) or Herod (Acts 12) and warnings against trusting wealth and the rich abusing their power (Ps 52:7; Prov 11:16; 1 Tim 6:17). However, a key difference in the OT is a few named people who have material wealth and a degree of righteousness.[424] This has no NT parallel.[425] I will discuss five of them below in canonical order. The righteous rich receive their wealth from God as a token of blessing,[426] respond in risky faith, and bless others.[427] Also, they had to work for their money, and suffered significant deprivation or testing.

Abram was so wealthy that the land could not support both his herds and those of Lot (Gen 13:6).[428] His refusal, with a solemn oath,[429] to rely on people for wealth is seen in rejecting the king of Sodom's offer of spoil (Gen 14:22–24). Abraham's true wealth is God (Gen 15:1), whose "Do not be afraid" frequently introduces oracles of salvation.[430] God remedies his greatest need by giving him the child of promise, Isaac (Gen 21:2).[431] His most significant test was God's command to sacrifice Isaac (Gen 22:2), which Abraham passed, and he received a very rare oath from the Lord, promising many descendants and great wealth by possessing his enemies' cities (Gen 22:17). Abraham had wealth and righteousness, and the former did not interfere with the latter.[432]

---

424. Called the righteous rich by Wright ("Rich," 255).

425. Barnabas (Acts 4:36–37) could be an exception but, like Lydia (Acts 16:14), his presumed wealth in owning land is never mentioned. Zacchaeus was described as πλούσιος (Luke 19:2), but he only received Jesus' explicit approval after he promised to give half of his goods to the poor and to repay any ill-gotten gains fourfold, far more than the fifth for theft (Lev 6; Nolland, *Luke 18:35—24:53*, 906).

426. Young, "Wealth," 818.

427. Wright, "Rich," 255.

428. Baker, *Wealth*, 15; Hoppe, *Poor*, 19. The mention of Abram's cattle, gold, and silver prefigures the Exodus generation plundering the Egyptians (Wenham, *Genesis 1–15*, 13:6).

429. Ibid., 14:22.

430. Ibid., 15:1. The two narratives, in Gen 15:1–6 and 6:7–21, have been reversed, and should be inverted; e.g., 6:5 seems to describe the night sky, but 6:12 describes twilight (Fidler, "Sequence," 164). Vv. 9–11 happens the next day (Kidner, *Genesis*, 123).

431. The birth had been predicted in 17:16–21; 18:10–15 indicates God's special interest in a person, whether for judgment or for blessing, as here (Wenham, *Genesis 16–50*, 21:1).

432. Abraham could still be cavalier with his dependants; e.g., letting Sarah so

Isaac inherited all of Abraham's wealth (Gen 25:5),[433] but is compared unfavorably with him,[434] as God acted to safeguard Sarai from Pharaoh (Gen 12:17) with a clear warning (Gen 20:3), but did nothing directly for Isaac (Gen 26:8). While Isaac was wealthy and in a right relationship with God, as God told him to stay in Gerar and subsequently blessed him (Gen 26:6, 12–14),[435] he did not have the same standing with God, whose blessing was for Abraham's righteousness (Gen 26:3), not his. Isaac is similar to Solomon, in that both inherited their wealth and were led by those around them, Isaac in relation to his children (Gen 27) and Solomon by his foreign wives in serving their gods (1 Kgs 11).[436]

David gained Saul's attention by killing Goliath, was attached to the court,[437] befriended Jonathan, and married Saul's daughter Michal (1 Sam 17–18).[438] His wealth grew, and he gave his own treasure for Solomon's Temple, but said that God must give Solomon and all Israel a perfect heart to build it.[439] His relationship with God showed that he was "a man after (God's) own heart" (1 Sam 13:14),[440] and also that he was grateful to God. In 2 Samuel 7/1 Chronicles 17, he was concerned that the Ark was in a tent while he was in a palace. Nathan[441] encouraged him, but the Lord gave an oracle on David's royal house and posterity. David expressed his amazement and gratitude to God by asking "Who am I?",[442] which links this passage,

---

mistreat Hagar that she took their son, Ishmael, and fled (Hoppe, *Poor*, 19).

433. Cf. the concubines' sons, who merely received presents (Wenham, *Genesis 16–50*, 25:5–6).

434. Ibid., 26:7–12.

435. Ibid., Hoppe, *Poor*, 19.

436. Baker, *Wealth*, 158.

437. God arranged matters for David to be at court, and to become Saul's eventual successor (Hertzberg, *I & II Samuel*, 147). Sellew notes Saul's deceitful interior monologue as he sought David's death by the Philistines (1 Sam 18:17b, 21a; "Interior," 241). David was (regrettably) more successful in doing something similar to Uriah.

438. Hoppe contrasts Hannah in 1 Sam 1 (whose infertility led her to prayer)with David (whose humble circumstances "led him to scheming" [Hoppe, *Poor*, 56]). This is difficult, as Saul makes an offer which David accepts and then meets Saul's conditions (1 Sam 18:27). Even when God's favor had left Saul for David, he refused to take matters into his own hands by killing Saul (1 Sam 26:9; Weitzman, "David's Lament," 354).

439. Braun, *1 Chronicles*, 29:16–18.

440. God's eyes are already on Saul's successor (Hertzberg, *I & II Samuel*, 106). This is true, even given David's involvement in warfare (Pierce, *War*, 82).

441. Solomon apparently had no court prophet to rebuke him for his unfaithfulness.

442. By contrast, Solomon's "Who am I?" is directed at Hiram (2 Chr 2:6), not God, at the start of his ruinous building program. He and David had very different attitudes toward money.

Saul's offer of his daughter Merab (1 Sam 18:18), and David's prayer for Solomon (1 Chr 29:14). Unlike Solomon, David's wealth did not impede his relationship with God or the people, as it was devoted to the future temple. His deficiencies as a father (s2.3.3), as well as being in Jerusalem and not with the army (2 Sam 11), were more harmful.

Solomon is the next one; he inherited most of his wealth. He was wealthy enough to spend seven years on the temple but "thirteen years, however," on his palace (1 Kgs 6:38—7:1). He used forced labor (1 Kgs 5:13-18) and fulfilled all Samuel's prophecies of royal greed (1 Samuel 8; 1 Kgs 10:14-29).[443] He had so many foreign wives that he worshiped their gods (1 Kgs 11:4-6)[444] and was succeeded by Rehoboam, whom God chose to divide Israel (1 Kgs 12:24).[445] His marriage to Pharaoh's daughter (1 Kgs 3:1) was his first significant act, which takes place before he prays for wisdom. While[446] not necessarily breaching Deuteronomy 17, which forbids "many wives" and returning to Egypt (vv. 16-17),[447] Solomon's reign began in this way and ended by worshiping foreign gods (1 Kgs 11). He went astray from the start.[448]

Sweeney is troubled by criticism of the excesses of Solomon, who is idealized as succeeding David.[449] He fails to distinguish between what a person is given and what they do with those gifts. Solomon did not earn the throne or wealth, but squandered both by sin. Contrary to the law against

---

443. Lowery, *Sabbath*, 13-14; Hoppe, *Poor*, 59-60; Domeris, *Heart*, 81.

444. While David had concubines, they did not appear to undermine his relationship with God, as they came from the local Jebusite population (Hill, "Concubines," 131) and were not necessarily idolators. The harem represents Solomon's formal political alliances with foreigners and, it might be added, their gods (Christensen, *Deuteronomy 1:1—21:9*, 17:16-17). Solomon's apostasy had serious consequences for Israel's future (Knoppers, "Rehoboam," 426).

445. The Chronicler does not mention Solomon's apostasy, so while there seems to be no reason for God dividing Israel, it comes down to Rehoboam's threatened harshness. It could be a possible anticipation of Jeroboam's apostasy, which is taken very seriously (ibid., 429).

446. It usually meant a treaty, which could endanger Israel's "treaty" with God (Craigie, *Deuteronomy*, 256).

447. The texts allow bigamy, but hope for better behavior (Rodd, *Glimpses*, 41).

448. Contra Nugent ("Politics," 83), that David and Solomon are "two of Israel's best kings," when Josiah is more deserving (Sweeney, *Solomon*, 620). The account of Josiah's reign is "totally positive," culminating in the "superlative judgement" of 2 Kgs 23:25 (Delamarter, "Josiah," 30). In fact, his untimely death needs explanation, as the result of Judah's prior sin. By contrast, Hoppe notes that Solomon's abuse of power led to revolts (Hoppe, *Poor*, 58).

449. Sweeney, *Solomon*, 608-10.

accumulating wives, horses, or wealth (Deut 17:17),[450] he had one thousand wives and concubines (1 Kgs 11:3) and traded in horses, chariots, and silver (1 Kgs 11:27–29). Money can corrupt even God's anointed king.

Solomon did not personally show his God-given wisdom by following David's example. Solomon illustrated what the conquest generation knew: when they sinned, God allowed the nations to take their wealth and land.[451] If David stored wealth for the temple, Solomon amassed more wealth for himself. Solomon's excessive building meant another breach of Deuteronomy 17 when, unable to pay Hiram, he gave him twenty Galilean towns (1 Kgs 9:11), breaking the law about a foreign king reigning over Israel (Deut 17:15).[452] This enslaved fellow Israelites (1 Kgs 11:28), caused resentment, led to Jeroboam's rise—whose administration of the forced labor led to popular discontent—and divided Israel.[453]

Job has already been mentioned (s3.4.2). He was so wealthy that Satan accused God of buying his loyalty (1:10).[454] To protect Job's reputation, God allowed him to be tried severely (within limits) by losing all of his assets—and worse, all his children—but Job emerged with integrity intact. After Job's repentance of his ignorance, God commended him (42:7),[455] doubled his wealth (42:12–17), and gave him more children.

A full discussion of the OT view of wealth is beyond this thesis, but there are some principles. All wealth is God's, who gives it to anyone he wants (Ps 24:1).[456] This gift will cause fewer problems when the person has earned their money to become wealthy, like Abraham and David, who are viewed more favorably than those who inherited their wealth, such as Isaac or Solomon, who are led by those around them. Secondly, wealth shows the nature of a person's relationship with God. While both Abraham and Isaac passed off their wives as their sisters, Abraham is viewed more favorably, particularly in trusting God (Gen 15:6). While David commit-

---

450. Baker, *Wealth*, 158; Christensen, *Deuteronomy 1:1—21:9*, 17:16–17.

451. Young, "Wealth," 818. God delayed judgment until Rehoboam's reign (1 Kgs 11:12).

452. Sweeney, "Solomon," 617; Baker, *Wealth*, 263. The monarchy was a concession by God, which was withheld from non-Israelites (Christensen, *Deuteronomy 1:1—21:9*, 17:15). Solomon's cession to Hiram is another example of the king showing he was above the law (Horsley, *Powers*, 56). This ignores the fact that a king hardly cedes territory willingly. It violated the writer of Deuteronomy's crucial description of Israel as "brothers"; e.g., Deut 3:18; 15; 17:15, et al. (Hoppe, *Poor*, 50, 176n13).

453. Baker, *Wealth*, 128; Hoppe, *Poor*, 59.

454. Habel, *Job*, 90.

455. Job's blunt speeches are closer to the truth than his friends' conventional wisdom (ibid., 583).

456. Young, "Wealth," 818.

ted the heinous[457] crime of ordering Uriah's murder (2 Sam 11), Solomon nearly broke his relationship with God by idolatry (1 Kgs 11). The gift of wealth is a double-edged sword, as seen in contrasting "rich"/"wicked" with "poor"/"righteous"/"godly."[458] Wealth may mean ungodly behavior.

The New Testament

By contrast, there are no named people in the NT, especially in Luke/Acts, who are described as both righteous and rich, a clear difference from the OT. At Jesus' purification, his family offered two turtledoves, the offering by the poor (Luke 2:24; Lev 12:6–8).[459] When someone is called wealthy, like the rich young ruler (Matt 19:22; Mark 10:22; Luke 18:23),[460] or the Pharisees as "lovers of money" (Luke 16:14),[461] their wealth is always a barrier to following Jesus.[462] No special sin is ascribed to the rich man in Luke 16, except not caring for Lazarus, the poor man, to whom no special merit is ascribed, but the rich man goes to hell.[463] The poor man, in a true reversal, seems to be lying on Abraham's bosom, the guest of honor at an eschatological feast.[464] However, when a named person who could be wealthy follows or is sympathetic to Jesus, like Lydia, a seller of purple (Acts 16:14), their presumed wealth[465] is downplayed; or like Zacchaeus, they give much of it to the poor (Luke 19). Barnabas (Acts 4) is a possible exception, as he has

---

457. It was completely unnecessary. What could Uriah do to the king? (See Anderson, *2 Samuel*, 5:15.)

458. Young, "Wealth," 818–19. Ben-Dov notes this pattern in Pss 10:2, 28:28, and 82:4 ("Curse," 448).

459. Nolland, *Luke 1—9:20*, 2:24; Marshall, *Luke*, 117; Pao and Schnabel, "Luke," 270.

460. Jesus omits the tithe (Baker, *Wealth*, 34). This is not unusual, given that Jesus is quoting the Decalogue; Baker speculates that his answer (Luke 18:21 "all these") may have been different if Jesus had asked.

461. Hoppe, *Poor*, 153. Their attitude to money shows the cracks in an otherwise impressive display (Nolland, *Luke 9:21—18:34*, 16:14). So Fitzmyer (*Luke X–XXIV*, 1112). The Pharisees may have scoffed at Luke 16:13 (Parsons, *Luke*, 249).

462. "their resistance to the new characterized ... by their attitude to money ... " (Barton, "Money," 51).

463. Zehnder, "Mammon," 35; Hoppe, *Poor*, 153. Bammel and Hauck claim that the point of the story is not "the failure of the rich man in relation to the poor" but "the ineluctable alienation ... of all rich men, from ... God" ("πτωχός," 906). This makes poverty the basis of acceptance by God and wealth that of rejection. This vastly oversimplifies matters.

464. Smith, "Table," 626.

465. Williams, *Acts*, 282.

land to sell, but like David he devotes his personal resources to the community. Implicitly, much is made of his right action.

While Ananias and Sapphira are not called wealthy, we may presume so, given that they had land to sell (Acts 5:1).[466] The text is framed by two summaries of an idealized view[467] of the church (Acts 4:32–35; 5:12–16), which highlight the central role of the apostles.[468] The text is stark: trying to deceive the church,[469] seemingly at Satan's behest (Acts 5:3),[470] after much thought,[471] following the example of a Cyprian Levite (Barnabas),[472] but only giving part of the money, they are struck down in response to Peter's rebuke.[473] Exegetes have struggled with the actual means of death, the main options being nervous shock, some form of magic, or the direct action of God.[474]

The severity of the judgment needs explanation before examining possible causes. It is the first serious sin in the early church and, moreover, the first involving money; "The wrong use of money is a serious sin."[475] Of the three rivals to God, a human acting like God (s3.2.2) and Satan (s3.4) were already present in the OT, but money was not. A named person in the OT could still be described as both rich and righteous, but there is no NT parallel. The severity of God's action on Ananias and Sapphira[476] is to show this changed state of affairs. No church member could have an improper relationship with money[477] any more than they could presume to act like God (Herod; s3.2.3) or have an improper relationship with evil (Simon Magus s3.2.3).

466. Hypothesising that they were forced to sell for economic reasons has no support from the text; rather they wanted to seem generous. Greed contributed to the downfall of Judas also (Oropeza, *Footsteps*,1:230).

467. "no needy persons" mirrors Deut 15:4 (Johnson, L.T., *Acts*, 86).

468. Sterling, "Virtue," 68; McCabe, "Words," 25. This is said twice, so it is important to Luke. Imperfect tenses show a pattern (Fernando, *Acts*, 179).

469. Pilgrim, *Good News*, 153.

470. Garrett, *Demise*, 50; Johnson, L.T., *Acts*, 88. v 4 assigns responsibility to Ananias (Fernando, *Acts*, 197).

471. Williams, *Acts*, 96–97.

472. The ancient law banning Levite ownership of land had been long disregarded (ibid., 94).

473. Kelly argues that Peter's question is a test, and that he acts worse than Satan by "miraculously" arranging their deaths (Kelly, *Satan*, 104). This is overdone, as Peter asks a direct question, which they answer with a lie.

474. McCabe lists contemporary explanations ("Words," 35).

475. Fernando, *Acts*, 198.

476. Importantly, the church saw it as God's judgment (ibid., 197).

477. Paul was aware of the danger, which they could do to the Corinthian church (Smith, *Hand This Man*, 37).

This same continuity (plus newness) is expressed somewhat differently in the secondary literature, particularly the Graeco-Roman ideal of friendship. Scholars argue that Luke was trying to portray the infant church as not threatening the existing social order, but still stressing some differences.[478] First, friendship was not just between equals—a landowner put money at the feet of a fisherman (Acts 5:2), hardly an option for a Roman in the Ancient Near East honor-shame culture.[479] Secondly, Luke's account rejects the reciprocity ethic where equals helped one other, particularly in a patron-client relationship, in exact anticipation of future help in return.[480] Next, rich members of the church should not expect, or be given, preferential treatment.[481] Lastly, there was a new communal, as opposed to an individual, aspect to property ownership.[482] They offended against each of these differences from the surrounding culture by deceiving the infant church. Given the new idolatrous status of money, and the distinctives of the infant church as against the dominant culture, they "suffer the fate their deceit deserves."[483]

We can now study possible causes. Did death come from nervous shock at the exposure of his deceit or Peter's "prophetic declaration"?[484] The text says nothing like this, but even if it did, it cannot explain Sapphira's death,[485] which happened the moment Peter spoke: "the apostles came down hard" and they were "struck so deeply by their curse that they died."[486]

---

478. D'Angelo, "Women," 449.

479. Mitchell, "Friendship," 259, 266.

480. Ibid., 266, 270; Gagnon, "Motives," 143.

481. Ibid., 143.

482. Kazen, "Christology," 605; Mitchell, "Friendship," 268.

483. Barrett, "First," 99. The narrative contains verbal echoes (so Williams [Acts, 96], the use of νοσφίζω) from Josh 7, the death of Achan (Sterling, "Virtue," 683). However, he does not address the clear factual differences: the items were under the ban, so they belonged to God, not Achan, whereas the land and its sale proceeds belonged to Ananias and Sapphira (Acts 5:4). Secondly, Achan's sin was theft, not deception. Lastly, Israel stoned Achan, whereas God seems to have acted unilaterally in the case of Ananias and Sapphira. It is not clear (contra Williams, Acts, 97; Fernando, Acts, 196) that Luke chose this verb to compare the two narratives. Marshall is on safer ground to highlight the differences ("Acts," 111).

484. Williams, Acts, 97; Johnson, Acts, 88.

485. Ananias's death shows a "possible indication of a curse," but Sapphira's death "is more suggestive of a curse" (Smith, Hand This Man, 174). This is overstated, as there is no mention of future delivery to evil; rather, evil has already been at work: Acts 5:3, "how is it that Satan has so filled your heart?"

486. Eberts, "Plurality," 313.

But the text only mentions Peter, not multiple apostles, and says nothing of a curse,[487] which is presumably forbidden in the NT (Luke 6:28; Rom 12:14).

King analyzed the text, given the widespread Ancient Near East belief in magic, likening the deaths to "uncanny" deaths like the Aboriginal and Torres Strait Islanders' "pointing the bone."[488] In the light of beliefs prevalent in the ancient world, they may have believed that Peter had certain powers to protect his apostolic authority, which they were unable to resist. This argument is unconvincing in addressing magic, the position of Peter, the parallel with Judas, and Ananias and Sapphira's beliefs. Magic is never shown as under a Christian's power, nor is it encouraged.[489] The power of evil is always constrained, but in both testaments God sovereignly strikes down serious, unrepentant sinners. Secondly, Peter seems petulant in being more concerned about a hitherto-invisible challenge to his own authority than Ananias and Sapphira's fate, and forgetful of his own history and of the teaching of Jesus about restoring a sinner. Moreover, given his own sin of denying Christ (far worse than withholding money) and subsequent restoration, why not go to them in private and seek to sort things out? Thirdly, to liken betraying Jesus to deceitfully withholding some of their money is a stretch. Lastly, why might they believe that they were doomed, as the text says nothing like this? Given the speed of events, it would be remarkable if they had time to think at all.

The last possibility is God's direct action.[490] Their powerlessness is seen when they are apparently struck down by the very God to whom they had just offered part of the proceeds.[491] There are a number of reasons for this being the most plausible, and the most confronting, solution. While the surrounding culture's use of magic may have been informative, the OT background is normative. Explanations deriving from magic are not only unproven, but unlikely, given the Biblical picture of magic. There is no hint that Peter used magic to buttress his authority, or that they would have understood him as acting this way. In the OT, God acted sovereignly to purge sin from his people by death. Williams cites Nadab and Abihu.[492] I

---

487. Ibid., 313.

488. King, "Pointing."

489. Garrett, *Demise*, 103. Luke's choice of vocabulary is designed to defeat any idea that apparently identical outcomes, miraculous signs, etc., can imply identical sources of power for the church and magicians; e.g., Bar Jesus and the sons of Sceva (ibid., 84–87, 92, 98). So also McCabe, "Words," 186.

490. Peter's words "effect divine judgment" (ibid., 48).

491. This is the closest example of money's association with evil, in that Satan appears to have empowered Ananias and Sapphira's greed with disastrous consequences.

492. Williams, *Acts*, 99.

would add Er, Onan (Gen 38; 46), and Jeroboam (2 Chr 13:20). This avoids importing ideas such as nervous shock, which has no precedent. Even a possible parallel like Nabal, where the truth meant "his heart failed him and he became like a stone," is ascribed to the Lord (1 Sam 25:37–38). Eli's death was caused by a fall (1 Sam 4), which was due to shock.

Finally, while they made no claims to deity, nor did others so describe them, their apparently unremarkable sin transgressed the idolatrous status of money in the NT and confused the clear distinction between the infant church and the surrounding culture. God's direct action in causing their deaths is the most probable cause.[493] Dying by God's direct action evidences money's new idolatrous status, as those who died at God's hand were invariably human rivals to God, like the prince of Tyre (s3.2.2), Herod (s3.2.3), and the "man of lawlessness" (s3.2.3), or had an improper relationship with Satan, the demonic rival to God, like the prince of Tyre and the "man of lawlessness." Death by God's immediate action shows that improper relationships with God's human, demonic, or material rivals are all offensive to God.

3.5.3. Πλοῦτος, πλουτέω, πλουτίζω

In moving from the OT to the NT, the canon takes an increasingly critical view of wealth. Torah references are few and insignificant (Gen 31:16; Deut 33:19),[494] but the criticism becomes more apparent in the historical and prophetic literature, where two key points emerge. God gives wealth, but few use it wisely, and there are warnings not to trust wealth, in addition to unflattering descriptions of the wealthy.

Firstly, God is recorded as giving wealth to four kings, but it is less a gift than a test of character, and usually ends problematically. I have already covered David and Solomon (s3.5.2). God was with Jehoshaphat[495] "in his early years" and gave "great wealth" as he served God (2 Chr 17:3–6.).[496] After initial hostility toward Israel,[497] his wealth led him into three problematic ventures which required God's rescue: an alliance with Ahab,

---

493. Fernando, *Acts*, 197.

494. The tribes' wealth from the sea would allow them to hold festivals to God (Craigie, *Deuteronomy*, 399).

495. Delamarter appears to confuse Ahab with Jehoshaphat by paralleling the supposed death of Jehoshaphat with that of Josiah ("Josiah," 34), when it is Ahab who died at Ramoth Gilead.

496. Wilcock, *Chronicles*, 188.

497. Dillard, *2 Chronicles*, 17:1.

a venture with Ahaziah where the ships were lost (2 Chr 18:31;[498] 20:37), showing "divine displeasure,"[499] and a near fatal raid on Moab (2 Kgs 3). God gave Hezekiah "very great riches,"[500] but his pride caused God's wrath on "Judah and Jerusalem" (2 Chr 32:29, 32:25). The visit of the Babylonian envoys was a test from God (2 Chr 32:31), which he failed.[501] When told that his wealth and descendants would be deported, he thought only of his own security (2 Kgs 20:19; Isa 39:8).[502] When God is said to give wealth to someone, it is likely that things will end problematically. It is a (serious) test of character, and the narratives warn of the dangers of wealth for someone not fully devoted to God.

This is heightened by the many warnings not to trust wealth and negative descriptions of the wealthy in the wisdom traditions and the prophets. God ruined the man who "trusted in his great wealth"; people must not trust in increased wealth or boast in riches (Pss 52:7; 62:10; Jer 9:23).[503] The images of the wealthy are truly confronting. They are sinners and wicked (ἁμαρτωλοὶ καὶ εὐθηνοῦνται; Ps 73:12),[504] lazy and ruthless (ὀκνηροὶ ἐνδεεῖς; Prov 11:16), deceitful (Prov 13:7), greedy (Prov 28:8),[505] and ungodly (ἀσεβείας; Mic 6:12). Πλουτέω and πλουτίζω are similar. God gives wealth, (πλουτίζει; 1 Sam 2:7),[506] but Abram is concerned not to be enriched by the king of Sodom, as this may mean a lack of trust in God (ἐπλούτισα Gen 14:23). Hard work enriches, but only God's blessing prevents sorrow (πλουτίζουσιν; Prov 10:4, 22).[507] The Prophets are mostly negative, like their images of the πλοῦτος in Isaiah 16 (Moab) and Isaiah 29 (Ariel). They boast

---

498. The Chronicler adds that God rescued Jehoshaphat, absent from 1 Kgs 22 (ibid., 18:32).

499. Ibid., 20:37.

500. Domeris, *Heart*, 81.

501. Dillard, *2 Chronicles*, 32:31.

502. Watts is too charitable in calling this "piety," but better when calling it "weakness" (*Isaiah 34–66*, 66).

503. Allen, *Jeremiah*. It is a contrast of "two triads: wisdom, power, and riches contrast with steadfast love, justice, and righteousness." (Craigie et al., *Jeremiah 1–26*, 9:23). So also Brueggemann (*Jeremiah 1–25*, 95).

504. Yet seemingly secure (Domeris, *Heart*, 98).

505. Ibid., 109.

506. Hertzberg, *I & II Samuel*, 30.

507. Murphy, *Proverbs*, 10:22; Domeris, *Heart*, 123. The wisdom literature was most likely written for those with some control over their lives whereas the poor could rarely become rich no matter how hard they worked (Hoppe, *Poor*, 68).

in their wealth (Hos 12:8),[508] are corrupt shepherds (Zech 11:5),[509] and deceitful (Jer 5:27).[510] All the named wealthy in the OT are either severely tested or their wealth is a trap. All generic references to the wealthy are deeply critical of their characters and their use of their wealth.

Perhaps the worst sin of the rich is not caring for the poor. In the MT, a number of words mean poverty. These include דַּלָּה (dallah), דַּל (dal), רוּשׁ (rush), אֶבְיוֹן (ebyon), and עָנִי (ani). The first three only mean economic poverty; e.g., דַּלָּה ("poorest of the land"; 2 Kgs 25:12; LXX: πτωχῶν);[511] דַּל ("a poor man in his lawsuit"; Exod 23:3; LXX: πένητα);[512] and רוּשׁ ("the other poor"; 2 Sam 12:1; LXX: πένης).[513] אֶבְיוֹן and עָנִי can mean economic poverty ("the poor and needy; Deut 15:11; אֶבְיוֹן; LXX: πένητι).[514] People must not oppress "a hired man," but pay wages daily (Deut 24:14–15;[515] עָנִי; LXX: πένης). Together, especially when rebuking those oppressing the poor, they mean economic poverty (Prov 31:20; Ezek 16:49; 18:12; 22:29; Amos 8:4).[516] The prophets starkly showed the sin of rich against poor by equating idolatry with oppression, not restoring a pledge garment and usury.[517]

אֶבְיוֹן and עָנִי can also mean non-economic dependence on God.[518] David is never shown as economically poor,[519] but calls himself "poor/poor

---

508. Stuart, *Hosea*, 12:8; Hoppe, *Poor*, 68. In effect, they defy God to show that they sinned in accumulating their wealth (Domeris, *Heart*, 102).

509. This is arguably for enslaving fellow Israelites (Foster, "Shepherds," 746).

510. Thompson, *Jeremiah*, 250; Allen, *Jeremiah*.

511. Hobbs, *2 Kings*, 24:14; Domeris, *Heart*, 15. Ironically, it took the fall of Judah to free the poorest from a rapacious system (Hoppe, *Poor*, 66).

512. Hauck, "πένης," 38. This insight is so perceptive that some have proposed modifying "poor" to "important" (Durham, *Exodus*, 23:3). The rich, not decisions favoring the poor, were subverting justice (Hoppe, *Poor*, 35).

513. Domeris, *Heart*, 17. In the face of such royal abuse of power, all the prophet could do was to formulate a telling story (Horsley, *Powers*, 166), but this is not all—Nathan also announces God's punishment. Nathan used the same word, רוּשׁ, for the poor man, as David used for himself (1 Sam 18:23; Hoppe, *Poor*, 57).

514. Horsley, *Powers*, 52; Domeris, *Heart*, 21; Hauck, "πένης," 39. Deut sees no positive value in poverty, so the rich are encouraged to be generous (Hoppe, *Poor*, 31).

515. Craigie, *Deuteronomy*, 309. Contrary to normal ideas, the fate of the rich man depends on the poor man's "recommendation" to God (Ben-Dov, "Curse," 439). Deut uses "poor and needy," but not אֶבְיוֹן on its own, for economic poverty, so they might be contract laborers with daily rations (Domeris, *Heart*, 20).

516. Hoppe, *Poor*, 105; Hauck, "πένης," 39; Mays, *Amos*, 143.

517. Hoppe, *Poor*, 94.

518. The wealth of the rich blinds them to their need for God (Myers, *Walking*, 145).

519. Except early in his life; e.g., 1 Sam 18:23: "I'm only a poor man."

and needy" (עָנִי; Pss 34:6; 40:17; 69:29;[520] 70:5;[521] 86:1; 109:16, 22;[522] LXX: πτωχός καὶ πένης)[523] or "the needy one" (וְאֶבְיוֹן; πένητος; LXX: Ps 108:31).[524] This means non-economic dependence on God, as Psalm 109 does not mention economic poverty:[525] "the Psalms of Lament … extend ebyon … into … one's need for God."[526] The LXX thus guards the distinction between economic and non-economic need, but only uses πτωχός and πένης, not ἐνδεής, as acceptable translations for non-economic need for God. The only GNT use of πένης is 2 Corinthians 9:9, citing Psalm 112:9, where Paul asked the Corinthians to give generously to the poor Christians in Jerusalem and promises them spiritual riches like thanksgiving (9:11–14).[527]

The New Testament

The OT's descriptions of the negative aspects of wealth are intensified in the NT, where most references to literal wealth are negative.[528] Wealth can block salvation when its deceitfulness chokes the gospel message (Matt 13:22/ Mark 4:19;[529] Luke 8:14[530]). It is untrustworthy (1 Tim 6:17),[531] less valu-

---

520. Tate, *Psalms 51–100*, 69:29. This prayer is like a curse, that God might harm his enemy (Smith, *Hand This Man*, 69–70).

521. Tate errs to describe the person as "needy-poor," when it is apparently David (*Psalms 51–100*, 70:5).

522. Bammel and Hauck say that אֶבְיוֹן and עָנִי is "the regular expression in the Ps. for the attitude" of the one praying ("πτωχός," 889). The issue is that most of these Pss have strongly autobiographical descriptions of David's dire circumstances; e.g., Ps 35:1, 4: "fight against me," "seek my life," etc., which are not "regular." It is another detailed imprecatory curse against the Psalmist's enemy (Smith, *Hand This Man*, 71).

523. "A self-designation of the righteous" (Hauck, "πένης," 39). The LXX blurs the contrast between πένης and πτωχός (Kittel, *Theological Dictionary*, 825).

524. "The psalms consistently portray God as the protector and deliverer of the poor e.g. Pss … 109:31." (Hoppe, *Poor*, 129). While not denied, a more nuanced interpretation is needed for David's self-referential Ps 109, as David is not poor economically.

525. "As a special proof of piety" (Hauck, "πένης," 40).

526. Domeris, *Heart*, 15.

527. Balla, *2 Corinthians*, 776.

528. Ellingworth, *Hebrews*, 613. The early church thought that the wealthy were captive to their wealth (Brown, "Prayer," 610).

529. France, *Mark*, 206; Capper, "Goods," 71.

530. Hagner, *Matthew 1–13*, 13:28; Zehnder, "Mammon," 36. Not only is anxiety about wealth a problem, but wealth itself is a problem (Nolland, *Luke 1—9:20*, 8:14).

531. A contrast between trusting in wealth and being rich in good deeds (Mounce, *Pastoral*, 6:17). 1 Tim 6 shows the rich manifesting greed, which disrupts normal social relationships (Brown, "Prayer," 610).

able than "disgrace for the sake of Christ" (Heb 11:26), rotten,[532] or transitory (Rev 18:17).[533] All positive references to πλοῦτος are non-material.[534] Phrases such as "God enriches all who call on Him" (πλουτῶν, Rom 10:12) could mean monetary wealth. However, as all the other positive references to wealth in Romans are non-material, like God's kindness, his glory, and his riches for the world and the Gentiles, etc. (Rom 2:4; 9:23; 11:12, 33),[535] 10:12 should also mean spiritual riches.[536] The same picture emerges in Ephesians, Philippians, and Colossians with "the riches of God's grace" (Eph 1:7)[537] or "the glorious riches of (the word of God)."[538] The only positive references to literal wealth are the Macedonians' generosity in the collection for the Jerusalem church (2 Cor 8:2),[539] symptomatic of a correct moral/spiritual attitude, where Paul says that they could not be true brothers and sisters of the Jerusalem church without giving.[540] This is like David giving his own wealth to Solomon to build the temple (1 Chr 29). Paul's reassurance that God could meet all the Philippians' needs (4:19) probably includes but is not limited to physical needs.[541]

NT references to literal wealth are mostly negative. The rich (πλουτοῦντας) are sent away empty, and those who are not rich toward God[542] will lose their wealth (πλουτῶν; Luke 1:53; 12:2).[543] Desiring wealth is a trap (πλουτεῖν; 1 Tim 6:9). The snare is linked to Satan (παγίς; 1 Tim 3:7; 2 Tim 2:26),[544] connecting inanimate money and evil. Wealth is based on luxury (Rev 18:3, 15, 19).[545] Rather, people are enriched to help others

---

532. Martin, *James*, 5:2; Davids, *James*, 175–76; Kamell, "Humility," 172.

533. Aune, *Revelation 6–16*, 18:17.

534. Schmidt, "Riches," 826.

535. Contrasting the abundance of God's gifts with Roman patronage (Downs, "Patronage," 146).

536. Regarding Rom 2:4: contra Morris, *Romans*, 112. πλοῦτος plus the genitive means abundance (Cranfield, *Romans*, 1:144).

537. Such phrases indicate the lavishness of God's gift (O'Brien, *Ephesians*, 107). While this is not doubted, O'Brien should have noted the uniformly spiritual nature of the blessings.

538. O'Brien, *Colossians*, 1:27.

539. Furnish, *II Corinthians*, 413.

540. Hoppe, *Poor*, 159; Schmidt, "Riches," 826.

541. Muller, *Philippians*, 152

542. For example, by using their money to help others (O'Brien, *Ephesians*, 107).

543. Nolland, *Luke 9:21—18:34*, 12:21; Bock, *Luke*, 157.

544. Mounce, *Pastoral*, 6:9.

545. Aune, *Revelation 6–16*; Resseguie, *Revelation*, 228. The kings of the earth were partners in Babylon's "worship of Mammon" (Beasley-Murray, *Revelation*, 265).

(πλουτιζόμενοι; 2 Cor 9:11)[546] and for good deeds (1 Tim 6:18),[547] or generous sharing[548] with such "beneficence [being] . . . beneficial for attaining eternal life."[549] Positive references are to the wealth of spiritual gifts (1 Cor 1:5, 7) and enriching others (2 Cor 6:10;[550] 9:11).[551]

Two examples show that the NT has kept the OT distinction of economic and non-economic need with its *hapax* πένης in 2 Corinthians 9:9, and its affirmation that there were "no needy persons" (ἐνδεής)[552] in the NT church due to the apostolic redistribution of wealth (Acts 4:34–35[553]), after the pattern of Mosaic law.

Firstly, in the Makarisms,[554] Luke 6:20 has Jesus saying Μακάριοι οἱ πτωχοί while Matt 5:3 adds (or Luke omits) τῷ πνεύματι. Luke 6:20 is confronting with its apparent blessing of economic poverty somehow conferring membership of the kingdom. Nolland confuses the issue by defining οἱ πτωχοί in contrast with τοῖς πλουσίος, who receive a woe instead.[555] More attention to MT and LXX usage may have avoided this dilemma.[556] If Jesus blessed the ἐνδεής, which always means economic poverty, this would need resolution. By blessing οἱ πτωχοί, Jesus does little more than affirm LXX usage, that "they"[557] can mean those who rely on God, regardless of economic circumstances, thus enabling participation in the kingdom. Matthew 5:3 only clarifies what Luke implies, that the correct internal attitude, poverty of spirit, is essential for the kingdom. Barton notes that the correct attitude

---

546. Furnish, *II Corinthians*, 450; Downs, "Patronage," 152.

547. Hoppe, *Poor*, 162.

548. Mounce, *Pastoral*, 6:18.

549. Hays, "Almsgiving," 275.

550. It cannot mean material wealth, as (true) apostles are πτωχοί, impoverished [Furnish, *II Corinthians*, 359]).

551. Schmidt, "Riches," 827.

552. This means economic need, as presumably everybody in the early church had a non-economic need for God. It alludes to Deut 15:4 (Johnson, *Acts*, 86).

553. Zehnder, "Mammon," 36. Acts 4:34–35 reproduces the LXX of Deut 15:4, which says that there will be no poverty in a Torah observant community, so Luke is implying that the infant church is the true Israel (Hoppe, *Poor*, 156).

554. Matthew consciously parallels Matt 5–7 and 23–25 with the contrasts of blessings/woes; reception/loss of the kingdom; inner/outer righteousness; true/false teaching, etc., to warn the disciples what to do/avoid given the certainty of judgment (Hood, "Extent," 540).

555. Nolland, *Luke 1—9:20*, 6:20.

556. So also Bammel and Hauck ("πτωχός," 904) and Arnal ("Scribes," 35), quoting Patterson, *Thomas*, 234.

557. Pao and Schnabel ("Luke," 296). The gospels could have achieved the same goal with Jesus' blessing (πένης), but it is a *hapax* (2 Cor 9:9).

is willingness to receive.[558] Hagner also confuses the issue when arguing for the primacy of the OT background of μακάριοι; he fails to do the same for οἱ πτωχοί τῷ πνεύματι, saying that it is "the frame of mind characteristic of the literally poor,"[559] which is not the only meaning. The evangelists have Jesus preserving the core LXX meaning of πτωχοί as dependence on God, but retaining the OT's dim view of τοῖς πλουσίοις (Luke 6:24).

Further support for this occurs in the narrative of the poor widow's offering (Mark 12:41–44/Luke 21:1–4).[560] She is described as χήρα πτωχή — not, for argument's sake, as ἐνδεής.[561] That this is about her real economic poverty, and her ensuing total reliance on God[562] is shown by giving "all she had to live on" (Mark 12:44/Luke 21:4),[563] so that she then needed help, to God's house, the temple.[564] She shows both dependencies of οἱ πτωχοί, and receives Jesus' approval that she gave relatively more than the πλουσίοι.[565]

Breyer is amiss by saying that Jesus is more concerned with a social/religious system which allowed her poverty than praising her tiny offering.[566] Whatever the validity of this point, the text shows Jesus' genuine appreciation of her offering. It is fair to say (if unsaid by Jesus) that she showed her relational dependency on God by her economic dependency. Jesus asked something similar of the rich (πλούσιος) young ruler (Luke 18:22; "sell all that you have . . . and give to the poor"[567]) and asked Levi to leave everything (Luke 5:28).[568] By contrast, none who are called wealthy in the NT are in an identifiably positive relationship with God.

558. Barton, "Money," 43.

559. Hagner, *Matthew 1–13*, 5:3.

560. Luke has Jesus reporting, but not commending, the poor widow's actions (Hoppe, *Poor*, 154). It is difficult to see how Jesus' words could not commend the widow, contrasting her with the rich.

561. "Widow" links this to previous criticism of scribes (12:38–40; Beavis, *Mark*, 184).

562. The "total commitment to God that the widow's gift represented" (Lane, *Mark*, 443).

563. Her gift prefigures Jesus' complete self-giving (Hoppe, *Poor*, 146). A Markan two-step progression clarifies "all . . . on" with "put in everything" (Resseguie, *Narrative*, 49). She held nothing back (Pilgrim, *Good News*, 95).

564. Bolt, *Cross*, 90.

565. France, *Mark*, 493; Bammel and Hauck, "πτωχός," 902. Paul praising the impoverished Macedonians' generosity (2 Cor 8:2) is similar (Kruse, *2 Corinthians*, 151).

566. Breyer, "Widow," 124. The text is about the widow's impoverishment due to her cultic obligations (Myers, *Binding*, 321). Nothing like this is said or implied. Her offering appears to be voluntary, if personally costly. If Jesus was angry at the system, he is not recorded as showing any anger, unlike his cleansing of the temple (Matt 21/Mark 11/Luke 19), where he overturned tables and rebuked the money-changers.

567. Horsley, *Powers*, 142.

568. Hoppe, *Poor*, 154.

3.5.4. Δουλεύειν

The next illustration of money's new status in the NT is the changed use of δουλεύειν from the OT.[569] Δουλεύειν in the LXX has four meanings, two with direct NT parallels. Someone can serve God (e.g., Judg 2:7; Rom 12:11) or one another freely (e.g., Gen 29:18, Jacob/Rachel; Gal 5:13). While someone in the OT could serve another involuntarily, like Israel serving Aram (Judg 3:8), δουλεύειν is not used in the GNT to describe the Roman occupation.[570] The fourth category, serving an inanimate object, is the most relevant. In the OT, this exclusively means Israel serving foreign or other gods as representatives of the nations, θεοῖς ἑτέροις or ἀλλοτρίοις; e.g., Deuteronomy 28:64.[571] In the NT, the situation is more complex, as no Jew or Christian was said to serve idols. No references to Rome/Romans in the Gospels or Acts mention idolatry. There are some continuities from the OT to the NT, in that Christians are not to worship θεοῖς (Gal 4:8),[572] but there are new emphases. No Israelite was warned not to serve sin or the στοιχεῖα.

Στοιχεῖα can have neutral meanings, like basic Christian teaching (Heb 5:12)[573] or the physical elements of the universe (2 Pet 3:10, 12),[574] but serving στοιχεῖα is linked to slavery (Gal 4:3[575]; Col 2:8) and contrasted with serving God.[576] The NT στοιχεῖα are described similarly to the OT idols in terminology or effect.

---

569. See Appendix 10 for the raw data.

570. For an alternative, see Horsley (s3.3.4). The Jewish denial in John 8:33 is very puzzling. The other two similar NT references—Acts 7:7 (Egypt) and Rom 9:12 (Jacob/Esau)—relate to Israel's past, not its future.

571. Given the close association between nation and deity in the Ancient Near East, the third and fourth meanings may, in some circumstances, be linked. Serving another nation may be like, or actually involve, serving its gods.

572. Paul notes the similarity of the pre-Christian experience of both Jew and Gentile (Longenecker, *Galatians*, 4:8; Bruce, *Galatians*, 201), even though only Gentiles "did not know God" (Dunn, *Galatians*, 223).

573. Ellingworth calls this "Repetition for emphasis." στοιχεῖα, milk (5:12–13), and "elementary teachings about Christ" (6:1) all mean essentially the same thing (Ellingworth, *Hebrews*, 303).

574. The planets or the spiritual powers allegedly controlling them or spiritual beings exercising control over the cosmos are possible meanings (Bauckham, *Jude, 2 Peter*, 3:10; O'Brien, *Colossians*, 2:15).

575. The emphatic καὶ ἡμεῖς stresses the Jewish nature of the audience, and links slavery with obeying the Law (Longenecker, *Galatians*, 4:3; Bruce, *Galatians*, 193). It is slavery for all (Myers, *Binding*, 126).

576. Longenecker, *Galatians*, 4:9; Bruce, *Galatians*, 202; Dunn, *Galatians*, 226; Bammel and Hauck, "πτωχός," 909; Col 2:20. Longenecker objects to the similarity of meaning of στοιχεῖα in different contexts (*Galatians*, 4:3). While context is crucial, he

In Matthew 6:24 and Luke 16:13, Jesus notes the impossibility of serving both God and money.[577] Like στοιχεῖα and θεοῖς, serving money is contrasted with serving God, so we can treat it with similar seriousness. Money is paralleled as an equally offensive object of service with things which are obviously wrong. The novelty in this command is that the OT never warned about the impossibility of serving both God and money. Money is the only material object which is portrayed in the NT as a direct rival to God. Wealth in the NT is an active barrier to serving God, as seen in Jesus' reason: "he will hate the one and love the other" (Matt 6:24; Luke 16:13). This Jewish idiom expresses the absolute commitment which God demands.[578] In Luke 14:26, Jesus said that those who did not hate their own family, or have them as a lesser commitment than him, could not be his disciples.[579] If money gains that place (which is only appropriate for God), lessening felt dependence on God, then we will prefer it to him. Jesus criticized religious opponents for loving money, and the Corban controversy prioritizes money for the temple (human tradition) over money for family duties (a Torah duty; Luke 16:14; Mark 7:11).

What does it mean to serve? This is not defined in the Bible, but could mean placing the needs of the object of service above one's own needs, and obeying where that object is God. To serve God means obedience in contrast with serving the Baals (Judg 2:7, 11).[580] To serve someone means placing their needs ahead of one's own, like Jesus ministering to outcasts (Matt 8:2). To serve money could then mean subordinating other, more legitimate needs like caring for others, even oneself, to an all-consuming desire to make more money. Zehnder's article "What Does It Mean to 'Serve Mammon'?" fails to answer this in the light of the NT. His answer concerns money's improper use, forbidden by the OT, but in the heightened atmosphere of the NT, he should have emphasized the danger of money itself.[581]

---

should note the uniformly negative tone of these texts. There is no encouragement to serve the στοιχεῖα. Wink believes they are basic religious practices of people, which may enslave them (*Naming*, 67, 72). Lynch argues (correctly, in my opinion) that Wink has not proven his basic thesis, that the στοιχεῖα have simultaneously a heavenly and an earthly pole ("Powers," 258).

577. This is the closest the Bible gets to ascribing deity to money. Such a stark choice would help Jesus encourage people to follow him (Allison, *Resurrecting*, 40). One cannot serve two masters with differing demands (Davies and Allison, *Matthew*, 1:642).

578. Hagner, *Matthew 1–13*, 6:24. So also Capper, "Goods," 71.

579. "Hate" is typical Semitic hyperbole, and the mention of "even his own life" shows that Jesus does not want hostility or sectarian division (Nolland, *Luke 9:21—18:34*, 14:26).

580. Hoppe, *Poor*, 47.

581. 1 Tim 6:10, "the love of money is the root of all kinds of evil," may be a slight softening, as it concludes a paragraph focused not so much on money as its misuse.

The New Testament

There are clear continuities between the OT and NT on wealth, but the NT strengthens the warnings considerably. Both warn against misusing wealth, but the NT emphasizes the danger of money itself. It is not only reified like fire (Jas 5:3),[582] it is also deified as an alternate object of worship to God (Matt 6:24; Luke 16:13)[583] with a similarly consuming effect (Jas 5:3; Heb 12:29[584]).[585] Kamell is only partly right to note James 5's condemnation of the rich for failing to care for the poor (which any OT prophet could and did say), but not to see the danger of money itself.[586] The OT has nothing like the NT's graphic personification of the danger of money, as in James 5:3: "Your gold and silver are corroded. Their corrosion will testify against you and eat your flesh like fire."[587] While fire is central in scenes of eschatological judgment,[588] ἐν ἐσχάταις ἡμέραις shows that the effect of this fire is present.[589] Next, in Deuteronomy 24:15, the laborers cry out to God for their unpaid wages,[590] but James 5:4 intensifies the warnings of Deuteronomy, with the unpaid wages also crying out.[591] This motif reaches its literal apotheosis in the deification of money. Like idolators, those who pursue money will follow it to its appointed destruction (1 Tim 6:9). The picture is completed by the NT having no named, righteous rich, unlike the OT. It is difficult to imagine a more compelling warning.

Next, in the teaching after the Sermon on the Mount/Plain, Jesus considerably strengthens OT moral teaching. Much debate, beyond the scope

582. The perfect tenses are "prophetic anticipation" of what will certainly happen (Martin, *James*, 5:3). The references to fire and "the last days" evoke images of eschatological judgment; the "treasure" they are laying up is the certainty of destruction. James accepted the wicked's eternal judgment (Sim, "Weeping," 130).

583. "Jesus and Paul do not condemn riches *as such*" (Zehnder, "Mammon," 36; his emphasis). While this is strictly true, Zehnder has not grappled with the far more negative picture of wealth in the NT. It is not just a matter of the proper use of money, as in the OT, but fundamentally a question of whom or what one serves.

584. 12:29 is based on Deut 4:24 and 31 and is designed to evoke God's faithfulness (Ellingworth, *Hebrews*, 692). While this may be true, the undeniable element of warning in chapter 12 should not be overlooked.

585. Lane, *Hebrews*, 12:29.

586. Kamell, "Humility," 171.

587. If money has the effect of fire, it is likened to God, who is "a consuming fire" (Heb 12:29).

588. Martin, *James*, 5:3; Hoppe, *Poor*, 163. This is as close as the NT gets to money's powerlessness and ultimate judgment by God.

589. Davids, *James*, 177.

590. Hoppe, *Poor*, 34.

591. Carson, "James," 1009.

of this thesis, has occurred about "the practicability of the sermon."[592] It has fourteen triads, most of which have a description of traditional righteousness, a vicious cycle, and finally a transforming initiative to free the person.[593] Murder was (and still is) unlawful, and its preliminary attitudes of hatred and abuse were and are forbidden for Christians (Matt 5:22–23).[594] "No command never to be angry is given,"[595] but Jesus identifies murder, then the cycles of anger and abuse leading to it, before concluding with behavior which could transfer a potentially murderous relationship into one of reconciliation.[596] It is not an impossible or interim ethic, but required of all disciples.[597] Stassen expends much effort in explaining that the Sermon is not dyadic, warning and prohibition, but triadic, as shown above.[598] But he misinterprets the pericope on "treasure in heaven" by not seeing that it does not follow the pattern. We would expect a warning against greed or the misuse of money, followed by examples of vicious cycles about money, followed by transforming initiatives.

Matthew 6:19–34 has a warning, a possible (if enigmatic) transforming initiative, and then teaching on light and two masters. Stassen joins 6:24 with 6:25–34 on not worrying.[599] However, Stassen cannot give an example of traditional teaching about not serving God and money, but worse, fails to recognize that the discussion of money applies more closely to treasure (6:19) than food and clothing, about which "your Father knows that you need them" (6:32), something never said of money. Finally, and breaking the triadic pattern, there are no transforming initiatives. Jesus gives specific

---

592. Hagner, *Matthew 1–13*, 5:22. The Sermon is like a covenant renewal ceremony based on Sinai and Josh 24 (Horsley, *Powers*, 137–41). He believes that Jesus was addressing Galilean village communities, crushed by the Romans, who blamed themselves for their predicament. Jesus called them to take appropriate actions so that God could bless them. In response, both Matt 5:1 and Luke 6:20 are clear that Jesus principally addressed his disciples, not Galileans in general. It is more like a new, rather than a renewed, covenant.

593. Stassen, "Triads," 268.

594. Keener, *Matthew*, 183.

595. Stassen, "Triads," 272.

596. Ibid., 272.

597. The primary audience in both Matt 5:1 and Luke 6:17 is "His disciples" (Hagner, *Matthew 1–13*, 5:1). Hoppe is right to note the eschatological rectification of all injustice (Hoppe, *Poor*, 148), but still should have emphasized that, in the meantime, Jesus has given his followers concrete steps to take. Hood contrasts Matt 5–7 and 23–25 (beatitudes/woes; reception/loss of the kingdom; inner/outer righteousness, etc.) to argue that they function as warnings for Christians that they must be prepared for judgment ("Extent," 540).

598. Stassen, "Triads," 268–69.

599. Ibid., 286.

directions about proper fasting and prayer, but his guidance on money is obscure. What does storing up "treasure in heaven" mean? Stassen believes that it means submitting oneself to God's sovereign rule,[600] which sounds reasonable, but cannot show this from the text. Jesus has transforming initiatives for all triads except for money, arguably implying that it is so powerful that (mere) initiatives are inadequate. No other physical object or activity in the NT is portrayed as a direct competitor to God, as in Matthew 6:24. This is more evidence of money's new and unique status.

Matthew 6:19–34 has many points of interest, but I will focus on two. Firstly, to serve money is to collect wealth on earth where "moth and rust destroy" (Matt 6:19), rather than having treasure in heaven, where no harm occurs.[601] Jesus' stark warning in 6:24 shows the impossibility of serving two masters.[602] Next, the verbs in this passage are usually plural, showing that our attitude to money and to neighbor (given the parallelism between Matthew 6:19–34 and 7:1–12) are similar and communal.[603] Matthew 6:33, the "climactic imperative,"[604] "seek first His kingdom," has a communal aspect, as ζητεῖτε is plural and the present tense means ongoing effort.[605]

Jesus' other warning on the impossibility of serving two masters is in the difficult parable[606] of the dishonest steward (Luke 16:1–13).[607] Interpre-

600. Ibid., 285.

601. Barton, "Money," 43.

602. Keener, *Matthew*, 233. It was possible, but involved divided loyalties (Hagner, *Matthew 1–13*, 6:24).

603. Stassen, "Triads," 267–308.

604. Barton, "Money," 44.

605. Hagner, *Matthew 1–13*, 6:33. Such texts address an educated rural elite facing real economic uncertainty (Arnal, "Scribes"). He argues that the construction of Sepphoris and Tiberias meant that goods and the wealthy flowed to them from surrounding villages (ibid., 147). This deepened existing divisions between rich and poor, leaving an educated class of village scribes managing their masters' affairs as the visible face of oppression (ibid., 153). In response, the scribes, facing an uncertain future, composed Luke's presumed source Q, addressed to the rich with something to sell or capable of lending, enjoining them to be generous in giving to the poor (ibid., 173). Arnal concludes that Q is mainly addressed to the affluent and only generally to the poor (ibid., 174). This may overstate matters as, while certain passages like 12:33–34 ("give to the poor") are clearly addressed to the rich, materialism and its attendant anxiety are presumably as much a temptation to those with too little as to those with too much. Moreover, if the scribes wanted to get the rich onside, it is strange that Luke's descriptions of the rich are so uniformly negative, and that the person most highly praised by Jesus for giving is the widow in non-Q Luke 21:1–4, who is not just poor but desperately so. If Arnal was right, the scribes' purpose would be better served by stories of the rich being blessed by God for their generosity, but there are none.

606. Beavis, *Slavery*, 44.

607. Zwiep compares Judas's "reward for his wickedness" (Acts 1:18) with "the

tations which show the master as foul of the law or commercial practice with the steward foregoing usurious interest[608] cannot show this from the text. The master knew what was on the bills, and it could not be falsified. The most likely setting was a respected master who cared enough about his image to dismiss a wasteful[609] steward. Beavis portrayed the steward favorably as a clever slave outwitting the master, like Aesop's fable,[610] but none of her examples have the master praising the steward. She argues that διαβάλλω shows that the steward was unfairly accused.[611] This word is a *hapax* in the GNT, and its only two LXX uses are Daniel 3:8 and 6:24 (English 6:25) where the accusations were true—the Jews were refusing to worship the image (Dan 3:8) and Daniel was praying (Dan 6:10)—but unfair. Ukpong argues that the steward was "unjust" by society's standards for giving to the poor.[612] This ignores the fact that the amount of debt reflected a large farm[613] and that the master praised the steward, undermining the social structure which benefited the master. Ukpong is on safer ground to note that each use of Ἄνθρωπός τις ἦν πλούσιος (Luke 12:16; 16:1, 19) is pejorative.[614]

Ukpong and Beavis (oddly) have the master praising the steward for revealing his sin[615] (16:8). Tenants paid a fixed annual rent and a fee to the steward for each contract. His trial is rapid, but the result is not communicated at once, hence the haste.[616] Landry and May argue that some would

---

manager of unrighteousness" (Luke 16:8; "Matthias," 89) and "the mammon of unrighteousness" (Luke 16:9), all using ἀδικίας.

608. Nolland, *Luke 9:21—18:34*, 798; Pilgrim, *Good News*, 127.

609. The same accusation applied to the Prodigal Son (Landry and May, "Honor," 287-309). Sellew doubts the prodigal's repentance due to similarities with Peter's inner dialogue in Acts 12:11, but Peter had no reason to repent ("Interior," 246). He was "a disloyal, dishonest . . . steward losing his status as one of the . . . trusted retainer class" (Capper, "Goods," 66). If so, the steward could face corporal punishment (Udoh, "Slave," 332).

610. Beavis, "Slavery," 47. So also Udoh, "Slave," 329.

611. Beavis, "Slavery," 48.

612. Ukpong, "Shrewd," 201. Ukpong calls the steward "shrewd" (ibid., 193), but Luke calls him τῆς ἀδικίας (16:8), like the money in 16:9 (Nolland, *Luke 9:21—18:34*, 16:9), which the NIV translates "worldly" and which will later be shown as an alternative to God (16:13). We may safely assume that Luke implies something worse than just "shrewd."

613. Nolland, *Luke 9:21—18:34*, 799; Parsons, *Luke*, 247.

614. Ukpong, "Shrewd," 198.

615. Ibid., 206; Beavis, "Slavery," 51. Mann is very optimistic to argue that the master praises the steward for making the best of a bad situation ("Steward," 234), when the whole affair is the steward's fault, due to his wastefulness. His proposed textual amendment that the manager is praised for his "experience" is unsupported by the text (ibid., 235).

616. Nolland, *Luke 9:21—18:34*, 16:2.

think that the reductions were done at the master's request.⁶¹⁷ This cannot be read from the text, and it is more likely that the steward has backed the master into a corner with his last move.⁶¹⁸ He could rewrite contracts⁶¹⁹ for the master, and the reciprocity culture meant that he would be an honored guest of the debtors.⁶²⁰ The master sees the shrewdness in a fellow "son of this age,"⁶²¹ whom Jesus contrasts with τοὺς υἱοὺς τοῦ φωτός. Neither master nor steward are seen as appropriate models for God's people,⁶²² especially in the light of Jesus' comments on misusing the wealth of others (16:9–13)⁶²³ and the climactic "You cannot serve both God and Mammon" (16:13).

The parable has many interpretations, and Luke 16:9–13 is a necessary corrective. Someone might be surprised that the steward is called unrighteous, whilst another may be surprised that such action could be praised. Only the one who has entrusted their whole future (holding nothing back, not even "unrighteous mammon" [Luke 16:9]⁶²⁴) to a supremely merciful Master, and looks after the poor in this life, can hope to be welcomed into heaven. This underlines Jesus' warnings that we must choose between God and money. The next parable is that of the rich man and Lazarus where this choice with all its consequences, is portrayed starkly. The gospel's view of money is much more negative than the OT. Money is not a neutral object over which we exercise power, but a powerful rival deity, "a possible master."⁶²⁵

---

617. Landry and May, "Honor," 301.

618. Ibid., 305. The sounds of praise of the master's "generosity" (a highly valued quality in an Ancient Near East ruler) were probably reaching the master's ears as he commended the steward.

619. This is like Aesop's tales of revenge, where the steward actually does what he is accused of: mishandling the master's affairs. But again, this does not account for the master's praise (Beavis, "Slavery," 50).

620. Nolland, *Luke 9:21—18:34*, 16:7.

621. Ibid., 16:8; Marshall, *Luke*, 620. His praise of the steward—because the master "needed at least to appear to be observing covenantal law," given impending judgment (Horsley, *Powers*, 146)—is forced.

622. Contra Pao and Schnabel, "Luke," 343.

623. The "friends" are the poor, reflecting Luke 12:33 and 18:22, so the contrast is between people using money for selfish purposes versus those caring for the poor (Nolland, *Luke 9:21—18:34*, 16:9).

624. Ibid., 16:9. This does not preclude wise use of money now, as the point of 16:9 is to use money properly while we can, for one day it will come to an end (Marshall, *Luke*, 621). Pao and Schnabel omit ἀδικίας ("Luke," 343).

625. Nolland, *Luke 9:21—18:34*, 16:13.

3.6. Conclusion to Section 3

Section 3 has studied the main three rivals to God: human, demonic, and material. Human and demonic rivals have the following features (and material rivals to a lesser extent): an ascription by others or presumption by the person of divinity, a malicious nature or an association with evil, a strange powerlessness, and a final judgment by God.

Human rivals to God are few but consistent. Adam and Eve in Genesis 3 and the king/prince of Tyre attempted to cross the divine/creature line and were judged by God (Gen 1:26; Ezek 28:7, 18). In the NT, Simon Magus with his magic, Herod with accepting worship, and the "man of lawlessness" proclaiming himself divine were/will be judged by God for failing to observe this boundary. In most cases, evil is present either overtly or covertly.

Supernatural rivals to God are also evident. The anti-idolatry polemic in Second Isaiah mirrors the Babylonian *mîs-pî* ritual, where an evil spirit indwelt the idol, animating it. In a clear contrast with secular Greek, the LXX uniformly uses εἴδωλον and δαιμόν negatively; e.g., the Baal of Peor incident (Num 25) and Deuteronomy 32:17 links idols and demons. The GNT intensifies these negative features so that the parallel warnings in the NT are more severe; e.g., Jesus himself will punish his idolatrous people (Rev 2:16, 23).

Finally, money is portrayed as an alternate object of worship to God and like God, a consuming fire, which calls out to God for justice (Matt 6:24; Luke 16:13; Jas 5:3–4). The OT has nothing like James's graphic warnings about wealth itself. The only positive references to wealth in the NT are spiritual like "the riches of (God's) kindness" (Rom 2:4), or the collection for the Jerusalem church (2 Cor 8–9).

The study of terms related to rivalry; idols; the supernatural; Satan; and money, from secular sources; the Jewish scriptures; intertestamental; Second Temple; and New Testament literature reveals that they may converge and coalesce to describe behavior that usurps roles which rightly belong to God. It is now appropriate to see whether similar patterns emerge in the NT's depiction of Judas.

Introduction to Section 4

So far, we have established that the Biblical and other uses of παραδίδωμι and ἑταῖρος are consistent with betrayal. In Section 3, we established that Satan, idols, and human rivals to God share remarkably similar characteristics. Inanimate money can be a rival to God. Allowing for their different states, either they falsely claim or were ascribed divinity, or they are linked with evil but are powerless, and will finally be judged by God. Having established these results, we are now in a position to examine the Biblical record on Judas for parallels to see whether the accounts of his behavior fit in such an environment.

S4.2 will examine the following synoptic texts which show Judas's presence:

- the call of the Twelve;[1]
- Jesus teaching the Twelve the meaning of the parable of the sower;
- Jesus sending out the Twelve on mission and their reporting back;
- the feeding of the five thousand;
- the warning that the greatest in the kingdom must be servant of all; and
- the third prediction of his death.

The evidence will show (based on Markan priority) that Mark establishes Judas's guilt and Matt/Luke intensify it.

Ss4.3–4 will examine the events in the Passion Narratives:

- the plot to betray Jesus;
- the anointing of Jesus at Bethany;

---

1. Here following Meier's point that both Mark and John prefer to talk of the Twelve as an absolute ("Twelve," 637).

- the Last Supper;
- Judas's betrayal of Jesus; and
- Judas after the betrayal.

It will repeat the methodology of s4.2.

From the vantage point reached, an attempt will then be made to consider whether Judas is treated as an idol. This will focus particularly on Luke/Acts, but it may be possible to extrapolate parallels to that material from the other gospels. Care will be taken to avoid basing the parallels on disputed views of the synoptic problem. Only parallels will be examined, not dependency.

Section 4

Judas in New Testament Narratives

4.1. Introduction

IN THE LIGHT OF previous work, ss4.1–2 will examine some synoptic passages which include at least one of: παραδίδωμι, ἑταῖρος, or a reference to Judas by name or as one of the Twelve. This requires addressing the synoptic problem, the literary relationship between the synoptics. It is beyond the scope of this thesis to solve what is unresolved after two centuries,[1] but a relationship seems indisputable.[2] McKnight gives three reasons: the phenomena of content, where 90 percent of Mark is found in Matt and 50 percent in Luke; of order, where almost always at least two evangelists agree on the order of events; and of words, where there is substantial similarity in parallels.[3]

Most scholars support Markan priority.[4] Patristic sources uniformly cite a Mark, assumed to be the NT companion of Barnabas, Paul, and Peter.[5] Next, it is hard to see how certain texts in Matthew or Luke could precede their Markan parallels. Jesus' temptation is four words in Mark 1:13,[6] but

---

1. Carlson, "Synoptic," http://www.mindspring.com/~scarlson/synopt/.s

2. Linnemann disagrees due to an analysis of words shared by the synoptics (*Criticism*) but it has not been widely accepted; e.g., she has not addressed the improbability of similar wording (Bock, *Studying*, 171).

3. McKnight, "Streeter," 75–77.

4. Goodacre, *Synoptic*, 56; Bock, *Blasphemy*, 185; Bock, *Historical*, 173; Muller, "Reception," 318.

5. France, *Mark*, 37; Beavis, *Mark*, 6; Guelich, *Mark*, xxviii.

6. Garrett warns us not to mistake brevity for lack of emphasis (*Temptations*, 59). The early placement, his use of the strong word ἐκβάλλει, and his integration of Jesus' baptism with the testing show its importance to Mark. Satan's temptations prefigure those of Jesus' political opponents to compromise himself (Myers, *Binding*, 130). It is difficult to see this. I argued in s3.4 that it is better to see this as Satan, having been

eleven verses in Matthew 4:1–11 and thirteen in Luke 4:1–13. It is hard to see how Mark could have known passages on Jesus resisting evil, and only used four words which say very little. It is more likely that Matthews and Luke expanded Mark. Last, Goodacre argues that "editorial fatigue" shows Markan priority when Matthew and Luke inconsistently include Markan material; e.g., the narrative of John the Baptist's death (Matt 14) which omits the crucial role of Herodias in Mark, and Luke 19's parable of the ten pounds which assumes just three servants.[7] I make no findings on the relationship of Matt, Luke, or John apart from Mark preceding them all.

4.2. Narratives with Judas's presence at key points in Jesus' ministry

I will discuss:

- The call of the Twelve;
- Jesus teaching the Twelve[8] the meaning of the parable of the sower;
- Jesus sending out the Twelve on mission and them reporting back to him;
- the feeding of the five thousand;
- the warning that the greatest in the kingdom must be servant of all; and
- the third prediction of his death.

---

defeated in and cast out of heaven, attempting to defeat Jesus on earth, but failing.

7. Goodacre, "Fatigue," 45. Foster, "Q," 328–30. I reject Matthean priority as per Farmer ("Case"), where Luke uses Matthew as a source and Mark uses both. It gives no reason for Mark writing if he is little more than a copyist (Osborne, "Response," 143), it ignores orality, and it smakes Luke wholly dependent on Matthew when Luke 1:2 mentions many sources (Gerhardsson, *Memory*; Allison, *Resurrecting*).

Huggins supports Markan priority, but believes that Matthew used Luke as a source, which neatly resolves the minor agreements ("Posteriority," 1). Schultz provides further support for Luke incorporating existing material by arguing that Jesus is alluding to Archelaus in Luke 19:12 when passing by the Herodian Palaces on the Jericho-Jerusalem road, to forestall any Messianic expectations by the crowd ("Archelaus," 118).

8. Mark and John prefer "the Twelve" absolutely—not, for example, "the twelve disciples" (Meier, "Twelve," 637).

4.2.1. The call of the Twelve[9]
(Mark 3:13-19;[10] Matt 10:1-4; Luke 6:12-16)

Mark

All exegetes highlight the disciples' importance.[11] From his first appearance in 1:16, "Jesus is seldom alone."[12] The call of the Twelve from the wider circle of Jesus' μαθηταὶ distinguishes those close to Jesus from the crowd, who are undecided about Jesus but given a way to be closer to him. Guelich notes "the prominence given the disciples" in the gospel's structure.[13] Hawkin has 1:14—6:34 showing "the two-pronged theme of the rejection of Jesus by his own and his acceptance by the nucleus of a new people."[14]

An inclusion (two pages on) (Mark 3:9—4:1) describes Jesus' separation from the crowd by geography or a boat. The verses in contrasting pairs show the meaning of insider/outsider (s3.3.5) and how this distance might be bridged. Mark's narrative passes through a number of points to detail Judas's shift from being an insider to an outsider.

First, Mark uses a number of features to separate the Twelve from others who encounter Jesus. He has mentioned the crowd twice: they obstruct the friends bringing the paralysed man (2:4) and Jesus taught them after they praised God for the healing (2:13). "Crowd" could seem slightly negative in that while they can listen to Jesus' teaching, important events like the call of the Twelve are done in their absence (3:13).[15]

Secondly, it is important to note those close to Jesus and those at a distance. Uniquely, Mark's Jesus called the Twelve to be "with him" (3:14),[16]

---

9. It is reasonable to see the Twelve as existing during Jesus' lifetime (ibid., 671).

10. Mark is considered first because of Markan priority.

11. Ellingworth notes Mark's strong preference for "His disciples" ("Disciples," 114–26).

12. France, *Mark*, 27.

13. Guelich, *Mark*, xl. Bock believes that, if the author is John Mark, his experience of leaving Paul under pressure in Acts 13:13 may be reflected in his depiction of the disciples' struggles in Mark 6–14 (*Mark*).

14. Hawkin, "Disciples," 495. The covenantal λαός replaces Mark's ὄχλος in Luke 20:45 (Minear, "Audience," 84).

15. Myers, *Binding*, 156.

16. Without wishing to interpret Mark by John, Martin argues, without understating the enormity of Judas's betrayal of Jesus, that his departure from Jesus may be his defining feature in John ("Judas," 145). He is the only one of the Twelve who joins the defectors (6:66–71). Ἀπῆλθον εἰς τὰ ὀπίσω links the defection in 6:66 with Judas in 18:6. Judas's failure to be "with" Jesus means that he is not cleansed (13:7–11), he is excluded from Jesus' blessing (13:15–18), Jesus' teaching (chs 14–16), and his prayer for protection (17:12). The new commandment as evidence of being Jesus' disciples is only

in his presence.[17] By contrast, his earthly family are "outside" (3:20-21,[18] 3:31-35).[19] This Markan sandwich, with severe warnings against attributing the work of God to evil, highlights Jesus' opposition. His family are apparent insiders who behave like outsiders. Mark 3:20 contrasts them with the crowd who sit at Jesus' feet and listen (3:31). Being outsiders, they must send someone in to call Jesus. They are not as bad as the scribes facing an unforgivable sin for attributing Jesus' work to evil.[20] The final opponent is Judas, the insider who will act as an outsider by handing Jesus over (3:19). Mark contrasts him with the crowd, apparent outsiders, who listen to Jesus (3:32) and are offered a way in (3:34). In summary, the distinction is between apparent insiders (Judas, Jesus' family, and the teachers) who are actually outsiders and apparent outsiders (the crowd) who sit at Jesus' feet as insiders.

In the LXX, God was usually the subject of "hand over" (Appendix 1). When a human was the subject, there were strictly limited conditions, like handing over the accused for trial (Deut 19:12). Mark gave a negative nuance to παραδίδωμι in John the Baptist's jailing (1:14),[21] so John and Jesus should have been charged with some crimes, but were not. John was executed due to Herod's promise to Herodias's daughter,[22] and Jesus was

---

given after he leaves (13:34-35). John's use of τρώγω links 13:18 with 6:54-58, showing Jesus' foreknowledge (Oropeza, *Footsteps*, 1:182).

17. Guelich, *Mark*, 158.

18. His own family and the scribes are trying to prevent Jesus obeying his calling from God. Jesus must relativize his relationships with his family for the sake of the kingdom (Ahearne-Kroll, "Family," 1-25).

19. The narratives about Jesus' family frame an accusation that he is demonized (Resseguie, *Narrative*, 55). It is very optimistic to limit "my mother and my brothers" to the all-male Twelve (Lane, *Mark*, 148).

20. Twelftree, "Blasphemy." Contra Busch, who argues that Jesus' assault on Satan's kingdom is an "inside job" because if, as Jesus says, Satan's kingdom will fall due to civil war, then Jesus' assaults are "demonic" ("Questioning," 485, 484). This odd reasoning fails to distinguish between Satan's kingdom falling because of civil war and other reasons, like Jesus' assaults. Mark never implies that Jesus and Satan are allies.

21. France, *Mark*, 163; Beavis, *Mark*, 43. Luke 3:20 ascribes John's arrest to Herod.

22. Discrepancies between the evangelists and between them and Josephus mean that Mark and Matthew reveal nothing useful on the acts of Herodias and her daughter (Kraemer, "Herodias," 345). He believes Herod's execution of John the Baptist is a Christian literary device to refute any idea that Jesus was John redivivus (ibid., 322), as decapitation made resurrection impossible (ibid., 341). However, he argues for the centrality of John's baptism of Jesus making this impossible, as both were alive at the same time (ibid., 348). There is thus no need for Kraemer's hypothesis on the method of execution. Secondly, I argued in s4.1 that editorial fatigue could explain Matthew's use of Mark, as much as Kraemer's Matthew doing textual surgery on Mark. Finally, he is probably on safer ground to note Herodias's manipulation of a weak Herod, although

executed despite everyone affirming his innocence. Both Herod and Judas usurped God's right to hand over.

Lastly, Jesus said that whoever obeys God can be as close to him as family (3:34),[23] significant in a family-centric culture.[24] He addresses the crowd (3:32), so outsiders can become insiders, "His true family,"[25] by following Jesus in obeying God. Jesus is forming a gap between himself and the crowd, his own family, and the scribes (in increasing degree of being "outsiders") not so that they might be excluded, but so that they might cross that gap through commitment to the will of the Father.

Mark

3:9 "because of the crowd"   separation[a]

3:13 "departed"   A physical separation between Jesus and the crowd.

3:14 "be with him"   Apostles appointed to be close to Jesus.

   3:19 "who betrayed Him"   An insider who becomes an outsider.

      3:20 "into"   Jesus inside the home.

         3:22–30   Presumed insiders, teachers of the law, who show their outsider status by accusing Jesus of being possessed.

      3:31 "outside"   Apparent insiders who remain outside.

3:32 "crowd around"   The crowd are normally outsiders.

3:32 "outside"   As for 3:31; Markan sandwich: 3:20–21 and 3:31–35.

3:35 "around him"   The crowd can be true insiders if they obey.

4:1 "got into a boat"   Jesus and the crowd are separated (4:1).[b]

a. This withdrawal provides the pattern for Matt's schema of "threefold pattern of hostility/withdrawal/prophetic fulfillment" (Good, "Verb," 1–12).

---

he had said that this was unhistorical (ibid., 346). I showed in s3.2.3 that (powerless) Herod was like an idol, a human rival to God, swayed either by the crowd (Acts 8) or, here, his wife.

23. It is overstating matters to say that there is "mutual alienation" between Jesus and his earthly family (Myers, *Binding*, 168), but rather Jesus' family must understand their new (lower) place in his life.

24. Beavis, *Mark*, 69.

25. France, *Mark*, 179–80.

b. This is more about tensions between the Pauline church and the Jerusalem church run by Mary and James, etc., as shown by gaps in the editing as 4:9, "whoever has ears," implies that some could hear contrary to 4:11–12 and 4:36 ("He was already in the boat") without any explanation how (Goulder, "Outside," 289–302). Neither carry much weight, as the first treats the narrative as a pretext for the ecclesiastical situation when Mark was writing and fails to see that Matt and Luke also have confronting statements about the purpose of the parables, but without Mark's pronounced insider/outsider distinction. The second point is an argument from silence. If it was important for the narrative, presumably Mark would have said so. The narrative makes sense as is, and highlights the distinction between insider and outsider. Thirdly, to say that "Jesus' family are in some way aligned with the scribes" (ibid., 295) is extreme.

Support for this is the next inclusion which starts in 4:2 with "many . . . parables" and ends in 4:33 with "many . . . similar parables" (Myers, *Binding*, 170). The three sea incidents, (1) calming the sea (4:35–41), (2) walking on the sea (6:45–52), and (3) conversation about loaves in the boat (8:13–21), group 4:1—8:21 into two sets of five miracles, which can be misunderstood like the parables (Malbon, "Echoes," 214, 218).

Matthew

There are only a few differences between Matthew and Mark. The first is the use of authority. Both record Jesus healing the paralytic as an expression of his authority (Matt 9:6; Mark 2:10),[26] which is "empirically verifiable."[27] While Mark 2:12 has the crowds glorifying God, Matthew 9:8 records the crowd glorifying God, "who had given such authority to men." The key difference in Matthew's use of authority is the centurion (8:9), who recognized the link between being under and exercising authority.[28] This prepares the way for the appointment of the Twelve, who will be asked both to receive authority from Jesus and then to exercise it (Matt 10:1, 8).

Secondly, Matthew 10:1 has ὥστε against Mark 3:14's ἵνα for Jesus giving authority to the Twelve.[29] ὥστε stresses the result of receiving authority, to

---

26. Horsley, illustrating his thesis that "miracle" is a modern construct that was foreign to ancient cultures who saw no distinction between the natural and the supernatural (*Magic*, 122, 8), argues that Jesus broke the connection between the man's sin and self-blame and his paralysis. It is debatable whether his conclusion that this shows humanity's ability to forgive sin fully explains the crowd's ἐξίστασθαι (2:12), elsewhere used of reactions to Jesus raising a dead girl or stilling the storm (Mark 5:42; 6:51).

27. Keener, *Matthew*, 290.

28. Ibid., 267.

29. Result: Blass and Debrunner, *Grammar*, 369; purpose: ibid., 391.

exorcize and heal.³⁰ We might conclude that, for obedient disciples, purpose and result could be much the same.³¹ It is better to note that, in Mark, ἵνα applies to both being with Jesus and also being sent out, as the two purpose clauses flowing from ἐποίησεν.³² Matt stresses the result of authority, rather than having been with Jesus, which is more relevant for later generations who could not have been with him, but could still exercise authority in his name.

Thirdly, Jesus warns the Twelve about persecution after instructing them for their first ministry tour. Matthew 10:4 calls Judas the one "who also betrayed him," and then has Jesus describing the persecutions awaiting the Twelve. The narrative ends at 11:1: "When Jesus had finished giving orders to his twelve disciples."³³ Jesus would suffer the same persecutions of being brought before kings and governors, of being flogged, etc., because Judas handed him over. This is arguably why these warnings are placed so early and in so much detail in Matthew, when actual persecution for the apostles lay years in the future.³⁴

Matthew is similar to Mark, but without the inside/outside feature, which is not as pronounced in Matthew 12:46–50.³⁵ His emphasis on people exercising Jesus' authority and being persecuted like him might reflect the later experience of the church.

Luke

Luke is quite different from Matthew and Mark, in that the insider/outsider and authority themes are absent. He introduces two new but not unexpected elements: Jesus prayed all night to God beforehand, and Judas is described unambiguously as "traitor," not just as he "who handed Jesus over."

Nolland sees the call narrative as the culmination of 5:1—6:16's structure of seven units. Calls are in the first (Simon, James, and John), the middle

---

30. The aim was to expel them, not to command their obedience (Davies and Allison, *Matthew*, 2:152).

31. Blass and Debrunner, *Grammar*, 391(3).

32. Guelich, *Mark*, 3:14; Blass and Debrunner, *Grammar*, 392(1e).

33. Matthew's refrain "when Jesus had finished" divides the gospel into five major discourses, each with a prologue and epilogue: 7:28–29; 11:1; 13:53; 19:1; and 26:1 (Resseguie, *Revelation*, 44).

34. Hagner "eschatological trouble" (*Matthew 1–13*, 10:22). Despite the specific nature of Matthew's Jesus' words to the Twelve, Matthew could also be addressing his readers' situation.

35. This is editorial fatigue, with Matthew copying from Mark, but forgetting that he did not describe Jesus as entering a house (Goodacre, "Fatigue," 48).

(Levi), and the last (the Twelve).³⁶ Only one name is in doubt: Thaddaeus or Judas son of James, which could be the Greek and patronymic names of the same person.³⁷ Having been called (including Judas) by Jesus, they are to call others to salvation.

Jesus spent the "whole night" (ἦν διανυκτερεύων) praying and then chose twelve apostles (Luke 6:12). This is the only time when Jesus is said to be awake all night, although he may have been awake all night before crucifixion.³⁸ Luke records many of Jesus' prayers, but this is the only time when he specifically prayed "to God." This is redundant:³⁹ to whom else would he pray? It highlights the importance of the occasion and Jesus' reliance on the Father. It was not Jesus who chose Judas so much as he obeyed God in calling Judas.⁴⁰ Did Jesus know from the start that Judas would turn traitor? There are a variety of pictures of Jesus' foreknowledge. Luke does not say, unlike Mark 13:32, which suggests that Jesus was only ignorant of when he would return. John 6:64 does seem decisive that Jesus did know.

Most damningly, Luke calls Judas⁴¹ προδότης or traitor (6:16),⁴² whose graphic power denies any ambiguous understandings of παραδίδωμι. Another NT use is⁴³ Stephen's penultimate accusation against the Sanhedrin of betraying and murdering Jesus (Acts 7:52): "without . . . 'mitigation by ignorance.'"⁴⁴ The GNT says "traitors and murderers you became," with an emphatic ὑμεῖς. This is paralleled in Luke 6:16 with Judas, who "became a traitor." The common vocabulary is a serious indictment of Judas, who is likened to a Sanhedrin who are guiltier than their ancestors⁴⁵ and who also handed over an innocent man, Stephen, to death (Acts 7:56).

---

36. Nolland, *Luke 1—9:20*, 264.

37. Bauckham, *Eyewitnesses*, 100-101. The name and patronymic should be enough differentiation from the traitor (Guelich, *Mark*, 3:18-19).

38. While not stated directly, there seems an unbroken series of events until "daybreak" (Luke 22:66).

39. Nolland (tactfully) calls it unusual (*Luke 1—9:20*, 6:12). Fitzmyer: "its awkwardness" (*Luke I-IX*, 616).

40. Marshall, *Luke*, 238.

41. Iscariot is derived from the Aramaic "the false one," evidencing unfaithfulness (ibid., 240).

42. Resseguie does not allow for this when arguing that παραδίδωμι is not treachery (*Narrative*, 159).

43. Its only LXX occurrences are the extra-canonical 2 and 3 Maccabees.

44. Johnson, *Acts*, 134.

45. Marshall, "Acts," 147.

For Klassen, Luke "deviates from his source" by calling Judas traitor.[46] He gives no evidence; it may make his argument more difficult, and he feels bound to oppose it. He does not show how he knew Luke's source or ask why Luke changed a less incriminating source,[47] a serious omission. Klassen says that this is "the only text in the New Testament in which Judas is called a traitor,"[48] as though it needs no response. Luke uses the same word for Judas as Josephus did for his treachery at Jotapata (which Klassen admits),[49] so a better explanation is needed. Josephus's (anguished) speech to his troops shows the pressure he felt and his awareness of the accusation of treachery (s2.3.7).[50]

Conclusions

The Markan account shows Judas's guilt established beyond reasonable doubt from the first. He contrasts Judas with the crowd, who are normally seen as outsiders but are offered a closer relationship with Jesus, even becoming his true family, by obeying the Father. By contrast, Judas, an apparent insider, is an outsider who will hand Jesus over. The normal LXX meaning of παραδίδωμι, plus the unsettling example of John the Baptist, leave little doubt that this is meant negatively. Matthew's account is similar to Mark, but with added emphases: like the centurion, the Twelve must accept Jesus' authority and use it. While Jesus warns them of future persecution, the early placement of this text, so soon after the mention of Judas's betrayal, may indicate that Jesus would experience these persecutions through Judas handing him over. Luke's account stresses that the selection of Judas was in response to Jesus praying, and that Judas is clearly called προδότης. In summary, Mark and Luke clearly establish Judas's guilt, and Matthew only slightly less.

---

46. Klassen, *Friend*, 116.

47. Klassen assumes that a later source must be wrong. A later source may clarify what an earlier source only implies. He suggested that Mark also blackened Judas's name by adapting his sources (ibid., 80).

48. Ibid., 116.

49. Ibid., 116.

50. For Josephus, παραδίδωμι and προδίδωμι can refer to the same incident: *J.W.* 4.521, 523 (s2.2.2).

4.2.2. Jesus teaching the Twelve: Insider Status (Mark 4:10-33; Matt 13:10-23; Luke 8:9-15)

All the synoptics agree that, some time after choosing the Twelve, Jesus spoke privately to them about the parable of the sower. While Matthew 13:10 and Luke 8:9 mention disciples, Mark 4:10 explicitly says that the Twelve and others around Jesus asked about the parable. While Matthew and Luke insert chapters of positive interactions between Jesus and outsiders, as Jesus showed God's nature and then gave his confronting explanation of the purpose of the parables, Mark's abruptness highlights the Twelve's insider status.

Mark

I showed Mark's inside/outside theme above,[51] where Judas and Jesus' family, usually considered insiders, are shown as outsiders, while the crowd, considered outsiders, are given a way in by obeying God (3:35). This (abrupt) motif forms the heart of this text and increases Judas's culpability. Petersen argues that Mark 4–8 is best seen as cycles of three. In the A cycle (e.g., 4:1-34) Jesus acts; the B cycle (e.g., 4:35-41) shows the disciples' incomprehension; while the C cycle (5:1-20) shows outsiders' (understandable) incomprehension.[52] Unlike obvious outsiders like the scribes, Judas is an apparent insider who particularly fulfills Jesus' prediction that some will be "ever seeing but never perceiving, and ever hearing but never understanding" (4:12). While the Eleven deserted Jesus, only Judas betrayed him for money (14:11).

In 4:10 and 34; Jesus taught plainly to "those around Him," a "reminiscence of 3:31-35,"[53] but in 4:11 "those on the outside" hear parables, lest they turn and be forgiven.[54] The seeming harshness may mask some relevant facts. Despite being with Jesus, even insiders may not understand,[55] as misunderstanding is a constant across all four gospels. The point is "the receptivity of the hearers."[56] Insiders only hear because they had previously been called into his presence and responded. Outsiders may become insiders by obeying God (3:35). The meaning of the "will of God" is unclear, as

---

51. Hawkin, "Disciples," 496-97.
52. Petersen, "Composition," 205, 214.
53. Guelich, *Mark*, 4:10; France, *Mark*, 194.
54. Malbon, "Echoes," 217; Petersen, "Composition," 207; Hawkin, "Disciples," 497.
55. Guelich, *Mark*, 4:10.
56. France, *Mark*, 198. With the increasing visibility of the kingdom, the present verdict may only be temporary, leading to eventual repentance (ibid., 201).

most religious people would claim this as an aim, but in context, may mean sharing with Jesus in proclaiming the kingdom.[57] These confronting verses preserve God's sovereignty.[58] As shown above, this process of teaching creates a gap between people and Jesus, which Jesus wants them to cross (Mark 3:35),[59] but which is not necessarily bridged by just being with Jesus.

Matthew

Rather than Mark's abrupt transition from choosing the Twelve, then a warning on the unforgivable sin to the parable of the sower, Matthew includes two chapters which distinguish between apparent insiders and outsiders. The lost sheep of Israel may reject the Twelve and their message (10:14).[60] They would be worse off at judgment than sinful Sodom and Gomorrah (10:15).[61] Families, the ultimate insiders, will betray their own (10:21),[62] and the Twelve may even witness to the ultimate outsiders, Gentiles (10:18). The text continues with Tyre and Sidon faring better at judgment than Korazin and Bethsaida (11:21) before dealing with two outsiders: a man in need of healing (12:10) and a demoniac (12:22). The passage concludes with the ultimate insider/outsider contrast: Jesus' family, who are outside (12:47).

Having established that apparent insiders may reject or not understand (10:14; 12:10) God, and that outsiders may be advantaged, only then does Matthew's Jesus give the parable and interpretation. Hagner argues that, while the participles can be understood concessively as "although seeing," the finite verbs speak of willfulness, or "they will not see."[63] In Matthew, the reader is better prepared, having seen Jesus ministering to apparent insiders/outsiders in previous chapters. Matthew 13:13's ὅτι indicates that the parables are to help, not hinder, understanding.[64] Jesus takes the initiative to preach to people (11:1), and imbues the disciples with a sense of urgency. God is not arbitrarily hardening people against their will.[65]

57. Ibid., 180.

58. This is Jesus' judicial response to stubbornness of heart (Watts, "Mark," 155).

59. Contra Hawkin ("Disciples," 498) who sees no explanation for the hardening.

60. They followed Jewish practice, where Jews shook off the dust of Gentile lands when entering Israel or even the (presumably higher grade) Jerusalem dust when entering the temple (Keener, *Matthew*, 320).

61. Hagner, *Matthew 1–13*, 10:15.

62. In an honor-shame culture, it was "an incomparably high allegiance" to Jesus (Keener, *Matthew*, 324).

63. Hagner, *Matthew 1–13*, 13:13.

64. Davies and Allison, *Matthew*, 2:392.

65. Given that the rejection appears to be solely from Jewish listeners, it may not

Luke

Luke is similar to Matthew in emphasis. After calling the Twelve (Luke 6), Jesus gives the Sermon on the Plain, saying that some unlikely people are insiders: the poor,[66] the hungry, the persecuted, etc., but that some apparent insiders are on the outer: the rich, the popular, and so forth. Luke then gives examples of outsiders who should be treated well: enemies, the centurion's servant, the sick, etc. Standard views of status are subverted. Obedience and faith are highlighted as essential. By the time Jesus gives the Parable of the Sower and its interpretation (Luke 8:9–15), the reader has the context to interpret Jesus' confronting words not as heartless rejection, but as the words of a God who will not compromise on sin. Jesus sows the seed of the kingdom extravagantly and challenges each member of the crowd to respond.[67]

Judas, having personal access to Jesus, is more culpable than the crowd, as he could hear Jesus' explanations, something denied the crowd. He may illustrate two negative categories in the parable. Jesus said that certain people were like seed sown on a path, where the Devil took the seed away (Luke 8:12).[68] Judas is one of only a small number of people in the NT who are closely associated with Satan (Luke 22:3).[69] Secondly, Jesus said that the seed would be choked by "life's . . . riches" (8:12). Judas was paid to betray Jesus (Luke 22:5). Judas is thus closely associated with both Satan and money, the demonic and material rivals to God respectively.

Conclusion

The earliest account in Mark is stark in moving directly from Jesus calling the Twelve through the confronting teaching on Beelzebub to Jesus' family, apparent insiders who remain outside, to the parable of the sower. Arguably, Judas will ultimately be revealed as the best example of Jesus' warning: those who see but do not perceive, showing that neither physical nor relational (his family) proximity is adequate alone. Matthew 10–12 and Luke 6–7 maintain this theme, but soften Mark's starkness with chapters of narratives of Jesus ministering to classic outsiders: Gentiles, the demonized, and the

---

be unreasonable to see this as an early outworking of Paul's emphasis in Rom 9–11 that a hardening came upon Israel, that the message of the gospel might go from them to the Gentiles, that the church might not be wholly Jewish.

66. This most likely means, like the MT and LXX, non-economic dependence on God (s3.5.3).

67. Nolland, *Luke 1—9:20*, 8:8.

68. Bock, *Luke*, 733.

69. Parsons, *Luke*, 135.

ill. Matthew 10 has Israel rejecting the Twelve and families betraying their own, and Luke 8 has Jesus ministering to classic outsiders like the Gerasene demoniac. This highlights Judas's guilt by contrast, as none of the aforementioned groups had anything like Judas's access to Jesus. These passages foreshadow Judas's actions, especially if we assume that the Jesus narrative is one in which the main details are already known by the readers, rather than being discovered for the first time.

4.2.3. Jesus sends the Twelve out (Mark 6:6b–13; Matt 10:5–10; Luke 9:1–6)

After calling and giving the Twelve further teaching and demonstrating his authority in various miracles, Jesus sent them on mission. Given the similarity between the three accounts, I will discuss these narratives thematically.

Firstly, each evangelist says explicitly that "the Twelve" were present (Matt 10:5; Mark 6:7; Luke 9:1).[70] Mark 6:7[71] alone records that Jesus sent them out[72] in pairs.[73] Both Mark and Luke record that the apostles, which must include Judas, returned to Jesus and "reported to Jesus all that they had done" (Luke 9:10). Mark 6:30 adds the phrase "and taught,"[74] showing his stress on Jesus' teaching and the close link between his ministry and theirs.[75] This apparently minor fact increases Judas's culpability as an insider. He apparently used the same authority as the Eleven[76] with similar success, as he was not singled out for censure.

70. Luke 9:1 and 10 is most likely for the close identification of the Twelve and the apostles. Apostle was not indiscriminate, but was not limited to the Twelve, as Paul was an apostle but not one of the Twelve (Meier, "Twelve," 641). Luke 9:1–50 prefigures 9:51–19:44 as the prophet Jesus recapitulates and consummates Moses' journey in Deuteronomy, particularly the necessity of Moses' death: Deut 1:37, 3:27, 4:21 (Moessner, "Preview," 582).

71. Texts on the mission of the Twelve frame the death of John the Baptist (Resseguie, *Revelation*, 55).

72. A link to the call scene was one of the two purposes in Jesus' call (Guelich, *Mark*, 6:7).

73. "Providing mutual support and companionship" (France, *Mark*, 247); Capper, "Goods," 73.

74. In Mark, "apostle" is someone sent out on a mission, like the Twelve (Meier, "Twelve," 639). Once they return, Mark does not use "apostle" again. Mark's "bare summary" of their mission means a relative lack of interest compared with the call to a discipleship of the cross (8:27–30; Myers, *Binding*, 213).

75. Guelich, *Mark*, 6:30.

76. It is a sharing of Jesus' authority, with those who had been "with him" (France, *Mark*, 248).

Next, Jesus' instructions include warnings which could function proleptically regarding Judas. He apparently taught to others what he did not apply personally. Mark 6:7 and Luke 9:1[77] agree that Jesus gave them authority over unclean spirits/demons, while Matthew 10:8 has Jesus' command to "drive out demons."[78] Mark 6:13 and Luke 9:6 record their success in exorcism. The evangelists never say how aware Judas was of Satan's role in the betrayal, but he could not claim ignorance of the potential for possession or satanic entrapment, as he had heard and seen Jesus' teaching and ministry concerning evil and done the same himself, but eventually failed to avoid evil personally.

Thirdly, all the evangelists have Jesus' warning about money (Mark 6:8; Matt 10:9; Luke 9:3).[79] This is at least a warning not to be encumbered materially, but to let God provide via "the beneficiaries of their ministry."[80] Jesus had already taught clearly on the blessedness of poverty of spirit (Matt 5:3; Luke 6:12; s3.5.4) and the dangers of wealth (Matt 6:19; Luke 6:24),[81] concluding with the stark "You cannot serve both God and Mammon" (Matt 6:24). It is notable that Matthew has this warning early, like that of persecution, so that Judas is a candidate to fulfill it, while Luke 16:13 has his parallel warning closer to Jesus' teaching to his disciples on the Mount of Olives. Judas would have heard all these warnings before the ministry tour, and as he is not stated as an exception to Mark 6:30, we may conclude that he also taught the dangers of wealth. Taking money to betray Jesus showed that he had not learned this lesson (Matt 26:16; Mark 14:11; Luke 22:5).[82]

Fourthly, they "preached that people should repent" (μετανοῶσιν; Mark 6:12), mirroring Jesus' first recorded words: "Repent and believe" (Mark 1:15).[83] Mark does not mention Judas after Gethsemane, but Matthew does not say that Judas repented when, remorseful, μεταμεληθείς,

---

77. Luke adds "all," highlighting their later failure in 9:40, "they could not" (Nolland, *Luke 1—9:20*, 9:1).

78. This is no weakening of authority because Matthew had just recorded the singular example of the centurion's understanding of authority (8:9), an outsider who is more praiseworthy than many insiders.

79. I covered the intensification of the dangers of wealth from OT to NT in s3.5.

80. Guelich, *Mark*, 6:10; Myers, *Binding*, 213.

81. "Mammon is the negative counterpart of God" (Bovon, *Studies*, 192). Matthew's more negative view of possessions is seen in Jesus not letting the Twelve take sandals or staff (10:10; Keener, *Matthew*, 318).

82. Oropeza, *Footsteps*, 1:76. He earned money at the cost of eternal life (ibid.,1:37).

83. The message of the Twelve would sound very similar to the message of John (France, *Mark*, 250), although he fails to note the extra elements of exorcism and healing, which John did not demonstrate.

he threw the money back into the temple (Matt 27:3-4).[84] It has five GNT uses. Two texts show that the person has changed their mind: the first son did go to work, and Judas threw the money into the temple (Matt 21:29,[85] 27:3). The other three uses are negative, showing no change in the person's/ group's mindset. In Matthew 21:32, the crowds hear that others will enter the kingdom ahead of them because they rejected John the Baptist. In 2 Corinthians 7:8, Paul tells the Corinthians that he does not regret causing them pain by his letter.[86] Lastly, in Hebrews 7:21, God will not change his mind. The positive uses show a mere change of mind, but no evidence of actual repentance of sin, which seems to be ignored. The negative uses show that the subject will not even take the first step toward changing their mind, much less repentance. Merenlahti has thus no warrant for saying of Judas "he repents," and that his suicide "looks like an effort to make amends."[87] Klassen cannot say that Judas "seeks repentance," but only that he may be heading toward repentance but commits suicide instead.[88] True repentance is better shown by μετάνοια.[89] Judas apparently failed to absorb Jesus' teaching on repentance.

Conclusion

Jesus' teaching at the sending out of the Twelve foreshadows some issues which figure later in Judas's betrayal: the dangers of evil and money and the need for repentance. Given the importance of these issues, it is significant that he is not singled out for censure on returning from the mission. Apparently, he taught and applied these teachings while on mission. The subsequent course of his life shows a close connection with both evil and money in betraying Jesus, and an inability to repent, even when he realized the enormity of his crime. Jesus strongly warned "his disciples" that

---

84. The response of the chief priests to Judas, σὺ ὄψῃ, is very similar to Pilate's response to the crowd, ὑμεῖς ὄψεσθε (Matt 27:4, 24; Bond, *Pilate*, 134). Oropeza (*Footsteps*, 1:76-77) thinks that Judas may have repented, but μεταμεληθείς argues against this.

85. Hagner optimistically sees this as "repent" (*Matthew 14-28*, 21:29), which requires addressing the original error, not just changing course.

86. See s4.2.4 for the parallels between Herod and Judas. Interestingly, 2 Cor 7:9-10 has λύπη, λυπέω, and μετάνοια, as Paul contrasts godly grief leading to repentance, which Judas is not said to do, with worldly grief leading to death, which happened to Judas. There is no evidence that Judas repented.

87. Merenlahti, "Characters," 61.

88. Klassen (*Friend*, 103) neither asks nor answers why, if Judas is obeying Jesus, there is any regret at all.

89. Blomberg, "Matthew," 95.

the consequences of hearing but not obeying him would be like the total destruction of a house (Luke 6:20, 49). Professed discipleship is assumed from the double "Lord, Lord" (Luke 6:46).[90] This severe warning comes after the call of the Twelve but before their ministry.

4.2.4. Feeding the five thousand (Mark 6:30-44; Matt 14:13-21; Luke 9:10-17)

The Feeding Narratives have much in common, but Mark and Matthew seem closer than Luke. Context is vital for interpretation, as both Mark and Matthew precede the feeding with Herod's feast. The main themes present in Herod's feast (a host who presumes to act like God by sending an innocent man to death [which God never did]) and the feeding (another host, Jesus, provides for God's people) coalesce in the Last Supper because of the many, telling parallels between Herod and Judas. At the Last Supper, Jesus as host provides for his people and a leader of God's people, while Judas sends an innocent man to death. In other words, the parallel is not eucharistic, but rather between Herod and Judas in their respective roles in the deaths of the innocent John the Baptist and Jesus in the context of a meal. Herod and Judas are paralleled as treacherous leaders under the old and new covenants respectively. We first consider Mark and Matthew.

Mark and Matthew

Immediately prior to the feeding, Mark and Matthew record Herod's birthday feast, during which he was incited to behead John the Baptist. Herod's treatment of John the Baptist arguably foreshadows Judas's treatment of Jesus. There are numerous parallels. Both are likened to God by presuming to act like God, in the act of handing over innocent people to custody (which, again, God never did; Herod: Mark 1:14; Matt 4:12; Judas: Mark 14:10; Matt 26:16), and the passive tense[91] is used in both cases (John: Mark 1:14; Matt 4:12; Jesus: Mark 9:31). Both start a series of events causing the death of an innocent man (Herod: Mark 6:26;[92] Matt 14:9; Judas: Mark 14:44; Matt

---

90. Nolland, *Luke 1—9:20*, 6:46.

91. This signifies God's purposes in John's imprisonment and death, paralleling the Son of Man (Guelich, *Mark*, 1:14). So also Hagner (*Matthew 1-13*, 4:12).

92. France, *Mark*, 259. Pilate makes a similar rash decision under crowd pressure (Mark 15:14-15; Guelich, *Mark*, 6:26).

27:3), as Herod betrays his responsibility to uphold the law[93] and Judas betrays Jesus. Both regret deeply what they have done (Herod:[94] Mark 6:26; Matt 14:9; Judas: Matt 27:4).

Mark uses περίλυπος for Herod's distress at having to order John's execution and Jesus' distress preparing for death in Gethsemane (6:26; 14:34). Matt uses λυπέω similarly for the disciples' reaction to Jesus' prediction of his death (17:23) which are juxtaposed[95] with uses at the Last Supper (26:22),[96] Gethsemane (26:37),[97] and the unforgiving servant (18:31). The words show grief which is intense,[98] apparently unavoidable, and linked with death. Judas's remorse after the betrayal led him to suicide (Matt 27:5). Both accounts are followed by Jesus walking on the water, with his veiled claim to deity, ἐγώ εἰμι (Mark 6:50; Matt 14:27). Matt expands Mark's account so that the disciples venerate him as the Son of God (Matt 14:33). Finally, both suffer an untimely death at God's hand (Herod: Acts 12:20–23;[99] Judas: Acts 1:18). Both opposed the infant church and failed. There are two differences: Herod ordered John's death, while Judas betrayed Jesus to his enemies; and Herod was host at his meal, unlike Judas. However, the similarities are far more meaningful than any differences.

Given the same context in Mark and Matthew of a death-feeding-nature miracle and the parallels between the two texts, any alleged comparisons[100] between Jesus' actions with the bread at the feeding and the Last

93. "Parody on the shameless methods of decision-making among the elite" (Myers, *Binding*, 216).

94. Jewish law had devised ways of breaking oaths so that greater evil did not result, but Herod was more concerned with his honor (Keener, *Matthew*, 401). See also Hagner (*Matthew 14–28*). It is editorial fatigue by Matthew, and evidence for Markan priority, as Matthew omits Herodias's role, thus making Herod's grief difficult to understand given his desire to kill John (14:5; Goodacre, "Fatigue," 46–47).

95. Hagner, *Matthew 14–28*, 17:23.

96. Judas is never said to call Jesus "Lord," only "Rabbi" Matt 26:22, 25, 49 (Resseguie, *Revelation*, 181).

97. Jesus was dying as "the bearer of sin" (Hagner, *Matthew 14–28*, 26:37).

98. Jesus: his grief could (almost) kill him (Keener, *Matthew*, 637). So Evans, *Mark 8:27—16:20*, 14:34.

99. The man who shone outwardly was rotting away inwardly (Fernando, *Acts*, 364).

100. Hagner, *Matthew 14–28*, 14:18–19. Nolland's convoluted and unconvincing explanation: "He [Jesus] then handles the food in a manner evocative of the Last Supper and therefore of eucharistic practice. Luke handles differently from Mark the difficulty of paralleling the bread and the fish: he drops separate description of the distribution of the fish and of the fragments left over; at the same time he adds 'them' to Mark's 'blessed,' probably intending that the following language, despite being better suited to the bread, should, nevertheless, be applied equally to the fish" (*Luke 1—9:20*, 9:10).

Supper require far more than shared words. The feeding has no mention of wine or Jesus' death, and Jesus' taking, blessing, breaking, and distributing the bread are ubiquitous, done by the father at every meal in a Jewish home;[101] it is improbable that they are meant eucharistically. Rather, the contexts contrast what a meal should be with what it was. A meal should not mean the death of an innocent man because of a host/guest, given the importance of hospitality within Judaism,[102] but rather God providing for his people in shared fellowship. The parallel is inexact because the feeding and Herod's feast are two distinct but nonetheless juxtaposed meals, whereas the Last Supper is by definition only one meal, which still incorporates both elements of innocent death and provision. Also, Jesus and John the Baptist have different roles: Jesus is both host and victim, while John is only the victim, not even a guest.

Secondly, Matthew and Mark address questions of deity. As argued above, both Herod and Judas presumed to act like God in handing over. Both record Jesus walking on the water after the feeding and his claim to deity (ἐγώ εἰμι, "I am"; Matt 14:27;[103] Mark 6:50[104]). Lest there be any doubt, Matthew has the disciples venerating Jesus as "Son of God" (14:33). Matthew lets them act more truly than they yet understood, venerating someone they regarded as God's unique messenger, but not yet as God's incarnation.[105] The Herod story foreshadows the betrayal by Judas, and potentially indicates that such treatment of God's chosen ones is blasphemous.

Moloney (whose work only applies to John): "Jesus' deliberate action of taking bread ... [reflects] the Eucharistic thought and practice of the early church" (*Love*, 112). This reads too much into an everyday act of taking bread using the very common λαμβάνω. He also says "Eucharist is a sub-theme to ... the gift of the piece of bread" to Judas. However, the most natural reading is that the sop identifies the traitor, as John 13 has no Eucharist. He argues that John replaces the LXX's ἐσθίω with τρώγω to link this passage with John 6 (Moloney, *Glory*, 21). But John 6 lacks clear references to Jesus' crucifixion, and John 13 lacks any reference to Jesus' blood, two essential elements in the Synoptics, so this approach may be eisegetical.

101. Hagner notes the example of Paul in Acts 27:35 (*Matthew 14-28*, 14:18-19). Beavis says "the text is dense with liturgical language" (*Mark*, 107), but she does not show that it is specifically eucharistic. Davies and Allison (*Matthew*) argue that the order of events is significant, being the same as 26:20-29, but ignore the fact that the actions could only be done in this order (2:481).

102. Keener, *Matthew*, 627.

103. Davies and Allison, *Matthew*, 2:506. "In a theophany-like context ... the words allude to the definition of ... Yahweh" (Hagner, *Matthew 14-28*, 14:27).

104. Evans, *Mark 8:27—16:20*, 6:50.

105. Hagner, *Matthew 14-28*, 14:33; Keener, *Matthew*, 408.

Luke

Luke has apparently departed from the Markan order[106] both before and after the feeding of the five thousand.[107] Instead of Mark and Matthew's description of John the Baptist's death, Luke's Herod admits responsibility for John's death and asks "Who, then, is this?" (9:9), which Peter will later answer by declaring that Jesus is "the Messiah of God." (9:20). While Mark and Matthews potentially show that Herod's treatement of John the Baptist is a type of blasphemy by action, Acts 13:23 argues that Herod's death was for a more overt blasphemy in accepting worship from the crowd. This makes explicit and public what was previously only implicit and private in Herod's treatment of John, that Herod transgressed the divine-human boundary.

Secondly, Moessner has argued that Luke's Jesus in 9:1–44 recapitulates Moses in Deut, so that the transfiguration replaces Horeb as "the mountain of revelation." Luke then has four narratives pre-transfiguration and four matching ones afterwards, so that Luke's feeding (9:10–17) matches Jesus' second prediction of his death (9:43b–45).[108] The feeding shows God's provision for the people through Jesus[109] but the matching prediction foreshadows betrayal. Luke has linked Judas with the feeding and in due course will reveal Judas as the traitor (22:4).

Conclusion

Mark and Matthew parallel the actions of Judas with Herod, in that both breach the Jewish understanding of hospitality[110] by causing the death of someone innocent. While there are differences—Jesus was present at the meal and John the Baptist appears not to have been—the impetus for both deaths stem from a meal. Judas and Herod both presume to act like God, abrogating to themselves decisions of life and death, which is potentially blasphemy. They experience grief or remorse and suffer an untimely death.

---

106. A "great omission" (Nolland, *Luke 1—9:20*, 9:10).

107. The five thousand represent Israel as a whole (Minear, "Audience," 84).

108. Moessner, "Preview," 599.

109. Jesus functions as host and servant, anticipating the messianic banquet (Smith, "Table," 632).

110. Fitzgerald, "Hospitality."

4.2.5. Who is the greatest?
(Mark 9:33–37; Matt 18:1–6; Luke 9:46–48)

Mark

Immediately after Jesus' second prediction of his death, the disciples argue about who is the greatest. Firstly, Mark indicates Jesus' initiative by having him question the Twelve. Either he overheard, was an astute judge of people, or had a supernatural ability to read minds (2:8).[111] The Twelve could seem insensitive in the light of Jesus' words, but we could interpret the situation as like Peter at Caesarea Philippi,[112] who sees, but does not fully perceive (8:32).[113] Perhaps the Twelve (9:35) saw that Jesus would die, and wondered who might lead them.[114] Jesus sits like a teacher, καθίσας, to rectify matters.[115]

Next, Jesus said that greatness meant being servant (διάκονος) of all. Its only other use in Mark is the antithetical 10:43,[116] where Jesus makes the same point. Judas was present both times, as Mark mentions the Twelve (9:35) and the ten (10:41), plus James and John. Jesus warned them that being first meant not being like Gentiles with an arbitrary exercise of power, but to serve the rest. Mark does not identify Judas, but his arbitrary handing over of Jesus sounds more like what Jesus forbade than servanthood.

Thirdly, Jesus brought a small child into their midst as a live teaching aid and took the child into his arms (ἐναγκαλισάμενος; 9:36). The other use is 10:16, where parents brought children for his blessing.[117] The point is not

---

111. France, *Mark*, 373.

112. Anderson notes the importance of misunderstanding, particularly in John 6, as Jesus' clarifications advance the dialogue ("Bread," 19). He argues that this is to correct misunderstandings in the Johannine community (ibid., 24). The most relevant issue is Peter's confession in 6:68–69, which Jesus seems to cut off abruptly. Anderson argues that this was to address the relative contributions of the Petrine and Johannine sections of the church under Domitian's persecution (ibid., 56). While the hierarchical Petrine churches may have had difficulties with the more familial Johannine churches, Simon Peter was not a devil; rather, that was Judas (ibid., 50). Alleged Petrine-Johannine difficulties may be reading more into the text than is there, as Anderson argues that Jesus' rhetorical question in 6:70, "Have I not chosen you?", should be interpreted as a statement: "I have not chosen you to avoid persecution." (ibid., 57). This is hardly the most likely reading, as there is no hint of persecution of the Twelve in John 6.

113. This is one of five narratives showing the disciples' opacity between Jesus healing the blind in Mark 8:22–26 and 10:46–62 (Resseguie, *Revelation*, 55).

114. France, *Mark*, 373.

115. Donahue, "Factor," 587.

116. Resseguie, *Revelation*, 179.

117. Derrett, "Children," 2.

becoming like a child to receive the kingdom[118] (10:15); rather, Jesus is inverting normal patterns by receiving the least of all, a child.[119] For Mark, the child (and the adult's reaction) is a surrogate for Jesus (9:37). Judas failed to take either teaching to heart when handing the innocent Jesus over to death. Κατακυριεύω means an arbitrary, unfair exercise of power (like Judas) and is forbidden (Matt 20:25; Mark 10:42; 1 Pet 5:3). Its only other use is the violent demoniac in Acts 19;16. Tragically, Judas[120] set in motion the events leading to Jesus' death, whose prediction led to this narrative.

Matthew

Matthew portrays the disciples more favorably.[121] Rather than arguing, they were "filled with grief" (17:23) at his impending death, Peter sought to resolve the temple tax issue (17:24–25),[122] and their question to Jesus is more neutral (18:1) than in Mark and does not immediately follow Jesus' prediction.

Matthew considerably strengthens Mark's teaching on the child who stood ἐν μέσῳ αὐτῶν. The disciples argued about who was the greatest, but Jesus answers indirectly by implying that it was the very least/servant/child. But Matthew strengthens this to require childlike humility for entry to the kingdom by linking humility, greatness, and servant.[123] The only uses of ταπεινόω are Matthew 18:4 and 23:12, but both require humbling oneself. By contrast, exalting oneself leads to humiliation like Capernaum (Matt 23:12;

---

118. "Adults who have the qualities of children will inherit the kingdom" (ibid., 17) overstates matters, as the text does not use such language.

119. France, *Mark*, 374; Myers, *Binding*, 261.

120. This is more credible than Jesus confronting the Roman authorities (ibid., 278).

121. Something similar happened in Jesus' explanation of the parable of the sower (s4.2.2).

122. This text is most likely historical, its core going back to Jesus (Harb, "Value," 257). While Peter, the "ideal disciple" (263), is portrayed positively, so is Jesus in relation to the temple tax. Jesus wanted to avoid giving (unnecessary) offense, so he instructed Peter on how to get the coin. By the time Matthew wrote, the temple had been destroyed, and Harb argues that he is using this incident to encourage Christians to pay the *Fiscus Judaicus*, introduced by Vespasian (ibid., 259), even though Gentile Christians were exempt. Matthew is portraying the pre-Easter disciples and the post-Easter church far more favorably than Mark.

123. Matthew uses Luke as a source (Huggins, "Posteriority," 1). If so, it is difficult to understand why he has then apparently omitted Luke's dispute between the disciples about greatness at the Last Supper (22:24), as this would show their continuing inability to understand what was about to unfold.

11:23). Mark simply locates this pericope in Capernaum (9:33), but Matthew[124] and Luke 10:15 have Capernaum as a potent symbol of judgment.[125]

Finally, Matthew's Jesus strongly encouraged the disciples to welcome in his name those lacking social standing like children,[126] and so to welcome him. It is difficult to see how Judas betraying Jesus to death for money is showing humility or welcoming him. Once again, Judas the insider hears clear teaching from Jesus, but apparently rejects it. Like Capernaum, Judas had seen Jesus' miracles, but still betrayed him, and was also severely rebuked. He is a human equivalent of Capernaum. This depiction of the disciples as more privileged will only intensify the gravity of his betrayal.

Luke

Luke portrays the disciples in confronting terms as he moves directly from Jesus' prediction of his death to the argument on greatness.[127] Luke keeps Mark's emphasis on Jesus' initiative, insight, or special knowledge (Luke 4:23; 5:22; 6:8), but he does not ask, only to be answered with silence.

Luke follows Mark 9:37 by stressing that the child[128] is to be compared with Jesus, not the disciples. The child is placed next to Jesus, not in their midst, and Jesus' first words compare the disciples' response to the child with their response to him. Greatness is "measured by the company one keeps."[129] This is clear in the case of being with Jesus, who makes the same point regarding those of low status, like children. This is highlighted by Jesus' "in my name" (9:48). Luke smoothes Mark's general ἕν τῶν τοιούτων παιδίων to a specific τοῦτο τὸ παιδίον.[130] It is not just children in general, but how the

---

124. Matt 17:24 places them all in Capernaum, and Jesus only leaves Galilee in 19:1.

125. Branden further argues that themes in the Capernaum passages all hint at conflict with evil (*Conflict*, 137). Capernaum is charged with unbelief (11:23), and chapter 12 calls unbelievers "evil" (12:34; ibid., 138). Matt 4:8-9 has Satan's control over political areas as the epitome of the temptations (ibid., 138).

126. Keener, *Matthew*, 448.

127. Marshall, *Luke*, 395. Luke moves Mark 10:35-45 to the Last Supper (Smith, "Table," 620). As all three synoptic texts are straight after Jesus' second prediction of his death, it is better to see Luke 22:25-27 as another example of Jesus' prediction, which leads to a dispute on greatness. Jesus' illustration (sitting at table versus serving) better fits the context of a meal than the base of a mountain (Luke 9).

128. This is not a baby; rather, it is a child who can speak but still relies on parents (Bovon, *Child*, 382).

129. Nolland, *Luke 9:21—18:34*, 9:48.

130. Marshall, *Luke*, 396.

Twelve will respond to situations like "this child."[131] The relevance for Judas is that Jesus links people's reaction to him with their reaction to God (9:48). So, Judas's betrayal of Jesus is akin to rejecting God.

Conclusion

The Twelve were present both times when Jesus discussed διάκονος (Mark 9:35; 10:41). He later warned them against arbitrary use of power, like the Gentiles (10:42), using his approaching death as the prime example. While Matt portrays the disciples more favorably, the sting is in the description of Capernaum which, like Judas, had seen Jesus' miracles, but not repented and was promised a severe judgment. Luke portrays the Twelve in very confronting terms, only concerned about status, when Jesus is going to die. These passages reiterate the insider status of the Twelve and show a variety of behaviors, either about status or relationship to Jesus, which may well become relevant to the depiction of Judas, as they highlight his tragic failure to learn as an insider.

4.2.6. The third prediction of Jesus' death (Mark 10:32–34; Matt 20:17–19; Luke 18:31–33).

Each text has the Twelve present (Matt 20:17; Mark 10:32; Luke 18:31).

Mark

We could see Mark 10:32–34 as opposing self-interest, as it is framed by Jesus teaching the disciples after the departure of the rich young ruler and James and John's request (an ABA' structure). Pursuing this train of thought through the surrounding dialogue with the disciples adds a question about imitating Jesus. It is better to ask what Jesus will (10:28–31, 32–34)[132] or will not provide for his disciples (10:35–39a, 39b–45; an ABA'B' structure) because of the question of imitating Jesus. This will enhance criticism of Judas's subsequent treatment of Jesus.

The NT critiques wealth/the wealthy, in that wealth may be a rival deity (s3.5.4; Matt 6:24; Luke 16:31). The rich man seemed blessed by God with wealth and a desire for eternal life (Mark 10:17), but when Jesus called

---

131. Ibid., 396.

132. "Astonishment" links 10:24 and 10:32 on the cost of discipleship (Myers, *Binding*, 277).

him to renounce wealth to follow God, he left (10:22). Responding to the Twelve's astonishment (10:26), Jesus promised them a reward in this life with trouble (10:31),[133] but finally eternal life.[134] This applies initially to the disciples, and then more broadly to later followers, as Jesus never received fields, houses, etc., even though all faced persecution. Arguably in response to this, Jesus warned the Twelve that he would die and be raised (10:33–34). There is no sense that the Twelve were to imitate this redemptive death.[135]

In a continuing pattern, Mark portrays the disciples in a harsher light than, say, Matthew. Mark 10:34 precedes James and John's singular request for places at Jesus' right and left hands (10:35).[136] Jesus asks if they understand, as "cup" and "baptism" in Mark mean "death."[137] Unlike 10:32–34, where there is no suggestion that they will follow Jesus to a similar death, James and John are promised that they will persevere to death and that their manner of life must imitate Jesus, who will die. The increasingly specific request for power and influence, despite Jesus' words to the rich man, require him to speak more pointedly to the Twelve. Judas apparently did not heed Jesus' warnings against personal advancement, but set in motion the events leading to Jesus' death.

Matthew

By contrast, and in a continuing pattern, Matthew is more sympathetic to the disciples. Firstly, and most importantly, he uses the verbal thread "friend" to narrow the issue down to increasing conflict between a figure representing God and one of a crowd.[138] Matt's uses of ἑταῖρε (20:13; 22:12; 26:50) have

---

133. "A fitting summary" of Jesus' teaching since his second prediction of death (France, *Mark*, 408–9). It is like s3.5.2, where only those faithful under testing were protected from money's destructive effects.

134. Evans, *Mark 8:27—16:20*, 10:30.

135. The Markan Jesus calls people to obey God, not imitate Jesus (Donahue, "Factor," 586).

136. They want to sit nearest Jesus when judging the twelve tribes of Israel (Evans, *Mark 8:27—16:20*, 10:35). This is the only time that they feature together in the gospel without Peter (France, *Mark*, 415).

137. Evans, *Mark 8:27—16:20*, 10:38.

138. Klassen says that "friend" normally shows that "the one addressed is committing an ungrateful act against the one who has been generous," but that in Matt 26:50, it shows "the relationship of trust that exists between Jesus and Judas" (Klassen, *Friend*, 103). He gives no reason for this discrepancy.

In Matt 20:13 and 22:12, the person will not receive what God wants to give, whether money or clothing. These people want to do things their way, not God's. They might complain, but they cannot answer God's judgment. Then, in Matt 26:50, Jesus calls

common features.[139] First, there is conflict between God, the owner/king in the kingdom of heaven (20:1; 22:12),[140] or Jesus (26:50), and an individual. Secondly, the person[141] called "friend" is one of a group of workers (20:13), guests (22:11-12), or the Twelve (26:47).

Next, the "friend" reneges on a prior request to work for a denarius (20:13), wear correct clothes (22:12) or be faithful to Jesus (26:48). They have "presumed on another's grace."[142] In response to God's rebuke,[143] they are silent or their response is not given (20:15; 22:12b[144]). Lastly, they are

---

Judas "friend" at the betrayal.

Is Judas the supreme example of the "friend" who rejects what God offers? Like the workers in God's vineyard, Judas had been there all along. When the church replaced Judas as apostle, the candidate had to "have been with us the whole time the Lord Jesus went in and out among us" (Acts 1:21). Jesus' comments about Judas at the Last Supper (the "woe" and the comment about it being better if he was not born) support Judas being sent to hell, the penalty for the man at the wedding. It is used three times where "the speaker has been wronged" (Davies and Allison, *Matthew*, 3:75).

The main reference is to Matthew's audience, warning them that some ostensible believers will be rejected at Jesus' return (Oropeza, *Footsteps*, 1:77). While true, ἑταῖρε shows that Judas is the primary reference.

Lachs ("Rabbinic," 164–65) critiques Davies ("Sermon," 396) for choosing the wrong Aramaic antecedent for ἑταῖρος, but both fail to see that, even if הבר means "learned colleague," all three uses are negative. Wright does not see this verbal thread, and sees the parable as a warning not to grumble ("Debtors," 19).

139. Each text has its own meaning. In Matt 20, God chooses to show the same grace to latecomers; Matt 22, where those originally invited do not come and so the invitation is extended to all (Hagner, *Matthew 14–28*); and Matt 26, where Jesus highlights the enormity of betrayal by calling Judas "friend," contra Hagner (*Matthew 14–28*, 26:50), who maintains that Jesus' words "should not be understood as involving a negative or sarcastic connotation." This is puzzling to say the least in an atmosphere of betrayal and violence.

140. Tasker, *Matthew*, 190.

141. Cripps follows Manson in suggesting that Judas is in mind ("Note," 30). Διάκονος is rare in the gospels, and διακονία is used for the ministry where Matthias replaces Judas. It is "more than a coincidence" that Jesus calls Judas ἑταῖρε. Matthew identifies Judas by name and alone discloses his fate (26:25; 27:3). "Many are called, but few are chosen" is very appropriate for him. The wedding guest being sent out is like Judas at the Last Supper, and being sent to outer darkness is fitting for the "son of perdition" (John 17:12). So also Tasker, *Matthew*, 208. The one with an evil eye was felt to be able to harm their friends and themselves (Elliott, "Parable," 53).

142. Keener, *Matthew*, 483. Grindheim, "Works," 326; it is a rejoinder to the reward promised in 19:28-29, emphasizing God's grace.

143. Saying that Matthew uses "friend" "to shame one who has presumed on another's grace" (Keener, *Matthew*, 483) is too general, as Matt's "friends" always presume on God's grace.

144. Hendriksen, *Matthew*, 798; 26:50. The host asks genuinely, but the man's silence means there is no misunderstanding (Keener, *Matthew*, 522).

sent from God's presence in increasingly severe terms. The worker must leave (20:14a), but the guest is sent to outer darkness, symbolizing judgment.[145] Jesus does not send Judas away,[146] but the reader knows that he had already pronounced the "birth woe" on Judas (26:24b),[147] said of nobody else. The first use of "friend" comes just before the third prediction, and shows that it is really just one of the Twelve, Judas, who will cause trouble. This is consistent with my results in s2.3, where a friend can betray.

Secondly, James and John's mother, not the men themselves, makes the request, and it is less sweeping (20:20).[148] Matthew contrasts this seeking of Jesus for personal gain with the heartfelt seeking of Jesus by the two blind men (20:29–34).[149] Leaders should be servants, not arbitrary overlords (20:25–28). James and John wanted to be close to Jesus for personal gain, but Judas betrayed Jesus for personal gain.

Luke

Like Matthew, Luke is more favorable to the disciples than Mark. They may be blind and uncomprehending, but not mercenary. Mark has the two-stage healing of the blind man at Bethsaida (8:22–26) and the healing of Bartimaeus (10:46–52) as an inclusion on blindness[150] around the predictions of Jesus' death. Luke has nothing so critical, but like Matthew, the healing of Bartimaeus is a comment on the disciples (18:35–43). They are spiritually blind,[151] but if they call out to the Son of David for mercy, they too can follow (ἠκολούθει) him.

Secondly, Luke stresses the disciples' incomprehension (9:45; 18:34). Despite their insider knowledge, some things they do not know, and moreover, the meaning had been hidden from them, a divine passive. They were too afraid to ask Jesus (9:45).

---

145. Hagner, *Matthew 14–28*, 22:13; Glancy, "Slaves," 84.

146. The closest is John 13:27–30.

147. It is unique in the NT, but rabbis said something similar as a general warning (Keener, *Matthew*, 626).

148. Davies and Allison, *Matthew*, 3:86.

149. Keener, *Matthew*, 485.

150. Horsley, *Magic*, 135.

151. Fitzmyer, *Luke X–XXIV*, 1214.

Conclusion

Mark's portrait of the Twelve is harsh, with two of the inner three only concerned about their prospects. All Twelve should have taken to heart Jesus' warnings against the desire for personal advancement. Matthew softens the picture, using "friend" to show that the real (and escalating) conflict will be between Jesus and just one of the Twelve. Having Judas as one of the "friends" will assist the lexical field of "betrayal." Luke portrays the Twelve more favorably—they are uncomprehending, but not mercenary.

4.2.7. Conclusion

The above are representative of Jesus' ministry prior to entering Jerusalem and show Judas negatively in retrospect. At the call of the Twelve, Mark's careful structure shows Judas, a presumed insider, as an outsider. Matt sharpens this picture with Jesus' warnings about being handed over and flogged, alluding to the personal effect of betrayal, when persecution for the Twelve lay well in the future. Luke emphasizes the Father's role in prompting Jesus to call Judas, and unambiguously calls him "traitor" (6:16).

Jesus' explanation of the Sower and sending the Twelve on mission show that Judas will not ultimately heed the warnings about the effects of Satan and/or money. Matthew and Luke sharpen this by having chapters of Jesus ministering to classic outsiders, such as the Gentiles, the ill, and demonized, before giving the parable. God does not heartlessly reject people but will not compromise on sin.

Mark and Matthew's feeding of the five thousand contrast Judas unfavorably with Herod as, while both are instrumental in sending innocent men to death, Judas's prior relationship with Jesus means betrayal is appropriate. Luke contrasts Judas unfavorably with Herod by stressing Herod's perplexity and wish to understand Jesus (9:9). Judas, on the other hand, simply fails/refuses to recognize Jesus despite all the opportunities he has had.

The narrative on the greatest in the kingdom shows how little Mark's Judas absorbed of Jesus' command to be the servant of all and not to lord it over others. Mark does not define lording it over others, but Judas's betrayal of the innocent Jesus for money is arguably an example. Matthew portrays the disciples more favorably by emphasizing their grief at Jesus' approaching death. This only heightens Judas's guilt as the one who handed Jesus to death. Luke's Jesus equates one's reaction to those of low standing with their response to Jesus, but it is precisely this Jesus whom Judas leaves to associate with those of high standing: the chief priests.

The third prediction of Jesus' death clearly says that the Twelve were there. Mark is harsh, sandwiching the narrative with Jesus teaching the Twelve after the departure of the rich ruler, an outsider who allows money to come between him and God, and James and John who, having heard of Jesus' approaching death, are more concerned with their own positions. While all are no doubt similarly concerned, only Judas betrays Jesus. Matthew heightens the enormity of Judas's act with "friend," which highlights in increasingly severe terms the tension between a figure representing God and an ungrateful individual from a group.

Judas can be placed at these narratives, so establishing that, whatever his level of understanding, his betrayal is inexcusable. The passages give prophetic warnings. They stress that insiders are privileged, but also flawed, and liable to misunderstand. The earliest gospel, Mark, establishes Judas's guilt, so making it less likely that this is a later invention by the church. Mark's harsh portrait of the disciples speaks volumes for Judas's guilt, in that while he views the Twelve dimly, only Judas hands Jesus over. We now turn to a consideration of Judas in the week leading up to Jesus' death.

Section 4.3. Judas in the Passion Narratives.

4.3.1. Introduction

This section will study key events involving Judas prior to Jesus' death:

- The plot to betray Jesus,
- the anointing of Jesus at Bethany,
- the Last Supper,
- Judas's betrayal of Jesus, and
- Judas after the betrayal.

4.3.2. The plot to betray Jesus
(Mark 14:1-2; Matt 26:3-5; Luke 22:1-6)

Mark links Judas with the temple authorities, Jesus' habitual enemies, by a sandwich (ζητέω, κρατέω, and Mark 13). Matthew uses Mark's material, but increases Judas's guilt by joining Jesus' woes on the Pharisees (chapter 23) with the apocalyptic chapter 24 and the three παρουσία parables in chapter 25 of presumed disciples exposed in increasingly severe terms. Luke adds the detail of Satan entering Judas (22:3).

Mark

The plot to arrest Jesus is a Markan sandwich[152] for the anointing at Bethany. Barton[153] argues that the little apocalypse (Mark 13) is framed by two sets of texts contrasting exemplary women with villainous men (12:38—14:9). We can assume the presence of Judas because of Mark 13:1. I extend this to contrast Jesus and Judas, who are in the temple precincts for very different reasons:

12:35–37: Jesus in the temple courts speaking to the crowds.

- 12:38–40: warnings against scribes and Pharisees.
  - 12:41–44: a poor widow.
    - 13: the little apocalypse, outside the temple (παραδίδωμι used three times).
  - 14:1–2: chief priests.
- 14:3–9: Jesus anointed by a faithful woman.[154]

14:10–11: Judas meets with the temple authorities about betraying Jesus (παραδοῖ used twice). Judas has changed sides and prepares the way for him to attend the Last Supper.[155]

Mark contrasts Jesus and Judas in three ways by linking Judas with the chief priests and the Pharisees. First, Mark uses ζητέω ten times with three uses by presumed insiders (1:37; 3:32; 16:6), framing seven negative uses,[156] which show Jesus' enemies seeking him for the wrong reason. In 8:11, Pharisees, who were planning to kill him (3:6), seek a sign. Jesus rebukes "this

---

152. A double sandwich around the Passover anointing and the plot by the chief priests (France, *Mark*, 547). Resseguie, *Narrative*, 55.

153. Barton, "Anointing," 232.

154. There are parallels between the poor widow and the anointing woman; e.g., each mentions πτωχός (12:42–43; 14:5, 7), the great contrast between the gifts of the rich and poor (12:41; 14:5), and the solemn ἀμὴν (12:43; 14:9; Grassi, "Heroine," 11). However, strictly speaking, the anointing woman did not give up ὅλον τον βίον αὐτῆς (12:44), and it is unlikely that the widow saw her gift as any preparation for Jesus' death, so the differences are significant. It may be better to argue that, in dependence on God (s3.5.3), the widow gave up everything like Jesus would in death, and the anointing woman prepared him for that death.

155. France, *Mark*, 557; Maritz, "Judas Iscariot," 304.

156. Parsenios makes the same point for John (*Rhetoric*, 58–59). Brant's review of Parsenios (Review, 390) makes the odd claim that "In the Synoptic Gospels, Jesus praises the act of seeking and promises its success (Matt 7:7; Luke 11:10)." As argued below, this is hardly representative of its Synoptic use.

generation" (8:12),[157] alluding to the generations of Noah and the wilderness, hinting that others are at fault.[158] The chief priests tried to arrest him, but the crowd intervened (12:12),[159] until Judas approached them (14:10) to hand Jesus over.[160] In 14:55, the Sanhedrin actively but unsuccessfully sought evidence to justify execution. We would normally expect those close to Jesus, like Judas, to seek him for proper reasons, but Judas is linked with those who have continually sought to kill Jesus.

Mark's use of κρατέω also shows Judas in a poor light. Jesus takes hold of others to help them (1:37; 5:41; 9:27). When people lay hold of an object, the result depends on the quality of their relationship with God, so Jesus rebukes the Pharisees as "hypocrites" for keeping the traditions of men instead of God (7:3–4, 6, 8),[161] but the disciples keep secret the transfiguration until after his resurrection (9:10).[162] But when Jesus is the object of κρατέω, the intent is harmful in wanting to arrest and/or kill him (12:12; 14:1, 44, 46, 49). Judas is aligned with those whom Jesus warned his disciples against:the Pharisees and Herodians (8:38), and the chief priests (11:18; 14:55). Mark uses παραδίδωμι twice and calls Judas ὁ εἷς τῶν δώδεκα (14:10–11), stressing his closeness to Jesus before his treachery.[163] Its next use is Jesus' devastating "birth woe" (14:20).

Thirdly, the juxtaposition of 14:1–2 after chapter 13 serves to link the impermanence of the temple with Jesus' death. Peter Bolt's Master of Theology thesis on Mark 13 has three basic interpretations: Jesus' παρουσία,[164] the fall of Jerusalem (AD 70), and his interpretation of an apocalyptic precursor to Jesus' death and post-Easter enthronement (13:24–27).[165] While Bolt has shown many connections between Mark 13 and Jesus' death, the final result

---

157. Contra Evans, who sees the "ominous turn" for ζητέω in 11:18, not here (*Mark 8:27—16:20*, 11:18).

158. Guelich, *Mark*; France, *Mark*, 312.

159. Evans, *Mark 8:27—16:20*, 14:1.

160. παραδίδωμι is "unexpected" (France, *Mark*, 548), but fails to note its function as a verbal thread. Jesus is handed over a number of times, but imputes less guilt the closer he gets to death (s4.3.5).

161. Usage establishes what is normative (ibid., 283).

162. This parallels παραδίδωμι with an inanimate object (s2.2).

163. The article reminds readers of Mark's earlier introduction of Judas (Evans, *Mark 8:27—16:20*, 14:10). He is the one of the Twelve who will betray Jesus.

164. So Donahue: Matt 24:3 adapts Mark 13:4 to be overtly eschatological ("Parable," 11–12).

165. Bolt, "Integrity," 3, 5, 15.

is unconvincing as he has overplayed his hand, not recognizing that some of Jesus' predictions fit his παρουσία better than his passion.[166]

Bolt rightly notes that, when the anonymous disciple called Jesus' attention to the stones of the temple, he alluded to the inviolability of God's earthly dwelling.[167] The three synoptic evangelists link the eventual historical destruction of the temple with the murder of Jesus by the tearing of the veil (Matt 27:51; Mark 15:38; Luke 23:45).[168] Judas is inextricably linked with the authorities of the temple which is facing destruction (Mark 13:2). His betrayal will lead to the very death which foreshadows that destruction.

Next, he rightly affirms that much of Mark 13 refers to Jesus' death, but wrongly believes that that is its sole focus. That some verses refer to his παρουσία[169] is confirmed by Bolt's exegesis. Jesus says that the gospel must first be preached πάντα τὰ ἔθνη, a monumental task (13:10). Bolt says "evangelising the nations is . . . the top priority," but ignores the scale of the task and its time frame.[170] The important thing for us is that Mark 13, the precursor to his passion, eloquently describes that death is not the last word for Jesus, but he whom Judas betrayed will return in glory, a very sobering thought. Finally, Mark 13 uses παραδίδωμι (vv. 9, 11) to refer to the apostles being handed over so that they can give witness.[171] Judas could not do this vital apostolic task, as he would be dead by then. The final use, 13:12, talks of family members betraying each other to death in an atmosphere of hatred (s2.2.4). If the inner circle is like a fictive family, Judas's actions anticipate betrayal by those within the church, not just outsiders.

Mark establishes Judas's guilt. Ζητέω, κρατέω, and παραδίδωμι link Judas with those who have always opposed Jesus, like the chief priests and the Pharisees. Mark 13 notes the impermanence of the temple, and that death

---

166. Evans, *Mark 8:27—16:20*, 13:24.

167. Bolt, "Integrity," 73.

168. France, *Mark*, 657.

169. Fusco, "Luke-Acts," 12.

170. Bolt, "Integrity," 90. Other questionable exegeses confirm that Jesus' return in the clouds (Bock [*Blasphemy*, 201] notes the mark of God in the OT) in power and glory is best seen as his παρουσία. Bolt says, "ἄγγελος can be a human or heavenly messenger" who will gather the elect ("Integrity," 116–17; France, *Mark*, 536–37). While strictly true, this is hardly fair, as the only reference in Mark to a human as ἄγγελος is John the Baptist (1:2). Mark 1:2b–3 conflates quotes from the LXX (Exod 23:20; Isa 40:3) and the MT (Mal 3:1; Guelich, *Mark*, 7). Exod 23:20 refers to a literal angel, and Mal 3:1 foretells the ministry of John the Baptist, so most references are to literal angels. Matt and Luke largely continue this pattern.

171. Mark is not portraying Roman power of any sort (e.g., Pilate) as weak (Bond, *Pilate*, 117–18).

is not the last word for Jesus, who will return in power and glory. Matthew and Luke will confirm and intensify this reading.

Matthew

Given Mark's trenchant criticism of Judas, one wonders how Matthew could possibly be more critical, but he is. Firstly, Matthew intensifies Mark's alignment of Judas with Jesus' enemies with a woe (26:24). Secondly, Matthew 25 has three parables showing presumed disciples sent from Jesus' presence in increasingly severe terms.

Ζητέω (Matt 21:46; 26:16, 59), κρατέω (21:46; 26:4, 48, 55–56), and παραδίδωμι (26:15–16, 25, 45–46, 48) reflect Markan usage, showing Judas aligned with Jesus' enemies.[172] By joining Matthew 23's woes with the apocalyptic material leading to the Last Supper, where Jesus pronounces a woe on Judas (26:24), Matthew shows Judas to be not only as culpable as the Pharisees, but worse. There is no record of Jesus applying the birth woe to a Pharisee or a scribe.[173] Via sees Matthew 23–25 as a unit, as its length and woes better parallel the Beatitudes. By omitting Mark's poor widow (12:41–44), Matthew joins together more sharply Jesus' denunciation of the scribes and the apocalyptic Matthew 24–26.[174] Variations on ταῦτα πάντα in 23:36 and 24:8, 33–34 confirm the link between Matthew 23 and 24.[175] Via rightly notes that the repeated woes of 23:13–16,[176] 23 highlight the threat of judgment in the last days.[177] They also place the scribes and Judas, the only named person to receive a woe from Jesus (26:24),[178] under a like judgment. The woe suggests another possible link in that Judas could be "a child

---

172. Judas's "Rabbi" to Jesus links him with those opposed to Jesus (Matt 23:8; Oropeza, *Footsteps*, 1.76).

173. "A pronouncement of frightful judgement" (Keener, *Matthew*, 626).

174. Via, "Ethical," 83. Chapters 23–25 are Matthew's fifth discourse, as the disciples are warned in chapter 23 not to imitate the Pharisees, etc. (Hood, "Extent," 532). References to hell (23:33, 36; 24:34), the loss of kingdom/house paralleling the loss of Jerusalem (23:13, 38; 24), and the inclusion of Jesus as king (21:1–11; 25:31–46) bind these chapters together, to warn the disciples not to be unprepared (ibid., 536).

175. Via, "Ethical," 83.

176. A woe was "a creative prophetic way of sounding impending judgement" (Keener, *Matthew*, 547).

177. Via, "Ethical," 83.

178. This is consistent with Matthew's other uses of οὐαί which are always spoken by Jesus. All of them indict people or cities for their poor behavior except for 24:19, where Jesus speaks a woe to pregnant or nursing mothers, not because of their sin, but because of added difficulty in fleeing. Alone of all the recipients of a woe, they are encouraged to pray that God will ameliorate the worst aspects of the flight.

of hell" (23:15), like the scribes and Pharisees, as demonic vilification of another teacher was quite rare.[179]

Matthew also inserts three παρουσία parables (the bridesmaids,[180] the talents,[181] and the sheep and goats[182])[183] between the apocalyptic Matthew 24 and the plot in Matthew 26, showing presumed disciples of Jesus exposed in increasingly harsh terms. They have the following in common: All have a figure representing God, the bridegroom or master of the kingdom of heaven (25:1, 14),[184] and the Son of Man[185] in his, not the Father's, glory

---

179. Pagels, "Part II," 33. Johnson begs to differ, arguing that the "slander of the NT is typical of that found among rival claimants to a philosophic tradition" ("Slander," 419–41). This is supported by the fact that most major players in the NT were Jews, just divided between Messianic and non-Messianic camps.

180. The parable of the bridesmaids is helpful in rebutting another claim by Charlesworth that Matthew's use of φρόνιμος in 10:16 "be as shrewd as snakes" shows that serpents represented wisdom (*Serpent*, 356). This is another example of applying secular categories to the Bible indiscriminately. The GNT's usage shows that it is always a warning. The wise man is warned to build his house on the rock (7:24), the "faithful and wise servant" to discharge his duties responsibly (Matt 24:45; Luke 12:42), the wise bridesmaids alone receive entry to the banquet (Matt 25:2, 4, 8–9), the self-serving steward is called "shrewd" to distinguish him from "the sons of light" (Luke 16:8), and Paul warns his readers not to be conceited (Rom 11:25; 12:16; 1 Cor 4:10; 10:15; 2 Cor 11:19). The ancients may have associated snakes with wisdom, but the Bible uses them to warn God's people; e.g., "brood of vipers," Matt 3:7; 12:34; 23:33 (ibid., 358).

181. Matthew and Luke do not rely on each other, as omitting "the pretender to the throne" motif causes Matt's parable to lose coherence because the third servant then seems to have no basis in the parable for his harsh view of the master, unlike Luke 19:14 (Schultz, "Archelaus," 126–27). I believe that my reconstruction of Matt 25 is better. Jesus is not a "hard man"; his presumed disciples are without excuse (25:24). They have acted in ways which are inconsistent with their (presumed) initial confession of Jesus as their Lord.

182. It is a climactic position at the end of Matt's five great discourses (Page, *Powers*, 117).

183. Edwards, *Matthew*, 68.

184. Marcus, "Entering," 663, 669.

185. "Son of Man" is Jesus' archetypal self-reference, used by him alone, except John 12:34, where the crowds appear to be quoting Jesus' words back to him (Marshall, "Son of Man"). A key question is whether it is generic, a periphrasis for "I/me" (France, *Mark*, 128; Barnett, *Early*, 168), or something more. This generic sense is inappropriate in Mark's and Luke's first uses (2:10; 5:24), where the miraculous healing of the paralytic evidences Jesus' claims, and also in Matt 8:20, which references Jesus' homelessness as "Son of Man." Similarly, John's first use (1:51) highlights Jesus' unique role linking heaven and earth (Ridderbos, *John*, 94). None of these first uses hint that "Son of Man" is generic.

The Synoptics use it in common ways: to show Jesus' present authority (Mark 2:10; Matt 9:6; Luke 5:24); to foreshadow his suffering and resurrection (Mark 8:31; Matt 16:13, 21; Luke 16:22); and his return (Mark 13:26; Matt 24:27; Luke 17:24). The earliest texts, Mark 13:62 and 14:26, are "clearly reminiscent" of Dan 7:13–14,s where a figure

(25:31).¹⁸⁶ Jesus called himself the bridegroom (9:15; 25:1¹⁸⁷) who would "be taken from them" (9:15), which sounds like a journey (25:14);¹⁸⁸ and Jesus' favorite self-reference was Son of Man (25:31).¹⁸⁹ The progression in chapter 25 further clarifies Jesus' identity.¹⁹⁰ In the bridesmaids, the κύριε merely passes judgment, but in the talents, he has gone away, been made king, and returned to judge (Matt 25:12, 19). If Jesus' "being taken" is his death, like the master returning from a journey, he would return from death.¹⁹¹ If the talents have Jesus returning as king, the scenario of the sheep and goats shows Jesus as king judging his people eschatologically, his identity as Son of Man, and his deity in "his glory" (25:31), all made clear.¹⁹²

All the interlocutors call Jesus Κύριε (25:11 [like "Lord, Lord"; 7:20-22],¹⁹³ 24, 37, 44), like a real/potential disciple.¹⁹⁴ It is Jesus judging the

---

like a son of man is given eternal authority by God (Marshall, "Son of Man"; France, *Mark*, 534). For Mark, Jesus is the "suffering, vindicated and authoritative Son of Man" who, when identified as the Christ (Mark 8:29), replies as the (arguably less nationalistic) Son of Man. Matthew continues Mark's usage, but especially emphasizes a person's present estimation of Jesus and their future judgment (Mark 8:38; Matt 16:27), and Jesus' role as coming savior (Matt 13:41; 19:28). Luke continues Matthew and Mark's themes, but adds the Son of Man's mission to save the lost (Luke 19:10) and his betrayal by Judas (Luke 22:48; cf. Mark 14:21b; Marshall, "Son of Man"). In short, there is no evidence that Jesus used it as a generic title; he explicitly based this self-reference on Dan 7.

186. Keener, *Matthew*, 602-3; Hagner, *Matthew 14-28*, 25:31. Matt 21:1-11 to 25:31-46 are an inclusion based on those who acknowledge Jesus' kingship. Matt 23 is a shift in audience without a break in theme. Jesus' opponents are negative examples which are not to be imitated by his disciples, so warning of the judgment which all his people will face (Hood, "Extent," 534).

187. Hagner, *Matthew 14-28*, 25:1. The archaic and elevated εὖ and οὐαί with its solemn OT associations are designed to increase reverence for Jesus (Lee, "Speech," 13, 23).

188. Ibid., 13.

189. Keener, *Matthew*, 602.

190. Contra Blomberg ("Matthew," 90), where the divine figure is God, not further defined.

191. Hagner, *Matthew 1-13*, 9:15. Most of the uses of the LXX cognate ἀπαίρεω concern Israel's forty-year journey after the Exodus, another link between the Exodus and Jesus' death; e.g., τὴν ἔξοδον refers to Jesus' death (Luke 9:31).

192. Matthew blends the judicial aspects (Jewish; Parables of Enoch) and the fact that Jesus would actually return with (Christian) usages of "Son of Man" (Sim, "Weeping," 116).

193. Hagner, *Matthew 14-28*.

194. "The foolish virgins belong to the Christian community" (Davies and Allison, *Matthew*, 3:400). Grindheim, "Works," 328; Kingsbury, "Kyrios," 248. Despite the NIV translating respectively "sir," "Master," and "Lord."

church.[195] Next, all had a task/expectation—to meet the groom, invest the talents or care for "the least of (Jesus') brothers"[196] (25:1, 14, 40), but not all obeyed (25:9, 19–23, 37–39). The disobedient are described as not knowing/being known by Jesus (25:12, 26 [irony], 44). A breakdown in the master-servant relationship is clear in their actions (25:8, 25, 42–43).[197] Jesus is not rebuking those who were consciously not his disciples.[198] Lastly, Jesus rejects the disobedient in increasingly harsh terms. The foolish bridesmaids are locked out (25:11),[199] as their conduct was an insult,[200] and the servant is sent to outer darkness/hell (25:30).[201] The goats,[202] originally Jesus' disciples but who later disobeyed, are sent to hellfire prepared for Satan and his angels (25:41, 46).[203]

195. Sim, "Weeping," 150; Via, "Ethical," 91; Grindheim, "Works," 328; Edwards, *Matthew*, 68. Contra Pagels ("Part II," 34) and Sim ("Weeping," 118), who gloss over problems in their exegeses. While affirming that Jesus will judge all people, here it is just the church. If,s as Keener says, it concerns the reception of Christian evangelists (*Matthew*, 605), why does Matthew's Jesus not focus on their response to the evangelists' message (the most important thing) more than their needs? Does Hagner really think that meeting the evangelists' physical needs will suffice for salvation for the unrepentant (*Matthew 14–28*, "Explanation")? This is salvation by works. It is far better to see the goats as those ostensibly converted (despite πάντα τὰ ἔθνη), hence calling Jesus "Lord," but whose later actions did not match their confession.

196. No unconverted gentile is ever called "brother" in the NT (Donahue, "Parable," 25).

197. Matthew uses προσέρχεσθαι with its cultic/reverential sense for a servant approaching the master (Edwards, *Matthew*, 68). This only increases the guilt of the third servant, who approaches reverentially and then rebukes the master (25:24).

198. Contra Blomberg ("Matthew," 90), who thinks that this is the final judgment of "the people of the nations." That Jesus judges πάντα τὰ ἔθνη is not fatal, as the risen Jesus commanded the Eleven to disciple this group, teaching them to obey him. It is more likely that the goats are those who heard the preaching, apparently converted but then did not obey, than those who never heard. This mirrors 13:41, where the angels remove those who cause evil "*out of the kingdom*" at judgment (Donahue, "Parable," 11; his emphasis).

199. Jesus is warning against "carelessly going against social demands" (Wright, "Debtors," 21). This hardly justifies the seriousness of the groom's response: "I never knew you."

200. Keener, *Matthew*, 598.

201. Via, "Ethical," 87; Keener, *Matthew*, 601; Hagner, *Matthew 14–28*, 25:30; Sim, "Weeping," 137.

202. The goats could be religious leaders opposed to Christ (Bligh, "Eternal," 11) but it is highly unlikely that they would call him κύριε.

203. Sim, "Weeping," 134. Talbott's rejection of an eternal hell is unconvincing ("Freedom"). He notes that the goats are surprised at their judgment, but fails to note that the sheep are equally surprised at their vindication (ibid., 417). He does not see that the main problem is a breakdown in the master-servant relationship: "you did

The parables show the dire consequences for those who presume they are Jesus' disciples, calling him "Lord," but whose actions show they are not. He is warning "the lazy within the church."[204] The servants were given different amounts, just as the apostles seemed to have different giftings and access to Jesus, but they still had to be faithful with what they received.[205] The text eloquently sets the scene for the one who looks like a disciple but is not—Judas—to plot Jesus' betrayal.

Luke

Like Matthew, Luke continues Mark's usage of ζητέω (11:16; 19:47; 20:19; 22:2, 6; 24:5) and παραδίδωμι (22:4, 6, 21-22, 48; 23:25), but uses συλλαμβάνω instead of κρατέω for the arrests of Jesus, Peter, and Paul (Luke 22:54; Acts 1:16; 12:3; 23:27; 26:21).

Luke adapts Mark's material in two ways to increase Judas's guilt. First, the plot to betray Jesus leads directly into the Last Supper.[206] Luke follows Mark closely from Luke 20:1 (Jesus' authority disputed) to 24:12 (his resurrection), only omitting Mark's discussion of the Great Commandment (12:28-34).[207] If Mark contrasts two Jews in the temple courts for very different reasons, stressing the difference between devoted women and villainous men,[208] Luke contrasts two meetings of Jews, one in the temple (22:1-6) and the other outside the temple (22:7-38) to increase Judas's guilt, as the only one present at both meetings.

---

not do for me" (25:45). Next, he argues that choosing without fully understanding the consequences means that it is not free (ibid., 419). This odd argument would mean that, as we never foreknow the full consequences of any of our actions, then we never make a free choice. He also fails to understand the strength of his argument that someone can have a valid, if incomplete, understanding of the consequences and still do wrong (ibid., 419). He asks how anyone could choose hell over heaven (ibid., 429), but fails to see that no one fully foresees consequences (e.g., the goats), and that the NT contains many warnings about hell from Jesus. Talbott has an impossible standard of proof. Walters ignores repentance and argues that God wears down the impenitent until they accept salvation ("Hell," 178). No human act "can be infinitely good or evil" (ibid., 183), but he does not see that any act can express acceptance or rejection of God to some degree.

204. Keener, *Matthew*, 601.

205. Hagner, *Matthew 14-28*, 25:15.

206. Marshall, *Luke*, 787. Luke restores Mark's original wording before the Markan sandwich (Nolland, *Luke 18:35—24:53*, 22:3).

207. Ibid., 22:1.

208. Barton, "Anointing," 331.

Secondly, Luke has Satan entering Judas,[209] who then goes to the chief priests to betray Jesus. Pagels has shown that, from the beginning of Jesus' public ministry, or after his defeat of Satan in the desert (4:1), Luke consistently has Jesus' Jewish opponents playing (doubtless unconsciously) Satan's role by opposing him.[210] Spiritual conflict intensifies as the opponents' attitude hardens. Jesus exults in Satan's expulsion from heaven (10:18–19).[211] At his arrest, Jesus hints that the power behind the chief priests (and all those involved in his arrest) is "darkness" (22:52–53).[212] These links show Judas aligned with evil and Jesus' opponents.

Conclusion

With a sandwich, Mark aligns Judas with the temple authorities, who want to harm Jesus. Mark 13 foretells the temple's destruction, which Jesus' death foreshadows, the curtain being torn when he died (Mark 15:38). Matthew 25's three parables show presumed disciples of Jesus being exposed in increasingly severe terms. This prepares the way for the presumed disciple Judas's plot in Matthew 26. While the evangelists have shown that, even those close to Jesus can be flawed (ss 4.2.5–6), Luke increases Judas's guilt by having the plot against Jesus leading into the Last Supper and by having Satan enter him (22:3).

4.3.3. Jesus anointed at Bethany
(Mark 14:3–9; Matt 26:6–13; Luke 7:36–50; John 12:1–8)

All four gospels have stories of Jesus being anointed. We must decide if all four accounts, particularly Luke, are related. Munro, Van Til, and Sellew note the common elements of Jesus being anointed with perfume by a woman at a private dinner to argue that all four refer to the same event.[213] Kent agrees, arguing that Mary Magdalene, Mary of Bethany, and the sinful woman of Luke 7 are the same, despite his table of comparison[214] showing

---

209. Judas is not thereby exonerated, but may explain how he could do something evil (Page, *Powers*, 127–28). So Pagels ("Part II," 37). Luke 22:3 and John 13:27 have variations of εἰσῆλθεν δὲ Σατανᾶς εἰς Ἰούδαν (Pagels, *Origin*, 128). According to Bovon (*Luke*, 135), Jesus' fate is mainly about conflict between God and Satan.

210. Pagels, "Part II," 36.

211. This refers to Michael's defeat of Satan in Rev 12:9 (Page, *Powers*, 110).

212. Pagels, "Part II," 38; Fitzmyer, *Luke X–XXIV*, 1449; Parsons, *Luke*, 323.

213. Munro, "Women," 52; Van Til, "Anointings," 82 and Sellew, "Interior," 250.

214. Kent, "Mary," 16–17.

substantial differences from Mark/Matthew/John. These are so great that one wonders if anyone would equate the accounts except for the (very) common name of Simon.

Mark 14:3, Matthew 26:6, and John 12:1 locate the anointing in Bethany, but Luke is silent. Luke 7:36 notes that the host, called Simon (7:40), was a Pharisee, while the others do not. Mark 14:3 and Matthew 26:6 call the host Σίμωνος τοῦ λεπροῦ, which John omits. Kent argues that Luke's Simon was a healed leper, but the text does not say this.[215] Simeon/Simon was by far the most popular male name for five hundred years amongst Palestinian Jews, and both he Bauckham and Holst argue that they are different events.[216] The only common factor is the very common name of Simon. That we are then most likely dealing with two separate incidents[217] is shown by the reason for the anointing. Gujarro and Rodriguez, Munro, and Nickelsburg argue for a royal/Messianic anointing in Mark/Matthew, largely based on Jesus being anointed on the head to inaugurate his Messiahship.[218]

By contrast, Bauckham argues that anointing the head was not confined to kings, but was common at feasts, and that Jesus' Messiahship is not stated explicitly in Mark.[219] Van Til argues that Luke's version also cannot be understood as regal, as Luke uses ἀλείφω, not the expected χρίω.[220] He believes that it is like a sacrifice, with the ointment poured out at the base of the altar, but the text says nothing like this.[221] In Mark 14:8, Matthew 26:12, and John 12:7,[222] Jesus describes the anointing as anticipating his burial, while in Luke 7:47, it shows the woman's gratitude for forgiveness. Sellew must conclude that Luke has substantially rewritten Mark's account,[223] but

---

215. Ibid., 18.

216. Bauckham, *Eyewitnesses*, 65, 81; Holst, "Anointing," 437.

217. Smith, "Table," 622.

218. Gujarro and Rodriguez, "Messianic," 137; Munro, "Women," 60; and Nickelsburg, "Passion," 170. Georgia argues strenuously that Mark's Jesus imitates but subverts the Roman triumph, where the victorious triumphator led the captives in procession before offering sacrifice to the gods and executing the defeated king ("Triumph," 19–20). Even given Georgia's concession that we can only access records of how Romans experienced the triumph, not the triumph itself, it is hard to see Jesus' entry into Jerusalem as anything like a Roman triumph, and Jesus was led away from the temple, not toward it, to die.

219. Bauckham, *Eyewitnesses*, 191; also Munro, "Women," 63.

220. Van Til, "Anointings," 79.

221. Bauckham, *Eyewitnesses*, 73, 78.

222. The anointing parallel texts associated with courtship or marriage (Brant, "Drama," 248). This is unconvincing, as Jesus explicitly describes the anointing as preparation for death (12:7).

223. Sellew, "Interior," 250.

the differences are so great that I take Luke to describe a different event.[224] I will examine how Matthew, Mark, and John describe the same incident.[225]

Mark

Mark 14:1–11 is a Markan sandwich with the frame (14:1–2, 10–11) and the inner narrative (14:3–9) interacting for interpretation.[226] The theme linking the frame and the narrative is Jesus' death, which is plotted in the frame but grieved and/or predicted in the narrative. This interaction has two important consequences for the purpose of the anointing and evaluating Judas's actions.

I showed above that it was wrong to see the anointing as regal/Messianic or sacrificial, as the text gives no support. These interpretations do not allow for the Markan sandwich, which is based on death, not a regal/Messianic anointing, but for his reign; it is similar for the Messiah. Gujarro and Rodriguez, Munro, Holst, and Nickelsburg expend much effort in deciding if anointing the head or feet[227] is important for their interpretation but fail to acknowledge the Markan sandwich.[228] It is far better to adopt the reason given by Jesus (that the anointing was to prepare him for death), as this most naturally unites the frame and the narrative, than to import ideas which only have slim support in the narrative and none in the frame.

Secondly, ζητέω, κρατέω, and παραδίδωμι align Judas with the chief priests (s4.3.2). Τοῖς ἀρχιερεῦσιν and γραμματεῦσιν plot the death of Jesus (8:31; 10:33–34; 11:18; 14:1–2). Judas's presence can be established at Jesus' third prediction of his death (s4.2.6; 10:32). Judas is linked with those plotting Jesus' death, and becomes the vital link in procuring it. The contrast with the unnamed woman who anointed Jesus and the woman who spent money rather than receiving it in anticipation of his death could not be greater.[229]

---

224. See also Bock, *Luke*, 690.

225. There is no critical consensus on whether John used Mark as a source (Beasley-Murray, *John*, xxxvii).

226. Edwards, *Mark*, 195; Resseguie, *Narrative*, 54.

227. Gujarro and Rodriguez, "Messianic"; Munro, "Women"; Nickelsburg, "Passion"; and Holst, "Anointing." This varies so much between the accounts that the original, if there is one, cannot be discerned.

228. This most naturally arises from trying to conflate Luke with the other three, which I argue is wrong.

229. Edwards, *Mark*, 209. Maritz contrasts the high price of the perfume with the much lower price of betrayal (*Testimony*, 306).

Matthew

Matthew reproduces Mark's account closely with a few differences. First, Matthew has prepared the way by focusing on the essential problem of a breakdown in the relationship between Jesus and a disobedient group of disciples by three parables in Matt 25 (s4.3.2). Secondly, Matthew heightens Mark's criticism of the disciples by substituting the explicit οἱ μαθηταὶ (26:8) for Mark's ἦσαν δέ τινες (14:4). Groups of *disciples* can deserve a sharp rebuke from Jesus. Thirdly, Matthew substitutes προσέρχεσθαι for Mark's plainer ἔρχεσθαι for the anointing woman approaching Jesus (Mark 14:3; Matt 26:7), one of ten amendments in Markan material.[230] Προσέρχεσθαι frequently carries a cultic meaning in the LXX of approaching a god or an altar and, in secular sources, it can also mean approaching someone of higher rank or dignity to ask a favor.[231] Like Matthew's more specific οἱ μαθηταὶ above, this also increases the disciples' culpability. While the (male) disciples criticize her, the woman alone approaches Jesus with appropriate reverence and insight. If all parties, obedient and disobedient, in the preceding parables (Matt 25) call Jesus κύριε, she is the only one here to treat him as such.

John

John shows Judas's guilt by an inclusion, achieving the notable feat of paralleling Caiaphas and Judas as examples of one of a group of Jews speaking against Jesus. Secondly, John highlights Judas's greedy nature by his habitual theft from the purse and his lack of concern for the poor, which can mean anyone who realizes their dependence on God (s3.5.3), a grave indictment of someone who was meant to lead people to Jesus.

Inclusion: John 11:45—12:11

John 11:45: many Jews believe in Jesus because he raised Lazarus ("Πολλοὶ οὖν ἐκ τῶν Ἰουδαίων ... ἐπίστευσαν εἰς αὐτόν).
11:46: division amongst the Jews about Jesus—some go to the Pharisees.
11:47-48: meetings of Jews opposed to Jesus—the Sanhedrin.
11:49-50: one Jew from the group speaks against Jesus—Caiaphas.[232]

---

230. Edwards, *Matthew*, 71.
231. Ibid., 66-67.
232. Caiaphas voices for the whole Sanhedrin their general opposition to Jesus. It is "a plausible and pragmatic concern to protect their own constituency from Roman

11:51–52: words by/about Jesus' death—prophecy.

11:53–54: a plot to kill Jesus.[233]

11:55–57: division amongst the Jews about Jesus.

12:1–3: meetings of Jews close to Jesus—Martha, Mary, and Lazarus.

12:4–6: one Jew from the group speaks (implicitly) against Jesus; the insider Judas Iscariot complains about the waste.

12:7–8: words by/about Jesus' death—by Jesus.

12:9–10: a plot to kill Jesus *and* Lazarus.

12:11: many Jews believe in Jesus because he raised Lazarus ("ὅτι πολλοὶ . . . τῶν Ἰουδαίων . . . ἐπίστευον εἰς τὸν Ἰησοῦν").

The belief of many of the Jews in Jesus for raising Lazarus to life (11:45; 12:10) forms the inclusion. It shows, not unnaturally, a deteriorating situation. John 11:46–54 contains nothing new, as those habitually opposed to Jesus meet and decide to kill him. John 11:51 mentions that Caiaphas (unconsciously) prophesied,[234] underlining God's sovereignty, which is often expressed by δεῖ in the Synoptics; e.g., Matt 16:21. The author never hints that Caiaphas is thereby absolved, any more than Judas.[235] What is worse is that it is now one of those close to Jesus, Judas, who is compared with Caiaphas by speaking implicitly against Jesus. Judas presumed to act like God by doing what God never did (arguably blasphemy by action): handing over an innocent person to death. Moreover, the plot is now enlarged to include Lazarus's death as well.[236] It is Johannine irony that the very act of Jesus which gave life to Lazarus becomes the motivating factor for his death (12:10).[237]

Secondly, Judas shows a quality of the rich: he does not care about the poor (John 12:6).[238] By choosing a word which does not just mean economic

---

reprisals, even at the possible cost of a wrongful execution" (Pagels, "Part II," 48). It was well within Jewish thought; e.g., Sheba (2 Sam 20; Köstenberger, *John*, 469).

233. It is ironic that the Jewish leadership condemns "their one hope to death," so ensuring that he will draw the scattered children of God to himself (12:32; Duke, *Irony*, 112).

234. It was prophecy associated with the high priest's office (Beasley-Murray, *John*, 11:51; Morris, *John*, 567) versus holder of the highest office that year, but not as prophet (Ridderbos, *John*, 410). Both God and Caiaphas spoke, but with vastly different meanings (Carson, *John*, 422).

235. Ridderbos, *John*, 409.

236. Not one but two innocent deaths gives the lie to Caiaphas being a true prophet (King, *John*, 153).

237. Keener, *John*, 2:866. Another parallel is that both Caiaphas and Judas seek the death of innocent men.

238. In general, he also shows key character traits of the rich (s3.5.3). He is ruthless,

need, but more generally, dependence on God (s3.5.3), John is saying that Judas did not care about those who were dependent on God, regardless of their presumed economic status. His habitual theft only completes a picture of not caring (John 12:6).[239]

Conclusion

Mark 14/Matthew 26/John 12 are recognizably the same incident, but with different emphases: an insightful woman anoints Jesus at Bethany to prepare for his looming death. Mark shows Judas's guilt by aligning him with Jesus' traditional enemies: the chief priests and teachers of the law, the very ones to whom Jesus predicted that he would be handed over (Mark 10:34). Matthew increases Judas's guilt by the preceding parables in Matthew 25 on disobedient disciples and by substituting the more reverent προσέρχεσθαι for Mark's more pedestrian ἔρχεσθαι, Matthew highlights just whom he

---

wicked for betraying an innocent man, deceitful for stealing from the purse (John 12:6), and greedy (Prov 11:16; 13:7; 28:8; Ps 73:12) for accepting the money. He shows no features which usually shield a person from money's destructive effects, like severe testing or generosity (s3.5.2). Judas continues the OT pattern of God's people mishandling money to their cost, but does so in the heightened NT atmosphere, with its almost-wholly negative view of wealth/the wealthy. Judas, an already negative character, is associated negatively with arguably the most dangerous physical object in the NT: money.

John's only mentions of "poor" (12:5-6, 8; 13:29) all portray Judas negatively (Xavier, "Paradigm," 254).

The author contrasts Mary's extravagance with Judas's venality (Ridderbos, *John*, 416). It is believable for anyone who could betray an innocent person for thirty pieces of silver (Carson, *John*, 429). [M]έλει (12:6; 10:13) and κλέπτης (10:1, 8, 10; 12:6) parallel Judas with the hirelings (Keener, *John*, 2:864).

There are similarities to the hirelings in John 10:13 (Morris, *John*, 578; Brown, *John I-XII*, 448). Brown wonders whether disappointed avarice may have been behind Judas's decision to betray Jesus (ibid., 578). The position of treasurer may indicate Judas's place of honor near Jesus at the Last Supper, and why Judas having thirty pieces of silver may not have aroused suspicion (ibid., 453). The poor are mentioned twice in John 12:5-8 and 13:27-29 where ironically, the Eleven think that Judas does care about the poor (Martin, *Judas*, 147). He argues that Judas has some close similarities with the secessionists of 1 John 3:17, who also do not care about the poor despite having the means to do so.

239. Judas is the representative defector. He is introduced in a context of defection (6:66-71), and while Jesus' command to "Leave her alone" could be taken as is, the ἵνα (12:7) implies that Judas's departure will result in Jesus' burial (Martin, *Judas*, 145). As a disciple within the infant Jesus movement, Judas is also ignoring his responsibilities to this community. Deut 24:14-15 warns the rich against withholding wages, lest the Lord hold this sin against the whole community (Craigie, *Deuteronomy*, 309; Christensen, *Deuteronomy 21:10—34:12*, 24:15). If this principle carries into the early church, Judas is theoretically risking God's wrath on the church.

will betray. John stresses his venal nature by his habitual theft and uses an inclusion to parallel Judas and Caiaphas in a deteriorating situation, where Lazarus is now under threat of death. In stressing the role of money, John comes closer to themes explored in Luke's quite different account.

4.3.4. The Last Supper[240] (Mark 14:12–26; Matt 26:17–30; Luke 22:7–23)

The Supper Narratives are quite complex and, accordingly, I will only deal with points relevant to Judas, particularly the "birth woe" texts (Mark 14:21; Matt 26:24; Luke 22:22). In the LXX, no woe is spoken without a cause, but for habitual drunkenness, on those who deliberately confuse good and evil, for injustice, etc. (Isa 5:11, 20; 10:1). God may speak a woe for a breach of covenantal obligations on those "who acquit the guilty for a bribe," as "they have rejected the law of the Lord" (Isa 5:23–24).[241] A woe may be spoken to Gentiles with a penalty: the king of Assyria is the "club of My (God's) wrath" but God also said that, after he had used the king to punish Jerusalem, he would punish him for thinking that God was no more real than idols (Isa 10:5, 8, 12).[242] All are accountable, even those inflicting a woe with God's permission.

Klassen queries whether the woe forms match, and suggests that the impersonal nature of the synoptic woe is a marked departure.[243] It does not, however, rule out the value of the OT precedents in illuminating those of the supper narratives. When a woe is spoken to an individual, they are named by their office or deed. God spoke a woe on "the Assyrian," but "my commanders," "shall I not deal with Jerusalem," and God's explicit identification make clear it is the king (Isa 10:8, 11–12). "That the person [is] unidentified" matters less than their deed.[244]

---

240. Moloney makes a brave but unconvincing attempt to minimize, in effect, Judas's treachery in John. He makes a number of helpful comments about how Jesus' love for his "ignorant and failing disciples" reveals God's and Jesus' unconditional love for the world (*Love,* 116, 113). He equates the failures of Peter and Judas as though they are similar, even though Jesus clearly said "I am not referring to all of you" (John 13:18) when referring to the fulfillment of Ps 41:9. Jesus' unconditional love for the world only heightens Judas's culpability, as it is precisely this love which Judas betrayed.

241. Repeated woes continue the funeral scene from the Song of the Vineyard (Watts, *Isaiah 1–33,* 63).

242. A woe is pronounced on Israel (Isa 9:8—10:4) for manifold sins and then on Assyria for gross presumption (Watts, *Isaiah 1–33,* 147).

243. Klassen, *Friend,* 82.

244. Ibid., 82.

Mark

The only individual woe in Mark is to the one who will hand Jesus over (Mark 14:21).[245] Jesus does not name Judas, except to say that the traitor is "one of the Twelve" (14:20). This is no more impersonal than the woe to the king of Assyria, as both are described by their deed. The king presumed to think like God (Isa 10:13–14), and Judas presumed to act like God by doing what is normally God's prerogative: handing people over to death (s2.2). They each received a woe directly from God, with the king promised near total destruction of his forces (Isa 10:16–19). However, Jesus said of Judas that it would have been better if he had not been born, a frightful judgment (Mark 14:21).[246] Klassen argues that Jesus pronounces a woe on the "one *chosen* to deliver him up."[247] He has imported the idea of choice, which is wholly absent from Mark 14:21.[248] In Mark, Judas initiates the betrayal (14:10). If he is obedient, why does Jesus pronounce a woe, not a blessing? If Jesus is expressing "sympathy for the rejection"[249] which the betrayal will cause Judas, surely there are better words. The natural understanding of his words, which caused the apostles such sadness (Mark 14:19), is that he was giving Judas a final chance not to betray him. Mark's only other woe is Jesus' on nursing mothers (13:17). They have done nothing to earn such a fate, and uniquely among the "woe" passages, he asks them to pray that the suffering might not be too great (Mark 13:18, 20). Judas has a choice, and the women can pray—these woes seem avoidable.

Matthew

Mark shows that Judas's judgment is avoidable. Matt shows how uniquely it applies to him. First, he adopts Jesus' words almost verbatim. Mark 14:21 reads "ὅτι ὁ μὲν υἱὸς τοῦ ἀνθρώπου . . . παραδίδοται. Καλόν αὐτῷ εἰ οὐκ ἐγεννήθη ὁ ἄνθρωπος ἐκεῖνος."[250] Matthew 26:24 omits ὅτι and adds ἦν after Καλόν, hardly significant changes. While (presumably) the Eleven

---

245. The anonymity is maintained by the double ὁ ἄνθρωπος ἐκεῖνος (France, *Mark*, 567). Jesus' words are intended to prompt Judas to repent (Oropeza, *Footsteps*, 1:37n112).

246. It suggests final condemnation, implying that his act was wrongful (ibid., 1:147).

247. Klassen, *Friend*, 82; my emphasis.

248. France, *Mark*, 567.

249. Klassen, *Friend*, 83.

250. "The offence . . . is, even if not unprecedented, serious" (King, *Fencing*, 19; citing Evans, *Mark 8:27—16:20*, 379)

question Jesus in sorrow with the emphatic ἐγώ εἰμι and call him κύριε (26:22), Matthew names Judas as the recipient of the woe (unlike Mark) and as questioning Jesus with the same ἐγώ εἰμι (26:25), but calling him ῥαββί. I argue in s4.3.5 that this is a calculated insult, rather than just "inadequate."[251]

Secondly, "woe" is a serious, eternal penalty[252] which is incurred by rejecting God, except for the nursing mothers (Matt 24:19). Jesus pronounces a woe on Jewish Korazin and Bethsaida for rejecting him despite his miracles, and for things which cause people to sin, particularly "the man through whom they come" (Matt 11:21; 18:7). Matthew linked Judas with Jesus' traditional opponents, the teachers of the law and Pharisees, in chapters 23–25, and inserted three παρουσία parables (s4.3.2) immediately before Judas's plot to betray Jesus. The last usage in this escalating series is on Judas at the Last Supper.

The common element is final judgment: on Korazin and Bethsaida (chapter 11), the entry to heaven or not (chapter 18), and "How will you escape being condemned to hell?" (23:33). Like Korazin and Bethsaida,[253] Judas had seen Jesus' miracles (s4.3.5), and yet had not repented. Judas could be an example of the woe on the man, τῷ ἀνθρώπῳ, through whom came enticements to sin (18:7).[254] Once the temple hierarchy had the means to kill Jesus, the temptation to do so would increase (Matt 26:3–5, 14–16). Jesus never rebukes the temple hierarchy as harshly as Judas.[255] We also see a pattern of increasing seriousness. Korazin and Bethsaida do not understand the miracles and the need to repent. Next, people do not see that serious sin disqualifies them from eternal life. Finally, the religious leadership of Israel are cursed because of unfaithfulness, culminating in handing over innocent blood (Matt 23:15, 23, 27, 30–32). The narrative sequence climaxes with the woe on Judas, which is worse than any of its predecessors.

Klassen thinks that the "birth woe" (Matt 26:24b) is a "reason to reject . . . betrayal";[256] if Judas had betrayed Jesus, then these words are Jesus'

251. Davies and Allison, *Matthew*, 3:464.

252. "A threat or warning" (ibid., 2:266).

253. Compared unfavorably with two notorious Gentile cities: Tyre and Sidon (Siker, "Gentiles," 87).

254. It is rated C, showing a considerable degree of doubt (Aland et al., *Greek New Testament*, xiii). The alternative looks like a conscious assimilation to Judas: οὐαὶ τῷ ἀνθρώπῳ ἐκείνῳ is almost written verbatim from Mark 14:21.

255. Some of Jesus' comments in ch 23 could apply to Judas: he is arguably twice as much a child of hell as the Pharisees as he was one of the Twelve and yet betrayed Jesus, he neglected justice and faithfulness in betraying Jesus, he may have been presentable on the outside but was full of wickedness on the inside (as a thief), and was about to hand over innocent blood (Matt 23:15, 23, 27, 30ff).

256. Klassen, *Friend*, 107.

encouragement to do so (which violates a fundamental rule of Judaism), so there was no betrayal.[257] He has ignored the possibility that Jesus might be highlighting Judas's looming betrayal to dissuade him. He does not explain how such confronting comments could mean "Judas faithfully carried out that mission for his master."[258]

Klassen is right that Jesus' comments stress the gravity of the act[259] but not the betrayer's identity. Jesus does not clearly identify Judas, so the Eleven do not know who will hand him over, but he uses the solemn amen to introduce his comments, pronounces a "woe" on the one handing over, concludes that it would have been better if he had not been born, and finally answers Judas to affirm what he is saying and to highlight the ominous nature of Judas's answer.[260] Matthew's Jesus, in that culture, could not have been any plainer.

Luke

Luke records the sovereignty of God in Jesus' chilling words, "The Son of Man will go as it has been decreed, but woe to that man who betrays him" (Luke 22:22), which are largely similar to Matthew and Mark. Like Mark, Luke's Jesus does not specifically identify the traitor, and while Luke does not repeat Mark's comment that it would have been better if the traitor had not been born, Luke 22:3 (cf. Mark and Matthew) says for the first time that Satan entered Judas, coloring all of Judas's later actions.[261]

---

257. Klassen has failed to give a single clear example where "woe" is an encouragement. The only other real possibility is necessity, but Jesus could simply have walked onto the temple grounds and been arrested.

258. Ibid., 107.

259. "A culpable and irrevocable decision" (France, *Mark*, 567).

260. Keener calls Jesus' manner of answering Judas "roundabout," which reflects Jesus' manner of answering "his opponents on that night" (*Matthew*, 626). This is significant: Judas the insider is being answered like an enemy of Jesus. Were one to propose hypothetically that Jesus' enigmatic answer is not confirmation of betrayal, then to rebut such an idea requires far more than agreeing with the speaker. At the very least, Jesus should have reassured Judas that his proposed actions were not treacherous.

261. Satanic entry is unusual, but must not be confused with possession (Nolland, *Luke 18:35—24:53*, 22:3). Page notes the similarity with Ananias and Sapphira, who were (also) motivated by greed (*Powers*, 132). The evangelists do not address Judas's motivation, but he is linked negatively with money. Smith seems not to have given Satanic entry due weight, as he agrees with Klassen that betrayal should not be assumed ("Hand this Man," 159; Klassen, *Friend*, 56). He does not explain how a Satanically inspired handing over could be so benign.

Only the Father could allow Jesus to die,[262] but a horrible fate, the emphatic πλὴν οὐαί,[263] awaits the one handing him over. This preserves God's sovereignty and Judas's accountability. The evangelists do not discuss Judas's motivation, but there is no evidence that he cooperated with God.[264] The very severity of God's judgment must count against any positive evaluation of Judas, contra Bovon, who sees "the hand of Judas and the hand of God . . . joined together" in the betrayal.[265]

Judas had not understood that the locus of God's people had passed from national Israel to a new people based around Jesus. This is broached in the Nazareth sermon (4:16–30) and comes to fruition in Acts.[266] If God warned the nations to submit to Israel or be judged (Isa 41:11–12; 52:1–2), then those who oppose his purposes under the new covenant might be judged similarly. Judas opposed Jesus by handing him over to the chief priests. Israel was to be a light to the nations (Isa 42:6), and Judas was a light of sorts on mission to Israel (s4.2.3), but his death prevented him from being a light to the nations. Jesus concludes his riposte to the arresting party with "But this is your hour—when darkness reigns" (Luke 22:53). Judas has aligned himself with the forces of darkness, and cannot be part of the Gentile mission because of death.

---

262. God decreed, but Jesus still had to agree: "not my [Jesus'] will but yours [the Father's] be done" (Luke 22:42); and there are times when Jesus escaped because his time had not yet come (Luke 4:30).

263. Fitzmyer, *Luke X–XXIV*, 1410.

264. Oropeza, *Footsteps*, 1:146

265. Bovon, *Luke*, 172.

266. Pao, *Acts*, 77, 227–35.

4.3.5. Judas's betrayal of Jesus
(Mark 14:43–50; Matt 26:47–56; Luke 22:47–53)

Matthew and Mark (but not Luke or John) have Judas calling Jesus "Rabbi" (Mark 14:45; Matt 26:25). Describing Judas calling Jesus "Rabbi," Judas regarding him "*only* as a teacher," does not capture its full meaning.[267] Comparing the first use of titles for/by Jesus in the Synoptics, shows that it is a calculated insult.[268]

Mark

The first use of a title for Jesus in Mark by a named character or Jesus himself, as opposed to the evangelist, is usually accompanied by a validating miracle.[269] Jesus was not simply given titles by himself or others, but miracles showed their truth. In most cases, the presence of the disciples, including Judas, can be established. Judas had enough information to suspect that Jesus was more than a rabbi (Mark 14:45).[270] This is shown in the following table. While the Eleven had deficits in understanding Jesus (s4.2.5), none of them betrayed him.

Title in Mark.	Disciples	First	By	Miracle
My Son[a]	n/a	1:11[b]	The Father	Heaven opened,[c] 1:10
Jesus of Nazareth	1:21	1:24	Evil spirit	Exorcism, 1:25
The Holy One of God	1:21	1:24[d]	Evil spirit	Exorcism, 1:25
Son of Man	n/a	2:10	Jesus	Healing, 2:12
Lord	2:23	2:28[e]	Jesus	nil

---

267. Keener, *Matthew*, 626.

268. John achieves something similar by a different method. In John 13:13, Jesus told the Twelve that it was entirely appropriate for them to call him "Teacher and Lord" because that was true. Also, the grammatically redundant ὑμεῖς (13:13) emphasizes that this is a collective, not an individual, attribute of the Twelve (Collins, "Teacher," 327). The repetition of ὑμεῖς in 13:14–15 emphasizes the collective responsibility of the Twelve to learn from and obey Jesus (ibid., 328). They call him "Lord" and should act appropriately. The key point is that Judas was present and close enough to Jesus to receive the sop (13:26) and, having had Jesus wash his feet and heard all that Jesus said, left to betray him (13:30). The enormity of this is only heightened by Jesus saying that servants are not greater than their master (13:16; ibid., 343), yet Judas was about to betray the one who was rightfully his master.

269. Exceptions are Lord (it is unclear why) and King of the Jews/Israel (miracles would have been inappropriate at his trial; Mark 2:28; 15:2, 32).

270. "Rabbi" used by Peter (9:5; 11:21) and Judas, the two who fail Jesus the most (Beavis, *Mark*, 216).

Title in Mark.	Disciples	First	By	Miracle
Son of God[f]	3:7, 9	3:11	Unclean spirits	Healing, 3:10
Teacher	4:35	4:38	Disciples	Stilling storm, 4:39
Jesus	5:1	5:7	Legion	Exorcism, 5:13
Son of the Most High God	5:1	5:7[g]	Legion	Exorcism, 5:13
"I am"	6:48	6:50[h]	Jesus	Walking on the sea, 6:48
Lord (by a Gentile)	n/a	7:28	Syrophoenician	Exorcism, 7:29
Christ	8:27	8:29	Peter	Revelation (Matt 16:17)
Rabbi	9:2 (the 3)	9:5	Peter	Transfiguration, 9:2[i]
Son of David	10:46	10:47	Bartimaeus	Healing, 10:52
Son of the Blessed One	n/a	14:61	High Priest	Prophecy, 14:62
King of the Jews[j]	n/a	15:2	Pilate	nil
King of Israel	n/a	15:32	Chief priests	nil

a. "Beloved" indicates Jesus' uniqueness (Guelich, Mark 1:1—8:26, 1:11).

b. This meant Jesus' deity, as it sounded like Zeus talking to his sons, Apollos or Hermes (Dixon, "Descending," 774). Where a heavenly voice calls Jesus "My Son" in 1:11 and 9:7; he is also called "beloved" (Donahue, "Factor," 592).

c. The descent of the Spirit as a dove has Greek antecedents (from Homer), not Jewish (Dixon, "Descending," 759). Homer had a pervasive influence on the Ancient Near East; he used birds to signify the arrival/departure of gods (766). Καταβαίνω εἰς does not mean movement toward, as all other NT examples have an impersonal object. Εἰς probably means the Spirit went "into" Jesus (ibid., 771–72).

d. It acknowledges Jesus' superiority (Guelich, Mark 1:1—8:26, 1:24).

e. Self-references by Jesus in 2:28, 11:3, and by the Syrophoenician in 7:28 (Donahue, "Factor," 565).

f. Collins notes the meanings of "Son of God," possibly held by Jesus' followers of diverse backgrounds. Greek/Roman converts may have likened Jesus to Empedocles and Asclepius, who either claimed or were ascribed immortality because of their healing powers ("Readers," 89). While Romans could apply "son of God" to a virtuous person, and Augustus called himself such (ibid., 96–97), the demons here worship him (cf. other claimants), and the Father called Jesus his (uniquely) beloved Son (1:11). Collins distinguishes the demonic confession "You are" from the centurion's lesser "this was" (3:11; 15:39).

g. 'Son . . . God' is a divine name for Zeus, but it is linked here with the human name Jesus (ibid., 90). Other people sometimes do what the Twelve are meant to, here to follow Jesus (Donahue, "Factor," 583).

h. The disciples did not appreciate the full significance of ἐγώ εἰμι (Guelich, Mark 1:1—8:26, 6:50). It is an epiphany of Jesus (ibid., 577).

i. This reflects Greek traditions that the gods walked on earth in human form (Collins, "Readers," 90).

j. The ancients would have seen the darkness (15:33) as the King of the Jews' apotheosis (ibid., 94). This title is only used in Mark by Pilate and his soldiers (Bond, Pilate, 106). Bond sees Pilate's question as an astute attempt to gauge the degree of danger in such an apparently seditious claim.

The Twelve were present except for Jesus' baptism, the healings of the paralytic and the Syrophoenician's daughter, and Jesus' trial. They would have heard the titles given to/by Jesus and seen the validating miracle. While Judas was not at the transfiguration, it is very likely that he was present at all the others (particularly those of Mark 3:7 and 9; 4:35; 6:48; and 10:46). In 3:7, Jesus took his disciples to the lake, where they heard the demon call him "son of God." Jesus then appointed the Twelve, so arguably Judas saw the exorcism. He explained the parable of the sower to them (Mark 4:10), and later, Judas is not excepted when they crossed the lake, heard "Teacher," and saw the storm stilled.[271] Similarly, Judas was present, heard Jesus' "I am," and saw him stilling the storm (Mark 6:48, 50; Matt 14:27). Judas would have heard Bartimaeus call Jesus "son of David," seen his restored sight (Matt 10:31; Mark 10:48), and heard "Rabbi" (Mark 10:51), used by him to Jesus in Gethsemane (Mark 14:45). The narrative shows Judas as an apostle and insider who should have had a better understanding of Jesus than (merely) calling him "Rabbi": it implies a deliberate slight.[272] Judas kissing Jesus, a traditional sign of respect and affection from a disciple to a rabbi, as the pre-arranged signal of identification, adds an element of hypocrisy to Judas's act[273] and completes the picture of deliberate insult from his "Rabbi." It breaches every cultural norm between teacher and disciple.

A similar situation, if not so pronounced, exists in Matthew and Luke. There is much evidence that Judas heard many of Jesus' titles and saw the validating miracles. It is difficult to see how he could not understand Jesus' uniqueness. Calling Jesus "Rabbi" in Gethsemane (14:45) is not just "presumptuous,"[274] but is an insult, as Judas had seen and heard many convincing proofs that Jesus was much more than a rabbi.

---

271. Luke 9:12 notes that the Twelve were at the feeding of the five thousand. The evangelists do not say that all Twelve were at Caesarea Philippi, but if John 6:66–71 is the Johannine version, John said three times that all Twelve were there (6:67, 70–71; Matt 16:13; Mark 8:29; Luke 9:20). Luke 18:31 has all Twelve present at the third prediction of Jesus' death.

272. Contra Zwiep ("Judas and the Jews," 73), who says that Mark's Judas only played "an ambiguous role" in the arrest.

273. Evans, *Mark 8:27—16:20*, 14:45.

274. Ibid., 14:45.

Matthew

Title	Disciples	First	By	Miracle
My Son	nil	3:17	The Father	Heaven opened, 3:16
Jesus of Nazareth	21:6	21:11?	The crowds	nil
The Holy One of God		nil		
Son of Man	8:18	8:20	Jesus	nil
Lord	5:1	8:2	Leper	Healing, 8:3
Son of God[a]	nil	4:3	Satan	
Teacher	8:18	8:19	Tchr of the law	nil
Jesus	nil	1:21	An angel	Annunciation, 1:21
Son of the Most High God		nil		
"I am"	14:26	14:27	Jesus	Walking on the water
Lord (by a Gentile)	nil	15:22.	Canaanite	Exorcism
Christ	16:13	16:16	Peter	Revelation, 16:17
Rabbi[b]	26:20	26:25	Judas	nil
Son of David[c]	nil	9:27	2 blind men	Healing, 9:29
Son of the Blessed One		nil		
King of the Jews		2:2	The Magi	Saw His star, 2:2
King of Israel		nil		

a. Mowery argues that Matthew has reversed the normal order ὁ υἱὸς τοῦ θεοῦ found in all the gospels, plus other NT books, to become θεοῦ υἱὸς to emphasise Jesus' divinity ("Son of God," 197). He cites examples of ὁ υἱὸς τοῦ θεοῦ, but misses the common thread of opposition by evil (4:3, 6; 8:29); Jewish leaders (26:63; 27:40) and Peter (16:16), later called "Satan" (16:23). Mowery notes that 16:16 and 26:63 share eight words: σὺ εἶ ὁ Χριστὸς ὁ υἱὸς τοῦ θεοῦ (ibid., 195), contrasting the responses to Jesus by two Jews. He gives three examples of θεοῦ υἱός, but does not notice that they cover the three possible responses to Jesus as Son of God: the disciples worship Jesus after hearing him say "I am" and watching him calm the storm (14:33); the chief priests mock him (27:43) and the centurion and others acknowledge him (27:54). Collins notes in Matt's source (Mark 15:39) that the centurion said Jesus "was (ἦν) the Son of God," which she distinguishes from demonic acclamation (3:11; Collins, "Readers," 93). The only other prepositive is the disdainful Matt 13:55: "the carpenter's son." The prepositive's emphasis on Jesus' divinity increases the culpability of those who reject or betray him.

b. Judas calling Jesus "Rabbi" links him to the scribes, who love being called such (23:7–8; Sim, "Weeping," 185).

c. Matthew links Jesus' healing acts to "Son of David," alluding to Ezekiel 34:5 in Matt 9:36 and Ezek 34:17 in Matt 25:32 (Baxter, "Son of David," 36). Israel's leadership are likened to Ezek 34's unfaithful shepherds (ibid., 43–44).

Matthew 26:49 also records Judas kissing Jesus, but adds a new element as Judas greets Jesus with Χαῖρε, the traditional greeting of peace. In the circumstances, this is of course ironic,[275] as he hands Jesus over to death. As in Mark 14:45, Matthew 26:49 keeps the intensive κατεφίλησεν for the

275. Hagner, *Matthew 14–28*, 26:49.

actual identifying kiss. As previously, Matthew highlights Judas's treachery, but intensifies it with the ironic Χαῖρε.

When Matthew 26:50 has Jesus calling Judas "Friend,"[276] this does not excuse him, but places him well within the frame of a close colleague who turned against his master. This is not established by the use of "friend" alone, but by Judas also satisfying all the other criteria (s2.3.1). Jesus went obediently to the cross (Matt 26:39), but like the other examples of treachery in s2.3, Judas is not thereby excused, not least because he was prompted by Satan, God's main spiritual rival, and rewarded with money, God's main material rival (s3.5). Judas's handing over of Jesus uses παραδίδωμι; Jesus, as Son of God, was superior to Judas—there was no reason for Judas to hand Jesus over, and finally, both Judas and Jesus died. The text provides firm support from the background of the LXX and Josephus for Judas's actions being treacherous.

In conclusion, like Mark, Matthew links first occurrences of titles with validating miracles, and Judas is not mentioned as an exception to hearing Jesus of Nazareth, Lord, "I am," and Christ, as well as those titles for which there was no validating miracle. The narrative progression in Matthew mirrors that of Mark and reinforces the insult.

Luke

Luke differs, as many of Jesus' titles are given in the disciples' absence, but most importantly for our purposes, Luke's Judas does not call Jesus "Rabbi." The complete lack of an honorific may imply an even greater degree of contempt. Even if this is not so, the lack of any such detail in Luke leaves the nature of their relationship uncertain, implying that Judas has drifted away from previous intimacy, despite the (attempted) kiss (22:48), "a gesture of affection, of love, or of respect."[277]

In summary, Mark and Matthew allow the reader with a high degree of probability to ascertain that Judas was present when titles were given to or by Jesus, and he would have seen the accompanying miracles which validated their truth. He would have realized that Jesus was more than just another rabbi. Calling Jesus "Rabbi" was a calculated insult to someone whom he had good reason to suspect was much more. Judas added insult to injury by kissing Jesus, a normal sign of respect and affection, to betray him.

---

276. Even less likely is "terms of intimacy" (Brant, *Drama*, 176) between them. Saying that Jesus "remains friendly" may overstate things compared with highlighting Judas's treachery (Davies and Allison, *Matthew*, 3:509).

277. Bovon, *Luke*, 215.

Blasphemy

Blasphemy most conveniently summarizes Judas's attitude to Jesus. Mark draws attention to the blasphemous[278] dimension of the charges against Jesus (14:63–64),[279] particularly due to his self-testimony.[280] Jesus was thought to be arrogating to himself a divine prerogative by his self-testimony, and prophesying that he would return and judge his accusers.[281] Jesus is culturally, if not legally, guilty of blasphemy.[282]

However, the real blasphemer is Judas, with whom they are colluding. This is shown by what he says and does. Bock cites many texts from the LXX, Philo, and Josephus to argue that the key element of blasphemy is verbal. Disrespectful words spoken against God show an underlying negative attitude which impugns his power, uniqueness, or goodness.[283] Judas calling Jesus "Rabbi" in Gethsemane may not just be simple incomprehension, as he had seen miracles which validated Jesus' claims (Matt 26:49; Mark 14:45). He impugned Jesus' power (otherwise, why hand him over?), his uniqueness (there were many rabbis, but only one Lord), and his goodness (Jesus' innocence [Matt 27:4]), and so fell within the Jewish understanding of blasphemy.

Blasphemy is not only verbal, but may manifest in actions which show an arrogation to oneself of the prerogatives of God. King argues that self-testimony, arrogating to oneself a right held only by God, is "an instance of blasphemy."[284] If we may extend the same principle to arrogating actions performed overwhelmingly by God, it is clear that Judas falls foul of this as well. Examining παραδίδωμι (s2.2) shows that, in the LXX, God is the subject almost 90 percent of the time. Many of the remaining cases are where people act in place of God, but with strict requirements for justice (Deut 19:12). By handing over Jesus, Judas was not just claiming to act in virtual equality with God—and so implicitly and blasphemously comparing himself with God—but he claimed a right which not even God claimed: hand-

---

278. See m. Sanh. 7.5: blasphemy is an inappropriate uttering of God's name, and the Jews used various circumlocutions, like the high priest's ὁ υἱὸς τοῦ Εὐλογητοῦ and Jesus' equally careful reply that he would be seen ἐκ δεξιῶν καθήμενον τῆς Δυνάμεως (Mark 14:61–62; Bock, *Blasphemy*, 2; Beavis, *Mark*, 221).

279. McKnight and Modica note other charges against Jesus, such as that he is demon-possessed, etc. (*Opponents*).

280. Bock, *Blasphemy*, 202, 231; King, "Giants," 73,77.

281. Bock, *Blasphemy*, 231.

282. Ironically, Jesus would be guilty of blasphemy if he was not who he said he was.

283. Ibid., 35, 42; Bock, "Blasphemer," 77.

284. King, "Giants," 77.

ing over "innocent blood" (Matt 27:4) to certain death. Judas's disrespect to Jesus, and his arrogation of what even God did not claim, is clear evidence that he was a blasphemer within existing Jewish norms. The irony is that, while the high priest was careful to avoid blasphemy by using a circumlocution for God's name, Jesus was only there because the temple authorities had paid a real functioning blasphemer, Judas, to hand him over for trial.

Arrest/Trial

There are two key points: Judas initiating the handing over of Jesus to a mob (Appendix 8) and the subsequent handing over of Jesus to unjust trials before Annas, Caiaphas, and finally Pilate, who hands him over for crucifixion. The use of παραδίδωμι in these circumstances is consistent with betrayal.[285] Secondly, I will show that the closer Jesus gets to the cross, the less guilt he imputes to those involved. These points are made so similarly in each gospel that little is gained by studying them separately.

The element of coercion is central. Jesus is not just handed over, he is arrested and bound by an armed mob like a common criminal (Matt 26:47; Mark 14:46; Luke 22:47; John 18:12).[286] While this could be in continuity with the LXX, no one who is wholly innocent is handed over for trial in the LXX (s2.2.3), so this is another new concept. Jesus is taken for an unsatisfactory trial before Annas and then Caiaphas (John 18:13ff), where the charge(s) are unclear.[287] The initial charge against Jesus is unstated but his insistence on the public nature of his teaching may counter insinuations by the high priest that he taught secretly like a false prophet.[288]

---

285. Oropeza, *Footsteps*, 1:143.

286. The Johannine Judas's passivity in Gethsemane is meant to highlight the control which "Jesus has over his destiny," as having Judas actively identify Jesus would have conflicted with this control (Maritz, "Judas Iscariot," 292). This argument presumes that having active disciples somehow lessens Jesus' control. Nothing like this is said. Jesus' problem with Judas is not that he is active, but that he is a traitor.

287. The high priest's procedure was unusual, as Jewish judges normally questioned the witnesses in detail, more so than the accused (Beasley-Murray, *John*, 18:19). This gives further weight to concerns that this was not a formal, legal trial, but a legal expedient.

288. Ibid., 18:19. The Sanhedrin sought evidence to justify execution (Matt 26:59; Mark 14:55), but the false witnesses (Baker, *Wealth*, 206) did not agree (Matt 26:60; Mark 14:56); it was only Jesus' self-revelation as the Christ which caused the charge of blasphemy, which had not been mentioned previously (Matt 26:65; Mark 14:63). Twelftree argues that the reply of Mark's Jesus began with "I am," apparently taking on a title which only God could bestow and was thus open to the charge of blasphemy ("Blasphemy"). Luke is more circumspect: the charge is not so much blasphemy as the more dangerous (in Roman eyes) treason (23:2), where Jesus is accused of opposing

Secondly, before the Sanhedrin,²⁸⁹ Jesus is silent in the face of false testimony and agrees with the high priest that he is the Christ, but replies in the language of the Son of Man (Matt 26:63-64; Mark 14:61-62;²⁹⁰ Luke 22:67) and Son of God (Luke 22:70).²⁹¹ The synoptics record Jesus' circumspection before Pilate,²⁹² even though he was accused of being the potentially treasonous King of the Jews (Matt 27:14; Mark 15:5; Luke 23:3).²⁹³ But in John 19:10, when Pilate said that he could free Jesus or crucify him, Jesus said that that was only because he had been given such authority by God.²⁹⁴ Jesus then relativized Pilate's guilt as "the one who handed me over to you is guilty of a *greater* sin." (John 19:11).²⁹⁵ The closer Jesus gets to the cross, the less guilt he is willing to attribute. Of the soldiers carrying out the crucifixion,²⁹⁶ Jesus said, "Father, forgive them, for they do not know what they are doing" (Luke 23:34).²⁹⁷ Jesus means the soldiers, as the rest of the verse mentions

---

taxation and claiming to be a king.

289. The question of whether this was an actual trial is vexed, and any standard commentary will review the evidence for and against. There are considerable difficulties, with it being a formal trial, and commentators like France, *Mark*, 602; Keener, *Matthew*, 645; *John*, 1086 and Nolland (*Luke 18:35—24:53*, 1104) argue that it is more like a pretrial hearing to see if an actual charge (again conjectural) could be sustained.

290. Garrett misses the point that Jesus' silence before the high priest was to deny Satan any evidence to use against Jesus "before the *divine* tribunal" (her emphasis; *Temptations*, 125). I argued in s3.4.4 that Satan and his angels had been expelled from heaven years before. The text itself provides nothing to support Garrett.

291. I will not discuss the significance of the different accounts of the trial by the evangelists. I will show that Jesus attributes less guilt the closer he gets to the cross. Hagner argues that Jesus is not evasive but affirmative, even though he is less "direct and emphatic" than in Mark 14:62 (*Matthew 14-28*, 26:63). Jesus is more circumspect in Luke than in Mark (Nolland, *Luke 18:35—24:53*, 1109).

292. Especially as the Romans equated silence by the accused with a guilty plea (Bond, *Pilate*, 109).

293. Jesus does not deny his kingship, but says that his main role is attesting to the truth (Brant, *Drama*, 191).

294. Bond, *Pilate*, 189.

295. Pagels, "Part II," 49; my emphasis. The identity of this person is not disclosed. Beasley-Murray suggests that it is not Judas (in spite of the parallel use of παραδίδωμι) because he is dead by this stage, and the singular precludes the Jewish leadership (*John*, 19:10). The most likely candidate is Caiaphas, who uttered the fateful prophecy in John 11:49-50 (Oropeza, *Footsteps*, 1:185). To argue that Judas is intended, given Jesus' reference to him in John 6:64 as ὁ παραδώσων, suffers from the fatal flaw that Judas did not hand Jesus to Pilate, but to an armed mob (John 18:3): "Jesus implies that Judas' guilt is greater than Pilate's" (MacKinnon, "Imagination," 199; MacKinnon, "Christology," 273).

296. Whitlark and Parsons, "Seven," 204.

297. At first glance, the external evidence can seem evenly divided between inclusion and exclusion. This evenness is more apparent than real, as the MSS which exclude

them casting lots;[298] they are identified as such in John 19:23. It is difficult to argue that Jesus referred to the Jewish authorities, who well knew that they were engineering his death. Even with the textual uncertainty of Luke 23:34, the pattern is clear that Jesus imputes less guilt to the participants, the closer he gets to crucifixion. Only of Judas, not even of Caiaphas or Pilate, did Jesus pronounce the "birth woe" (Matt 26:24, Mark 14:21, and Luke 22:22 "woe to that man").

---

are spread across different texts (which is better), while those which include are all Western (not so good; ibid., 189–91). The external evidence therefore favors omission, and the authors seek to explain its incorporation into Luke as being necessitated by gospel harmonizations which had only six words by Jesus from the cross, as opposed to the theologically significant seven. The inclusion of this material into Luke then gave canonical balance in the seven words: three each from Luke and John, and one from Matthew/Mark (ibid., 204). Luke 23:34a seems a secondary inclusion, most likely to form seven sayings from the cross, but it also neatly fits the pattern of decreasing attribution of guilt by Jesus as he gets closer to the cross.

It is very optimistic to extend Jesus' prayer "to all who had a hand in securing Jesus' present position upon the cross" (Nolland, *Luke 18:35—24:53*, 23:34). At least, genuine repentance would seem necessary for forgiveness. This would be impossible for the dead Judas, especially given Jesus' "woe to that man," and highly unlikely for a Caiaphas, who had seen his plans fulfilled. Pilate's washing of his hands hardly equates with repentance. Only the soldiers, under authority (contra Fitzmyer, *Luke X–XXIV*, 1504) could be forgiven for executing what they would no doubt have thought to be yet another troublesome Jew. Parsons correctly notes the theme of forgiveness, but not the limitation, γάρ, of ignorance (*Luke*, 337).

Aland, et al., give Luke 23:34 a C grade, showing much doubt as to whether the text or the apparatus has the superior reading (*Greek New Testament*, xiii). There is an impressive list of early witnesses which omit this prayer, but as Nolland says, given Luke's conscious paralleling of the death of Jesus with that of his first martyr Stephen, it is hard to see how Luke could have produced Acts 7:60 while unaware of this tradition (*Luke 18:35—24:53*, 1141). Even if we omit this verse, the pattern of decreasing guilt is clear. Jesus never says of those who actually condemned or executed him that it would have been better if they had not been born.

The bystanders would have understood Jesus' prayer as referring to the forgiveness of the ignorant for their unintentional sin (King, "Kol Nidre"). He argues that the Yom Kippur ritual contained echoes of Num 15 to this effect (ibid., 135). He argues that Jesus specifies no particular audience (ibid., 146), but the prayer seems to refer only to the ignorant. There are two other problems. King refers (ibid., 142) to the generosity of Jesus' forgiveness, but fails to allow for the fact that the Yom Kippur ritual meant asking for forgiveness and Num 15 required sacrifice. It is difficult to see the authorities meeting either condition. Secondly, given that King approvingly quotes Schultz allowing "wilful disobedience" (ibid., 136), and Daube allowing "presumptuous sins" to be unwitting and therefore unintentional, one wonders what it would require for a sin to be intentional, especially as the authorities ride roughshod over legal procedure in order to secure a conviction and rapid execution. It is unclear in what sense they are not intending Jesus' death.

298. The whole scene is reminiscent of the treatment given to defeated warriors (Brant, "Drama," 215).

The circumstances of Jesus' handing over to Annas, Caiaphas, and Pilate are in s2.2.4. The most important thing for our purposes is that Judas starts a series of events which culminate in Jesus' death. Annas, Caiaphas, and Pilate all act in flagrant disregard of the most basic standards of justice, and yet none are reproached by Jesus like Judas.

4.4. Judas after the betrayal (Matt 27:1–10; Acts 1:15–26)

Matthew has three further significant events which show Judas's guilt. He is remorseful; he disposes of the thirty shekels; and he dies. By contrast, Mark, Luke, and John have nothing on Judas post-betrayal. Acts 1 records his death at Akeldama.

Matthew

Matthew's account of Judas post-betrayal highlights slavery (δουλεύειν) in relation to money and the monetary precedent found in Zechariah 11. This shows the change in δουλεύειν from OT to NT (s3.5.4), with Judas potentially trying to serve both Jesus and money. As an apostle, he was called to serve Jesus, but by taking the money to betray an innocent Jesus, he was arguably serving it. Klassen argues that, although the wages of thirty shekels in Zechariah 11 may have had a bearing on Matthew's account, it cannot be determinative.[299] However, he does not recognize the ways in which Zechariah 11 informs Matthew's narrative.

There are many parallels between the LXX of Zechariah 11 and Matthew 26:14–16/27:1–10.[300] Both have a form of παραδίδωμι: παραδώσω (Matt 26:15) and παραδίδωμι (Zech 11:6). Matthew 27 has παραδίδωμι in 27:2 (παρέδωκαν), 27:3 (παραδιδοὺς), and 27:4 (παραδοὺς), in a context of Judas's remorse at Jesus' arrest. Both are negative: the Lord handing over his people in Zechariah 11:6 is caused by a lack of pity for them from exasperation, and Judas's handing over of the Lord is at least for money.

Second, both have thirty pieces of silver:[301] τριάκοντα ἀργύρια (Matt 26:15) and τριάκοντα ἀργυροῦς (Zech 11:12–13). Both refer to a/the potter

---

299. Klassen, *Friend*, 98.

300. It is typology, as the fit with Judas is "quite loose" (Blomberg, "Matthew," 96). This overstates matters.

301. Exegeting OT passages which only mention thirty shekels is unhelpful. The shepherd's wages in Zech 11 may have influenced Matthew's account, but Zechariah cannot be determinative because its message does not apply in the Matthean situation: Klassen, *Friend*, 98. He cites Exod 21:32 (money for a slave gored by a bull; Rodd,

τὸν ἀγρὸν τοῦ κεραμέως (Matt 27:7) and εἰς τὸ χωνευτήριον (Zech 11:13), as well as throwing money into the House of the Lord (Zech 11:13; Matt 27:5).³⁰² Thirty pieces of silver were the wages for the faithful shepherd who sought to rescue Israel from the worthless shepherds, but was rejected.³⁰³ One might argue that buying the potter's field and throwing money at the potter are different, but Keener suggests, following Longenecker, that Matthew has revocalized יֹצֵר ("potter") as אוֹצָר ("treasury"),³⁰⁴ so that the Scriptures are fulfilled by the money reaching the potter's field, if not the treasury.³⁰⁵ By citing Jeremiah in 27:9, Keener argues that Matthew is asking readers to consider an analogous passage in Jeremiah 32:6-14, where Jeremiah exercises the right of redemption at God's command.³⁰⁶ Hendriksen notes correctly that it is not a potter's field, but that Jeremiah 19 has parallels with Matthew 27: shedding of innocent blood (Jer 19:4; Matt 27:4), prominence of senior priests (Jer 19:1; Matt 27:3, 6-7), a potter (Jer 19:1; Matt 27:7, 10), and the Potter's Field was in Topheth (Jer 19:6; Matt 27:8), a place of burial (Jer 19:11; Matt 27:7).³⁰⁷

Third, both have money thrown into the temple. Zechariah 11:13 has καὶ ἐνέβαλον αὐτός εἰς τον οἶκον κυρίου, and Matthew 27:5 has καὶ ῥίψας τὰ ἀργύρια εἰς τὸν ναόν.³⁰⁸ Last, both Zechariah 11:12 and Matthew 26:15 use ἔστησαν for money being weighed or counted. This is a notable number of parallels which cannot easily be dismissed. By contrast, Klassen's passages of Exodus 21:32 and Leviticus 27:1-8 contain no such parallels bar the thirty shekels.³⁰⁹ Leviticus 27:3 has the value of a male between twenty and sixty years (Jesus' age range) as fifty shekels, not thirty. The parallels with

---

Glimpses, 128) and Lev 27:1-8 (redemption of a woman dedicated to the Lord), which also mention thirty shekels. He has not considered Zechariah in enough detail to draw this conclusion.

302. Hendriksen, *Matthew*, 947.

303. Keener, *Matthew*, 620.

304. Ibid., 657.

305. McGarry, "Angel," 225. A Second Temple official called יֹצֵר melted metal into pottery jars, which were broken as required (Smith [*Micah-Malachi*, 11:13] cites Torrey ["Foundry," 256], referring to Herodotus). This establishes a link between "potter" and (the temple) "treasury." So also Foster, "Shepherds," 750; and Blomberg, "Matthew," 95.

306. Keener, *Matthew*, 657; Domeris, *Heart*, 133; Davies and Allison, *Matthew*, 3:569. This links Jeremiah buying the field and the chief priests buying the potter's field (Smith, *Micah-Malachi*, 11:13). It is the only positive symbolic action in Jeremiah (Allen, *Jeremiah*).

307. Hendriksen, *Matthew*, 948.

308. Judas was trying to avoid the curse for taking a bribe to shed innocent blood: Deut 27:25 (Talbert, *Matthew*, 300).

309. Klassen, *Friend*, 98.

Zechariah are better than Levitivus/Deuteronomy and arguably show that Matthew was at least aware of Zechariah.

Klassen dismisses the connection between Zechariah 11 and Matthew 26–27 as "the message of the Zechariah story surely does not apply" in Matthew, but gives no evidence.[310] Zechariah 11 said that God's appointed shepherd of Israel had wearied of the flock's enmity and left them to their own devices. As in John 10:19 and 39, Matthew's use of shepherd imagery from Zechariah indicates an increasing tension between Jesus and the Jewish establishment, culminating in abuse (10:19)[311] and attempted capture (10:39).

Matthew also shows increasing tension between the shepherd and those to whom he was sent. Matthew 2:6 quotes Micah 5:2 in referring to Jesus as the one to be shepherd of God's people.[312] Matthew 9:36 portrays the people as sheep without a shepherd.[313] This is paralleled in Zechariah 11:5, where the shepherds do not spare the people;[314] in Zechariah 11:9, with the bold statement "I will not be your shepherd"; and in Zechariah 11:15, with the Lord's promise to raise up an uncaring shepherd, arguably a non-shepherd. Matthew's parable of the sheep and the goats (his last parable prior to betrayal) has Jesus dividing his people into two groups based on obedience to him (s4.3.2). Similarly, in Zechariah 11, the narrator distinguishes between the flock (the majority) who rejected the shepherd, and the afflicted of the flock who recognized the "word of the Lord" (Zech 11:11) and were the special objects of his care (11:7). The last reference to shepherds is Matthew 26:31, citing Zechariah 13:7, where Jesus predicts that, when he is struck, his disciples will be scattered.[315] Jesus' voluntary death is paralleled in Zechariah 11:8, where the narrator leaves his office and foretells serious consequences for the flock.[316]

310. Ibid., 98.

311. Beasley-Murray, *John*, 10:19, 10:39.

312. Hagner also argues for dependency on 2 Sam 5:2 where the Lord commissions David as shepherd of Israel (*Matthew 1–13*, 2:6). This would emphasize Jesus' Davidic ancestry.

313. Keener argues that this is an invitation for "the Lord to shepherd his people himself" (*Matthew*, 309), but it is difficult to see how this fits the context with God, far from doing the job himself, proposing to raise up a worthless shepherd (11:16) who will consume the flock.

314. Tran argues that this is defamiliarization, where familiar symbols are removed from their normal context and placed in a new one to prompt reinterpretation so that, for example, people do not rely on their own resources, but on God ("Shepherd," 534). The uncaring shepherd is not only remiss but also self-destructive, as he relies on the sheep for food, wool, etc.

315. Hendriksen, *Matthew*, 913; Keener, *Matthew*, 635.

316. Tran says that the shepherd abandons the flock ("Shepherd," 537), but this may

Given the above, it is fair to argue that we have similar themes of God's chosen shepherd experiencing increasing friction with God's people and leaving his position.[317] In both cases, Israel rejected God's appointed shepherd. There are differences between the readings: in Zechariah, the shepherd throws the money into the temple, whereas in Matthew it is Judas, but Matthew's purpose is portraying Scripture as fulfilled in the entire Christ-event. Given the above, it is disingenuous to claim that Zechariah's message does not apply in Matthew. Moreover, Klassen makes no attempt to show the relevance of Exodus 21:32 and Leviticus 27:1–8. A failure to consider each passage from Matthew and Zechariah in sufficient detail led him to consider these other passages, which have no bearing on Judas. The relevance for Judas is considerable, as he is shown to be fulfilling prophetically[318] the rejection of God's appointed shepherd by his people for the sake of money alone.

---

be too harsh because the trigger was the flock detesting the shepherd. There are also parallels between Zech 9–11 and the gospels in general. Smith cites Lamarche, that Zech 9–14 is the most quoted section of the Prophets in the gospel Passion narratives (*Micah–Malachi*, "Zech Intro"). The King comes to Jerusalem riding on a donkey (Zech 9:9 in Matt 21:5; McGarry, "Angel," 224). The king in Zech 9:9 is described as "righteous and having salvation," and the inscription on Jesus' (God our Savior) cross is "Jesus, King of the Jews" (Matt 27:37). God's people were harassed and helpless, like sheep without a shepherd (Zech 10:2; Matt 9:36). Israel's shepherds are useless (Zech 10:3; 11:5; John 10:8; Ridderbos, *John*, 358). The include "Pharisees who claimed to hold the keys of the kingdom (cf. Matt 23:13; Luke 11:52) and in the perspective of the Gospel their successors in contemporary Judaism" (Beasley-Murray, *John*, 10:8). When the good shepherd proclaims his identity, conflict escalates (Zech 11:8; John 10:14–19; Beasley-Murray, *John*, 10:19; Ridderbos, *John*, 366). The Lord particularly cares for the faithful of the flock (Zech 11:7; John 10:10). The payment of the thirty shekels ended the relationship between the shepherd and those in authority over God's people (Zech 11:12; Matt 26:15). Thirty shekels was the wages of Zech's faithful shepherd who sought to rescue Israel from unfaithful shepherds, but was rejected (ibid., 620). People will look on the shepherd whom they have pierced (Zech 12:10; John 19:37). Lastly, the shepherd will be struck and the sheep scattered (Zech 13:7–9; Matt 26:31; Keener, *Matthew*, 635). It is not just the number of parallels which needs addressing but their type. Those relevant to the Passion Week illustrate the consequences of the handing over. Those which relate to Jesus' self-description as the Good Shepherd in John 10 are also important. This incident led to serious division in the crowd and the second attempt to stone Jesus after his claim that "I and the Father are one" (John 10:30). His claim to give eternal life (John 10:28) was shown in raising Lazarus, and after this there was a plot by the Jewish authorities to kill Jesus, with Caiaphas unknowingly prophesying the effect of his death (John 11:50–51).

317. As the Judean elites broke faith with God by enslaving fellow Israelites, therefore Zech 11 revokes the earlier promises of restoration from Isa 44 (Foster, "Shepherds," 752).

318. "The long established will of God" (Dowd and Malbon, "Significance," 289).

Acts

Finally, there are apparent similarities in the deaths by hanging of Judas and Ahithophel (s2.3.5).[319] Matthew 27:5 records that Judas hanged himself, but Acts 1 records a more gruesome death at Akeldama. Whilst gruesome death is a common element, it is arguably less significant than the theme of betrayal. If Jesus was betrayed by Judas, David was also betrayed by Joab and Ahtithophel.[320] If Joab, as head of the army, used military force to betray David, then Ahithophel, "David's counselor" (2 Sam 15:12), used his advisory capacity similarly. He was in a trusted relationship with David (2 Sam 15:12), although not called his "friend," but was inferior to David as king. Ahithophel's treachery is shown by his cogent advice on how David might be killed quickly (s2.3.5).

Another parallel between Ahithophel and Judas is the comparison with God. 2 Samuel 16:23 said, "the advice Ahithophel gave was like that of one who inquires of God."[321] I have shown in Appendix 1 that in the LXX, almost 90 percent of the occurrences of παραδίδωμι either have God as the subject or the divine passive. By handing over Jesus, Judas was presuming to act like God.[322] Both Ahithophel and Judas show a treacherous presumption in acting like God.

The nature of the texts makes it difficult to ascertain Judas's actual fate, but each has used the tradition of his death to draw a particular conclusion. In Matthew, the Zechariah parallels have Judas fulfilling the prophetic rejection of God's appointed shepherd, while in Acts, Judas's gruesome death illustrates the fate of one who presumed to act like God.

4.5. Conclusion

Judas was present at these key events in the week before Jesus' death. Each text has Mark establishing Judas's guilt, and then Matthew and Luke heighten his guilt.

---

319. Anderson argues concerning his name, "The name 'Ahithophel' raises certain questions since it may mean 'my brother is folly' (cf. BDB, 27). In view of such names as Ishbosheth and Mephibosheth . . . it is probable that 'Ahithophel' is a deliberate distortion of some such name as 'Ahibaal' (so Mazar, "Military," 317 n.1) which may mean 'My divine brother is Baal'" (2 *Samuel*, 15:12). His suicide is an implied criticism of his reputation, which equated his advice "with the oracle of God" (Janzen, *Ethics*, 131).

320. Zwiep fails to note this ("Matthias," 41).

321. Daube, "Absalom," 320.

322. I argued in s4.3.5 that Judas's conduct would fit the Jewish cultural understanding of blasphemy.

Mark links Judas with the chief priests and other temple officials by ζητέω, κρατέω, and παραδίδωμι. Judas is aligned with them and is the lynchpin in Jesus' betrayal and arrest. Mark 13 highlights Jesus' looming death, but also his future vindication in divine glory, so Judas and the chief priests will not have the final say. Matthew's omission of Mark's poor widow (12:41–44) highlights even more starkly Judas's treachery by removing intervening text between the plot and the Last Supper. The parables of the bridesmaids, the talents, and the sheep and goats show a breakdown in the relationship between Jesus and presumed disciples, so Matthew 25 prepares us for the betrayal. Luke clearly identifies Satan (as does John 13:2, 27) as entering and presumably motivating Judas (22:3).

Matthew, Mark, and John all describe essentially the same event at Bethany where Jesus is anointed by a woman in anticipation of his looming death.[323] Mark's sandwich passage in 14:1–11 links Judas with Jesus' historical enemies (τοῖς ἀρχιερεῦσιν καὶ γραμματεῦσιν) in plotting his death. Matthew has prepared the way with three parables in chapter 25 on the breakdown of the relationship between Jesus and some of his presumed followers. Matthew portrays the Twelve more harshly than Mark, but preserves the Markan sandwich to highlight the one who was turning traitor: Judas (26:14–15). John parallels Caiaphas and Judas by way of an inclusion and hints at Judas's possible motive as a habitual thief (12:6). All three show an unflattering contrast between the woman and Judas.

At the Last Supper, Jesus' only recorded topic of conversation common to all four gospels is the impending betrayal. The narratives in Mark 14:21, Matthew 26:24, and Luke 22:22 share Jesus' woe on the one who will betray him. Mark's Jesus pronounces the "birth woe" on the unidentified traitor, an unparalleled judgment. Matthew's Jesus has Mark's wording almost verbatim, but the sting is using "woe" many times in increasing seriousness and linking chapter 23's teachers of the law and Pharisees with Judas, who he names. Luke/Acts stresses the importance of the mission to the Gentiles. However, Judas not only cooperates with the leaders of national Israel by betraying Jesus to them, but cannot take part in the Gentile mission because he committed suicide instead.

In Gethsemane, Judas calls Jesus "Rabbi" (Mark 14:45), and Keener argues that this shows that he regarded Jesus "*only* as a teacher."[324] The first use of titles by/about Jesus shows that Judas would have heard new titles for Jesus with miracles which validated their truth. Judas is not just uncomprehending, but insulting: he had enough evidence to know that Jesus was

---

323. Luke 7:36–50 describes another anointing for different purposes (s4.3.3).
324. Keener, *Matthew*, 626.

far more than a teacher. While none of the Twelve fully understood Jesus' identity and ministry during the three years of his public ministry, only Judas became a traitor. Matthew continues this pattern similarly, although not to the same extent. Luke has a different approach, as many of Jesus' titles are given in the disciples' absence, but Judas is not mentioned as an exception to 8:26, "Son of the Most High God"; 9:18, "The Christ of God"; or 10:23, "The Son." His true opinion of Jesus is shown by kissing him (a mere attempt, in Luke) to betray him, when that was normally a sign of respect by a disciple to a rabbi (Mark 14:45; Matt 26:49; Luke 22:47–48). Judas sets in motion a series of events which culminate in Jesus' death. In the interrogations which follow, Annas, Caiaphas, and Pilate all act in flagrant disregard of the most elementary standards of justice, and yet none are reproached by Jesus as much as Judas.

Even after the betrayal, Judas still does not repent, but shows the lesser quality of mere remorse. The parallels between Zechariah 11 and Matthew 27 establish that Judas is prophetically fulfilling the role of the one who betrays the Lord's appointed shepherd to death for the sake of money alone. The outcome in Luke is different. Whilst commentators may relate the nature of Judas's death in Acts to that of Ahithophel, this is not the strongest parallel: the ways in which both seek the deaths of their masters and are likened to God are much more significant. The shared manner of death is used to draw this out. Zwiep argues (wisely) that the different accounts in Matthew 27 and Acts 1 cannot be harmonized, and we should respect their integrity.[325]

---

325. Zwiep, "Matthias," 16.

Section 5

Summary of Findings

THE PRELIMINARY AIM OF this study was to determine whether the evangelists' uses of two words closely associated with Judas, παραδίδωμι, and ἑταῖρος, were consistent with him betraying Jesus, responding particularly to visible concerns with previous lexical and philological studies. The middle section then investigated whether Judas, though a human being, functioned within the text as an idol, a created thing indwelt by evil and treated as divine by those in a negative relationship with the God of the Bible, particularly within Luke/Acts. The final section compared in close detail the evangelists' views of Judas.

5.1. Παραδίδωμι and ἑταῖρος

Too many scholars have not investigated παραδίδωμι sufficiently rigorously, but have tried to acquit Judas through a superficial examination, like Klassen and Greenberg in s2.1. Rather than recognizing polysemy, where the same word can take different meanings in different contexts, they assumed that, since some examples of παραδίδωμι cannot mean "betray," then it never or only rarely means "betray." We cannot rule out possible meanings of a word before thoroughly examining the evidence.

We began with the fact that, in secular Greek and the work of Flavius Josephus, παραδίδωμι can mean betrayal or the unjustified breach of an existing relationship for other than legal or military reasons (ss2.2.1, 2.2.2). There is a universal restriction on παραδίδωμι: the person being handed over has no say, and when the handing over is not done under legal or military authority, it is always coercive. LXX usage mirrors this, but includes a different emphasis: God is the subject of παραδίδωμι either directly, or by a divine passive almost 90 percent of the time (Appendix 1). Handing over is overwhelmingly a divine activity, normally due to serious and unrepented sin. God may hand the nations over to Israel, or Israel to the nations, or even nations to other nations (s2.2.3) under such circumstances. The crucial thing to note is that a sovereign action by God cannot be called betrayal, as the handing over is not unjustified—as God repeatedly told Israel (s2.2.3)—but for their breach of the covenant with God. That said, παραδίδωμι in the LXX may still be translated "betray" in the case of Samson, who was handed over by fellow Israelites to the Philistines (s2.3.2).

The GNT continues this pattern with some new additions. While God may hand over his sinful people for discipline (s2.2.4), as in the LXX, he may also hand them over for testing or bearing witness. In a new emphasis, God's people may feel an internal compulsion to hand themselves over to God for his purposes, following the example of Jesus (s2.2.4). I separated the handing over of Jesus by the Jewish and Roman authorities from that by Judas due to Jesus' reaction. Jesus never reproaches them like he does Judas, upon whom he pronounced the "birth woe" (Matt 26:24), a "frightful judgment."[1] Judas illustrates the coercive element of παραδίδωμι by handing Jesus over to an armed mob (Matt 26:47). Using a word which in the LXX overwhelmingly has God as the subject hints at something worse: Judas may be presuming to divinity, as even God never handed over to death a manifestly innocent person, as Judas said of Jesus (Matt 27:4). By the standard and definitions of the time, he is a blasphemer, arrogating to himself what properly belongs to God (s4.3.5).

The usage of ἑταῖρος is also striking: no "friend" in secular Greek ever betrays, but in the LXX and Josephus, there is a remarkably consistent pattern where a friend, or one of whom friendly relations can be assumed, betrays their superior in the hope of personal gain, and normally a death results as the outworking of God's judgment (Appendix 9). Samson was betrayed by the Timnite, her father, Delilah, and later three thousand armed Israelites (s2.3.2); Jonadab betrayed Amnon and King David betrayed Tamar (s2.3.3); and Hushai only pretended to betray David, while Joab (s2.3.4) and Ahithophel (s2.3.5) actually did. Josephus gives two graphic examples of betrayal in Eurycles and Noarus, but arguably the best example is Josephus himself at Jotapata (s2.3.7). Judas illustrates in Appendix 9 the essential features of a friend who betrays. He is easily recognizable as a traitor against the background of the LXX and Josephus. Nothing is ever said to exonerate or excuse him, and the "birth woe" (Matt 26:24; Mark 14:21) is simply unparalleled.

---

1. Keener, *Matthew*, 626.

The three NT uses of ἑταῖρος sum up its attitude to this "friend" of Jesus (Matt 20:13; 22:12; 26:50; s4.2.6). They show, with increasing seriousness, conflict between a member of a group and a figure representing God, with the person sent from God's presence in increasingly severe terms. Matthew has softened Mark's somewhat harsh picture of the disciples to show that the problem is just one disciple, not all twelve. The NT has shown the potential from the LXX and Josephus for a friend to betray but unlike them has no positive examples of ἑταῖρος, the word with which Jesus addresses Judas (Matt 26:50).

In summary for this section, the GNT use of both παραδίδωμι and ἑταῖρος is sufficient to establish that Judas betrayed Jesus. Παραδίδωμι can mean betrayal, but more importantly, the context of Judas's handing over of the Jesus who he later said was innocent (Matt 27:4) into the hands of those who were plotting his death, for personal gain, is conclusive proof that Judas betrayed Jesus. The lack of any positive reference to Judas or his behavior in the NT only confirms this picture. The use of ἑταῖρος further highlights Judas's culpability as one of the Twelve, as Matthew's three parables using this term show in increasing seriousness the complete breakdown in relationship between God and one of a group, eloquently setting the scene for Jesus to address Judas as such in Gethsemane. These two terms alone establish Judas's guilt beyond reasonable doubt.

5.2. Rivals to God

While Judas's betrayal of Jesus is rightly condemned, he is even guiltier than a (mere) traitor by uniquely embodying God's three main rivals: human, demonic, and material. Both testaments have examples of human or idol rivals to God, who either claim divinity or allow it to be ascribed to them, who are associated with evil and who are judged or struck down directly by God. Pao argued that Luke/Acts is reworking certain themes from Second Isaiah to show the church, not the synagogue, as the true heirs of the Exodus traditions (Acts 5; s3.2.1). In particular, the idols and their makers are singled out for mockery, pretending to divinity like the idol-makers or being ascribed divinity like the idols.[2] The parallel with Judas is clear: both are treated as divine, both are empowered by evil, and both are paid to do what properly belongs to God.

Adam and Eve are like God, being in God's image, but are tempted by the serpent identified as Satan in Romans 16. While they did not die immediately, they became mortal and were driven from Eden (s3.2.2). A

---

2. Holter, "Idol," 58.

clear example in the LXX is the prince/king of Tyre in Ezekiel 28. Ezekiel describes the human king of Tyre as only a prince, despite being a king. Behind him lay a fallen, malevolent figure who was called "king." The intertwining of their guilt and their judgment is unparalleled anywhere else in the Bible. The two most important features are as follows: firstly, Ezekiel's use of Eden, not a reference to Genesis 3, but more broadly as a motif of places where God entered into judgment with creatures, some of whom had hitherto been perfect. Secondly, God's grief at the king, a fallen angelic being whom I argue is Satan, is unparalleled in the Bible (s3.2.2).

Luke/Acts strongly reworks both themes. Both Simon Magus and Herod allowed themselves to be acclaimed as divine—Simon by working magic, and Herod by handing James over to death, accepting worship, and being asked for food and peace (s3.2.3). Their powerlessness is shown in Simon's need to ask for power to give the Holy Spirit, and Herod being struck down by an angel and dying five days later. Μαγεύω is a *hapax* in Acts 8:9, but its cognate μάγος occurs in Acts 13:6 and 8 about Elymas, whom Paul calls υἱὲ διαβόλου (13:10). We can reasonably assume that the source of Simon's power is demonic. No such doubt exists regarding the eschatological "man of lawlessness" (2 Thess 2), whose power is explicitly ascribed to Satan and whom Jesus will destroy at his παρουσία (s3.2.3). S4.3.5 shows Judas exhibiting these same features. He presumes to divinity by handing over an innocent Jesus. Handing over is overwhelmingly a divine act (s2.2), but not even God handed over an innocent person to death.

The link with evil is shown by Satan entering Judas (Luke 22:3) to effect the betrayal. This is an example of a theme which is strong in Luke/Acts, but also found elsewhere (John 13:2, 27). It is ironic that both had been hitherto powerless: Satan had not been able to oppose Jesus after his defeat in the wilderness, and Judas was apparently unable to betray Jesus until Satan entered him. Judas's ultimate powerlessness is shown when he is arguably struck down by God and dies at Akeldama (Acts 1). The temple authorities treated Judas as divine by paying him to do the divine-like task of handing Jesus over to death. In essence, they were repeating the sin of earlier generations of leaders of God's people in what is arguably idolatry.

The next rival to God is the demonic, particularly the prince of evil, Satan. Here the role of evil was established in the rite of *mîs-pî*, where the deity represented by the idol was invited to indwell and enliven it. Judah most likely saw this rite during the Babylonian captivity (s3.3.2).[3] Judas is the only named individual in the Bible whom Satan was said to enter, and this entry produced an immediate, verifiable effect: he was then able to betray Jesus.

---

3. Boden, "Mesopotamian," 28–29.

Such a demonic influence must rule out any positive evaluation of Judas's behavior, as God is never recorded approving anything which Satan did.

The NT has an intensified picture of evil with references which are both more numerous and graphic. I argued that this was because Satan and his angels had been expelled from heaven around the time of the Massacre of the Innocents (Matt 2; s3.4.4). While disputed, I argue that this best accounts for the complete lack of any references to Satan's presence in heaven in the NT, unlike the OT, despite a book like Revelation having many chapters describing heaven. I further argue that the final defeat of evil in Revelation 19 is best taken literally, and not as a metaphor for the cross (s3.4.5).

There are clear parallels between the accounts of Satan and Judas. Jesus had known *ab initio* that Judas, ὁ παραδώσων, would betray him (John 6:64), and Judas's presence can be established at key points in Jesus' ministry (Section 4). Like those between Satan and God in the OT, the recorded interactions between Judas and Jesus are tense. This holds true across all the gospels, like John 12's account of Jesus' anointing (12:7; s4.3.3) and Judas's mockery in Gethsemane, calling Jesus (merely) "Rabbi" when he had compelling evidence that Jesus was much more (Matt 26:49; Mark 14:45; s4.3.5).

A further rival to God appears in the NT, as compared with the OT, namely money. While greed and the misuse of money were condemned in the OT (s3.5.3), there is a clear movement in the discussion of wealth from the OT to the NT. The NT not only retains but markedly intensifies the OT's warnings on wealth. It is not just the misuse of wealth which the NT condemns; but with a few, limited exceptions, the NT portrays the problem as wealth itself. This is shown in three parts: the named and righteous rich, wealth itself, and the meaning of service. These frames show a consistent hardening of the Bible's attitude against wealth and the wealthy in the move to the NT.

In the OT, a few individuals combine a degree of righteousness with substantial material wealth (s3.5.2): Abraham, Isaac, David, Solomon, and Job. Those that were generous or had earned (as opposed to inheriting) their money, like Abraham, David, and Job, were best protected from money's destructive effects. Isaac inherited Abraham's wealth, but was led by those around him, like Solomon, whose wives led him to idolatry. The contrast with the NT could not be greater, as no named person in the NT has both righteousness and material wealth. When a named person who could be wealthy follows, or is sympathetic to, Jesus, like Lydia (Acts 16), their assumed wealth is never mentioned. For those described as wealthy, like the Pharisees or the rich young ruler (Luke 16, 18), their wealth is a significant, even insuperable, barrier to discipleship (s3.5.2). The parable of Dives (Luke 16) and the narrative of Ananias and Sapphira (Acts 5) show the dramatically changed status of money in the NT. Their apparently unremarkable sin, lying to the Holy Spirit, was met with a rapid and fatal response by God, to show that the church could not have an improper relationship with money without serious consequences. There is simply no OT parallel.

Πλοῦτος and its cognates are also illuminating. When God made several OT kings wealthy, it was more of a test than a gift, and usually ended problematically (s3.5.3). The OT is full of unflattering descriptions of wealth and the wealthy, and the NT only intensifies this, particularly by analyzing the attitude of the rich to the poor. By examining the MT words for poverty, a clear pattern emerges. These include דַּלָּה (dallah), דַּל (dal), רוּשׁ (rush), אֶבְיוֹן (ebyon), and עָנִי (ani). The first three terms only mean economic poverty: דַּלָּה, "poorest of the land" (2 Kgs 25:12); דַּל, "a poor man in his lawsuit" (Exod 23:3); and רוּשׁ, "the other poor" (2 Sam 12:1). אֶבְיוֹן and עָנִי can mean economic poverty, "the poor and needy" (Deut 15:11; אֶבְיוֹן). People must not oppress "a hired man," but pay wages daily (Deut 24:14-15; עָנִי; LXX: πένης). However, אֶבְיוֹן and עָנִי can also mean non-economic dependence on God. David is never shown as economically poor,[4] but calls himself "poor/ poor and needy" (עָנִי; Pss 34:6; 40:17; 69:29; 70:5; 86:1; 109:16, 22). The LXX guards the distinction between economic and non-economic need, but only uses πτωχός and πένης—not, say, ἐνδεής as an acceptable translation for non-economic need for God.

The NT keeps this distinction in the Sermon on the Mount/Plain. Luke 6:20 has Jesus saying Μακάριοι οἱ πτωχοί, while Matthew 5:3 adds (or Luke omits) τῷ πνεύματι. Jesus is not blessing material poverty, but an attitude of dependence on God. The text of the poor widow's offering (Mark 12:41-44/ Luke 21:1-4) is similar: she illustrates personally both economic and non-economic dependencies of οἱ πτωχοί and receives Jesus' approval that she gave relatively more than all the πλούσιοι. It is precisely these poor, those reliant on God, τῶν πτωχῶν, about whom Judas was said not to care (John 12:6).

The final point concerns the intensification of Δουλεύειν, whose OT usages concerning material objects exclusively mean Israel serving θεοῖς ἑτέροις or ἀλλοτρίοις; e.g., Deuteronomy 28:64 (s3.5.4). The NT continues this by warning Christians not to serve θεοῖς (Gal 4:8) or the στοιχεῖα linked with slavery (Gal 4:3; Col 2:8) and contrasted with serving God (Gal 4:9). Jesus notes the impossibility of serving both God and money (Matt 6:24; Luke 16:13). Like the στοιχεῖα and the θεοῖς, serving money is contrasted with serving God, so we can treat this with similar seriousness. Money is paralleled as an equally offensive object of service with things which are obviously wrong. The novelty in this command is that the OT never warned

---

4. Except early in his life; e.g., 1 Sam 18:23: "I'm only a poor man."

about the impossibility of serving both God and money. Several NT passages illustrate the stark warnings attached to serving money. James 5:3 has silver and gold eating the flesh of the damned, and 5:4 cites Deuteronomy 24:1 on unpaid wages; but in James, the wages themselves cry out for justice.

Next, in the teaching after the Sermon, Jesus strengthens considerably OT moral teaching. While Jesus gives clear teaching on upholding the NT's higher standards, his teaching on money is enigmatic, but culminates in the graphic "You cannot serve" (Matt 6:24; Luke 16:13), hinting at money's uniquely negative status as a rival to God. This is confirmed in the difficult parable of the dishonest steward (Luke 16). The master's praise notes the shrewdness in a fellow "son of this age,"[5] whom Jesus contrasts with (his people) τοὺς υἱοὺς τοῦ φωτὸς. Neither the master nor the steward are held up as appropriate models for God's people, although Luke 16:9, "use worldly wealth," could be interpreted as Jesus encouraging his people to follow the characters' actions, but not their presumed motivation of self-interest.

There is an immediate relevance for these rivals to God in our discussion of Judas, in that he is uniquely linked with all three. Judas has all the features of a human rival to God. He is ascribed divinity implicitly by the temple authorities, by being asked to do the divine-like task of handing someone over to death. While Herod also hands over an innocent John the Baptist to death, he at least seems distressed by being manipulated into such an action, something conspicuously absent in Gethsemane. It is a notable feat to be compared unfavorably with Herod (s4.2.4). While there are a number of other human rivals to God (s3.2), what makes Judas unique is that Satan is explicitly said to enter him (Luke 22; John 13), arguably like the rite of *mîs-pî*, where the god represented by the statue was asked to indwell and empower it. It was only after Satan entered Judas that he could do the divine-like task of handing Jesus over. Idol temples were paid money by worshipers to ensure a favorable response from the god, and Judas was also paid, the only person in the NT paid a nominated sum to do a divine-like task. Judas is uniquely linked with all three rivals to God and arguably functions like an idol.

5.3. The identity of Judas Iscariot

We are now in a position to define more accurately the identity of Judas Iscariot. He uniquely exemplifies the essential traits of an idol so completely that, allowing for the fact that he was a flesh and blood human being and not an object of stone or wood, he would be recognized as such.

---

5. Nolland, *Luke 9:21—18:34*, 16:8; Marshall, *Luke*, 620.

5.3.1. *A created being acting like God*

Firstly, Judas was a human being who acted like God in handing over Jesus to trial and death (s4.3.5). In chapter 4, I described various people in both testaments who were consciously or unconsciously human rivals to God. All either claimed divinity or divine prerogatives, or allowed such to be ascribed to them and were struck down directly by God or an angel. I showed in s2.2 that handing over is overwhelmingly a divine activity for serious, unrepented sin, but by handing over the innocent Jesus, Judas was doing what even God never did. While a person may claim to be divine, Judas was also treated as such by the temple authorities, who paid him to do this divine-like task of handing someone over for trial. Like the idol-makers (s3.2.1), once Judas used his undoubted authority against its source, Jesus, there is increasing alienation, as reflected in "that man" (Luke 22:22). Moreover, Isaiah mocked the idols and their makers for their weakness (s3.2.1), and Judas was similarly weak, only able to betray Jesus after Satan entered him (Luke 22:3). We might summarize that Satan, Judas, and idols form an ungodly trio who share significant common features: they are likened to God, associated with evil, powerless, and usually receiving the direct judgment of God.

5.3.1.1. MÎS-PÎ

In Babylon, exiled Judah saw the rite of *mîs-pî*, where the Babylonian priests asked the god to indwell its image (s3.3.2). Given the OT's strong condemnation of idolatry (Exod 20:4), the animating spirit must have been evil. Something must have happened, as such a belief could not have been sustained across almost the entire Ancient Near East for centuries without some manifestation. Studying the δαιμόν and εἴδωλον word groups and the Beelzebul incident (Mark 3/Matt 12/Luke 12; s3.3.5) shows a marked differentiation from the surrounding culture, as well as an intensification in the move from the OT to the NT.

In secular Greek, the δαιμόν word group can refer either to humans or supernatural beings, who are sought for guidance or who ensure justice (s3.3.4).[6] Similarly, Josephus uses this group respectively to signify spiritual beings, whether good or evil, a providential visitation by such, and finally, the incorporeal aspect of someone who has died (*J.W.* 1.69, 1.82, 6.47). Josephus

---

6. Xenophon, *Mem.* 1.1.2; Xenophon, *Opera Omnia*, vol 1; Herodotus, *Historiae*, 5.87.2

uses this group positively, either for God's providence or for other spiritual beings guiding the living or ensuring justice for the dead (s3.3.4).

The contrast between Josephus and the LXX could hardly be greater (s3.3.4), with Deuteronomy 32:17 explicitly linking sin, idols, and evil. Every OT use of δαίμονιον involves idolatry or God's judgment—there are no neutral or positive references. If Israel behaved like the Canaanites, God would use such to punish them.[7] We also hear God's anger at unfaithful Israel, who have rejected him like an unfaithful wife (Hos 4:12). The same πνεύματι πορνείας, which prevents them acknowledging the Lord (Hos 5:4), is "in their heart," the first reference to evil inside a person. The GNT preserves the LXX's negative view, that evil is always inimical to people, and thoroughly refutes the idea from secular Greek and Josephus that evil could in any way be aligned with God. This is eloquently shown in the Beelzebul incident (Mark 3/Matt 12/Luke 12; s3.3.5) where, unlike Socrates above, deliberately confusing good and evil may mean a frightful punishment.

Mark's Jesus calls οἱ γραμματεῖς to explain that, contrary to their accusation, he is not demonized, as his exorcisms weaken Satan's position (s3.3.5). He addresses them ἐν παραβολαῖς (3:23), the distinctive address to an outsider (s4.2.2). Jesus' exorcisms show that he is indeed ὁ ἰσχυρότερος, who can restrain Satan and plunder his kingdom. To ascribe evil to such manifest good may merit eternal punishment (3:29). Mark's treatment of the Beelzebul accusations immediately follows the call of Judas as one of the Twelve, arguably highlighting the connection between Judas and Satan and also between Judas and οἱ γραμματεῖς, who will become his co-conspirators. Matthew's Jesus reiterates Mark's argument, but also asks if, because the Pharisees' disciples did exorcisms, they are similarly in league with Satan (s3.3.5)? Jesus' miracles are more than enough evidence, so later requests for a sign (12:24, 38) further show what was in their hearts (12:34). Luke's Jesus gives a number of illustrations of different types of evil, from the disciples to the crowds to unclean spirits, showing an uncomfortable similarity (s3.3.5).

There is no middle ground between God and evil, and ascribing evil to good may merit eternal punishment (Matt 12:32). The problem for Judas is that he so neatly parallels Satan. Both Satan and Judas, although rebellious, were allowed to stay in God's presence, despite increasing tension (s3.4.2). Satan rebukes God (Job 1–2), and Judas, the Pharisees, and scribes[8] all showed significant tension toward Jesus, despite having seen his miracles. Tensions came to a head, and evil was expelled from heaven at the time

---

7. Allen, *Psalms 101–150*, 106:40.

8. The passersby mirror Satan's words in the wilderness: "If you are the Son of God," and the chief priests call Jesus "King of Israel," mirroring Ps 2:6–7 (Ferda, "Matthew's *Titulus*," 573).

of the Massacre of the Innocents (s3.4.4); similarly, Judas was sent from the Last Supper (John 13:27). The nature of Judas's death looks like divine retribution, and Revelation 19 portrays a final defeat of evil (s3.4.5). Judas is not only aligned with Jesus' enemies, but parallels Satan.

In secular Greek, the εἴδωλον word group means something either insubstantial, like false friendship, or someone or thing which is not/no longer alive, like a dead person or a statue (s3.3.3). It has no life of its own, but it is never spoken of negatively nor is it linked with evil. Josephus uses the word for idols and young men dying during a siege (*Ant.* 9.273; 10.65–66; *J.W.* 5.513; 7.452; see s3.3.3). Unlike the LXX, Josephus never links idols with evil by such words as δαιμόνιον.

By contrast, the LXX emphasizes repeatedly that God is a jealous God who allows no rivals (s3.3.3). Idolatry was specifically forbidden on the most serious grounds that it conflicted with God's nature and the Exodus, through which he constituted Israel as a nation (Exod 20:2). The adultery metaphor makes this clear, as God expresses a deep desire that his people not be linked to lifeless idols (Exod 20:4; Deut 7:4). Reform in Israel inevitably meant the destruction of idols (2 Kgs 11; 23:24–25; 2 Chr 14:5; 17:6).

As expected, the GNT reinforces the LXX's negative elements, but takes them to a new level by including harsher punishments for similar offenses from the LXX (s3.3.3). Jesus himself will punish his people who adopt Jezebel's teaching of εἰδωλόθυτος and immorality (Rev 2:23–24). Greed is equated with εἰδωλολατρία and εἰδωλολάτρης (Col 3:5; Eph 5:5), and the penalty is losing eternal life (1 Cor 6:9; Eph 5:5; Rev 21:8). The worst condemnation is in Paul's charge that eating εἰδωλόθυτος is worshiping evil (1 Cor 10:20). While idols are nothing, he is fully persuaded that the demonic lies behind idols/sacrifices, so the idols become significant when treated as divine,[9] as eating actualizes the fellowship between guests and demons (1 Cor 10:20).[10]

While not an exact parallel, Judas acts like an idol, so there is no possible compromise between him and Jesus if he will not repent. Judas exhibits a key parallel of idolatry in the NT. He is greedy, habitually stealing from the purse (John 12:6) and accepting the thirty shekels to betray Jesus (Matt 26:15). Jesus never rebukes anyone else as severely.

---

9. Fotopoulos, *Food*, 235.
10. Willis, *Meat*, 189; Page, *Powers*, 225; Smit, "Idolaters," 52.

5.3.2. Indwelt by evil

There are two main points here. Firstly, Satan entering Judas is somewhat like evil indwelling idols in the Babylonian rite of *mîs-pî*. Secondly, there are four profound parallels between Satan and Judas. For convenience, I have used the same headings as in s3.4 to describe Judas.

5.3.2.1. Parallels between Satan and Judas

Following on from s3.4, where I considered Satan and demons in the OT, I have used the same headings to show explicit parallels between Satan and Judas, particularly in the light of the Beelzebul incident, which shows the implacable hostility between good and evil and the necessity of not (deliberately) confusing them.

The demonic in God's immediate presence

The OT has passages which show evil able to speak with God personally (s3.4.2). Jesus' interaction with the Twelve is something like a "heavenly council" on earth. The Son presides like the Lord in heaven. Decisions are not made by vote, but by Jesus. Unlike heaven, with God and his holy angels, the earthly group only has one perfect member. The earthly group also has one rebellious member who has continued access to Jesus' presence, even though he is trying to betray him. The synoptic accounts of the Beelzebul incident give eloquent warnings about criticizing the work of God in the light of miraculous validation and being on the wrong side of the God/evil demarcation. There is no middle ground, and criticism of God may mean siding with evil. Like the Pharisees, Judas had enough miraculous evidence to know that Jesus was much more than another rabbi (s4.3.5). Whilst the narrative appears to present the Pharisees and Judas as insiders, it is really saying that they are outsiders because of their identification with evil.

John's Jesus remains in control. John 6:64, "For Jesus had known from the beginning . . . who would betray him," should be given its full weight.[11] In John 13, like the Synoptics, Jesus raises the treachery, and in John 13:26,

---

11. He went to his godly task with "eyes wide open" (Carson, *John*, 302). So, see Ridderbos, *John*, 248.

he identifies the traitor as the disciple next to him.[12] Jesus sent Judas away (13:27) when all hope of repentance was gone.[13]

Spiritual evil in God's presence was tolerated until it was finally expelled around the time of the Massacre of the Innocents (Matt 2; s3.4.4). In the Beelzebul incident, spiritual evil had just been cast out by Jesus. But Judas is arguably worse, as in Jesus' presence, Satan entered Judas (Luke 22:3; John 13:2, 27), enabling him to betray the innocent Jesus.

Tension toward God

In the OT, there seems to have been real tension between God and Satan (s3.4.2). In the Beelzebul incident, the Pharisees, scribes, and even some of the crowd show the most awful tension toward Jesus by accusing him of the capital charge of being possessed and/or helped by Satan. While unaware of Jesus' deity, the illogicality of their accusations and the evidence of the healings/exorcisms was sufficient to establish that their accusations were baseless. Jesus sent the Twelve on mission (Matt 10:5; Mark 6:7; Luke 9:1),[14] and then heard their reports on their return. Judas was not singled out for censure.[15] Apparently, he was as faithful as the rest (s4.2.3). Surprisingly, the next Synoptic references to Judas by name are his looming betrayal of Jesus (Matt 26:14/Mark 14:10/Luke 22:3). While not changing sides as quickly as Ahithophel (s2.3.5), he approached the chief priests (Matt 26:14; Mark 14:10; Luke 22:4) to betray Jesus. At the Last Supper, Jesus called Judas "that man" (Matt 26:23; Mark 14:21; Luke 22:22), showing significant tension between them.

Judas, the Pharisees, and the scribes all showed significant tension toward Jesus, despite having seen his miracles. However, Judas is the most culpable; as he was one of the Twelve, he heard and saw much of Jesus' teaching and miracles and yet still betrayed him. His closeness with Jesus

---

12. Zwiep, "Matthias," 38. If Judas was the guest of honor, Jesus could easily pass him the sop (Carson, *John*, 474). Brant overinterprets the sop by calling it "wine-soaked bread," a "parody of the Eucharist" ("Drama," 203). It is not clear that the bread was dipped into wine as opposed to the more usual common bowl.

13. Ridderbos, *John*, 471; Brown, *John XIII–XXI*, 575. "Judas goes forth into the night, wholly allied with the forces of darkness." (Kovacs, "Ruler," 234). Jesus, knowing what Judas will do, still includes him in a eucharistic-like setting (King, "Fencing," 30).

14. Luke 9:1 and 10 is most likely for the close identification of the Twelve and the apostles (Meier, "Twelve," 641). "Apostle" was not random, but was not synonymous with the Twelve. Paul was an apostle, but not one of the Twelve.

15. Contra the Synoptics, Judas is shown as a fake disciple throughout John (Oropeza, *Footsteps*, 1.202).

makes the nature of his betrayal worse by the conventions of the time. Jesus pronounced the "birth woe" (Mark 14:21; Matt 26:24) on no one else.

Crisis and irrevocable casting out

Satan's attempt to kill the infant Jesus using Herod in the Massacre of the Innocents was the defining crisis in the relationship between God and Satan which led to the expulsion of Satan and his angels (s3.4.4). In the Beelzebul incident, Jesus said that blaspheming the Holy Spirit is such an irrevocable breakdown in the relationship with God that the penalty is αἰωνίου (Mark 3:29; variations in Matt 12:31; Luke 12:10). Jesus does not define this blasphemy exactly, but in context, he probably means deliberately calling evil the work of God.[16] I argued that the best explanation of Jesus raising the impending betrayal was to dissuade Judas (s4.3.4), but once all hope of that appeared lost, he told Judas to go, although the Eleven did not understand what was happening.

Once more, Judas is the worst offender. While the Pharisees and scribes had judged the Galilean Jesus from far off Jerusalem, Judas had been with him night and day for the whole length of his ministry and seen and heard many miracles and much teaching. This would have been sufficient evidence for anyone that Jesus was working with God to break the power of evil in people's lives. If the Pharisees and scribes could be potentially guilty of an αἰωνίου ἁμαρτήματος (Mark 3:29), Judas was arguably even more guilty and deserving of a worse punishment, if that were possible. Moreover, Satan is never described as entering a Pharisee or scribe, but only Judas (Luke 22:3; John 13:2, 27).

God's punishment of Judas

Revelation 19's description of a final defeat of evil by Jesus in battle is best taken at face value,s and not as heaven's view of the cross (s3.4.5). The previous section shows Jesus warning the Pharisees and scribes of a possible eternal punishment if they deliberately portrayed good as evil. There is no easy way to reconcile the accounts of Judas's death in Matthew 27 and Acts 1, except that both show a violent death. Explanations such as Judas hanging himself, the rope breaking, and his body decomposing are "forced."[17] The

---

16. France, *Mark*, 177; Keener, *Matthew*, 366; Nolland, *Luke 9:21—18:34*, 680. The demons testify truly to Jesus, but the scribes do not (Watts, "Mark," 150).

17. Williams, *Acts*, 33. They cannot be harmonized (Zwiep, "Matthias," 16). Such attempts are "not very convincing" (Oropeza, *Footsteps,1*, 144).

imprecise nature of Judas's death in Acts 1 could indicate some direct action of God,[18] and so mirror the deaths of others who claimed equality with God.

In summary, sinful creatures had access to God's immediate presence for a time in both OT[19] and NT, and God used Satan and the lying spirit for his purposes to test his servants or punish his enemies in the OT, but there is no hint of a reward. As this same pattern of access and eventual expulsion happened in both OT and NT, it does not reflect a limitation of the incarnation, as per Cane,[20] but the consistent reaction of a holy God to evil in his presence. The parallels are clear in the behavior of Satan and Judas, and the Satan who was expelled from heaven was precisely the one who later entered Judas. Cane's argument must be assessed as wrong on this point.

5.3.3. Paid with money

In the move from OT to NT, the image of money darkens considerably. In the OT, a few named individuals are described as both rich and righteous, but without exception only those who had earned their money or suffered serious testing and/or deprivation like Abraham and David were protected from its negative effects. When God was described as giving money to the four kings, it was a test of character, which most failed. While the OT has many warnings not to trust wealth or misuse it, the NT intensifies this to warnings about wealth itself. The OT views money as neutral (and either good or bad outcomes may result), but the NT is not so optimistic; money is a rival to God in the hearts of humanity, and so cannot be either good or neutral. It is portrayed as an alternate object of worship to God and, like God, a consuming fire, which calls out to God for justice (Matt 6:24; Luke 16:13; Jas 5:3–4). The OT has nothing like these graphic warnings about wealth itself. The only positive references to wealth in the NT are spiritual like "the riches of (God's) kindness" (Rom 2:4) or the collection for the Jerusalem church (2 Cor 8–9).

By contrast, while the NT acknowledges the poor and the believer's duty to support them, it preserves the OT's distinction between economic and non-economic need by using one of the two LXX words for "poor," πτωχός, which expresses non-economic dependence on God, as in the Davidic Psalms of Lament. As king, David was hardly economically poor,

---

18. Judas's death fits the ancient pattern of a retributive death by the gods/God (Zwiep, "Matthias," 63).

19. If Pagels had considered all the OT data on Satan, she need not have asked "When was the dragon ever up 'in heaven'?" ("Social Three," 488).

20. Cane, *Place*, 185.

given his gift of one thousand talents for Solomon's temple (1 Chr 29), but still called himself "poor and needy." Recognizing this dual meaning may explain Jesus' words in the Sermon on the Mount/Plain. Far from blessing material poverty, he blesses those who sense their reliance on God, regardless of economic circumstances. The NT intensifies the negative aspects of the OT's picture of wealth and the wealthy in passages like the Parable of the Dishonest Steward (Luke 16:1–13), while omitting mitigating factors apart from personal generosity in the Collection for Jerusalem (2 Cor 8–9).

For Judas to be paid with money, the material rival to God, and empowered by Satan, the demonic rival to God—to arrogate God's privilege of handing over the Son of God—sums up the idolatrous nature of his actions.

5.4. The Synoptic Gospels

5.4.1. Events during Jesus' ministry

Six synoptic passages establish Judas's presence during Jesus' ministry: the call of the Twelve, the parable of the sower, the Twelve on mission, Jesus feeding the five thousand, discussion on the greatest in the kingdom, and the final prediction of Jesus' death (s4.2). I assumed Markan priority and examined how Matt and Luke built on Mark. A clear pattern emerges: Mark establishes Judas's guilt beyond reasonable doubt, and Matthew/Luke build on this to emphasize how much of Jesus' teaching Judas ignored in betraying him. From this, Judas emerges uniquely as the one who betrays Jesus, even if the others are all shown or assumed to waver in their discipleship.

Mark's call of the Twelve stresses their role in being with Jesus (3:14), and is based on an insider/outsider theme (s4.2.1). Judas, an apostle and insider who will betray Jesus (3:19), is contrasted with the crowd, who are normally outsiders, but listen to Jesus (3:32). Matthew stresses the persecutions awaiting the Twelve (s4.2.1). Persecution for them lay in the future, but Jesus would be brought before governors, flogged, etc., because of Judas. Luke 6 stresses that Jesus prayed "to God," a redundant phrase, and then obediently chose Judas, whom Luke explicitly calls προδότης (s4.2.1). If Judas is an outsider for Mark, in Matthew he will cause Jesus to be persecuted, and he will be a traitor for Luke.

Mark's parable of the sower (s4.2.2) neatly illustrates the insider/outsider motif, where Judas may be physically close to Jesus and hear his explanation, but still be an outsider at heart. Moreover, by being uniquely linked with Satan and money in the betrayal, Judas may personally illustrate two reasons why he did not respond to Jesus. Matthew and Luke emphasize

Judas's guilt by inserting two chapters of Jesus ministering to classic outsiders—the demonized, the mentally ill, etc.—before including the parable (s4.2.2). Jesus ministered to all, but would not dilute the gospel.

Jesus sending the Twelve on mission is similar (s4.2.3) and shows vital points of teaching and practice, which Judas apparently taught to others but did not personally obey. Jesus gave them authority over unclean spirits/demons, so despite Judas being the only person in the NT whom Satan was said to enter, he could not claim ignorance of evil. Jesus warned them about money in the confronting statement, "You cannot serve both God and Mammon" (Matt 6:24), but Judas later accepted money to betray Jesus. The Twelve apparently preached that people should repent, but even after betraying Jesus, Judas only felt the lesser remorse.

Immediately before the feeding of the five thousand, Mark and Matthew record Herod's birthday feast, where he was incited to behead John the Baptist. There are numerous, unique parallels between Judas and Herod, in that both were human rivals to God (s4.2.4), both caused the death of innocent men, were remorseful, and were struck down by God. The main themes present in Herod's feast (a host who presumes to act like God by sending an innocent man to death, which God never did) and the feeding (another host, Jesus, provides for God's people) coalesce in the Last Supper because of the many, telling parallels between Herod and Judas. Luke (s4.2.4) notably compares Herod favorably with Judas: Herod, an outsider, at least wants to understand who Jesus is (9:9); which Judas ought to have understood as one of the Twelve.

Just after Jesus' second prediction of his death, the Twelve argued about who was the greatest. This may be natural curiosity about which of them, presumably the greatest, would lead when Jesus died. Mark's Jesus warns the Twelve not to lord it over others, but to be the servant of all, which Judas arguably ignored in betraying Jesus (s4.2.5). Matthew strengthens this by linking humility, greatness, and servitude. Matthew only uses ταπεινόω in 18:4 and 23:12, but both require humbling oneself. Mark simply locates this pericope in Capernaum (9:23), but Matthew 11:23 and Luke 10:15 make Capernaum a potent symbol of judgment. Like Judas (s4.2.5), it had seen Jesus' miracles but had not repented. Luke portrays the disciples in confronting terms, moving directly from Jesus' prediction of his death to the argument on greatness. While the Eleven had been insensitive in arguing about greatness, and would all ultimately desert Jesus, Judas was the only traitor. This rejection of Jesus, the opposite of welcoming, would also be a rejection of the Father.

Each evangelist said that all twelve heard the third prediction of Jesus' death (Matt 20:17; Mark 10:32; Luke 18:31; s4.2.6). Mark portrays the disciples harshly, moving directly from the prediction to James and John's extraordinary request for places at Jesus' right and left hands (10:35). While James and John unwittingly request death in so asking, Judas will set in motion the events leading to Jesus' death. By contrast, Matthew is more sympathetic to the disciples, and uses the verbal thread of "friend" to narrow the issue down to increasing conflict between a figure representing God and one of a crowd. This is also established by Judas, satisfying all the criteria of "friend" (Appendix 9).

5.4.2. Events in the week prior to Jesus' death

Five events show Judas's presence and continue the pattern where Mark establishes Judas's guilt and Matthew/Luke intensify it. These events are the plot to betray Jesus, the anointing of Jesus at Bethany, the Last Supper, Judas betraying Jesus, and Judas after the betrayal.

The plot against Jesus is a Markan sandwich for Jesus' anointing at Bethany,[21] contrasting the presence of two Jews, Jesus and Judas, in the temple precincts for very different reasons. Mark links Judas with Jesus' habitual opponents, the chief priests and the Pharisees, with ζητέω, κρατέω, and παραδίδωμι. Finally, Mark 13, the precursor to the passion, eloquently describes that he whom Judas betrayed will return in glory, a very sobering thought (s4.3.2). Matthew continues Mark's use of these key terms, but Matthew 23's woes against the Pharisees parallel Jesus' woe on Judas (26:24). But Jesus never spoke the "birth woe" about a Pharisee or scribe. Moreover, Matthew inserts three παρουσία parables (the bridesmaids, the talents, and the sheep and goats)[22] between the apocalyptic Matthew 24 and the plot in Matthew 26 to show a terminal breakdown in the relationship between Jesus and presumed disciples. It is in a climactic position at the end of Matthew's five great discourses.[23] Luke also increases Judas's guilt by eliminating Jesus' anointing at Bethany (s4.3.3), so the plot to betray leads directly to the Last Supper. Lastly, Luke said explicitly that Satan entered Judas, presumably empowering him to betray Jesus (s4.3.2).

Matthew, Mark, and John all describe recognizably the same anointing of Jesus at Bethany, while Luke records a different event. In the previous paragraph, I drew out the connotations of the Markan sandwich for interpreting the anointing: Judas is linked with those who will condemn Jesus to death. Matthew has focused on Judas's guilt in the three παρουσία parables,

---

21. Resseguie, *Narrative*, 55.
22. Edwards, "Matthew," 68.
23. Page, *Powers*, 117.

but by using the reverential προσέρχεσθαι for the anointing woman approaching Jesus, he clearly contrasts the woman who treats Jesus as Lord with Judas who betrays him (s4.3.3). In a damning parallel within an inclusion based on belief in Jesus (11:45—12:11), John achieves the notable feat of paralleling Judas and Caiaphas. While both speak against Jesus (s4.3.3), Judas is more culpable as a disciple. Judas, a habitual thief, objected to the supposed waste of money in the anointing, but John 12:6 said that he did not care about the poor, which can mean whoever senses their dependence on God (s3.5). Judas showed many of the traits which the OT condemned in the rich, and showed none of the traits which protected people from the negative effects of money.

At the Last Supper, Mark's Jesus spoke the "birth woe." This is well within standard OT practice, where the recipient was identified by their deed (s4.3.4). The most reasonable interpretation was to dissuade Judas, and perhaps to alert the Eleven one final time as to what would happen. Jesus' final comment, that it would have been better if the traitor had not been born, is devastating and simply unparalleled (14:21). Matthew intensifies Judas's guilt, using "woe" as a verbal thread in escalating seriousness from Korazin and Bethsaida (ch 11)—who, like Judas, had seen Jesus' miracles (s4.3.5), and yet had not repented through the confronting question of entry to heaven (ch 18)—to the open rebuke of the scribes and Pharisees (ch 23), to the final woe on Judas, whom Jesus identified at the Last Supper (26:25). Judas is arguably the most culpable example of the warnings which Jesus gave in these passages (s4.3.4). Luke records Jesus' woe on Judas (22:22), but has a new emphasis: the locus of God's people has passed from Judaism (with whose leaders Judas aligned himself) to a new people based around Jesus, particularly in its mission to the Gentiles, from which Judas is absent due to his death.[24] Mark establishes Judas's guilt, Matthew has Judas as the most culpable recipient of a woe, and Luke (in Acts) shows Judas's absence from a key point of the gospel: the Gentile mission.

In Gethsemane, Judas calls Jesus "Rabbi" (Mark 14:45), and this is commonly seen as evidence that Judas is uncomprehending,[25] only seeing Jesus as a teacher. However, an analysis of the first use of titles in Mark for Jesus by a named character or by Jesus himself shows a clear pattern. Almost always, they are accompanied by a miracle which validated their truth (s4.3.5). Judas can be shown to be present at many of those occasions—not that he is specifically described as absent from the others. He had enough evidence that Jesus was much more than another rabbi, so this address is arguably a calculated in-

---

24. Pao, *Acts*, 77.
25. Keener, *Matthew*, 626.

sult. Matthew links eight first occurrences with validating miracles, and Judas is not mentioned as an exception to hearing Jesus of Nazareth, Lord, "I am," and Christ, as well as those titles for which there was no validating miracle (s4.3.5). Luke is different, as many of the titles are given in the disciples' absence, six of them before or at Jesus' birth. But Judas is not mentioned as an exception to 8:26, "Son of the Most High God"; 9:18, "The Christ of God"; or 10:23, "the Son," which had no associated miracle (s4.3.5).

Each evangelist preserves a key feature of the OT use of παραδίδωμι, that it is coercive (Matt 26:47; Mark 14:46; Luke 22:47; John 18:12). Judas betrays Jesus to an armed mob, who take him for clearly unsatisfactory hearings before Caiaphas and then Pilate. Judas's (attempted) kiss only completes the picture of deliberate insult (Mark 14:45; Matt 26:49; Luke 22:47–48). As handing over is overwhelmingly a divine action (s2.2), but not even God handed over an innocent person, Judas's betrayal of Jesus could be fairly described as blasphemy by action (s4.3.5). As Jesus gets closer to death, he imputes less guilt to those trying/executing him. He spoke a frightful judgment on Judas, but on the reading adopted from Luke 23:34, asked the Father to forgive the Roman soldiers as they acted in ignorance (s4.3.5).

5.4.3. Events after the betrayal

Afterward, Judas threw the money into the temple (Matt 27:3, 5). There are many parallels between Zechariah 11 and Matthew 26:14–16/27:1–10. All have forms of παραδίδωμι, both refer to thirty pieces of silver (Matt 26:15; Zech 11:12–13), a/the potter (Matt 27:7; Zech 11:13), and throwing money into the temple (Zech 11:13; Matt 27:5), and Zechariah 11:12 and Matthew 26:15 use ἔστησαν for money being weighed or counted. Both Zechariah 11 and the gospels show increasing tension between God's appointed shepherd and his people, leading to a breakdown in the relationship.

The accounts of Judas's death in Matthew 28 and Acts 1 cannot easily be reconciled, but there are two interesting parallels with the death of Ahithophel, in that both advised how their former masters, Jesus and King David, could be killed quickly, and both were likened to God—Judas for the divine-like task of handing over, and Ahithophel for the quality of his advice (2 Sam 16:23). These are more compelling parallels than their manner of death.

In summary, the synoptic accounts have Mark clearly establishing Judas's guilt from the start in the most graphic terms. He is an insider who acts like an outsider, he is aligned with those seeking to harm Jesus, and Jesus speaks a frightful judgment on him at the Last Supper. Far from exonerating him, Matthew and Luke only make his guilt clearer. He is the "friend" who betrays Jesus and the worst example of the sins which Jesus criticizes in the "woe" passages. Nothing is ever said to relativize his guilt, much less acquit him.

5.5. Conclusion

Studies of παραδίδωμι and ἑταῖρος show conclusively that Judas betrayed Jesus. The evangelists arguably used παραδίδωμι as a verbal thread linking Jesus' four handings-over, with Jesus imputing less guilt the closer he gets to death. Ἑταῖρος mirrors other examples in the LXX and Josephus where a previously close friend betrays.

Sections 3.1–4 show Judas as more than a mere traitor, but a rival to God. He presumed to divinity in handing over Jesus, and received God's final and direct punishment. Judah in exile in Babylon would have seen the rite of *mîs-pî*, where a/an (unclean) spirit was invited to indwell and enliven a statue. This and many other parallels between Judas and Satan portray his betrayal starkly, as God is never seen to approve anything done by Satan.

Section 3.5 shows the darker, even idolatrous, portrayal of money in the NT, compared with the OT. Judas uniquely satisfies three essential criteria for an idol. He is a created being who presumes to divinity and is treated as such by the leaders of God's people, the Jews; he is empowered by Satan, God's demonic rival, and paid with money, God's material rival. This is particularly clear in Luke and Acts, but also in the other gospels.

Section 4 shows a consistent picture where Mark establishes Judas's guilt beyond any reasonable doubt, and Matthew and Luke build on this to show how much his guilt is uniquely Judas's, and how closely he is linked with Jesus' enemies, human and demonic. Nothing is said to exonerate Judas, and only on him did Jesus pronounce the "birth woe" (Mark 14:21; Matt 26:24). Given the identity of Jesus and his supreme importance in the gospels, it is difficult to imagine guilt portrayed more starkly than Judas's.

Appendices

Appendix 1

The LXX's use of παραδίδωμι.

παραδίδωμι in the LXX: A Summary.	Torah	Prophets	Writ	Total
1. God hands over nations.				
God the subject	22		46	68
Divine Passive	2			2
Total				70
2. God hands over Israel.				
God the subject	2	15	23	40
Divine Passive	1	13		14
Total				54
3. Do not/will not hand over.				
God the subject	0	0	9	9
Divine Passive		2	2	4
Under authority	1			1
Coercive		2	5	7
Total				21
4. God hands nations to others.				
God the subject		8		8
Divine Passive		6		6
Total				14
5. One of God's people handed over.				
God the subject			5	5

παραδίδωμι in the LXX: A Summary (cont.)	Torah	Prophets	Writ	
Divine Passive		3	1	4
Self-offering		3	1	4
Coercion			5	5
				0
Total			18	0
6. Other.				0
God the subject	2	2	1	5
Divine Passive			4	4
Authority	1		1	2
Thing as object		2	3	5
Coercion			1	1
				0
Total			17	0
Grand Total	31	56	107	194
God as subject/divine passive	169	%	87.1	

Appendix 2

God hands the nations over to Israel.

All texts have God as subject or the divine passive.

No.	Book	Ch	Ver	Nper	Vo	Mo	Tens	Text
1	Gen	14	20	3s	A	Ind	Aor	"And blessed be God Most High, who delivered (παρέδωκεν) your enemies into your hand."
2	Exod	23	31	1s	A	Ind	Fut	"I will establish your borders from the Red Sea to the Sea of the Philistines, and from the desert to the River. I will hand over (παραδώσω) to you the people who live in the land and you will drive them out before you."
3	Num	21	2	2s	A	Subj	Aor	"Then Israel made this vow to the Lord: 'If you will deliver (παραδῷς) these people into our hands, we will totally destroy their cities.'"
4	Num	21	3	3s	A	Ind	Aor	"The Lord listened to Israel's plea and gave (παρέδωκεν) the Canaanites over to them. They completely destroyed them and their towns; so the place was named Hormah."

No	Book	Ch	Ver	Nper	Vo	Mo	Tens	Text
5	Num	21	34	1s	A	Ind	Perf	"The Lord said to Moses, 'Do not be afraid of him, for I have handed (παραδέδωκα) him over to you, with his whole army and his land. Do to him what you did to Sihon king of the Amorites, who reigned in Heshbon.'"
6	Num	32	4	3s	A	Ind	Aor	"The land the Lord subdued (παρέδωκεν) before the people of Israel—are suitable for livestock, and your servants have livestock."
7	Deut	1	8	1s	A	Ind	Perf	"See, I have given (παραδέδωκα) you this land. Go in and take possession of the land that the Lord swore he would give to your fathers—to Abraham, Isaac and Jacob—and to their descendants after them."
8	Deut	1	21	3s	A	Ind	Perf	"See, the Lord your God has given (παραδέδωκεν) you the land. Go up and take possession of it as the Lord, the God of your fathers, told you. Do not be afraid; do not be discouraged."
9	Deut	2	24	1s	A	Ind	Perf	"Set out now and cross the Arnon Gorge. See, I have given (παραδέδωκα) into your hand Sihon the Amorite, king of Heshbon, and his country. Begin to take possession of it and engage him in battle."

GOD HANDS THE NATIONS OVER TO ISRAEL.

No	Book	Ch	Ver	Nper	Vo	Mo	Tens	Text
10	Deut	2	30	3s	Pass	Subj	Aor	"But Sihon king of Heshbon refused to let us pass through. For the Lord your God had made his spirit stubborn and his heart obstinate in order to give him (παραδοθῇ) into your hands, as he has now done."
11	Deut	2	31		A	Inf	Aor	"The Lord said to me, 'See, I have begun to deliver (παραδοῦναι) Sihon and his country over to you. Now begin to conquer and possess his land.'"
12	Deut	2	33	3s	A	Ind	Aor	"The Lord our God delivered him over (παρέδωκεν) to us and we struck him down, together with his sons and his whole army."
13	Deut	2	36	3s	A	Ind	Aor	"From Aroer on the rim of the Arnon Gorge, and from the town in the gorge, even as far as Gilead, not one town was too strong for us. The Lord our God gave us (παρέδωκεν) all of them."
14	Deut	3	2	1s	A	Ind	Perf	"The Lord said to me, 'Do not be afraid of him, for I have handed him over (παραδέδωκα) to you with his whole army and his land.'"
15	Deut	3	3	3s	A	Ind	Aor	"So the Lord our God also gave into (παρέδωκεν) our hands Og king of Bashan and all his army."
16	Deut	7	2	3s	A	Ind	Fut	"... and when the Lord your God has delivered them (παραδώσει) over to you and you have defeated them, then you must destroy them totally."

No	Book	Ch	Ver	Nper	Vo	Mo	Tens	Text
17	Deut	7	23	3s	A	Ind	Fut	"But the Lord your God will deliver them over (παραδώσει) to you, throwing them into great confusion until they are destroyed."
18	Deut	7	24	3s	A	Ind	Fut	"He will give (παραδώσει) their kings into your hand, and you will wipe out their names from under heaven."
19	Deut	20	13	3s	A	Ind	Fut	"When the Lord your God delivers (παραδώσει) it into your hand, put to the sword all the men in it."
20	Deut	20	20	3s	Pass	Subj	Aor	"However, you may cut down trees that you know are not fruit trees and use them to build siege works until the city at war with you falls (παραδοθῇ)."
21	Deut	21	10	3s	A	Subj	Aor	"When you go to war against your enemies and the Lord your God delivers (παραδῷ) them into your hands and you take captives."
22	Deut	23	15		A	Inf	Aor	"For the Lord your God moves about in your camp to protect you and to deliver (παραδοῦναι) your enemies to you." (Deut 23:14)
23	Deut	28	7	3s	A	Subj	Aor	"The Lord will grant that the enemies who rise up against you will be defeated (παραδῷ) before you. They will come at you from one direction but flee from you in seven."

No	Book	Ch	Ver	Nper	Vo	Mo	Tens	Text
24	Deut	31	5	3s	A	Ind	Aor	"The Lord will deliver them (παρέδωκεν) to you, and you must do to them all that I have commanded you."
25	Josh	2	14	3s	A	Subj	Aor	"'Our lives for your lives!' the men assured her. 'If you don't tell what we are doing, we will treat you kindly and faithfully when the Lord gives (παραδῷ) us the land.'"
26	Josh	2	24	3s	A	Ind	Aor	"They said to Joshua, 'The Lord has surely given (παρέδωκεν) the whole land into our hands; all the people are melting in fear because of us.'"
27	Josh	6	2	1s	A	Ind	Pres	"Then the Lord said to Joshua, 'See, I have delivered (παραδίδωμι) Jericho into your hands, along with its king and its fighting men.'"
28	Josh	6	16	3s	A	Ind	Aor	"The seventh time around, when the priests sounded the trumpet blast, Joshua commanded the people, 'Shout! For the Lord has given (παρέδωκεν) you the city!'"
29	Josh	8	18	1s	A	Ind	Perf	"Then the Lord said to Joshua, 'Hold out toward Ai the javelin that is in your hand, for into your hand I will deliver (παραδέδωκα) the city.' So Joshua held out his javelin toward Ai."
30	Josh	10	8	1s	A	Ind	Perf	"The Lord said to Joshua, 'Do not be afraid of them; I have given (παραδέδωκα) them into your hand. Not one of them will be able to withstand you.'"

No	Book	Ch	Ver	Nper	Vo	Mo	Tens	Text
31	Josh	10	12	3s	A	Ind	Aor	"On the day the Lord gave (παρέδωκεν) the Amorites over to Israel, Joshua said to the Lord in the presence of Israel: 'O sun, stand still over Gibeon, O moon, over the Valley of Aijalon.'"
32	Josh	10	19	3s	A	Ind	Aor	"But don't stop! Pursue your enemies, attack them from the rear and don't let them reach their cities, for the Lord your God has given (παρέδωκεν) them into your hand.
33	Josh	10	30	3s	A	Ind	Aor	The Lord also gave (παρέδωκεν) that city and its king into Israel's hand."
34	Josh	10	32	3s	A	Ind	Aor	"The Lord handed (παρέδωκεν) Lachish over to Israel, and Joshua took it on the second day."
35	Josh	10	35	3s	A	Ind	Aor	"They captured (παρέδωκεν) it that same day and put it to the sword and totally destroyed everyone in it, just as they had done to Lachish."
36	Josh	11	6	1s	A	Ind	Pres	"The Lord said to Joshua, 'Do not be afraid of them, because by this time tomorrow I will hand (παραδίδωμι) all of them over to Israel, slain. You are to hamstring their horses and burn their chariots.'"
37	Josh	11	8	3s	A	Ind	Aor	"... and the Lord gave (παρέδωκεν) them into the hand of Israel. They defeated them and pursued them all the way to Greater Sidon."

GOD HANDS THE NATIONS OVER TO ISRAEL. 249

No	Book	Ch	Ver	Nper	Vo	Mo	Tens	Text
38	Josh	21	44	3s	A	Ind	Aor	"The Lord gave them rest on every side, just as he had sworn to their forefathers. Not one of their enemies withstood them; the Lord handed (παρέδωκεν) all their enemies over to them."
39	Josh	24	8	3s	A	Ind	Aor	"I brought you to the land of the Amorites who lived east of the Jordan. They fought against you, but I gave (παρέδωκεν) them into your hands. I destroyed them from before you, and you took possession of their land."
40	Josh	24	11	3s	A	Ind	Aor	"Then you crossed the Jordan and came to Jericho. The citizens of Jericho fought against you, as did also the Amorites, Perizzites, Canaanites, Hittites, Girgashites, Hivites and Jebusites, but I gave (παρέδωκεν) them into your hands."
41	Judg	1	4	3s	A	Ind	Aor	"When Judah attacked, the Lord gave (παρέδωκεν) the Canaanites and Perizzites into their hands and they struck down ten thousand men at Bezek."
42	Judg	3	10	3s	A	Ind	Aor	"The Spirit of the Lord came upon him, so that he became Israel's judge and went to war. The Lord gave (παρέδωκεν) Cushan-Rishathaim king of Aram into the hands of Othniel, who overpowered him."
43	Judg	3	28	3s	A	Ind	Aor	"'Follow me,' he ordered, 'for the Lord has given (παρέδωκεν) Moab, your enemy, into your hands.'"

No	Book	Ch	Ver	Nper	Vo	Mo	Tens	Text
44	Judg	4	7	1s	A	Ind	Fut	"I will lure Sisera, the commander of Jabin's army, with his chariots and his troops to the Kishon River and give (παραδώσω) him into your hands."
45	Judg	4	14	3s	A	Ind	Aor	"Then Deborah said to Barak, 'Go! This is the day the Lord has given (παρέδωκεν) Sisera into your hands. Has not the Lord gone ahead of you?'"
46	Judg	7	2		A	Inf	Aor	"The Lord said to Gideon, 'You have too many men for me to deliver (παραδοῦναι) Midian into their hands. In order that Israel may not boast against me that her own strength has saved her...'"
47	Judg	7	7	1s	A	Ind	Fut	"The Lord said to Gideon, 'With the three hundred men that lapped I will save you and give (παραδώσω) the Midianites into your hands. Let all the other men go, each to his own place.'"
48	Judg	7	9	1s	A	Ind	Aor	"During that night the Lord said to Gideon, 'Get up, go down against the camp, because I am going to give (παρέδωκα) it into your hands.'"
49	Judg	7	14	3s	A	Ind	Aor	"His friend responded, 'This can be nothing other than the sword of Gideon son of Joash, the Israelite. God has given (παρέδωκεν) the Midianites and the whole camp into his hands.'"

No	Book	Ch	Ver	Nper	Vo	Mo	Tens	Text
50	Judg	7	15	3s	A	Ind	Aor	"When Gideon heard the dream and its interpretation, he worshiped God. He returned to the camp of Israel and called out, 'Get up! The Lord has given (παρέδωκεν) the Midianite camp into your hands.'"
51	Judg	8	3	3s	A	Ind	Aor	"'God gave (παρέδωκεν) Oreb and Zeeb, the Midianite leaders, into your hands. What was I able to do compared to you?'" At this, their resentment against him subsided.
52	Judg	11	9	3s	A	Subj	Aor	Jephthah answered, 'Suppose you take me back to fight the Ammonites and the Lord gives (παραδῷ) them to me—will I really be your head?'"
53	Judg	11	21	3s	A	Ind	Aor	"Then the Lord, the God of Israel, gave (παρέδωκεν) Sihon and all his men into Israel's hands, and they defeated them. Israel took over all the land of the Amorites who lived in that country."
54	Judg	11	30	2s	A	Subj	Aor	"And Jephthah made a vow to the Lord: 'If you give (παραδῷς) the Ammonites into my hands.'"
55	Judg	11	32	3s	A	Ind	Aor	"Then Jephthah went over to fight the Ammonites, and the Lord gave (παρέδωκεν) them into his hands."

No	Book	Ch	Ver	Nper	Vo	Mo	Tens	Text
56	Judg	12	3	3s	A	Ind	Aor	"When I saw that you wouldn't help, I took my life in my hands and crossed over to fight the Ammonites, and the Lord gave (παρέδωκεν) me the victory over them. Now why have you come up today to fight me?"
57	Judg	18	10	3s	A	Ind	Aor	"When you get there, you will find an unsuspecting people and a spacious land that God has put (παρέδωκεν) into your hands, a land that lacks nothing whatever."
58	1Sam	14	10	3s	A	Ind	Perf	"But if they say, 'Come up to us,' we will climb up, because that will be our sign that the Lord has given (παραδέδωκεν) them into our hands."
59	1Sam	14	12	3s	A	Ind	Aor	"The men of the outpost shouted to Jonathan and his armor-bearer, 'Come up to us and we'll teach you a lesson.' So Jonathan said to his armor-bearer, 'Climb up after me; the Lord has given (παρέδωκεν) them into the hand of Israel.'"
60	1Sam	14	37	2s	A	Ind	Fut	"So Saul asked God, 'Shall I go down after the Philistines? Will you give (παραδώσεις) them into Israel's hand?' But God did not answer him that day" (Jonathan not handed over; 1 Sam 14:45, Eng).

GOD HANDS THE NATIONS OVER TO ISRAEL. 253

No	Book	Ch	Ver	Nper	Vo	Mo	Tens	Text
61	1Sam	17	47	3s	A	Ind	Fut	"All those gathered here will know that it is not by sword or spear that the Lord saves; for the battle is the Lord's, and he will give (παραδώσει) all of you into our hands."
62	1Sam	23	4	1s	A	Ind	Pres	"Once again David inquired of the Lord, and the Lord answered him, 'Go down to Keilah, for I am going to give (παραδίδωμι) the Philistines into your hand.'"
63	1Sam	30	23		A A	Inf Ind	Aor Aor	"David replied, 'No, my brothers, you must not do that with what the Lord has given (παραδοῦναι) us. He has protected us and handed (παρέδωκεν) over to us the forces that came against us.'"
64	2Sam	5	19	2s	A A A	Ind Ptc Ind	Fut Pres Fut	"So David inquired of the Lord, 'Shall I go and attack the Philistines? Will you hand (παραδώσεις) them over to me?' The Lord answered him, 'Go, for I will surely hand (παραδιδοὺς παραδώσω) the Philistines over to you.'"
65	2Kgs	3	18	1s	A	Ind	Fut	"This is an easy thing in the eyes of the Lord; he will also hand (παραδώσω) Moab over to you."
66	2Chr	16	8	3s	A	Ind	Aor	"Were not the Cushites and Libyans a mighty army with great numbers of chariots and horsemen? Yet when you relied on the Lord, he delivered (παρέδωκεν) them into your hand."

Appendix 3

God hands Israel over to the nations.

All texts have God as subject or the divine passive.

No.	Book	Ch	Ver	Nper	Vo	Mo	Tens	Text
1	Lev	26	25	2p	P	Ind	Fut	"And I will bring the sword upon you to avenge the breaking of the covenant. When you withdraw into your cities, I will send a plague among you, and you will be given (παραδοθήσεσθε) into enemy hands."
2	Deut	1	27		A	Inf	Aor	"You grumbled in your tents and said, 'The Lord hates us; so he brought us out of Egypt to deliver us (παραδοῦναι) into the hands of the Amorites to destroy us'" (see Deut 1:44, Eng).
3	Deut	32	30	3s	A	Ind	Aor	"How could one man chase a thousand, or two put ten thousand to flight, unless their Rock had sold them, unless the Lord had given (παρέδωκεν) them up?"
4	Josh	7	7		A	Inf	Aor	"And Joshua said, 'Ah, Sovereign Lord, why did you ever bring this people across the Jordan to deliver us (παραδοῦναι) into the hands of the Amorites to destroy us? If only we had been content to stay on the other side of the Jordan!'"

GOD HANDS ISRAEL OVER TO THE NATIONS.

No	Book	Ch	Ver	Nper	Vo	Mo	Tens	Text
5	Josh	24	33	3s	A	Ind	Aor	"And the Lord gave (παρέδωκεν) them into the hands of Eglon, king of Moab."
6	Judg	2	14	3s	A	Ind	Aor	"In his anger against Israel the Lord handed (παρέδωκεν) them over to raiders who plundered them. He sold them to their enemies all around, whom they were no longer able to resist."
7	Judg	6	1	3s	A	Ind	Aor	"Again the Israelites did evil in the eyes of the Lord, and for seven years he gave (παρέδωκεν) them into the hands of the Midianites."
8	Judg	6	13	3s	A	Ind	Aor	"'But sir,' Gideon replied, 'if the Lord is with us, why has all this happened to us? Where are all his wonders that our fathers told us about when they said, "Did not the Lord bring us up out of Egypt?" But now the Lord has abandoned us and put us (παρέδωκεν) into the hand of Midian.'"
9	Judg	13	1	3s	A	Ind	Aor	"Again the Israelites did evil in the eyes of the Lord, so the Lord delivered (παρέδωκεν) them into the hands of the Philistines for forty years."
10	Judg	20	28	1s	A	Ind	Fut	"They asked, 'Shall we go up again to battle with Benjamin our brother, or not?' The Lord responded, 'Go, for tomorrow I will give (παραδώσω) them into your hands.'"

APPENDIX 3

No.	Book	Ch	Ver	Nper	Vo	Mo	Tens	Text
11	1Sam	28	19	3s	A	Ind	Fut	"The Lord will hand (παραδώσει) over both Israel and you to the Philistines, and tomorrow you and your sons will be with me. The Lord will also hand over the army of Israel to the Philistines."
12	1Kgs	8	46	2s	A	Ind	Fut	"When they sin against you—for there is no one who does not sin—and you become angry with them and give them (παραδώσεις) over to the enemy, who takes them captive to his own land, far away or near."
13	2Kgs	3	13		A	Inf	Aor	"Elisha said to the king of Israel, 'What do we have to do with each other? Go to the prophets of your father and the prophets of your mother.' 'No,' the king of Israel answered, 'because it was the Lord who called us three kings together to hand (παραδοῦναι) us over to Moab.'"
14	2Kgs	21	14	1s	A	Ind	Fut	"I will forsake (παραδώσω) the remnant of my inheritance and hand them over to their enemies. They will be looted and plundered by all their foes."
15	2Chr	6	36	2s	A	Ind	Fut	"When they sin against you—for there is no one who does not sin—and you become angry with them and give (παραδώσεις) them over to the enemy, who takes them captive to a land far away or near."
16	2Chr	13	16	3s	A	Ind	Aor	"The Israelites fled before Judah, and God delivered (παρέδωκεν) them into their hands."

No.	Book	Ch	Ver	Nper	Vo	Mo	Tens	Text
17	2Chr	24	24	3s	A	Ind	Aor	"Although the Aramean army had come with only a few men, the Lord delivered (παρέδωκεν) into their hands a much larger army. Because Judah had forsaken the Lord, the God of their fathers, judgment was executed on Joash."
18	2Chr	25	20		A	Inf	Aor	"Amaziah, however, would not listen, for God so worked that he might hand (παραδοῦναι) them over to [Jehoash], because they sought the gods of Edom."
19	2Chr	28	5	3s	A	Ind	Aor	"Therefore, the Lord his God handed (παρέδωκεν) him over to the king of Aram. The Arameans defeated him and took many of his people as prisoners and brought them to Damascus.
20	2Chr	28	9	3s	A	Ind	Aor	"He said to them, 'Because the Lord, the God of your fathers, was angry with Judah, he gave (παρέδωκεν) them into your hand. But you have slaughtered them in a rage that reaches to heaven.'"
21	2Chr	30	7	3s	A	Ind	Aor	"Do not be like your fathers and brothers, who were unfaithful to the Lord, the God of their fathers, so that he made them an object of horror (παρέδωκεν), as you see."
22	2Chr	36	17	3s	A	Ind	Aor	"He brought up against them the king of the Babylonians, who killed their young men with the sword in the sanctuary, and spared neither young man nor young woman, old man or aged. God handed (παρέδωκεν) all of them over to Nebuchadnezzar."

APPENDIX 3

No.	Book	Ch	Ver	Nper	Vo	Mo	Tens	Text
23	Ps	77	48	3s	A	Ind	Aor	"He gave over (παρέδωκεν) their cattle to the hail, their livestock to bolts of lightning" (Ps 78:48, Eng).
24	Ps	77	61	3s	A	Ind	Aor	"He sent (παρέδωκεν) [the ark of] his might into captivity, his splendor into the hands of the enemy" (Ps 78:61, Eng).
25	Ps	105	41	3s	A	Ind	Aor	"He handed (παρέδωκεν) them over to the nations, and their foes ruled over them" (Ps 106:41, Eng).
26	Hos	8	10	3p	Pass	Ind	Fut	"Although they have sold (παραδοθήσονται) themselves among the nations, I will now gather them together. They will begin to waste away under the oppression of the mighty king."
27	Mic	6	14	3p	Pass	Ind	Fut	"You will eat but not be satisfied; your stomach will still be empty. You will store up but save nothing, because what you save I will give (παραδοθήσονται) to the sword."
28	Mic	6	16	1s	A	Subj	Aor	"You have observed the statutes of Omri and all the practices of Ahab's house, and you have followed their traditions. Therefore, I will give (παραδῶ) you over to ruin and your people to derision; you will bear the scorn of the nations."
29	Zech	11	6	1s	A	Ind	Pres	"'For I will no longer have pity on the people of the land,' declares the Lord. 'I will hand (παραδίδωμι) everyone over to his neighbor and his king. They will oppress the land, and I will not rescue them from their hands.'"

No.	Book	Ch	Ver	Nper	Vo	Mo	Tens	Text
30	Isa	64	6	2s	A	Ind	Aor	"No one calls on your name or strives to lay hold of you; for you have hidden your face from us and made us waste away (παρέδωκας) because of our sins" (Isa 64:7, Eng).
31	Isa	65	12	1s	A	Ind	Fut	"I will destine (παραδώσω) you for the sword, and you will all bend down for the slaughter; for I called but you did not answer, I spoke but you did not listen. You did evil in my sight and chose what displeases me."
32	Jer	2	24	3s	Pass	Ind	Aor	"... a wild donkey accustomed to the desert, sniffing the wind in her craving—in her heat who can restrain her (παρεδόθη)? Any males that pursue her need not tire themselves; at mating time they will find her."
33	Jer	15	4	1s	A	Ind	Fut	"I will make them abhorrent (παραδώσω) to all the kingdoms of the earth because of what Manasseh son of Hezekiah king of Judah did in Jerusalem."
34	Jer	21	10	3s	Pass	Ind	Fut	"I have determined to do this city harm and not good, declares the Lord. It will be given (παραδοθήσεται) into the hands of the king of Babylon, and he will destroy it with fire."
35	Jer	22	25	1s	A	Ind	Fut	"I will hand (παραδώσω) you over to those who seek your life, those you fear—to Nebuchadnezzar king of Babylon and to the Babylonians."

No.	Book	Ch	Ver	Nper	Vo	Mo	Tens	Text
36	Jer	24	8	1s	A	Ind	Fut	"'But like the poor figs, which are so bad they cannot be eaten,' says the Lord, 'so will I deal (παραδώσω) with Zedekiah king of Judah, his officials and the survivors from Jerusalem, whether they remain in this land or live in Egypt.'"
37	Jer	39	4	3s	Pass	Ind	Fut	"Zedekiah king of Judah will not escape out of the hands of the Babylonians but will certainly be handed (παραδοθήσεται) over to the king of Babylon, and will speak with him face to face and see him with his own eyes" (Jer 32:4, Eng).
38	Jer	39	28	3s	Pass	Ind	Fut	"Therefore, this is what the Lord says: I am about to hand (παραδοθήσεται) this city over to the Babylonians and to Nebuchadnezzar king of Babylon, who will capture it" (Jer 32:28, Eng).
39	Jer	39	36	3s	Pass	Ind	Fut	"You are saying about this city, 'By the sword, famine and plague it will be handed (παραδοθήσεται) over to the king of Babylon'; but this is what the Lord, the God of Israel, says" (Jer 32:36, Eng).
40	Jer	39	43	3p	Pass	Ind	Aor	"Once more fields will be bought in this land of which you say, 'It is a desolate waste, without men or animals, for it has been handed (παραδόθησαν) over to the Babylonians'" (Jer 32:43, Eng).

GOD HANDS ISRAEL OVER TO THE NATIONS.

No.	Book	Ch	Ver	Nper	Vo	Mo	Tens	Text
41	Jer	41	2	3s	Pass	Ind	Fut	"This is what the Lord, the God of Israel, says: Go to Zedekiah king of Judah and tell him, 'This is what the Lord says: I am about to hand (παραδοθήσεται) this city over to the king of Babylon, and he will burn it down'" (Jer 34:2, Eng).
42	Jer	44	17	2s	Pass	Ind	Fut	"Then King Zedekiah sent for him and had him brought to the palace, where he asked him privately, 'Is there any word from the Lord?' 'Yes,' Jeremiah replied, 'you will be handed (παραδοθήσῃ) over to the king of Babylon'" (Jer 37:17, Eng).
43	Jer	45	3	3s	Pass	Ind	Fut	"And this is what the Lord says: 'This city will certainly be handed (παραδοθήσεται) over to the army of the king of Babylon, who will capture it'" (Jer 38:3, Eng, Eng).
44	Ezek	7	21	1s	A	Ind	Fut	"I will hand (παραδώσω) it all over as plunder to foreigners and as loot to the wicked of the earth, and they will defile it."
45	Ezek	11	9	1s	A	Ind	Fut	"I will drive you out of the city and hand (παραδώσω) you over to foreigners and inflict punishment on you."
46	Ezek	16	27	1s	A	Ind	Fut	"So I stretched out my hand against you and reduced your territory; I gave (παραδώσω) you over to the greed of your enemies, the daughters of the Philistines, who were shocked by your lewd conduct."

No.	Book	Ch	Ver	Nper	Vo	Mo	Tens	Text
47	Ezek	16	39	1s	A	Ind	Fut	"Then I will hand (παραδώσω) you over to your lovers, and they will tear down your mounds and destroy your lofty shrines. They will strip you of your clothes and take your fine jewelry and leave you naked and bare."
48	Ezek	21	20	3p	Pass	Ind	Perf	"So that hearts may melt and the fallen be many, I have stationed (παραδέδονται) the sword for slaughter at all their gates. Oh! It is made to flash like lightning, it is grasped for slaughter" (Ezek 21:15, Eng).
49	Ezek	23	9	1s	A	Ind	Aor	"Therefore I handed (παρέδωκα) her over to her lovers, the Assyrians, for whom she lusted."
50	Ezek	23	28	1s	A	Ind	Pres	"For this is what the Sovereign Lord says: I am about to hand (παραδίδωμι) you over to those you hate, to those you turned away from in disgust."
51	Ezek	25	4	1s	A	Ind	Pres	"Therefore, I am going to give (παραδίδωμι) you to the people of the East as a possession. They will set up their camps and pitch their tents among you; they will eat your fruit and drink your milk."
52	Ezek	39	23	1s	A	Ind	Aor	"And the nations will know that the people of Israel went into exile for their sin, because they were unfaithful to me. So I hid my face from them and handed (παρέδωκα) them over to their enemies, and they all fell by the sword."

Appendix 4

Do not/will not hand over.

References to God in italics.

No.	Book	Ch	Ver	Nper	Vo	Mo	Tens	Text
1	Deut	23	16	2s	A	Ind	Fut	"If a slave has taken refuge with you, do not hand (παραδώσεις) him over to his master" (Deut 23:15, Eng).
2	Josh	24	10	3s	A	Ind	Aor	"*But I would not listen to Balaam, so he blessed you again and again, and I delivered (παρέδωκεν) you out of his hand.*"
3	Judg	2	23	3s	A	Ind	Aor	"*The Lord had allowed those nations to remain; he did not drive them out (παρέδωκεν) at once by giving them into the hands of Joshua.*"
4	1Sam	11	12	2s	A	Imp	Aor	"The people then said to Samuel, 'Who was it that asked, "Shall Saul reign over us?" Bring (παραδός) these men to us and we will put them to death.'"

No.	Book	Ch	Ver	Nper	Vo	Mo	Tens	Text
5	1Sam	23	14	3s	A	Ind	Aor	"David stayed in the desert strongholds and in the hills of the Desert of Ziph. Day after day Saul searched for him, but God did not give (παρέδωκεν) David into his hands."
6	1Sam	30	15		A	Inf	Aor	"David asked him, 'Can you lead me down to this raiding party?' He answered, 'Swear to me before God that you will not kill me or hand (παραδοῦναι) me over to my master, and I will take you down to them.'"
7	2Kgs	18	30	3s	Pass	Subj	Aor	"Do not let Hezekiah persuade you to trust in the Lord when he says, 'The Lord will surely deliver us; this city will not be given (παραδοθῇ) into the hand of the king of Assyria.'"
8	2Kgs	19	10	3s	Pass	Subj	Aor	"Say to Hezekiah king of Judah: Do not let the god you depend on deceive you when he says, 'Jerusalem will not be handed (παραδοθῇ) over to the king of Assyria.'"
9	1Chr	12	18		A	Inf	Aor	"David went out to meet them and said to them, 'If you have come to me in peace, to help me, I am ready to have you unite with me. But if you have come to betray (παραδοῦναι) me to my enemies when my hands are free from violence, may the God of our fathers see it and judge you'" (1 Chr 12:17, Eng).

No.	Book	Ch	Ver	Nper	Vo	Mo	Tens	Text
10	2Chr	32	11		A	Inf	Aor	"When Hezekiah says, 'The Lord our God will save us from the hand of the king of Assyria,' he is misleading you, to let you (παραδοῦναι) die of hunger and thirst."
11	Ps	26	12	2s	A	Subj	Aor	"Do not turn me over (παραδῷς) to the desire of my foes, for false witnesses rise up against me, breathing out violence" (Ps 27:12, Eng).
12	Ps	40	3	3s	A	Opt	Aor	"The Lord will protect him and preserve his life; he will bless him in the land and not surrender (παραδῴη) him to the desire of his foes" (Ps 41:2, Eng).
13	Ps	73	19	2s	A	Subj	Aor	"Do not hand over (παραδῷς) the life of your dove to wild beasts; do not forget the lives of your afflicted people forever" (Ps 74:19, Eng).
14	Ps	117	18	3s	A	Ind	Aor	"The Lord has chastened me severely, but he has not given me over (παρέδωκεν) to death" (Ps 118:18, Eng).
15	Ps	118	121	2s	A	Subj	Aor	"I have done what is righteous and just; do not leave (παραδῷς) me to my oppressors" (Ps 119:121, Eng).
16	Ps	139	9	2s	A	Subj	Aor	" . . . do not grant (παραδῷς) the wicked their desires, O Lord; do not let their plans succeed, or they will become proud" (Ps 140:8, Eng).

No.	Book	Ch	Ver	Nper	Vo	Mo	Tens	Text
17	Prov	30	10	2s	A	Subj	Aor	"Do not slander (παραδῷς) a servant to his master, or he will curse you, and you will pay for it."
18	Isa	36	15	3s	Pass	Subj	Aor	"Do not let Hezekiah persuade you to trust in the Lord when he says, 'The Lord will surely deliver us; this city will not be given (παραδοθῇ) into the hand of the king of Assyria.'"
19	Isa	37	10	3s	Pass	Subj	Aor	"Say to Hezekiah king of Judah: Do not let the god you depend on deceive you when he says, 'Jerusalem will not be handed over (παραδοθῇ) to the king of Assyria.'"
20	Jer	33	24		A	Inf	Aor	"Furthermore, Ahikam son of Shaphan supported Jeremiah, and so he was not handed over (παραδοῦναι) to the people to be put to death" (Jer 26:24, Eng).
21	Jer	45	20	3p	A	Subj	Aor	"They will not hand (παραδῶσίν) you over, Jeremiah replied. 'Obey the Lord by doing what I tell you. Then it will go well with you, and your life will be spared'" (Jer 38:20, Eng).

Appendix 5

God hands nations to other nations.

All texts have God as subject or the divine passive.

No.	Book	Ch	Ver	Nper	Vo	Mo	Tens	Text
1	Isa	19	4	1s	A	Ind	Fut	"I will hand (παραδώσω) the Egyptians over to the power of a cruel master, and a fierce king will rule over them," declares the Lord, the Lord Almighty."
2	Isa	23	7		Pass	Inf	Aor	"Is this your city of revelry, the old, old city, whose feet have taken her to settle (παραδοθῆναι) in far-off lands [Tarshish]?"
3	Isa	25	5	2s	A	Ind	Aor	"... and like the heat of the desert. You silence the uproar of foreigners; as heat is reduced by the shadow of a cloud, so the song of the ruthless is stilled (παρέδωκας)."
4	Isa	33	1	3p	Pass	Ind	Fut	"Woe to you, O destroyer, you who have not been destroyed! Woe to you, O traitor, you who have not been betrayed! When you stop destroying, you will be destroyed; when you stop betraying, you will be betrayed (παραδοθήσονται) [Assyria]."

No.	Book	Ch	Ver	Nper	Vo	Mo	Tens	Text
5	Isa	34	2		A	Inf	Aor	"The Lord is angry with all nations; his wrath is upon all their armies. He will totally destroy them, he will give (παραδοῦναι) them over to slaughter."
6	Isa	47	3	1s	A	Subj	Aor	"Your nakedness will be exposed and your shame uncovered. I will take vengeance; I will spare no one (παραδῷ)."
7	Jer	26	24	3s	Pass	Ind	Aor	"The Daughter of Egypt will be put to shame, handed (παρεδόθη) over to the people of the north" (Jer 46:24, Eng).
8	Jer	27	2	3s	Pass	Ind	Aor	"Announce and proclaim among the nations, lift up a banner and proclaim it; keep nothing back, but say, 'Babylon will be captured; Bel will be put to shame, Marduk filled with terror (παρεδόθη). Her images will be put to shame and her idols filled with terror'" (Jer 50:2, Eng).
9	Ezek	21	32	1s	A	Ind	Fut	"A ruin! A ruin! I will make it a ruin! It will not be restored until he comes to whom it rightfully belongs; to him I will give (παραδώσω) it [Ammon]" (Ezek 21:27, Eng).
10	Ezek	21	34		A	Inf	Aor	"Despite false visions concerning you and lying divinations about you, it will be laid (παραδοῦναι) on the necks of the wicked who are to be slain, whose day has come, whose time of punishment has reached its climax [Ammon]" (Ezek 21:29, Eng).

GOD HANDS NATIONS TO OTHER NATIONS. 269

No.	Book	Ch	Ver	Nper	Vo	Mo	Tens	Text
11	Ezek	21	36	1s	A	Ind	Fut	"I will pour out my wrath upon you and breathe out my fiery anger against you; I will hand (παραδώσω) you over to brutal men, men skilled in destruction [Ammon]" (Ezek 21:31, Eng).
12	Ezek	31	11	1s	A	Ind	Aor	"I handed (παρέδωκα) it over to the ruler of the nations, for him to deal with according to its wickedness. I cast it aside."
13	Dan	11	6	3s	Pass	Ind	Fut	"After some years, they will become allies. The daughter of the king of the South will go to the king of the North to make an alliance, but she will not retain her power, and he and his power will not last. In those days she will be handed (παραδοθήσεται) over, together with her royal escort and her father and the one who supported her."
14	Dan	11	11	3s	Pass	Ind	Fut	"Then the king of the South will march out in a rage and fight against the king of the North, who will raise a large army, but it will be defeated (παραδοθήσεται)."

Appendix 6

One of God's people handed over.

References to God in italics.

No.	Book	Ch	Ver	Nper	Vo	Mo	Tens	Text
1	Judg	15	12	Nil 2s	A A	Inf Imp	Aor Aor	"They said to him, 'We've come to tie you up and hand (παραδοῦναι) you over to the Philistines.' Samson said, 'Swear to me that you won't kill (παράδοτε) me yourselves.'"
2	Judg	15	13	1p	A	Ind	Fut	"'Agreed,' they answered. 'We will only tie you up and hand (παραδῶσομέν) you over to them. We will not kill you.' So they bound him with two new ropes and led him up from the rock."
3	Judg	16	23	3s	A	Ind	Aor	"Now the rulers of the Philistines assembled to offer a great sacrifice to Dagon their god and to celebrate, saying, 'Our god has delivered (παρέδωκεν) Samson, our enemy, into our hands.'"

ONE OF GOD'S PEOPLE HANDED OVER.

No.	Book	Ch	Ver	Nper	Vo	Mo	Tens	Text
4	Judg	16	24	3s	A	Ind	Aor	"When the people saw him, they praised their god, saying, 'Our god has delivered (παρέδωκεν) our enemy into our hands, the one who laid waste our land and multiplied our slain.'"
5	1Sam	24	5		A	Inf	Aor	"The men said, 'This is the day the Lord spoke of when he said to you, "I will give (παραδοῦναι) your enemy into your hands for you to deal with as you wish."' Then David crept up unnoticed and cut off a corner of Saul's robe" (1 Sam 24:4, Eng).
6	1Sam	24	11	3s	A	Ind	Aor	"This day you have seen with your own eyes how the Lord delivered (παρέδωκεν) you into my hands in the cave. Some urged me to kill you, but I spared you; I said, 'I will not lift my hand against my master, because he is the Lord's anointed'" (1 Sam 24:10, Eng).
7	1Sam	26	23	3s	A	Ind	Aor	"The Lord rewards every man for his righteousness and faithfulness. The Lord delivered (παρέδωκεν) you into my hands today, but I would not lay a hand on the Lord's anointed."

No.	Book	Ch	Ver	Nper	Vo	Mo	Tens	Text
8	Ps	9	35		A	Inf	Aor	"But you, O God, do see trouble and grief; you consider it to take it in hand. The victim commits (παραδοῦναι) himself to you; you are the helper of the fatherless" (Ps 10:14, Eng).
9	Ps	87	9	1s	Pass	Ind	Aor	"You have taken from me my closest friends and have made me repulsive to them. I am confined (παρεδόθην) and cannot escape" (Ps 88:8, Eng).
10	Job	2	6	1s	A	Ind	Pres	"The Lord said to Satan, 'Very well, then, he is in your hands (παραδίδωμι); but you must spare his life.'"
11	Job	16	11	3s	A	Ind	Aor	"God has turned (παρέδωκεν) me over to evil men and thrown me into the clutches of the wicked."
12	Isa	38	12	1s	Pass	Ind	Aor	"Like a shepherd's tent my house has been pulled down and taken from me. Like a weaver I have rolled up my life, and he has cut me off (παρεδόθην) from the loom; day and night you made an end of me."
13	Isa	38	13	1s	Pass	Ind	Aor	"I waited patiently till dawn, but like a lion he broke all my bones; day and night you made an end of me (παρεδόθην)."
14	Isa	53	6	3s	A	Ind	Aor	"We all, like sheep, have gone astray, each of us has turned to his own way; and the Lord has laid (παρέδωκεν) on him the iniquity of us all."

ONE OF GOD'S PEOPLE HANDED OVER.

No.	Book	Ch	Ver	Nper	Vo	Mo	Tens	Text
15	Isa	53	12	3s	Pass	Ind	Aor	"Therefore, I will give him a portion among the great, and he will divide the spoils with the strong, because he poured (παρεδόθη) out his life unto death, and was numbered with the transgressors. For he bore the sin of many, and made intercession for the transgressors."
16	Dan	3	95	3p	A	Ind	Aor	"Then Nebuchadnezzar said, 'Praise be to the God of Shadrach, Meshach and Abednego, who has sent his angel and rescued his servants! They trusted in him and defied the king's command and were willing to give up (παρέδωκαν) their lives rather than serve or worship any god except their own God'" (Dan 3:28, Eng).

Appendix 7

Other.

References to God in italics.

No.	Book	Ch	Ver	Nper	Vo	Mo	Tens	Text
1	Gen	27	20	3s	A	Ind	Aor	"Isaac asked his son, 'How did you find it so quickly, my son?' 'The Lord your God gave me (παρέδωκεν) success,' he replied."
2	Exod	21	13	3s	A	Ind	Aor	"However, if he does not do it intentionally, but God lets it happen (παρέδωκεν), he is to flee to a place I will designate."
3	Deut	19	12	3p	A	Ind	Fut	"... the elders of his town shall send for him, bring him back from the city, and hand (παραδώσουσιν) him over to the avenger of blood to die."
4	2Chr	35	12		A	Inf	Aor	"They set aside the burnt offerings to give them to the subdivisions of the families of the people to offer (παραδοῦναι) to the Lord, as is written in the Book of Moses."

OTHER.

No.	Book	Ch	Ver	Nper	Vo	Mo	Tens	Text
5	Esth	2	3	3p	Pass	Imp	Aor	"Let the king appoint commissioners in every province of his realm to bring all these beautiful girls into the harem at the citadel of Susa. Let them be placed under (παραδοθήτωσαν) the care of Hegai, the king's eunuch, who is in charge of the women; and let beauty treatments be given to them."
6	Esth	2	13	3s	A	Ind	Fut	"And this is how she would go to the king: Anything she wanted was given (παραδώσει) her to take with her from the harem to the king's palace."
7	Ps	62	11	3p	Pass	Ind	Fut	"They will be given over (παραδοθήσονται) to the sword and become food for jackals" (Ps 63:10, Eng).
8	Prov	6	1	2s	A	Ind	Fut	"My son, if you have put up (παραδώσεις) security for your neighbor, if you have struck hands in pledge for another."
9	Prov	11	8	3s	Pass	Ind	Pres	"The righteous man is rescued from trouble, and it comes (παραδίδοται) on the wicked instead."
10	Prov	24	22	3s	Pass	Subj	Aor	"... for those two will send sudden destruction (παραδοθῇ) upon them, and who knows what calamities they can bring?"
11	Prov	27	24	3s	A	Ind	Pres	"... for riches do not endure forever, and a crown is not secure (παραδίδωσιν) for all generations."

No.	Book	Ch	Ver	Nper	Vo	Mo	Tens	Text
12	Job	9	24	3s	Pass	Ind	Perf	"When a land falls (παραδέδονται) into the hands of the wicked, he blindfolds its judges. If it is not he, then who is it?"
13	Job	24	14	3s	A	Ind	Aor	"When daylight is gone, the murderer rises up and kills (παρέδωκεν) the poor and needy; in the night he steals forth like a thief."
14	Isa	25	7	2s	A	Imp	Aor	"On this mountain he will destroy (παραδός) the shroud that enfolds all peoples, the sheet that covers all nations."
15	Isa	33	6	3p	Pass	Ind	Fut	"He will be the sure foundation for your times, a rich store (παραδοθήσονται) of salvation and wisdom and knowledge; the fear of the Lord is the key to this treasure."
16	Isa	33	23	3s	Pass	Subj	Aor	"Your rigging hangs loose: The mast is not held secure, the sail is not spread. Then an abundance of spoils will be divided and even the lame will carry off (παραδοθῇ) plunder."
17	Dan	4	17	3s	A	Ind	Fut	"The decision is announced by messengers, the holy ones declare the verdict, so that the living may know that the Most High is sovereign over the kingdoms of men and gives (παραδώσει) them to anyone he wishes and sets over them the lowliest of men."

Appendix 8

The GNT.

Book	Ch	Ver	Nper	Vo	Mo	Tens	
1. God the subject of the verb/handing over for a blessing:							
Matt	11	27	3S	PA	IND	AO	"All things have been committed (παρεδόθη) to me by my Father. No one knows the Son except the Father, and no one knows the Father except the Son and those to whom the Son chooses to reveal him."
Luke	10	22	3S	PA	IND	AOR	"All things have been committed (παρεδόθη) to me by my Father. No one knows who the Son is except the Father, and no one knows who the Father is except the Son and those to whom the Son chooses to reveal him."
John	19	30	3S	ACT	IND	AOR	"When he had received the drink, Jesus said, 'It is finished.' With that, he bowed his head and gave up (παρέδωκεν) his spirit."
Acts	14	26	MP	PA	PART	PER	"From Attalia they sailed back to Antioch, where they had been committed (παραδεδομένοι) to the grace of God for the work they had now completed."

APPENDIX 8

Book	Ch	Ver	Nper	Vo	Mo	Tens	
Acts	15	26	3P	AC D	PART	PER	"... men who have risked (παραδεδωκόσι) their lives for the name of our Lord Jesus Christ."
Acts	15	40	3P	PA MS	PART	AOR	"... but Paul chose Silas and left, commended (παραδοθεὶς) by the brothers to the grace of the Lord."
Rom	4	25	3S	PA	IND	AO	"He was delivered (παρεδόθη) over to death for our sins and was raised to life for our justification."
Rom	8	32	3S	ACT	IND	AOR	"He who did not spare his own Son, but gave (παρέδωκεν) him up for us all—how will he not also, along with him, graciously give us all things?"
2 Cor	4	11	1P	PA	IND	PR	"For we who are alive are always being given over (παραδιδόμεθα) to death for Jesus' sake, so that his life may be revealed in our mortal body."
Gal	2	20	MS G	ACT	PART	AOR	"I have been crucified with Christ and I no longer live, but Christ lives in me. The life I live in the body, I live by faith in the Son of God, who loved me and gave (παραδόντος) himself for me."
Eph	5	2	3S	ACT	IND	AOR	"... and live a life of love, just as Christ loved us and gave (παρέδωκεν) himself up for us as a fragrant offering and sacrifice to God."
Eph	5	25	3S	ACT	IND	AOR	"Husbands, love your wives, just as Christ loved the church and gave (παρέδωκεν) himself up for her."

THE GNT. 279

Book	Ch	Ver	Nper	Vo	Mo	Tens	
1 Pet	2	23	3S	ACT	IND	IMP	"When they hurled their insults at him, he did not retaliate; when he suffered, he made no threats. Instead, he entrusted (παρεδίδου) himself to him who judges justly."
1 Cor	15	24	3S	ACT	SUBJ	PRE	"Then the end will come, when he hands over (παραδιδῷ) the kingdom to God the Father after he has destroyed all dominion, authority and power."

2. Judas handing over Christ.

Book	Ch	Ver	Nper	Vo	Mo	Tens	
Matt	10	4	MS N	ACT	PART	AOR	"Simon the Zealot and Judas Iscariot, who betrayed (παραδοὺς) him."
Matt	17	22		PA	INF	PRE	"When they came together in Galilee, he said to them, 'The Son of Man is going to be betrayed (παραδίδοσθαι) into the hands of men.'"
Matt	20	18	3S	PA	IND	FUT	"We are going up to Jerusalem, and the Son of Man will be betrayed (παραδοθήσεται) to the chief priests and the teachers of the law."
Matt	20	19	3P	ACT	IND	FUT	"... and will turn him over (παραδώσουσιν) to the Gentiles to be mocked and flogged and crucified."
Matt	26	2	3S	PA	IND	PRE	"As you know, the Passover is two days away—and the Son of Man will be handed over (παραδίδοται) to be crucified."
Matt	26	15	1S	ACT	IND	FUT	"... and asked, 'What are you willing to give me if I hand him over (παραδώσω) to you?' So they counted out for him thirty silver coins."
Matt	26	16	3S	ACT	SUBJ	AOR	"From then on Judas watched for an opportunity to hand him over (παραδῷ)."

APPENDIX 8

Book	Ch	Ver	Nper	Vo	Mo	Tens	
Matt	26	21	3S	ACT	IND	FUT	"And while they were eating, he said, 'I tell you the truth, one of you will betray (παραδώσει) me.'"
Matt	26	23	3S	ACT	IND	FUT	Jesus replied, "The one who has dipped his hand into the bowl with me will betray (παραδώσει) me."
Matt	26	24	3S	PA	IND	PRE	"The Son of Man will go just as it is written about him. But woe to that man who betrays (παραδίδοται) the Son of Man! It would be better for him if he had not been born."
Matt	26	25	MS N	ACT	PART	PRE	"Then Judas, the one who would betray (παραδιδοὺς) him, said, 'Surely not I, Rabbi?' Jesus answered, 'Yes, it is you.'"
Matt	26	45	3S	PA	IND	PRE	"Then he returned to the disciples and said to them, 'Are you still sleeping and resting? Look, the hour is near, and the Son of Man is betrayed (παραδίδοται) into the hands of sinners.'"
Matt	26	46	MS N	ACT	PART	PRE	"Rise, let us go! Here comes my betrayer (παραδιδοὺς)!"
Matt	26	48	MS N	ACT	PART	PRE	"Now the betrayer (παραδιδοὺς) had arranged a signal with them: 'The one I kiss is the man; arrest him.'"
Matt	27	3	MS N	ACT	PART	PRE	"When Judas, who had betrayed him (παραδιδοὺς), saw that Jesus was condemned, he was seized with remorse and returned the thirty silver coins to the chief priests and the elders."
Matt	27	4	MS N	ACT	PART	AOR	"'I have sinned,' he said, 'for I have betrayed (παραδοὺς) innocent blood.'"

Book	Ch	Ver	Nper	Vo	Mo	Tens	
Mark	3	19	3S	ACT	IND	AOR	"... and Judas Iscariot, who betrayed (παρέδωκεν) him."
Mark	9	31	3S	PA	IND	PRE	"He said to them, 'The Son of Man is going to be betrayed (παραδίδοται) into the hands of men.'"
Mark	10	33	3S	PA	IND	FUT	"'We are going up to Jerusalem,' he said, 'and the Son of Man will be betrayed (παραδοθήσεται) to the chief priests and teachers of the law.'"
Mark	14	10	3S	ACT	SUBJ	AOR	"Then Judas Iscariot, one of the Twelve, went to the chief priests to betray (παραδοῖ) Jesus to them."
Mark	14	11	3S	ACT	SUBJ	AOR	"They were delighted to hear this and promised to give him money. So he watched for an opportunity to hand him over (παραδοῖ)."
Mark	14	18	3S	ACT	IND	FUT	"While they were reclining at the table eating, he said, 'I tell you the truth, one of you will betray (παραδώσει) me—one who is eating with me.'"
Mark	14	21	3S	PA	IND	PRE	"The Son of Man will go just as it is written about him. But woe to that man who betrays (παραδίδοται) the Son of Man! It would be better for him if he had not been born."
Mark	14	41	3S	PA	IND	PRE	"Returning the third time, he said to them, 'Are you still sleeping and resting? Enough! The hour has come. Look, the Son of Man is betrayed (παραδίδοται) into the hands of sinners.'"
Mark	14	42	MS N	ACT	PART	PRE	"Rise! Let us go! Here comes my betrayer (παραδιδοὺς)!"

Book	Ch	Ver	Nper	Vo	Mo	Tens	
Mark	14	44	MS N	ACT	PART	PRE	"Now the betrayer (παραδιδοὺς) had arranged a signal with them: 'The one I kiss is the man; arrest him and lead him away under guard.'"
Luke	9	44		PA	INF	PRE	"Listen carefully to what I am about to tell you: The Son of Man is going to be betrayed (παραδίδοσθαι) into the hands of men."
Luke	18	32	3S	PA	IND	FUT	"He will be handed over (παραδοθήσεται) to the Gentiles. They will mock him, insult him, spit on him, flog him and kill him."
Luke	22	4	3S	ACT	SUBJ	AOR	"And Judas went to the chief priests and the officers of the temple guard and discussed with them how he might betray (παραδῷ) Jesus."
Luke	22	6		ACT	INF	AOR	"He consented, and watched for an opportunity to hand Jesus over (παραδοῦναι) to them when no crowd was present."
Luke	22	21	MS G	ACT	PART	PRE	"But the hand of him who is going to betray (παραδιδόντες) me is with mine on the table."
Luke	22	22	3S	PA	IND	PRE	"The Son of Man will go as it has been decreed, but woe to that man who betrays (παραδίδοται) him."
Luke	22	48	2S	ACT	IND	PRE	"... but Jesus asked him, 'Judas, are you betraying (παραδίδως) the Son of Man with a kiss?'"
Luke	24	7		PA	INF	AOR	"The Son of Man must be delivered (παραδοθῆναι) into the hands of sinful men, be crucified and on the third day be raised again."

THE GNT.

Book	Ch	Ver	Nper	Vo	Mo	Tens	
John	6	64	MS N	ACT	PART	FUT	"'Yet there are some of you who do not believe.' For Jesus had known from the beginning which of them did not believe and who would betray (παραδώσων) him."
John	6	71		ACT	INF	PRE	"(He meant Judas, the son of Simon Iscariot, who, though one of the Twelve, was later to betray (παραδιδόναι) him.)"
John	12	4		ACT	INF	PRE	"But one of his disciples, Judas Iscariot, who was later to betray (παραδίδοναι) him, objected . . ."
John	13	2	3S	ACT	SUBJ	AOR	"The evening meal was being served, and the devil had already prompted Judas Iscariot, son of Simon, to betray (παραδοῖ=) Jesus."
John	13	11	MS A	ACT	PART	PRE	"For he knew who was going to betray (παραδιδόντα) him, and that was why he said not every one was clean."
John	13	21	3S	ACT	IND	FUT	"After he had said this, Jesus was troubled in spirit and testified, 'I tell you the truth, one of you is going to betray (παραδώσει) me.'"
John	18	2	MS N	ACT	PART	PRE	"Now Judas, who betrayed (παραδιδοὺς) him, knew the place, because Jesus had often met there with his disciples."
John	18	5	MS N	ACT	PART	PRE	"'Jesus of Nazareth,' they replied. 'I am he,' Jesus said. (And Judas the traitor (παραδιδοὺς) was standing there with them.)"
John	19	11	MS N	ACT	PART	AOR	"Jesus answered, 'You would have no power over me if it were not given to you from above. Therefore, the one who handed me (παραδοὺς) over to you is guilty of a greater sin.'"

Book	Ch	Ver	Nper	Vo	Mo	Tens	
John	21	20	MS N	ACT	PART	PRE	"Peter turned and saw that the disciple whom Jesus loved was following them. (This was the one who had leaned back against Jesus at the supper and had said, 'Lord, who is going to betray (παραδιδοὺς) you?')"
1 Cor	11	23	3S	PA	IND	IMP	"The Lord Jesus, on the night he was betrayed (παρεδίδοτο), took bread."

3. An inanimate object being handed over.

Book	Ch	Ver	Nper	Vo	Mo	Tens	
Matt	25	14	3S	ACT	IND	AOR	"Again, it will be like a man going on a journey, who called his servants and entrusted (παρέδωκεν) his property to them."
Matt	25	20	2S	ACT	IND	AOR	"The man who had received the five talents brought the other five. 'Master,' he said, 'you entrusted (παρέδωκας) me with five talents.'"
Matt	25	22	2S	ACT	IND	AOR	"The man with the two talents also came. 'Master,' he said, 'you entrusted (παρέδωκας) me with two talents; see, I have gained two more.'"
Mark	4	29	3S	ACT	SUBJ	AOR	"As soon as the grain is ripe (παραδοῖ), he puts the sickle to it, because the harvest has come."
Mark	7	13	2P	ACT	IND	AOR	"Thus you nullify the word of God by your tradition that you have handed down (παρεδώκατε). And you do many things like that."
Luke	1	2	3P	ACT	IND	AOR	"... just as they were handed down (παρέδοσαν) to us by those who from the first were eyewitnesses and servants of the word."

THE GNT. 285

Book	Ch	Ver	Nper	Vo	Mo	Tens	
Luke	4	6	3S	PA	IND	PER	"And he said to him, 'I will give you all their authority and splendor, for it has been given to me (παραδέδοται), and I can give it to anyone I want to.'"
Acts	6	14	3S	ACT	IND	AOR	"For we have heard him say that this Jesus of Nazareth will destroy this place and change the customs Moses handed down (παρέδωκεν) to us."
Acts	16	4	3P	ACT	IND	IMP	"As they traveled from town to town, they delivered (παρεδίδουν) the decisions reached by the apostles and elders in Jerusalem for the people to obey."
Rom	6	17	2P	PA	IND	AOR	"But thanks be to God that, though you used to be slaves to sin, you wholeheartedly obeyed the form of teaching to which you were entrusted (παρεδόθητε)."
1 Cor	11	2	1S	ACT	IND	AOR	"I praise you for remembering me in everything and for holding to the teachings, just as I passed them on (παρέδωκα) to you."
1 Cor	11	23	1S	ACT	IND	AOR	"For I received (παρέδωκα) from the Lord what I also passed on to you . . ."
1 Cor	13	3	3S	ACT	SUBJ	AOR	"If I give all I possess to the poor and surrender (παραδοῖ=) my body to the flames, but have not love, I gain nothing."
1 Cor	15	3	1S	ACT	IND	AOR	"For what I received I passed on (παρέδωκα) to you as of first importance: that Christ died for our sins according to the Scriptures."

Book	Ch	Ver	Nper	Vo	Mo	Tens	
2 Pet	2	21	FS G	PA	PART	AOR	"It would have been better for them not to have known the way of righteousness, than to have known it and then to turn their backs on the sacred command that was passed on (παραδοθείσης) to them."
Jude	3		FS D	PA	PART	AOR	"Dear friends, although I was very eager to write to you about the salvation we share, I felt I had to write and urge you to contend for the faith that was once for all entrusted (παραδοθείση) to the saints."

4. Jews hand Jesus over for trial, Pilate sends Jesus to the cross.

Book	Ch	Ver	Nper	Vo	Mo	Tens	
Matt	27	2	3P	ACT	IND	AOR	"They bound him, led him away and handed him over (παρέδωκαν) to Pilate, the governor."
Matt	27	18	3P	ACT	IND	AOR	"For he knew it was out of envy that they had handed Jesus over (παρέδωκαν) to him."
Matt	27	26	3S	ACT	IND	AOR	"Then he released Barabbas to them. But he had Jesus flogged, and handed him over (παρέδωκεν) to be crucified."
Mark	10	33	3S	PA	IND	FUT	"They will condemn him to death and will hand him over (παραδοθήσεται) to the Gentiles"
Mark	15	1	3P	ACT	IND	AOR	"Very early in the morning, the chief priests, with the elders, the teachers of the law and the whole Sanhedrin, reached a decision. They bound Jesus, led him away and handed him over (παρέδωκαν) to Pilate."
Mark	15	10	3P	ACT	IND	PLP	"... knowing it was out of envy that the chief priests had handed Jesus over (παραδεδώκεισαν) to him."

THE GNT.

Book	Ch	Ver	Nper	Vo	Mo	Tens	
Mark	15	15	3S	ACT	IND	AOR	"Wanting to satisfy the crowd, Pilate released Barabbas to them. He had Jesus flogged, and handed him over (παρέδωκεν) to be crucified."
Luke	20	20		ACT	INF	AOR	"They hoped to catch Jesus in something he said so that they might hand him over (παραδοῦναι) to the power and authority of the governor."
Luke	23	25	3S	ACT	IND	AOR	"He released the man who had been thrown into prison for insurrection and murder, the one they asked for, and surrendered (παρέδωκεν) Jesus to their will."
Luke	24	20	3P	ACT	IND	AOR	"The chief priests and our rulers handed him over (παρέδωκαν) to be sentenced to death, and they crucified him . . ."
John	18	30	1P	ACT	IND	AOR	"'If he were not a criminal,' they replied, 'we would not have handed him over (παρεδώκαμεν) to you.'"
John	18	35	3P	ACT	IND	AOR	"'Am I a Jew?' Pilate replied. 'It was your people and your chief priests who handed you over (παρέδωκαν) to me. What is it you have done?'"
John	18	36	1S	PA	SUBJ	AOR	"Jesus said, 'My kingdom is not of this world. If it were, my servants would fight to prevent my arrest (παραδοθῶ=) by the Jews. But now my kingdom is from another place.'"
John	19	16	3S	ACT	IND	AOR	"Finally Pilate handed him over (παρέδωκεν) to them to be crucified. So the soldiers took charge of Jesus."

Book	Ch	Ver	Nper	Vo	Mo	Tens	
Acts	3	13	2P	ACT	IND	AOR	"You handed him over (παρέδωκατε) to be killed, and you disowned him before Pilate, though he had decided to let him go."

5. Christians, John the Baptist, etc., handed over to the synagogue.

Book	Ch	Ver	Nper	Vo	Mo	Tens	
Matt	4	12	3S	PA	IND	AOR	"When Jesus heard that John had been put (παρεδόθη) in prison, he returned to Galilee."
Matt	10	17	3P	ACT	IND	FUT	"Be on your guard against men; they will hand you over (παραδώσουσιν) to the local councils and flog you in their synagogues."
Matt	10	19	3P	ACT	SUBJ	AOR	"But when they arrest you (παραδῶσιν), do not worry about what to say or how to say it. At that time you will be given what to say."
Matt	10	21	3S	ACT	IND	FUT	"Brother will betray (παραδώσει) brother to death, and a father his child; children will rebel against their parents and have them put to death."
Matt	24	9	3P	ACT	IND	FUT	"Then you will be handed over (παραδώσουσιν) to be persecuted and put to death, and you will be hated by all nations because of me."
Matt	24	10	3P	ACT	IND	FUT	"At that time many will turn away from the faith and will betray (παραδώσουσιν) and hate each other…"
Mark	1	14		PA	INF	AOR	"After John was put in prison (παραδοθῆναι), Jesus went into Galilee, proclaiming the good news of God."

Book	Ch	Ver	Nper	Vo	Mo	Tens	
Mark	13	9	3P	ACT	IND	FUT	"You must be on your guard. You will be handed over (παραδώσουσιν) to the local councils and flogged in the synagogues. On account of me you will stand before governors and kings as witnesses to them."
Mark	13	11	MP N	ACT	PART	PRE	"Whenever you are arrested and brought to trial (παραδιδόντες), do not worry beforehand about what to say. Just say whatever is given you at the time, for it is not you speaking, but the Holy Spirit."
Mark	13	12	3S	ACT	IND	FUT	"Brother will betray (παραδώσει) brother to death, and a father his child. Children will rebel against their parents and have them put to death."
Luke	21	12	MP N	ACT	PART	PRE	"But before all this, they will lay hands on you and persecute you. They will deliver you (παραδιδόντες) to synagogues and prisons, and you will be brought before kings and governors, and all on account of my name."
Luke	21	16	2P	PA	IND	FUT	"You will be betrayed (παραδοθήσεσθε) even by parents, brothers, relatives and friends, and they will put some of you to death."
Acts	8	3	3S	ACT	IND	IMP	"But Saul began to destroy the church. Going from house to house, he dragged off men and women and put them (παρεδίδου) in prison."

APPENDIX 8

Book	Ch	Ver	Nper	Vo	Mo	Tens	
Acts	12	4	MS N	ACT	PART	AOR	"After arresting him, he put him in prison, handing him over (παραδοὺς) to be guarded by four squads of four soldiers each. Herod intended to bring him out for public trial after the Passover."
Acts	21	11	3P	ACT	IND	FUT	"Coming over to us, he took Paul's belt, tied his own hands and feet with it and said, 'The Holy Spirit says, "In this way the Jews of Jerusalem will bind the owner of this belt and will hand him over (παραδώσουσιν) to the Gentiles."'"
Acts	22	4	MS N	ACT	PART	PRE	"I persecuted the followers of this Way to their death, arresting both men and women and throwing them (παραδιδοὺς) into prison ."
Acts	27	1	3P	ACT	IND	IMP	"When it was decided that we would sail for Italy, Paul and some other prisoners were handed over (παρεδίδουν) to a centurion named Julius, who belonged to the Imperial Regiment."
Acts	28	17	1S	PA	IND	AOR	"Three days later he called together the leaders of the Jews. When they had assembled, Paul said to them: 'My brothers, although I have done nothing against our people or against the customs of our ancestors, I was arrested in Jerusalem and handed over (παρεδίδουν) to the Romans.'"

THE GNT. 291

Book	Ch	Ver	Nper	Vo	Mo	Tens	

6. The ungodly, the sinning Christian or angel handed over to sin, Satan, etc.

Book	Ch	Ver	Nper	Vo	Mo	Tens	
Matt	5	25	3S	ACT	SUBJ	AOR	"Do it while you are still with him on the way, or he may hand you over (παραδῷ) to the judge, and the judge may hand you over to the officer, and you may be thrown into prison."
Matt	18	34	3S	ACT	IND	AOR	"In anger his master turned him over (παρέδωκεν) to the jailers to be tortured, until he should pay back all he owed."
Luke	12	58	3S	ACT	IND	FUT	"As you are going with your adversary to the magistrate, try hard to be reconciled to him on the way, or he may drag you off to the judge, and the judge turn you over (παραδώσει) to the officer, and the officer throw you into prison."
Acts	7	42	3S	ACT	IND	AOR	"But God turned away and gave them over (παρέδωκεν) to the worship of the heavenly bodies."
Rom	1	24, 26, 28	3S	ACT	IND	AOR	"Therefore God gave them over (παρέδωκεν) in the sinful desires of their hearts to sexual impurity for the degrading of their bodies with one another. Because of this, God gave them over (παρέδωκεν) to shameful lusts. Even their women exchanged natural relations for unnatural ones. Furthermore, since they did not think it worthwhile to retain the knowledge of God, he gave them over (παρέδωκεν) to a depraved mind, to do what ought not to be done."

APPENDIX 9

Book	Ch	Ver	Nper	Vo	Mo	Tens	
1 Cor	5	5		ACT	INF	AOR	"... hand this man over (παραδοῦναι) to Satan, so that the sinful nature may be destroyed and his spirit saved on the day of the Lord."
Eph	4	19	3P	ACT	IND	AOR	"Having lost all sensitivity, they have given themselves over (παρέδωκαν) to sensuality so as to indulge in every kind of impurity, with a continual lust for more."
1 Tim	1	20	1S	ACT	IND	AOR	"Among them are Hymenaeus and Alexander, whom I have handed over (παρέδωκα) to Satan to be taught not to blaspheme."
2 Pet	2	4	3S	ACT	IND	AOR	"For if God did not spare angels when they sinned, but sent them to hell, putting them (παρέδωκεν) into gloomy dungeons ..."

Appendix 9
Friendship and treachery.

Narrative	"Friend"	Relationship	παραδίδωμι or situational markers (SM).	Inferior/Superior (in bold)	Betrayal	Death(s): T: traitor V: victim O: other	God's action
LXX							
1. Jael/Sisera	Judg 4:17 "friendly"	Judg 4:17	παραδίδωμι Judg 4:7, 14	Judg 4:2, 21	Judg 4:21	V: Judg 4:21; O: Judg 4:16.	Judg 4:6–7, 9, 14–15, 23
2. Samson. Wife/F-in-law	Judg 14:11 30, friends; 14:20, given to friend	14:10 wedding feast	SM: bride given to "friend" (Judg 14:20).	Judg 14:15–16	Judg 14:15–16	T: Judg 15:6; O: Judg 14:19, 15:8.	Judg 14:4. NB assumed idolatry (Judg 14:3).
Samson and Delilah	Nil but 16:4, "love".	Judg 16:4	παραδίδωμι Judg 16:23–24	Judg 16:4	Judg 16:5, 9, 12, 15, 20. Love three times	O: Judg 16:30 V: Judg 16:30	Judg 16, 20, 28 NB idolatry: 16:23
Samson and Israel.	Judg 13:2	Judg 15:20	παραδίδωμι Judg 15:12–13.	Judg 13:24; 14:19	Judg 15:12–13.	O: Judg 15:15	Judg 14:4, 6, 19; 15:14, 19; 16:20, 28.
3. Jonadab/Amnon	2 Sam 13:3 (Jonadab)	2 Sam 13:3 (Jonadab)	SM: 2 Sam 13:5	2 Sam 13:4 (David; superior)	2 Sam 13:14, 34	O: 2 Sam 13:29	2 Sam 12:10
4. Hushai/Joab/David. Hushai.	2 Sam 15:32, 37; 16:16–17	2 Sam 15:32; "friend" omitted in NIV	Does not betray David.	2 Sam 15:32	Does not betray, despite appearances	Nil	2 Sam 12:10 (betrayal of David's role as king) 2 Sam 12:10; 17:14
5. Hushai/Joab/David. Joab	1 Kgs 2:22	1 Kgs 2:22; 8:16	SM: 1 Kgs 1:7	1 Kgs 2:22	2 Sam 3:27; 11:14; 18:15; 20:10; 1 Kgs 1:7	O: 2 Sam 3:27, 39; 18:15; 20:10. T: 1 Kgs 2:5–6	1 Kgs 2:34

294 APPENDIX 9

Narrative	"Friend"	Relationship	παραδίδωμι or situational markers (SM).	Inferior/Superior (in bold)	Betrayal	Death(s): T: traitor V: victim O: other	God's action
6. Ahithophel.	Nil but 2 Sam 15:12 Like God (2 Sam 16:23)	2 Sam 15:12	SM: 2 Sam 17:1–4	2 Sam 15:12	2 Sam 15:31, 16:20, 17:1–4; juxtaposed with Hushai (1 Chr 27:33).	T: 2 Sam 17:23	2 Sam 17:14
7. Eurycles. Josephus.	J.W. 1.515	J.W. 1.515	SM: J.W. 1, 529, 550, 551.	King Herod: friend	J.W. 1.530	Nil, but not for lack of effort; J.W. 1:520.	unstated
8. Noarus	J.W. 2, 481	J.W. 2, 481	SM: J.W. 2, 481.	J.W. 2, 481	J.W. 2, 481	O: J.W. 2, 481.	unstated
9. Josephus	J.W. 3.362, 379	J.W. 2.360	παραδίδωμι J.W. 3.354; 3.360; 3.361; 3.370; 3.381.	J.W. 2.360; 2.568 (superior)	J.W. 3.360	V: his soldiers	unstated
GNT. 10. Judas	Matt 26:50	Matt 26:49 (disciple)	παραδίδωμι Matt 26:48	Inferior: disciple	Matt 26:47	T: Matt 27:4 V: Matt 27:50	presumed

Appendix 10

Δουλεῦειν in the OT/NT.

Item	OT		%	NT		%
1. Serve God	Torah	0	0.0			
	Writings	18	14.5			
	Prophets	16	12.9			
Total		34	27.4		9	36.0
2. Serve voluntarily	OT			NT		
	T	14	11.3			
	W	9	7.3			
	P	3	2.4			
Total		26	21.0		4	16.0
3. Enslaved another person	OT			NT		
	T	8	6.5			
	W	16	12.9			
	P	9	7.3			
Total		33	26.6		3	12.0
4. Enslaved inanimate object	OT			NT		
	T	2	1.6	money	4	16.7
	W	20	16.1	sin	2	8.3
	P	9	7.3	idols	3	12.5
Total		31	25.0	Total	9	36.0
Grand Total		124			25	

Bibliography

ALL REFERENCES TO COMMENTARIES in the WORD series and some theological dictionaries are from electronic versions, unless stated otherwise. Usually, this means that page numbers are unavailable, so references are to the relevant chapter and verse or the article being referenced.

Abbott, H. Porter. *The Cambridge Introduction to Narrative*. 2nd ed. Cambridge: Cambridge University Press, 2008.
Abrams, Daniel. "The Boundaries of Divine Ontology: The Inclusion and Exclusion of Meṭaṭron in the Godhead." *The Harvard Theological Review* 87 (1994) 291–321.
Abramson, Glenda. "Israeli Drama and the Bible: Kings on the Stage." *Australian Jewish Studies Review* 28 (2004) 63–82.
Ackerman, James S. "Knowing Good and Evil: A Literary Analysis of the Court History in 2 Samuel 9–20 and 1 Kings 1–2." *Journal of Biblical Literature* 109 (1990) 41–60.
Ackerman, Susan. "The Personal Is Political: Covenantal and Affectionate Love ('āhēb, 'ahăbâ) in the Hebrew Bible." *Vetus Testamentum* 52 (2002) 437–58.
Adams, Karin. "Metaphor and Dissonance: A Reinterpretation of Hosea 4:13–14." *Journal of Biblical Literature* 127 (2008) 291–305.
Aeschylus. *Agamemnon*. Edited by Arthur Sidgwick. 6th edition. Oxford: Clarendon, 1905.
Aghiorgoussis, Maximos. "The Meaning of Christian Baptism for the Baptized and for the Church." *Greek Orthodox Theological Review* 55 (2010) 19–48.
Ahearne-Kroll, Stephen P. "'Who Are My Mother and My Brothers?' Family Relations and Family Language in the Gospel of Mark." *The Journal of Religion* 81 (2001) 1–25.
Aimers, Geoffrey. "'Give the Devil His Due': The Satanic Agenda and Social Justice in the Book of Job." *Journal for the Study of the Old Testament* 37 (2012) 57–66.
Aland, Kurt, et al., eds. *The Greek New Testament*. 3rd ed. Stuttgart: UBS, 1983.
Alighieri, Dante. "Divine Comedy." http://etcweb.princeton.edu/dante/pdp/.
Allen, Leslie C. *Ezekiel 1–19*. WORD 28. Dallas: Word, 1994.
———. *Ezekiel 20–48*. WORD 29. Dallas: Word, 1990.
———. *Jeremiah: A Commentary*. Louisville: Westminster John Knox, 2008.
———. *Psalms 101–150*. Rev. ed. WORD 21. Dallas: Word, 2002.
Allison, Dale C. *Resurrecting Jesus. The Earliest Christian Tradition and its Interpreters*. Grand Rapids: Eerdmans, 2005.
Alter, Robert. *The Art of Biblical Narrative*. New York: Basic, 1981.

———. *The World of Biblical Literature*. London: SPCK, 1992.

Anderson, A. A. *2 Samuel*. WORD 11. Dallas: Word, 1989.

Anderson, Gary. "Celibacy or Consummation in the Garden? Reflections on Early Jewish and Christian Interpretations of the Garden of Eden." *The Harvard Theological Review* 82 (1989) 121–48.

Anderson, Paul N. "The Sitz im Leben of the Johannine Bread of Life Discourse and its Evolving Context." http://www.academia.edu/12953224/_The_Sitz_im_Leben_of_the_ Johannine_Bread_of_Life_Discourse_and_its_Evolving_Context_.

"The Arabic Gospel of the Infancy of the Saviour." http://www.newadvent.org/fathers/0806.htm.

Arbel, Daphna. "Questions about Eve's Iniquity, Beauty, and Fall: The 'Primal Figure' in Ezekiel 28:11–19 and Genesis Rabbah Traditions of Eve." *Journal of Biblical Literature* 124 (2005b) 641–55.

———. "'Seal of Resemblance, Full of Wisdom, and Perfect in Beauty': The Enoch/Metatron Narrative of 3 Enoch and Ezekiel 28." *The Harvard Theological Review* 98 (2005a) 121–42.

Arcand, Denys, dir. *Jesus of Montreal*. 1989; Richmond, Australia: Madman Cinema, 1989.

Arnal, William E. *Jesus and the Village Scribes: Galilean Conflicts and the Setting of Q*. Minneapolis: Fortress, 2001.

Asheri, David, et al. *A Commentary on Herodotus Books I–IV*. Edited by Oswyn Murray and Alfonso Moreno. Oxford: Oxford University Press, 2007.

Ashton, John. "The Identity and Function of the Ἰουδαῖοι in the Fourth Gospel." *Novum Testamentum* 27 (1985) 40–75.

Atkinson, Kenneth. "Taxo's Martyrdom and the Role of the Nuntius in the 'Testament of Moses': Implications for Understanding the Role of Other Intermediary Figures." *Journal of Biblical Literature* 125 (2006) 453–76.

Aune, David E. *Revelation 6–16*. WORD 52b. Dallas: Word, 1998.

———. *Revelation 17–22*. WORD 52c. Dallas: Word, 1998.

Aus, Roger. "God's Plan and God's Power: Isaiah 66 and the Restraining Factors of 2 Thess 2:6–7." *Journal of Biblical Literature* 96 (1977) 537–53.

Avioz, Michael. "Divine Intervention and Human Error in the Absalom Narrative." *Journal for the Study of the Old Testament* 37 (2013) 339–47.

———. "The Motif of Beauty in the Books of Samuel and Kings." *Vetus Testamentum* 59 (2009) 341–59.

Baker, David L. *Tight Fists or Open Hands? Wealth and Poverty in Old Testament Law*. Grand Rapids: Eerdmans, 2009.

Bal, Mieke. *Death & Dissymmetry: The Politics of Coherence in the Book of Judges*. Chicago Studies in the History of Judaism. Chicago: Chicago University Press, 1988.

———. *Murder and Difference: Gender, Genre and Scholarship on Sisera's Death*. Translated by Matthew Gumpert. Bloomington, IN: Indianapolis University Press, 1992.

Balla, Peter. "2 Corinthians." In *Commentary on the New Testament Use of the Old Testament*, edited by Gregory Beale and Don Carson, 753–83. Grand Rapids: Baker Academic, 2007.

Bammel, Ernst, and Friedrich Hauck. "πτωχός." In *The Theological Dictionary of the New Testament* 6, edited by Gerhard Kittel and Gerhard Friedrich, translated by Geoffrey W. Bromiley, 815–915. Grand Rapids: Eerdmans, 1969.

Baragwanath, Emily. *Motivation and Narrative in Herodotus*. Oxford: Oxford University Press, 2008.

Barclay, John M. G. "Jesus and Paul." In *Dictionary of Paul and His Letters*, edited by G. F. Hawthorne et al., 492–503. Downers Grove: InterVarsity, 1993.

Barker, Margaret. *The Great Angel: A Study of Israel's Second God*. Louisville: Westminster John Knox, 1992.

———. *The Revelation of Jesus Christ*. Edinburgh, UK: T & T Clark, 2000.

Barnett, Paul. *Apocalypse Now and Then: Reading Revelation Today*. Sydney: Anglican Information Office, 1989.

———. *Jesus & the Rise of Early Christianity: A History of New Testament Times*. Downers Grove: InterVarsity, 1999.

Barr, James. *The Semantics of Biblical Language*. Oxford: Oxford University Press, 1961.

———. "'Thou Art the Cherub': Ezekiel 28:14 and the Post-Ezekiel Understanding of Genesis 2–3." In *Priests, Prophets and Scribes: Essays on the Formation of Second Temple Judaism in Honour of Joseph Blenkinsopp*, edited by Eugene Ulrich et al., 213–23. JSOT Supplement Series 149. Sheffield: Sheffield Academic, 1992.

Barrett, Anthony A. "Sohaemus, King of Emesa and Sophene." *The American Journal of Philology* 98 (1977) 153–59.

Barrett, C. K. "The First New Testament?" *Novum Testamentum* 38 (1996) 94–104.

———. *The Gospel According to St. John*. 2nd ed. London: SPCK, 1982.

Barth, Karl. *Church Dogmatics*. Translated by G. T. Thomson et al. Edinburgh, UK: T & T Clark, 1936–1977.

Bartlett, John R. *Jews in the Hellenistic World*. Cambridge Commentaries on Writings of the Jewish and Christian World 1, Part 1. Cambridge: Cambridge University Press, 1985.

Barton, John. *The Nature of Biblical Criticism*. Louisville: Westminster John Knox, 2007.

———. *Understanding Old Testament Ethics: Approaches and Explorations*. Louisville: Westminster John Knox, 2003.

Barton, Stephen C. "Mark as Narrative: The Story of the Anointing Woman (Mark 14:3–9)." *The Expository Times* 102 (1991) 230–34.

———. "Money Matters: Economic Relations and the Transformation of Value in Early Christianity." In *Engaging Economics: New Testament Scenarios and Early Christian Reception*, edited by Bruce Longenecker and Kelly Liebengood, 37–59. Grand Rapids: Eerdmans, 2009.

Baruchi-Unna, Amitai. "The Story of Hezekiah's Prayer (2 Kings 19) and Jeremiah's Polemic Concerning the Inviolability of Jerusalem." *Journal for the Study of the Old Testament* 39 (2015) 281–97.

Bauckham, Richard. *The Gospels for All Christians: Rethinking Gospel Audiences*. Edinburgh, UK: T & T Clark, 1998.

———. *Jesus and the Eyewitnesses: The Gospels as Eyewitness Testimony*. Grand Rapids: Eerdmans, 2006.

———. *Jude, 2 Peter*. WORD 50. Dallas: Word, 1983.

Bauer, Walter, et al. *Greek-English Lexicon of the New Testament and Other Early Christian Literature*. Chicago: University of Chicago Press, 1957.

Baxter, Wayne. "Healing and the 'Son of David': Matthew's Warrant." *Novum Testamentum* 48 (2006) 36–50.
Beale, G. K. "Isaiah VI 9–13: A Retributive Taunt against Idolatry." *Vetus Testamentum* 41 (1991) 257–78.
Beale, G. K., and Sean M. McDonough. "Revelation." In *Commentary on the New Testament Use of the Old Testament*, edited by Gregory Beale and Don Carson, 1081–116. Grand Rapids: Baker Academic, 2007.
Beale, Gregory, and Don Carson, eds. *Commentary on the New Testament Use of the Old Testament*. Grand Rapids: Baker Academic, 2007.
Beasley-Murray, George R. *John*. WORD 36. 2nd ed. Dallas: Word, 1999.
———. *Revelation*. New Century Version. Grand Rapids, Eerdmans, 1974.
Beavis, Mary Ann. "Ancient Slavery as an Interpretive Context for the New Testament Servant Parables with Special Reference to the Unjust Steward (Luke 16:1–8)." *Journal of Biblical Literature* 111 (1992) 37–54.
———. *Mark*. Paideia Commentaries on the New Testament. Grand Rapids: Baker Academic, 2011.
Beck, Peter, "The Fall of Man and the Failure of Jonathan Edwards." *Evangelical Quarterly* 79 (2007) 209–25.
Bellemore, Jane. "Josephus, Pompey and the Jews." *Historia: Zeitschrift für Alte Geschichte* 48 (1999) 94–118.
Ben-Dov, Jonathan. "The Poor's Curse: Exodus XXII 20–26 and Curse Literature in the Ancient World." *Vetus Testamentum* 56 (2006) 431–51.
Bertoluci, Jose M. "The Son of the Morning and the Guardian Cherub in the Context of the Controversy Between Good and Evil." http://digitalcommons.andrews.edu/dissertations/17.
Best, Ernest. *The Temptation and the Passion: The Markan Soteriology*. SNTSMS Series 2. Edited by Graham Stanton. 2nd ed. Cambridge: Cambridge University Press, 1965.
Bevan, Edwyn. *Holy Images. An Inquiry into Idolatry and Image-Worship in Ancient Paganism and in Christianity*. London: Allen & Unwin, 1979.
Biddle, Mark. "Ancestral Motifs in 1 Samuel 25: Intertextuality and Characterization." *Journal of Biblical Literature* 121 (2002) 617–38.
Biguzzi, G. "A Figurative and Narrative Language Grammar of Revelation." *Novum Testamentum* 45 (2003) 382–402.
Black, David, and David Beck, eds. *Rethinking the Synoptic Problem*. Grand Rapids: Baker Academic, 2001.
Black, David, and David Dockery, eds. *New Testament Criticism & Interpretation*. Grand Rapids: Zondervan, 1991.
Blass, Friedrich, and Albert Debrunner. *A Greek Grammar of the New Testament and Other Early Christian Literature*. Translated and revised by Robert W. Funk. Chicago: University of Chicago Press, 1961.
Blenkinsopp, Joseph. "Another Contribution to the Succession Narrative Debate (2 Samuel 11–20; 1 Kings 1–2)." *Journal for the Study of the Old Testament* 38 (2013) 35–58.
Blevins, James L. *Revelation*. Knox Preaching Guides. Edited by John H. Hayes. Atlanta: John Knox, 1973.
Bligh, Philip H. "Eternal Fire, Eternal Punishment, Eternal Life (Mt 25:41, 46)." *The Expository Times* 83 (1971) 9–11.

Blomberg, Craig. "Matthew." In *Commentary on the New Testament Use of the Old Testament*, edited by Gregory Beale and Don Carson, 1–109. Grand Rapids: Baker Academic, 2007.

Blue, B. B. "Food, Food Laws, Table Fellowship." in *Dictionary of the Later New Testament and its Development,* edited by Ralph Martin and Peter Davids, 306–10. Downers Grove: InterVarsity, 1997.

———. "Food Offered to Idols and Jewish Food Laws." In *Dictionary of Paul and His Letters*, edited by Gerald F. Hawthorne, Ralph P. Martin, and Daniel G. Reid, 306–10. Downers Grove: InterVarsity, 1993.

Boase, Elizabeth. "Life in the Shadows: The Role and Function of Isaac in Genesis: Synchronic and Diachronic Readings." *Vetus Testamentum* 51 (2001) 312–35.

Bock, D. L. *Blasphemy and Exaltation in Judaism. The Charge Against Jesus in Mark 14:53–65*. Grand Rapids: Baker, 1998.

———. *The Gospel of Mark*. Cornerstone Biblical Commentary 11. Edited by Philip W. Comfort. Carol Stream, IL: Tyndale, 2005.

———. "Jesus as Blasphemer." In *Who Do My Opponents Say That I Am? An Investigation of the Accusations against the Historical Jesus,* edited by Scot McKnight and Joseph B. Modica, 76–94. The Library of New Testament Studies 327. London: T & T Clark, 2008.

———. *Luke, Volume 1: 1:1—9:50*. Baker Exegetical Commentary on the New Testament 3A. Edited by Moises Silva. Grand Rapids: Baker, 1994.

———. *Studying the Historical Jesus: A Guide to Sources and Methods*. Grand Rapids: Baker, 2002.

Boden, Peggy Jean. "The Mesopotamian Washing of the Mouth (mīs pî) Ritual: an Examination of Some of the Social and Communication Strategies Which Guided the Development and Performance of the Ritual Which Transferred the Essence of the Deity into the Temple Statue." PhD diss., Johns Hopkins University, 1998.

Bodner, Keith. "The Locutions of 1 Kings 22:28: A New Proposal." *Journal of Biblical Literature* 122 (2003) 533–43.

Bolt, Peter G. *The Cross from a Distance: Atonement in Mark's Gospel*. New Studies in Biblical Theology 18. Downers Grove: InterVarsity, 2004.

———. "The Narrative Integrity of Mark 13:24–27." MTh diss., Australian College of Theology, Kensington, NSW, 1991.

Bond, Helen K. *Pontius Pilate in History and Interpretation*. SNTS Monograph Series 100. Edited by Richard Bauckham. Cambridge: Cambridge University Press, 2004.

Bovell, Carlos R. "Genesis 3:21: The History of Israel in a Nutshell?" *Expository Times* 115 (2004) 361–66.

Bovon, François. "The Child and the Beast: Fighting Violence in Ancient Christianity." *The Harvard Theological Review* 92 (1999) 369–92.

———. *A Commentary of the Gospel of Luke 19:28—24:53*. Hermeneia Commentaries. Edited by Helmut Koetser. Translated by James Crouch. Minneapolis: Fortress, 2012.

———. "Studies in Luke-Acts: Retrospect and Prospect." *The Harvard Theological Review* 85 (1992) 175–96.

Boyd-Taylor, C. "Linguistic Register and Septuagintal Lexicography." In *Biblical Greek Language and Lexicography: Essays in Honor of Frederick W. Danker*, edited by Bernard A. Taylor et al., 149–66. Grand Rapids: Eerdmans, 2004.

Branden, Robert Charles. *Satanic Conflict and the Plot of Matthew*. Studies in Biblical Literature 89. New York: Lang, 2006.
Brant, Jo-Ann A. *Dialogue and Drama: Elements of Greek Tragedy in the Fourth Gospel*. Peabody, MA: Hendrickson, 2004.
———. *John*. Paideia Commentaries on the New Testament. Grand Rapids: Baker Academic, 2011.
———. Review of "Rhetoric and Drama in the Johannine Lawsuit Motif" by George L. Parsenios. *The Catholic Biblical Quarterly* 74 (2012) 390–91.
Braun, Roddy. *1 Chronicles*. WORD 14. Dallas: Word, 1986.
Brenk, Frederick E. "'A Most Strange Doctrine': Daimon in Plutarch." *The Classical Journal* 69 (1973) 1–11.
Brenner, Athalya. "A Triangle and a Rhombus in Narrative Structure: A Proposed Integrative Reading of Judges IV and V." *Vetus Testamentum* 40 (1990) 129–38.
Breyer, Chloe. "The Widow's Might." *Journal of Religion and Health* 43 (2004) 123–26.
Brondos, David A. *Paul on the Cross: Reconstructing the Apostle's Story of Redemption*. Minneapolis: Fortress, 2006.
Brown, Derek R. "The Devil in the Details: A Survey of Research on Satan in Biblical Studies." *Currents in Biblical Research* 9 (2011) 200–227.
Brown, Michael Joseph. "'Panem Nostrum': The Problem of Petition and the Lord's Prayer." *The Journal of Religion* 80 (2000) 595–614.
Brown, Raymond E. *The Gospel According to John I–XII*. Anchor 29. Edited by W. F. Albright and D. N. Freedman. Doubleday: New York, 1966.
———. *The Gospel According to John XIII–XXI*. Anchor 29. Edited by W. F. Albright and D. N. Freedman. Doubleday: New York, 1970.
Brown, Scott G. "Factualizing the Folklore: Stephen Carlson's Case against Morton Smith." *The Harvard Theological Review* 99 (2006) 291–327.
Bruce, F. F. *1 & 2 Thessalonians*. WORD 45. Dallas: Word, 1982.
———. *The Book of the Acts*. The New International Commentary on the New Testament. Grand Rapids: Eerdmans, 1986.
———. *The Epistle to the Galatians*. The New International Greek Testament Commentary. Exeter, UK: Paternoster, 1982.
Brueggemann, Walter. *Jeremiah 1–25: To Pluck Up, To Tear Down*. International Theological Commentary. Grand Rapids: Eerdmans, 1988.
———. *Jeremiah 26–52: To Build, To Plant*. International Theological Commentary. Grand Rapids: Eerdmans, 1991.
Budd, Philip J. *Numbers*. WORD 5. Dallas: Word, 1984.
Bultmann, R. "New Testament and Mythology." In *Kerygma and Myth: A Theological Debate*, edited by H.W. Bartsch, 1–44. 2 vols. Translated by R. H. Fuller. London: SPCK, 1972.
Bunta, Silviu. "Yhwh's Cultic Statue after 597/586 B.C.E.: A Linguistic and Theological Reinterpretation of Ezekiel 28:12." *Catholic Biblical Quarterly* 69 (2007) 222–41.
Busch, Austin. "Questioning and Conviction: Double-Voiced Discourse in Mark 3:22–30." *Journal of Biblical Literature* 125 (2006) 477–505.
Butler, Trent C. *Joshua*. WORD 7. Dallas: Word, 1984.
Caesar, Lael O. "Job: Another New Thesis." *Vetus Testamentum* 49 (1999) 435–47.
Caird, G. B. *The Revelation of St John the Divine*. Black's New Testament Commentaries. Edited by Henry Chadwick. 2nd ed. London: A & C Black, 1984.

Calhoun, George Miller. "The Jurisprudence of the Greek City." *Columbia Law Review* 24 (1924) 154-71.
Cancik, Hubert. "The History of Culture, Religion, and Institutions in Ancient Historiography: Philological Observations Concerning Luke's History." *Journal of Biblical Literature* 116 (1997) 673-95.
Cane, Anthony. *The Place of Judas Iscariot in Christology*. Aldershot: Ashgate, 2005.
Capper, Brian. "Jesus, Virtuoso Religion, and the Community of Goods." In *Engaging Economics: New Testament Scenarios and Early Christian Reception*, edited by Bruce Longenecker and Kelly Liebengood, 60-80. Grand Rapids: Eerdmans, 2009.
Carasik, Michael. "The Limits of Omniscience." *Journal of Biblical Literature* 119 (2000) 221-32.
Carlson, S. "The Synoptic Problem Home Page." http://www.hypotyposeis.org/synoptic-problem/.
Carr, David. "The Politics of Textual Subversion: A Diachronic Perspective on the Garden of Eden Story." *Journal of Biblical Literature* 112 (1993) 577-95.
Carson, D. A. "1 Peter." In *Commentary on the New Testament Use of the Old Testament*, edited by Gregory Beale and Don Carson, 1015-45. Grand Rapids: Baker Academic, 2007.
———. "2 Peter." In *Commentary on the New Testament Use of the Old Testament*, edited by Gregory Beale and Don Carson, 1047-61. Grand Rapids: Baker Academic, 2007.
———. *The Gospel According to John*. Grand Rapids: Eerdmans, 1991.
———. "James." In *Commentary on the New Testament Use of the Old Testament*, edited by Gregory Beale and Don Carson, 997-1013. Grand Rapids: Baker Academic, 2007.
———. "Jude." In *Commentary on the New Testament Use of the Old Testament*, edited by Gregory Beale and Don Carson, 1069-79. Grand Rapids: Baker Academic, 2007.
Casey, Maurice. *Jesus of Nazareth: An Independent Historian's Account of his Life and Teaching*. London: T & T Clark, 2010.
Charlesworth, James. *The Good & Evil Serpent. How a Universal Symbol Became Christianized*. The Anchor Yale Bible Reference Library. New Haven: Yale University Press, 2010.
Childs, Brevard S. *Isaiah: A Commentary*. Louisville: Westminster John Knox, 2001.
Christensen, Duane F. *Deuteronomy 1:1—21:9*. Rev. ed. WORD 6a. Dallas: Word, 2001.
———. *Deuteronomy 21:10—34:12*. WORD 6b. Dallas: Word, 2002.
Ciampa, R. E., and Brian Rosner. "1 Corinthians." In *Commentary on the New Testament Use of the Old Testament*, edited by Gregory Beale and Don Carson, 695-752. Grand Rapids: Baker Academic, 2007.
Clines, David. *Job 1-20*. WORD 17. Dallas: Word, 1989.
Coakley, J. F. "The Anointing at Bethany and the Priority of John." *Journal of Biblical Literature* 107 (1988) 241-56.
Cohen, Edward. *The Athenian Nation*. Princeton: Princeton University Press, 2000.
———. "Free and Unfree Sexual Work: An Economic Analysis of Athenian Prostitution." In *Prostitutes and Courtesans in the Ancient World*, edited by Christopher Faraone and Laura McClure, 95-124. Madison: University of Wisconsin Press, 2006.
Cohen, Shaye J. D. "Judaism without Circumcision and 'Judaism' without 'Circumcision' in Ignatius." *The Harvard Theological Review* 95 (2002) 395-415.

Cohen, Sol, and Victor Avigdor Hurowitz. "הקוח העמים הבל הוא" (Jer 10:3) in Light of Akkadian Parṣu and Zaqīqu Referring to Cult Statues." *The Jewish Quarterly Review* 89 (1999) 277–90.
Collins, Adela Yarbro. *The Apocalypse*. New Testament Message. Edited by W. Harrington and D. Senior. Wilmington, DE: Glazier, 1979.
———. *The Combat Myth in the Book of Revelation*. Harvard Dissertations in Religion 9. Missoula: Scholars, 1976.
———. *Crisis and Catharsis: The Power of the Apocalypse*. Philadelphia: Westminster, 1984.
———. "The Function of 'Excommunication' in Paul." *The Harvard Theological Review* 73.1/2 (January–April 1980) 251–63.
———. "Mark and His Readers: The Son of God among Greeks and Romans." *The Harvard Theological Review* 93 (2000) 85–100.
Collins, R. F. "You Call Me Teacher and Lord—and You Are Right. For That Is What I Am." In *Studies in the Gospel of John and its Christology: Festschrift Gilbert van Belle*, edited by Joseph Verheyden et al., 328–48. Leuven, Belgium: Peeters, 2014.
Comfort, Philip. "Idolatry." In *Dictionary of Paul and his Letters*, edited by Gerald Hawthorne and Ralph Martin, edited by Daniel Reid, 424–26. Downers Grove: InterVarsity, 1993.
Cooper, Lamar Eugene. *Ezekiel*. Nashville: Broadman and Holman, 1994.
Corner, Sean. "The Politics of the Parasite (Part One)." *Phoenix* 67 (2013) 43–80.
Cosgrove, Charles H. "The Divine Δεῖ in Luke–Acts: Investigations into the Lukan Understanding of God's Providence." *Novum Testamentum* 26 (1984) 168–90.
Craigie, Peter. *The Book of Deuteronomy*. The New International Commentary on the Old Testament. Eerdmans: Grand Rapids, 1976.
———. *Ezekiel*. The Daily Study Bible. Edinburgh, UK: St Andrews Press, 1983.
Craigie, Peter, et al. *Jeremiah 1–26*. WORD 26. Dallas: Word, 1991.
Cranfield, C. E. B. *Romans*. 2 vols. International Critical Commentary. Edinburgh, UK: T & T Clark, 1979.
Cripps, K. J. R. "A Note on Matthew xxii.12." *The Expository Times* 69 (1957) 30.
Cross, Frank M. *Canaanite Myth and Hebrew Epic: Essays in the History of the Religion of Israel*. Cambridge, MA: Harvard University Press, 1973.
Crossan, J. D. *Who Killed Jesus? Exposing the Roots of Anti-Semitism in the Gospel Story of the Death of Jesus*. San Francisco: HarperSanFrancisco, 1996.
Crown, Alan D. "Redating the Schism between the Judaeans and the Samaritans." *The Jewish Quarterly Review* 82 (1991) 17–50.
Croy, N. Clayton. "Hellenistic Philosophies and the Preaching of the Resurrection (Acts 17:18, 32)." *Novum Testamentum* 39 (1997) 21–39.
D'Angelo, Mary Rose. "Theology in Mark and Q: Abba and "Father" in Context." *The Harvard Theological Review* 85 (1992) 149–74.
———. "Women in Luke–Acts: A Redactional View." *Journal of Biblical Literature* 109 (1990) 441–61.
Danker, F. W. "Lexical Evolution and Linguistic Hazard." In *Biblical Greek Language and Lexicography: Essays in Honor of Frederick W. Danker*, edited by Bernard A. Taylor et al., 1–31. Grand Rapids: Eerdmans, 2004.
Daube, David. "Absalom and the Ideal King." *Vetus Testamentum* 48 (1998) 315–25.

———. "After The Deed." In *The Deed and the Doer in the Bible: David Daube's Gifford Lectures, Volume 1*, edited by Calum Carmichael, 222–40. West Conshohocken, PA: Templeton Foundation, 2008.

Davids, Peter. *Commentary on James*. The New International Greek Testament Commentary. Grand Rapids: Eerdmans, 1982.

Davies, William. *The Setting of the Sermon on the Mount*. Cambridge: Cambridge University Press, 1964.

Davies, William, and Dale Allison. *Matthew*. The International Critical Commentary. Edited by J. A. Emerton, C. E. B. Cranfield, and G. N. Stanton. 3 vols. Edinburgh, UK: T & T Clark, 1991.

Day, Peggy L. "Adulterous Jerusalem's Imagined Demise: Death of a Metaphor in Ezekiel XVI." *Vetus Testamentum* 50 (2000) 285–309.

———. *An Adversary in Heaven: sātān in the Hebrew Bible*. Harvard Semitic Monographs 43. Atlanta: Scholars Press, 1988.

Delamarter, Steve. "The Death of Josiah in Scripture and Tradition: Wrestling with the Problem of Evil?" *Vetus Testamentum* 54 (2004) 29–60.

Demosthenes. "Orations." http://www.perseus.tufts.edu/hopper/morph?l=paradedom e%2Fna&la=greek&can=paradedome%2Fna0&prior=kala\&d=Perseus:text:1999 .01.0073:speech=23:section=65&i=1.

Denzey, Nicola. "What Did the Montanists Read?" *The Harvard Theological Review* 94 (2001) 427–48.

De Quincey, Thomas. "Judas Iscariot and Other Writings." http://books.google.com.au/ books/download/Judas_Iscariot_and_Other_Writings.pdf?id=xP0XAAAAYAAJ &output=pdf&sig=ACfU3U3SPYD3t7xYJukeMTpvH03n4XWFzw.

Derrett, J. Duncan M. "Why Jesus Blessed the Children (Mark 10:13–16 par.)." *Novum Testamentum* 25 (1983) 1–18.

De Villiers, Pieter G. R. Review of *The War Between the Two Beasts and the Two Witnesses*, by Antoninus K. W. Siew. *Review of Biblical Literature* 02 (2007) 458–62.

De Voragine, Jacobus. "The Golden Legend." http://www.fordham.edu/halsall/basis/ goldenlegend/index.htm.

DeVries, Simon J. *1 Kings*. WORD 12. 2nd ed. Dallas: Word, 2003.

Dewald, Carolyn. "Humour and Danger." In *The Cambridge Companion to Herodotus*, edited by Carolyn Dewald and John Marincola, 145–64. Cambridge: Cambridge University Press, 2006.

Dewald, Carolyn, and John Marincola, eds. *The Cambridge Companion to Herodotus*. Cambridge: Cambridge University Press, 2006.

Dick, Michael B. "Prophetic Parodies of Making the Cult Image." In *Born in Heaven, Made on Earth: The Making of the Cult Image in the Ancient Near East*, edited by Michael B. Dick, 1–44. Winona Lake, IN: Eisenbrauns, 1999.

Dickerson, Patrick L. "The Sources of the Account of the Mission to Samaria in Acts 8:5–25." *Novum Testamentum* 39 (1997) 210–34.

Dillard, Raymond B. *2 Chronicles*. WORD 15. Dallas: Word, 1987.

Dixon, Edward P. "Descending Spirit and Descending Gods: A 'Greek' Interpretation of the Spirit's 'Descent as a Dove' in Mark 1:10." *Journal of Biblical Literature* 128 (2009) 759–80.

Domeris, William R. *Touching the Heart of God. The Social Construction Among Biblical Peasants*. Library of Hebrew Bible/Old Testament Studies 466. Edinburgh, UK: T & T Clark, 2007.

Donahue, John R. "A Neglected Factor in the Theology of Mark." *Journal of Biblical Literature* 101 (1982) 563–94.

———. "The 'Parable' of the Sheep and the Goats: A Challenge to Christian Ethics." *Theological Studies* 47 (1986) 3–31.

Donaldson, James, ed. "Constitutions of the Holy Apostles." http://www.ccel.org/ccel/schaff/anf07.ix.html.

Dowd, Sharyn, and Elizabeth Struthers Malbon. "The Significance of Jesus' Death in Mark: Narrative Context and Authorial Audience." *Journal of Biblical Literature* 125 (2006) 271–97.

Downs, David J. "Is God Paul's Patron? The Economy of Patronage in Paul's Economy." In *Engaging Economics. New Testament Scenarios and Early Christian Reception*, edited by Bruce Longenecker and Kelly Liebengood, 129–56. Grand Rapids: Eerdmans, 2009.

Droge, A. J. "Sabbath Work/Sabbath Rest: Genesis, Thomas, John." *History of Religions* 47 (2007/2008) 112–41.

Duff, Paul B. "Wolves in Sheep's Clothing: Literary Opposition and Social Tension in the Revelation of John." In *Reading the Book of Revelation*, edited by David L. Barr, 65–79. SBL Resources for Biblical Study 44. Atlanta: Society of Biblical Literature, 2003.

Duke, Paul D. *Irony in the Fourth Gospel*. Atlanta: John Knox, 1985.

Duling, Dennis C. "'[Do Not Swear . . .] by Jerusalem Because It Is the City of the Great King' (Matt 5:35)." *Journal of Biblical Literature* 110 (1991) 291–309.

Dunn, James D. G. *The Epistle to the Galatians*. Black's New Testament Commentary. Peabody, MT: Hendrickson, 1993.

———. *Romans 1–8*. WORD 38a. Dallas: Word, 1984.

———. *Romans 9–16*. WORD 38b. Dallas: Word, 1984.

———. *The Theology of Paul the Apostle*. Grand Rapids: Eerdmans, 1998.

Durham, John. *Exodus*. WORD 3. Dallas: Word, 1987.

Dutcher-Walls, Patricia. "The Circumscription of the King: Deuteronomy 17:16–17 in Its Ancient Social Context." *Journal of Biblical Literature* 121 (2002) 601–16.

Eberts, Harry W., Jr. "Plurality and Ethnicity in Early Christian Mission." *Sociology of Religion* 58 (1997) 305–21.

Eddy, Paul Rhodes. "Jesus as Diogenes? Reflections on the Cynic Jesus Thesis." *Journal of Biblical Literature* 115 (1996) 449–69.

Edwards, James R. "Markan Sandwiches: The Significance of Interpolations in Markan Narratives." *Novum Testamentum* 31 (1989) 193–216.

———. "The Use of ΠΡΟΣΕΡΧΕΣΘΑΙ in the Gospel of Matthew." *Journal of Biblical Literature* 106 (1987) 65–74.

Edwards, Mark, ed and trans. *Andocides. Greek Orators IV*. Warminster, PA: Aris and Phillips, 1995.

Edwards, Richard A. *Matthew's Narrative Portrait of Disciples. How the Text-Connoted Reader is Informed*. Harrisburg, PN: Trinity, 1997.

Ellingworth, Paul. *The Epistle to the Hebrews*. The New International Greek Testament Commentary. Grand Rapids: Eerdmans, 1993.

———. "(His) Disciples." *Novum Testamentum* 42 (2000) 114–26.

Elliott, J. K., ed. *The Principles and Practice of New Testament Textual Criticism: Collected Essays of G.D. Kilpatrick*. Leuven, Belgium: Leuven University Press, 1990.

Elliott, John H. "Matthew 20:1-15: a Parable of Invidious Comparison and Evil Eye Accusation." *Biblical Theology Bulletin: A Journal of Bible and Theology* 22 (1992) 52-65.

Emerton, J. A. "Looking on One's Enemies." *Vetus Testamentum* 51 (2001) 186-96.

Enslin, Martin S. "How the Story Grew: Judas in Fact and Fiction." In *Festschrift to Honor F. Wilbur Gingrich, Lexicographer, Scholar, Teacher, and Committed Christian Layman*, edited by Eugene Howard Barth and Ronald Edwin Cocroft, 123-41. Leiden, Belgium: Brill, 1972.

Eslinger, Lyle M. "The Enigmatic Plurals Like 'One Of Us' (Genesis I 26, III 22, and XI 7) in Hyperchronic Perspective." *Vetus Testamentum* 56 (2006) 171-84.

Evans, Craig A. *Mark 8:27—16:20*. WORD 34b. Dallas: Word, 2001.

Evans, Craig A., and Stanley E. Porter, eds. *Dictionary of New Testament Background*. Downers Grove, IL: InterVarsity, 2000.

Eynikel, Erik, and Katrin Hauspie. "The Use of δράκων in the Septuagint." In *Biblical Greek Language and Lexicography: Essays in Honor of Frederick W. Danker*, edited by Bernard A. Taylor et al, 126-35. Grand Rapids: Eerdmans, 2004.

Farmer, William R. "The Case for the Two-Gospel Hypothesis." In *Rethinking the Synoptic Problem*, edited by David Black and David Beck, 97-135. Grand Rapids: Baker Academic, 2001.

Fee, Gordon D. *The First Epistle to the Corinthians*. The New International Commentary on the New Testament. Grand Rapids: Eerdmans, 1987.

———. *New Testament Exegesis: A Handbook for Students and Pastors*. 3rd ed. Louisville: Westminster John Knox, 2002.

Fekkes, John. "Isaiah and Prophetic Traditions in the Book of Revelation: Visionary Antecedents and their Development." PhD diss., University of Manchester, 1988.

Feldman, Louis H. "Josephus' *Jewish Antiquities* and Pseudo-Philo's *Biblical Antiquities*." In *Josephus, the Bible and History*, edited by Louis H. Feldman and Gohei Hata, 59-80. Leiden: Brill, 1989.

———. "The Portrayal of Phinehas by Philo, Pseudo-Philo, and Josephus." *The Jewish Quarterly Review* 92 (2002) 315-45.

Ferda, Tucker S. "Matthew's *Titulus* and Psalm 2's King on Mount Zion." *Journal of Biblical Literature* 133 (2014) 561-81.

Fernando, Ajith. *Acts*. NIV Application Commentary Series. Grand Rapids: Zondervan, 1998.

Ferreiro, Alberto. "Simon Magus, Nicolas of Antioch, and Muhammad." *Church History* 72 (2003) 53-70.

Fidler, Ruth. "Genesis xv: Sequence and Unity." *Vetus Testamentum* 57 (2007) 162-80.

Fitzgerald, J. T. "Hospitality." In *Dictionary of New Testament Background*, edited by Craig A. Evans and Stanley E. Porter, 512-25. Downers Grove: InterVarsity, 2000.

Fitzmyer, J. A. *The Gospel According to Luke I-IX*. Anchor Bible 28. Edited by W. F. Albright and D. N. Freedman. New York: Doubleday, 1979.

———. *The Gospel According to Luke X-XXIV*. Anchor Bible 28A. Edited by W. F. Albright and D. N. Freedman. New York: Doubleday, 1983.

Fleming, Daniel E. "Job: The Tale of Patient Faith and the Book of God's Dilemma." *Vetus Testamentum* 44 (1994) 468-82.

Flint, Valerie, et al. *Witchcraft and Magic in Europe, Volume 2: Ancient Greece and Rome*. London: The Athlone, 1999.

Fossum, Jarl E. *The Name of God and the Angel of the Lord: Samaritan and Jewish Concepts of Intermediation and the Origin of Gnosticism*. Wissenschaftliche Untersuchungen zum Neuen Testament 36. Tübingen, Germany: Mohr, 1985.

Foster, Benjamin R. *Before the Muses: An Anthology of Akkadian Literature*. Vol. 1, *Archaic, Classical, Mature*. Bethesda, MD: CDL, 1993.

Foster, Paul. "Is It Possible to Dispense with Q?" *Novum Testamentum* 45 (2003) 313–37.

Foster, Robert L. "Shepherds, Sticks, and Social Destabilization: A Fresh Look at Zechariah 11:4–17." *Journal of Biblical Literature* 126 (2007) 735–53.

Fotopoulos, John. *Food Offered to Idols in Roman Corinth*. Wissenschaftliche Untersuchungen zum Neuen Testament 151. Tübingen, Germany: Mohr, 2003.

France, R. T. *The Gospel of Mark*. The New International Greek Testament Commentary. Carlisle, UK: Paternoster, 2002.

Franke, Chris A. "The Function of the Satiric Lament over Babylon in Second Isaiah (XLVII)." *Vetus Testamentum* 41 (1991) 408–18.

Frankel, David. "The Deuteronomic Portrayal of Balaam." *Vetus Testamentum* 46 (1996) 30–42.

Freedman, David Noel. "On the Death of Abiner." In *Love and Death in the Ancient Near East: Essays in Honour of Marvin H. Pope*, edited by Marvin Pope, John Marks, and Robert Good, 125–28. Guildford, CT: Four Quarters, 1987.

Friesen, Gary. "Myth and Symbolic Resistance in Revelation 13." *Journal of Biblical Literature* 123 (2004) 281–313.

Frolov, Serge. "How Old Is the Song of Deborah?" *Journal for the Study of the Old Testament* 36 (2011) 163–84.

Furnish, Victor Paul. *II Corinthians*. Anchor Bible, Vol 32A. Edited by William Albright and David Freedman. New York: Doubleday, 1984.

Furstenberg, Yair. "The Rabbinic View of Idolatry and the Roman Political Conception of Divinity." *The Journal of Religion* 90 (2010) 335–66.

Fusco, Vittorio. "Luke–Acts and the Future of Israel." *Novum Testamentum* 38 (1996) 1–17.

Gagnon, Robert A. J. "Luke's Motives for Redaction in the Account of the Double Delegation in Luke 7:1–10." *Novum Testamentum* 36 (1994) 122–45.

Galpaz-Feller, Pnina. *Samson: The Hero and the Man: The Story of Samson (Judges 13–16)*. Bible in History. Bern, Switzerland: Lang, 2006.

Garrett, Susan R. *The Demise of the Devil: Magic and Demonic in Luke's Writings*. Minneapolis: Fortress, 1989.

———. "'Lest the Light in You Be Darkness': Luke 11:33–36 and the Question of Commitment." *Journal of Biblical Literature* 110 (1991) 93–105.

———. *The Temptations of Jesus in Mark's Gospel*. Grand Rapids: Eerdmans, 1998.

Gaston, L. "Beelzebul." *Theologische Zeitschrift* 18 (1962) 247–55.

Georgia, Allan T. "Translating the Triumph: Reading Mark's Crucifixion Narrative against Roman Ritual of Power." *Journal for the Study of the New Testament* 36 (2013) 17–38.

Gerhardsson, B. *Memory and Manuscript: Oral Tradition and Written Transmission in Rabbinic Judaism and Early Christianity*. The Biblical Resource Series. Edited by A. Beck and David Freedman. Translated by Eric J. Sharpe. Grand Rapids: Eerdmans, 1998.

———. *The Reliability of the Gospel Tradition*. Peabody, MA: Hendrickson, 2001.

Gilbert, George Holley. "The Hellenization of the Jews between 334 B. C. and 70 A. D." *The American Journal of Theology* 13 (1909) 520–40.
Glancy, Jennifer A. "Slaves and Slavery in the Matthean Parables." *Journal of Biblical Literature* 119 (2000) 67–90.
Gockel, Matthias. *Barth and Schleiermacher on the Doctrine of Election: A Systematic-Theological Comparison.* Oxford: Oxford University Press, 2006.
Goddard, Cliff. *Semantic Analysis: A Practical Introduction.* Oxford Textbooks in Linguistics, edited by K. Brown, et al. Oxford: Oxford University Press, 1998.
Goering, Greg Schmidt. "Proleptic Fulfillment of the Prophetic Word: Ezekiel's Dirges over Tyre and Its Ruler." *Journal for the Study of the Old Testament* 36 (2012) 483–505.
Goldingay, John E. *Daniel.* WORD 30. Dallas: Word, 1989.
Goldingay, John E., and Christopher J. H. Wright. "Yahweh our God Yahweh One." In *One God, One Lord: Christianity in a World of Religious Pluralism*, edited by Andrew D. Clarke and Bruce W. Winter, 43–62. Grand Rapids: Baker, 1992.
Good, Deirdre. "The Verb ἀναχωρέω in Matthew's Gospel." *Novum Testamentum* 32 (1990) 1–12.
Goodacre, Mark. "Fatigue in the Synoptics." *New Testament Studies* 44 (1998) 45–58.
———. *The Synoptic Problem: A Way through the Maze.* Biblical Seminar 80. London: Sheffield Academic, 2001.
Goulder, Michael. "2 Cor. 6:14—7:1 as an Integral Part of 2 Corinthians." *Novum Testamentum* 36.1 (Jan 1994) 47–57.
———. "Behold My Servant Jehoiachin." *Vetus Testamentum* 52.2 (Apr 2002) 175–90.
———. "Those Outside (Mark. 4:10–12)." *Novum Testamentum* 33 (1991) 289–302.
Grabiner, Steven. *Revelation's Hymns: Commentary on the Cosmic Conflict.* Library of New Testament Studies 511. Edited by Chris Keith. London: Bloomsbury, 2015.
Grassi, Joseph A. "The Secret Heroine of Mark's Drama." *Biblical Theology Bulletin: A Journal of Bible and Theology* 18 (1988) 10–15.
Gray, Patrick. "Athenian Curiosity (Acts 17:21)." *Novum Testamentum* 47 (2005) 109–16.
Greenberg, George. *The Judas Brief: Who Really Killed Jesus?* New York: Continuum, 2007.
Greenspahn, Frederick E. "Syncretism and Idolatry in the Bible." *Vetus Testamentum* 54 (2004) 480–94.
Griffiths, Alan. "Stories and Storytelling." In *Herodotus*, edited by Carolyn Dewald and John Marincola, 130–44. Cambridge: Cambridge University Press, 2006.
Grindheim, Sigurd. "Ignorance Is Bliss: Attitudinal Aspects of the Judgment according to Works in Matthew 25:31–46." *Novum Testamentum* 50 (2008) 313–31.
Grossman, Allen. "'The Death of the Beloved Companion': Brief Notes on a Master Narrative of Poetic Knowledge, in Relation to the Human Interest in the Ethical." *Harvard Review* 2 (1992) 53–58.
Grudem, Wayne. *1 Peter.* Tyndale New Testament Commentaries. Grand Rapids: Eerdmans, 1988.
Gruen, Erich S. "The Use and Abuse of the Exodus Story." *Jewish History* 12 (1998) 93–122.
Gruenwald, Ithamar. "God the 'Stone/Rock': Myth, Idolatry, and Cultic Fetishism in Ancient Israel." *The Journal of Religion* 76 (1996) 428–49.

Grundke, Christopher L. K., "A Tempest in a Teapot? Genesis III 8 Again." *Vetus Testamentum* 51 (2001) 548–51.

Grundmann, W. "μέγας." In *Theological Dictionary of the New Testament*. Translated and abridged by G. W. Bromiley, 573–76. Eerdmans: Grand Rapids, 1985.

Guelich, Robert A. *Mark 1:1—8:26*. WORD 34a. Dallas: Word, 1989.

Guillaume, Philippe. "Dismantling the Deconstruction of Job." *Journal of Biblical Literature* 127 (2008) 491–99.

Gujarro, Santiago, and Ana Rodríguez. "The 'Messianic' Anointing of Jesus (Mark 14:3–9)." *Biblical Theology Bulletin* 41 (2011) 132–43.

Gunn, David M. *Judges*. Blackwell Bible Commentaries. Malden, ME: Blackwell, 2005.

Gunton, Colin. "Salvation." In *The Cambridge Companion to Karl Barth*, edited by John Webster, 143–58. Cambridge: Cambridge University Press, 2000.

Guthrie, Donald. *New Testament Introduction*. London: Tyndale, 1970.

———. *New Testament Theology*. Leicester: InterVarsity, 1981.

Habel, Norman. *The Book of Job*. Old Testament Library. London: SCM, 1985.

Hagner, Donald. *Matthew 1–13*. WORD 33a. Dallas: Word, 1993.

———. *Matthew 14–28*. WORD 33b. Dallas: Word, 1995.

Hahn, Scott Walker, and John Sietze Bergsma. "What Laws Were 'Not Good'? A Canonical Approach to the Theological Problem of Ezekiel 20:25–26." *Journal of Biblical Literature* 123 (2004) 201–18.

Hamilton, Jeffries M. "Hāʾāreṣ in the Shemitta Law." *Vetus Testamentum* 42 (1992) 214–22.

Hanks, Thomas D. "Poor, Poverty." In *The Anchor Bible Dictionary* 6, 402–24. New York: Doubleday, 1992.

Hanson, Paul. "The Birth of the Covenant." In *Moral Business: Classical and Contemporary Resources for Ethics in Economic Life*, edited by Max Stackhouse, 56–59. Grand Rapids: Eerdmans, 1995.

Harb, Gertraud. "Matthew 17.24–27 and its Value for Historical Jesus Research." *Journal for the Study of the Historical Jesus* 8 (2010) 254–27.

Hartley, John E. *Leviticus*. WORD 4. Dallas: Word, 1992.

Hauck, Friedrich. "πένης" In *The Theological Dictionary of the New Testament* 6, edited by Gerhard Kittel and Geoffrey W. Bromiley, translated by Geoffrey W. Bromiley, 37–40. Grand Rapids: Eerdmans, 2006.

Havrelock, Rachel. "The Two Maps of Israel's Land." *Journal of Biblical Literature* 126 (2007) 649–67.

Hawkin, David J. "The Incomprehension of the Disciples in the Marcan Redaction." *Journal of Biblical Literature* 91 (1972) 491–500.

Hawthorne, G. F. *Philippians*. Revised by R. P. Martin. WORD 43. Dallas: Word, 2004.

Hays, Christopher. "By Almsgiving and Faith Sins Are Purged: The Theological Underpinnings of Early Christian care for the Poor." In *Engaging Economics: New Testament Scenarios and Early Christian Reception*, edited by Bruce Longenecker and Kelly Liebengood, 260–80. Grand Rapids: Eerdmans, 2009.

Hedrick, Charles W. "Vestigial Scenes in John: Settings without Dramatization." *Novum Testamentum* 47 (2005) 354–66.

Hendriksen, William. *Matthew*. New Testament Commentary. Edinburgh, UK: Banner of Truth, 1973.

Hepner, Gershon. "Abraham's Incestuous Marriage with Sarah a Violation of the Holiness Code." *Vetus Testamentum* 53 (2003) 143–55.

Herodotus. *The Greek History: The Fourth, Fifth and Sixth Books*, edited by R. W. Macan. 2 vols. New York: Arno, 1973.
———. *Historiae*. Scriptorum Classicorum Bibliotheca Oxoniensis 1–2. Edited by Carolus Hude. Oxford: Oxford University Press, 1927.
Hertzberg, H. W. *I & II Samuel: A Commentary*. Old Testament Library. Translated by J. Bowden. 2nd ed. London: SCM, 1960.
Hill, Andrew E. "On David's 'Taking' and 'Leaving' Concubines (2 Samuel 5:13; 15:16)." *Journal of Biblical Literature* 125 (2006) 129–39.
Hill, John S. "τὰ βαΐα τῶν φοινίκων (John 12:13) Pleonasm or Prolepsis?" *Journal of Biblical Literature* 101 (1982) 133–35.
Hirsch, Eric. *The Aims of Interpretation*. Chicago: University of Chicago Press, 1976.
———. "Current Issues in Theory of Interpretation." *Journal of Religion* 55 (1975) 298–312.
———. *Validity in Interpretation*. New Haven: Yale University Press, 1967.
Hobbs, T. R. *2 Kings*. WORD 13. Dallas: Word, 1985.
Holst, Robert. "The One Anointing of Jesus: Another Application of the Form-Critical Method." *Journal of Biblical Literature* 95 (1976) 435–46.
Holter, Knut. *Second Isaiah's Idol-Fabrication Passages*. Beitrage zur biblischen Exegese und Theologie 28. Frankfurt am Main, Germany: Lang, 1995.
Homer. *Opera*. Scriptorum Classicorum Bibliotheca Oxoniensis 1–3. Edited by T. W. Allen. Oxford: Oxford University Press, 1920.
Homsher, Robert S. "Mythological Apocalypses: Eschatological Mythopoeic Speculation of the Combat Myth in Biblical Apocalyptic Literature." MA diss., Abilene Christian University, 2005.
Hood, Jason B. "Evangelicals and the Imitation of the Cross: Peter Bolt on Mark 13 as a Test Case." *Evangelical Quarterly* 81 (2009) 116–125.
———. "Matthew 23–25: The Extent of Jesus' Fifth Discourse." *Journal of Biblical Literature* 128 (2009) 527–43.
Hoppe, Leslie J. *There Shall Be No Poor Among You: Poverty in the Bible*. Nashville: Abingdon, 2004.
Horsley, Richard A. *Jesus and Magic: Freeing the Gospel Stories from Modern Misconceptions*. Eugene, OR: Cascade, 2014.
———. *Jesus and the Powers: Conflict, Covenant and the Hope of the Poor*. Minneapolis: Fortress, 2011.
Huggins, Ronald V. "Matthean Posteriority: A Preliminary Proposal." *Novum Testamentum* 34 (1992) 1–22.
Hughes, P. E. *The Second Epistle to the Corinthians*. The New International Commentary on the New Testament. Grand Rapids: Eerdmans, 1986.
Humphrey, Edith M. "A Tale of Two Cities and (At Least) Three Women: Transformation, Continuity and Contrast in the Apocalypse." In *Reading the Book of Revelation*, edited by David Barr, 81–96. SBL Resources for Biblical Study 44. Atlanta: Society of Biblical Literature, 2003.
———. "To Rejoice or Not? Rhetoric and the Fall of Satan in Luke 10:17–24 and Revelation 12:1–17." In *The Reality of Apocalypse: Rhetoric and Politics in the Book of Revelation*, edited by David Barr, 113–25. SBL Symposium Series 39. Atlanta: Society of Biblical Literature, 2006.

Hunsinger, George. "Karl Barth's Christology." In *The Cambridge Companion to Karl Barth*, edited by John Webster, 127–42. Cambridge: Cambridge University Press, 2000.

Hunt, Peter. "The Slaves and the Generals of Arginusae." *The American Journal of Philology* 122 (2001) 359–80.

Hurtado, L. W. "Son of God." In *Dictionary of Paul and his Letters*, edited by Gerald Hawthorne, Ralph Martin, and David Reid, 900–906. Downers Grove: InterVarsity, 1993.

Ilan, Tal, and Jonathan J. Price. "Seven Onomastic Problems in Josephus' 'Bellum Judaicum.'" *The Jewish Quarterly Review* 84 (1993–1994) 189–208.

Irenaeus. "Against Heresies." http://www.ccel.org/ccel/schaff/anf01.ix.ii.html.

Jacobsen, Thorkild. "The Graven Image." *Ancient Israelite Religion*, edited by P. Miller Jr., et al., 15. Philadelphia: Fortress, 1987.

Janowitz, Naomi. "Good Jews Don't: Historical and Philosophical Constructions of Idolatry." *History of Religions* 47 (Nov 2007/Feb 2008) 239–52.

Janzen, David. "'What He Did For Me': David's Warning about Joab in 1 Kings 2.5." *Journal for the Study of the Old Testament* 39 (2015) 265–79.

Janzen, Waldemar. *Old Testament Ethics: A Paradigmatic Approach*. Louisville: Westminster John Knox, 1994.

Japhet, Sara. "The Ideology of the Book of Chronicles and Its Place in Biblical Thought." *Beiträge zur Erforschung des Alten Testaments und des Antiken Judentums* 9. Frankfurt am Main, Germany: Lang, 1989.

Jebb, R. C., ed. *Selections from the Attic Orators*. London: Macmillan, 1962.

Jennings, Theodore W., Jr., and Tat-Siong Benny Liew. "Mistaken Identities but Model Faith: Rereading the Centurion, the Chap, and the Christ in Matthew 8:5–13." *Journal of Biblical Literature* 123 (2004) 467–94.

Johnson, Luke Timothy. *The Acts of the Apostles*. Sacra Pagina 5. Edited by D. J. Harrington. Collegeville, MN: Liturgical, 1992.

———. "The New Testament's Anti-Jewish Slander and the Conventions of Ancient Polemic." *Journal of Biblical Literature* 108 (1989) 419–41.

Johnson, William A. "Greek Electronic Resources and the Lexicographical Function." In *Biblical Greek Language and Lexicography: Essays in Honor of Frederick W. Danker*, edited by Bernard A. Taylor et al., 75–84. Grand Rapids: Eerdmans, 2004.

Jones, A. H. "The Urbanization of the Ituraean Principality." *The Journal of Roman Studies* 21 (1931) 265–75.

Joosten, Jan. "A Note on the Text of Deuteronomy xxxii 8." *Vetus Testamentum* 57 (2007) 548–55.

Josephus, Flavius. "Antiquities of the Jews." In *Whiston's Josephus*, by William Whiston, 22–426. Edinburgh, UK: Nimmo, Hay, and Mitchell, n.d.

———. "The Life of Flavius Josephus." In *Whiston's Josephus*, by William Whiston, 1–21. Edinburgh, UK: Nimmo, Hay, and Mitchell, n.d.

———. *The New Complete Works of Josephus*. Translated by William Whiston and commentary by Paul L. Maier. Rev. ed. Grand Rapids: Kregel, 1999.

Kaler, Michael. "Was Heracleon a Valentinian? A New Look at Old Sources." *The Harvard Theological Review* 99 (2006) 275–89.

Kalimi, Isaac. "The Capture of Jerusalem in the Chronistic History." *Vetus Testamentum* 52 (2002) 66–79.

Kamell, Marian. "The Economics of Humility: The Rich and the Humble in James." In *Engaging Economics: New Testament Scenarios and Early Christian Reception*, edited by Bruce Longenecker and Kelly Liebengood, 157–75. Grand Rapids: Eerdmans, 2009.

Kaminsky, Joel. "Reflections on Associative Word Links in Judges." *Journal for the Study of the Old Testament* 36 (2012) 411–34.

Kasser, Rodophe, et al., eds and trans. "The Gospel of Judas." http://www.nationalgeographic.com/lostgospel/_pdf/GospelofJudas.pdf?fs=www7.nationalgeographic.com&fs=magma.nationalgeographic.com.

Kaye, B. N. "Eschatology and Ethics in 1 and 2 Thessalonians." *Novum Testamentum* 17 (1975) 47–57.

Kazen, Thomas. "The Christology of Early Christian Practice." *Journal of Biblical Literature* 127 (2008) 591–614.

Keener, Craig. *A Commentary on the Gospel of Matthew*. Grand Rapids: Eerdmans, 1999.

———. *The Gospel of John: A Commentary*. 2 vols. Peabody, MA: Hendrickson, 2003.

Kelhoffer, James A. "Did John the Baptist Eat like a Former Essene? Locust-Eating in the Ancient Near East and at Qumran." *Dead Sea Discoveries* 11 (2004) 293–314.

Kelley, Nicole. "The Cosmopolitan Expression of Josephus's Prophetic Perspective in the 'Jewish War.'" *The Harvard Theological Review* 97 (2004) 257–74.

Kelly, Henry. "Adam Citings before the Intrusion of Satan: Recontextualizing Paul's Theology of Sin and Death." *Biblical Theology Bulletin* 44 (2014) 13–28.

———. *Satan: A Biography*. Cambridge: Cambridge University Press, 2006.

Kelly, J. N. D. *A Commentary on the Epistles of Peter and of Jude*. Black's New Testament Commentaries. Edited by Henry Chadwick. London: A & C Black, 1982.

Kennedy, James M. "Hebrew pithôn peh in the Book of Ezekiel." *Vetus Testamentum* 41 (1991) 233–35.

Kent, Grenville. "Mary Magdalene, Mary of Bethany and the Sinful Woman of Luke 7: the Same Person?" *Journal of Asia Adventist Seminary* 13 (2010) 13–28.

Keown, Gerald L., et al. *Jeremiah 26–52*. WORD 27. Dallas: Word, 1995.

Kerkeslager, Allen. "Apollo, Greco-Roman Prophecy, and the Rider on the White Horse in Rev 6:2." *Journal of Biblical Literature* 112 (1993) 116–21.

Kidner, Derek. *Genesis*. Tyndale Old Testament Commentaries. Edited by D. J. Wiseman. London: InterVarsity, 1974

King, Fergus J. "'De Baptista nil nisi bonum': John the Baptist as a Paradigm for Mission." *Mission Studies* 26 (2009) 173–91.

———. "'Father, Forgive Them, For They Know Not What They Do': Reflections on Luke 23:34a, Kol Nidre and the Atonement." *Australian Journal of Jewish Studies* 24 (2010) 134–60.

———. "'Fencing the Altar': Jesus, Judas and Eucharistic Discipline." *The Journal of Anglican Studies* 50.1 (Autumn 2016) 30–38. "Fencing"

———. *A Guide to St John's Gospel*. SPCK International Study Guide 51. London, Society for Promoting Christian Knowledge, 2015. ("John, 2015")

———. "He Descended to the Dead: Towards a Pastoral Strategy For Making Peace With the Living Dead." *Soma: an International Journal of Theological Discourses and Counter-Discourses* (2012) 2–19.

———. "Lex Orandi, Lex Credendi: Worship and Doctrine in Revelation 4–5." *Scottish Journal of Theology* 67 (2014) 33–49.

———. "More Than a Passover: Inculturation in the Supper Narratives of the New Testament." PhD diss., Frankfurt am Main, Germany: Lang, 2007.

———. *Opening the Scroll: An Introductory Commentary on the Revelation of John*. Köln, Germany: Lambert Academic, 2009. "Scroll"

———. "'Pointing the Bone': Sorcery Syndrome, Uncanny Death and the Fate of Ananias and Sapphira." *Irish Biblical Studies* 30 (2012) 1–22. "Pointing"

———. "'Standing on the Shoulders of Giants': Re-tuning John O'Neill's Theory of the Blasphemy Charge against Jesus." *Irish Biblical Studies* 28 (2010) 52–77.

———. "Revelation 21:1—22:5: An Early Christian Locus Amoenus?" *Biblical Theology Bulletin: Journal of Bible and Culture* 45 (2015) 174–83.

Kingsbury. Jack Dean. "The Title 'Kyrios' in Matthew's Gospel." *Journal of Biblical Literature* 94 (1975) 246–55.

Kirk, Alan. "'Love Your Enemies,' the Golden Rule, and Ancient Reciprocity (Luke 6:27–35)." *Journal of Biblical Literature* 122 (2003) 667–86.

Kittel, Gerhard, and Friedrich, Gerhard, eds. *Theological Dictionary of the New Testament*. Translated and abridged by Geoffrey W. Bromiley. Eerdmans: Grand Rapids, 1985.

Klassen, William. *Judas: Betrayer or Friend of Jesus?* Minneapolis: Fortress, 1996.

Klauck, Hans-Josef. *Judas—ein Jünger des Herrn*. Freiburg im Breisgau, Germany: Herder, 1987.

———. *Judas un disciple de Jésus: Exégèse et repercussions historiques*. Paris: Cerf, 2006.

Klawans, Jonathan. "Notions of Gentile Impurity in Ancient Judaism." *Australian Jewish Studies Review* 20 (1995) 285–312.

Klein, Ralph W. *1 Samuel*. WORD 10. Dallas: Word, 1983.

Klein, William, et al. *Introduction to Biblical Interpretation*. Rev. ed. Nashville: Thomas Nelson, 2004.

Kleist, James. *The Didache: The Epistle of Barnabus, the Epistles and the Martyrdom of St. Polycarp, the Fragments of Papias, the Epistle to Diogn*. Ancient Christian Writers 6. Edited by Johannes Quasten and Joseph C. Plumpe. New York, Paulist, 1948.

Knoppers, Gary N. "Rehoboam in Chronicles: Villain or Victim?" *Journal of Biblical Literature* 109 (1990) 423–40.

Konstan, David. "Greek Friendship." *The American Journal of Philology* 117 (1996), 71–94.

Köstenberger, A. J. "John." In *Commentary on the New Testament Use of the Old Testament*, edited by Gregory Beale and Don Carson, 415–512. Grand Rapids: Baker Academic, 2007.

Kovacs, Judith. "'Now Shall the Ruler of This World Be Driven Out': Jesus' Death as Cosmic Battle in John 12:20–36." *Journal of Biblical Literature* 114 (1995) 227–47.

Kraemer, Ross S. "Implicating Herodias and Her Daughter in the Death of John the Baptizer: A (Christian) Theological Strategy?" *Journal of Biblical Literature* 125 (2006) 321–49.

Krentz, Edgar. *The Historical-Critical Method*. Guides to Biblical Scholarship. Edited by D. O. Via. Minneapolis: Fortress, 1977.

Kruse, Colin. *2 Corinthians*. Tyndale New Testament Commentaries. Edited by Leon L. Morris. London: InterVarsity, 1987.

Kuecker, Aaron J. "The Spirit and the 'Other,' Satan and the Self." In *Engaging Economics: New Testament Scenarios and Early Christian Reception*, edited by Bruce Longenecker and Kelly Liebengood, 81–103. Grand Rapids: Eerdmans, 2009.

Kugel, James L. and Greer, Rowan A. *Early Biblical Interpretation*. Library of Early Christianity. Edited by W. A. Meeks. Philadelphia: Westminster, 1986.

Kurz, William S. "Luke 22:14–38 and Greco-Roman and Biblical Farewell Addresses." *Journal of Biblical Literature* 104 (1985) 251–68.

Laato, Antti. "The Composition of Isaiah 40–55." *Journal of Biblical Literature* 109 (1990) 207–28.

Lachs, Samuel T. "Rabbinic Sources for New Testament Studies: Use and Misuse." *The Jewish Quarterly Review* 74 (1983) 159–73.

Lacocque, André. "The Deconstruction of Job's Fundamentalism." *Journal of Biblical Literature* 126 (2007) 83–97.

Ladd, George Eldon. *A Commentary on the Revelation of John*. Grand Rapids, Eerdmans, 1972.

Lakoff, George. *Women, Fire and Dangerous Things: What Categories Reveal About the Mind*. Chicago: University of Chicago Press, 1987.

Lamarche, P. *Zacharie i–xiv: Structure, Litteraire, et Messianisme*. Paris: Gabalda, 1961.

Landry, David and Ben May. "Honor Restored: New Light on the Parable of the Prudent Steward (Luke 16:1–8a)." *Journal of Biblical Literature* 119 (2000) 287–309.

Lane, William L. *The Gospel of Mark*. The New International Commentary on the New Testament. Grand Rapids: Eerdmans, 1974.

———. *Hebrews 9–13*. WORD 47b. Dallas: Word, 1991.

Langton, Karen. "Job's Attempt to Regain Control: Traces of a Babylonian Birth Incantation in Job 3." *Journal for the Study of the Old Testament* 36 (2012) 459–69.

Launderville, Dale. "Ezekiel's Cherub: A Promising Symbol or a Dangerous Idol?" *The Catholic Biblical Quarterly* 65 (2003) 165–83.

Layton, Bentley. *The Gnostic Scriptures*. London: SCM, 1987.

Lee, Dorothy. "In the Spirit of Truth: Worship and Prayer in the Gospel of John and the Early Fathers." *Vigiliae Christianae* 58 (2004) 277–97.

Lee, Geoff. "Matthew xxvi : 50. Ἑταῖρε, ἐφ' ὃ πάρει." *The Expository Times* 81 (1969) 55.

Lee, John. *A History of New Testament Lexicography*. Studies in Biblical Greek 8. Edited by D. A. Carson. New York: Lang, 2003.

———. "A Note on Septuagint Material in the Supplement to Liddell and Scott." *Glotta* 47 (1969) 234–42.

———. "Some Features of the Speech of Jesus in Mark's Gospel." *Novum Testamentum* 27 (1985) 1–26.

Leech, Geoffrey. *Semantics: The Study of Meaning*. 2nd ed. Harmondsworth, UK: Penguin, 1981.

Leeming, David. "Religion and Sexuality: The Perversion of a Natural Marriage." *Journal of Religion and Health* 42 (2003) 101–9.

Leloup, Jean-Yves. *Judas and Jesus. Two Faces of a Single Revelation*. Translated by Joseph Rowe. Rochester, VT: Inner Traditions, 2006.

Lemos, Tracy. "Shame and Mutilation of Enemies in the Hebrew Bible." *Journal of Biblical Literature* 125 (2006) 225–41.

Levine, Nachman. "The Curse and the Blessing: Narrative Discourse Syntax and Literary Form." *Journal for the Study of the Old Testament* 27 (2002) 189–99.

Levinson, Bernard M. "The Reconceptualization of Kingship in Deuteronomy and the Deuteronomistic History's Transformation of Torah." *Vetus Testamentum* 51 (2001) 511–34.

———. "You Must Not Add Anything to What I Command You: Paradoxes of Canon and Authorship in Ancient Israel." *Numen* 50 (2003) 1–51.
Lewis, Theodore J. "The Ancestral Estate (אלהים הלח) in 2 Samuel 14:16." *Journal of Biblical Literature* 110 (1991) 597–612.
Liddell, H. G., and R. Scott. *A Greek-English Lexicon*. Oxford: Clarendon, 1996.
Lindsay, Mark R. *Barth, Israel and Jesus: Karl Barth's Theology of Israel*. Barth Studies. Edited by John Webster et al. Aldershot, UK: Ashgate, 2007.
Ling, Trevor. *The Significance of Satan*. London: SPCK, 1961.
Linnemann, Eta. *Biblical Criticism on Trial*. Translated by Robert Yarborough. Grand Rapids: Kregel, 2001.
Loftus, Francis. "The Anti-Roman Revolts of the Jews and the Galileans." *The Jewish Quarterly Review New Series* 68 (1977) 78–98.
Longenecker, Bruce, and Kelly Liebengood, eds. *Engaging Economics: New Testament Scenarios and Early Christian Reception*. Grand Rapids: Eerdmans, 2009.
Longenecker, Richard. *Galatians*. WORD 41. Dallas: Word, 1990.
Longman, Tremper, III. *Literary Approaches to Biblical Interpretation*. Foundations of Contemporary Interpretation 3. Grand Rapids: Academie, 1987.
Lorton, David. "The Theology of Cult Statues in Ancient Egypt." In *The Induction of the Cult Image in Ancient Mesopotamia: The Mesopotamian Mīs Pî Ritual*, edited by Christopher Walker and Michael Dick, 123–210. State Archives of Assyria Ritual 1. Helsinki, Finland: Neo-Assyrian Text Corpus Project, 2001.
Louw, Johannes, and Eugene Nida, eds. *Greek-English Lexicon of the New Testament Based on Semantic Domains*. 2 vols. New York: United Bible Societies, 1989.
Lowery, Richard. *Sabbath and Jubilee*. Understanding Biblical Themes. St. Louis: Chalice, 2000.
Luck, Georg. *Arcana Mundi: Magic and the Occult in the Greek and Roman Worlds: A Collection of Ancient Texts*. Baltimore: Johns Hopkins University Press, 2006.
Lull, David J. "The Servant-Benefactor as a Model of Greatness (Luke 22:24–30)." *Novum Testamentum* 28 (1986) 289–305.
Luz, Ulrich. "Intertexts in the Gospel of Matthew." *The Harvard Theological Review* 97 (2004) 119–37.
Lynch, Chloe. "How Convincing is Walter Wink's Interpretation of Paul's Language of the Powers?" *Evangelical Quarterly* 83 (2011) 251–66.
Lyons, John. *Linguistic Semantics: An Introduction*. Cambridge: Cambridge University Press, 1995.
Macaskill, Grant. "Critiquing Rome's Economy: Revelation and Its Reception in the Apostolic Fathers." In *Engaging Economics: New Testament Scenarios and Early Christian Reception*, edited by Bruce Longenecker and Kelly Liebengood, 243–59. Grand Rapids: Eerdmans, 2009.
Maccoby, Hyam. *Judas Iscariot and the Myth of Jewish Evil*. London: Halban, 1992.
MacKinnon, D. M. *The Borderlands of Theology: An Inaugural Lecture*. Cambridge: Cambridge University Press, 1961.
———. *The Borderlands of Theology and Other Essays*. Edited by George W. Roberts and Donovan E. Smucker. London: Lutterworth, 1968.
———. "Christology and Protest (1988)." In *Philosophy and The Burden of Theological Honesty: A Donald MacKinnon Reader*, edited by John McDowell, 265–75. T & T Clark Theology. London: T & T Clark, 2011.

---. "The Evangelical Imagination (1986)." In *Philosophy and The Burden of Theological Honesty: A Donald MacKinnon Reader*, edited by John McDowell, 189–99. T & T Clark Theology. London: T & T Clark, 2011.

---. "Teleology and Redemption (1995)." In *Philosophy and The Burden of Theological Honesty: A Donald MacKinnon Reader*, edited by John McDowell, 307–11. T & T Clark Theology. London: T & T Clark, 2011.

MacMullen, Ramsay. *Paganism in the Roman Empire*. New Haven: Yale University Press, 1981.

Malbon, Elizabeth Struthers. "Echoes and Foreshadowings in Mark 4–8: Reading and Rereading." *Journal of Biblical Literature* 112 (1993) 211–30.

Malina, Bruce J. *The New Testament World: Insights from Cultural Anthropology*. London: SCM, 1983.

---. "Wealth and Poverty in the New Testament World." In *Moral Business: Classical and Contemporary Resources for Ethics in Economic Life*, edited by Max Stackhouse, 88–93. Grand Rapids: Eerdmans, 1995.

Mann, C. S. "Unjust Steward or Prudent Manager?" *The Expository Times* 102 (1991) 234–35.

Marcus, Joel. "Entering into the Kingly Power of God." *Journal of Biblical Literature* 107 (1988) 663–75.

Mardaga, Hellen. "*Hapax Legomena*: A Neglected Field in Biblical Studies." *Currents in Biblical Research* 10 (2012) 264–74.

Margalith, Othniel. "Samson's Riddle and Samson's Magic Locks." *Vetus Testamentum* 36 (1986) 225–34.

Maritz, Petrus. "Judas Iscariot: Ironic Testimony of the Fallen Disciple in John 12:1–11." In *Studies in the Gospel of John and Its Christology: Festschrift Gilbert Van Belle*, edited by Joseph Verheyden et al., 289–316. Leuven, Belgium: Peeters, 2014.

Marsh, Noah M. "Idolatry." In *The Lexham Bible Dictionary*, edited by Jonh Barry and Lazarus Wentz. Bellingham, WA: Lexham, 2012.

Marshall, I. Howard. "Acts." In *Commentary on the New Testament Use of the Old Testament*, edited by Gregory Beale and Don Carson, 513–606. Grand Rapids: Baker Academic, 2007.

---. *Commentary on Luke*. The New International Greek Testament Commentary. Eerdmans: Grand Rapids, 1978.

---. *New Testament Interpretation: Essays in Principles and Methods*. Exeter, UK: Paternoster, 1977.

---. "Son of Man." In *Dictionary of Jesus and the Gospels*, edited by Joel B. Green et al., 775–81. Downers Grove: InterVarsity, 1992.

Marshall, I. Howard, and R. V. G. Tasker, eds. *Acts*. Tyndale New Testament Commentaries. Leicester, UK: InterVarsity, 1980.

Martin, Michael W. *Judas and the Rhetoric of Comparison*. New Testament Monographs 25. Edited by Stanley E. Porter. Sheffield: Sheffield Phoenix, 2010.

Martin, Ralph P. *2 Corinthians*. WORD 40. Dallas: Word, 1986.

---. *James*. WORD 48. Dallas: Word, 1988.

Martin, Troy W. "Watch during the Watches (Mark 13:35)." *Journal of Biblical Literature* 120 (2001) 685–701.

Mason, Steve. "Contradiction or Counterpoint? Josephus and Historical Method." In *Josephus, Judea and Christian Origins: Methods and Categories*, edited by Michael W. Helfield, 103–37. Peabody, MT: Hendrickson, 2009.

———. "The Essenes of Josephus's *Judean War*: From Story to History." In *Josephus, Judea and Christian Origins: Methods and Categories*, edited by Michael W. Helfield, 239–79. Peabody, MT: Hendrickson, 2009.

———. "Figured Speech and Irony in T. Flavius Josephus." In *Josephus, Judea and Christian Origins: Methods and Categories*, edited by Michael W. Helfield, 69–102. Peabody, MT: Hendrickson, 2009.

———. "Josephus as Authority for First-Century Judea." In *Josephus, Judea and Christian Origins: Methods and Categories*, edited by Michael W. Helfield, 7–43. Peabody, MT: Hendrickson, 2009.

———. "Of Audience and Meaning." In *Josephus, Judea and Christian Origins: Methods and Categories*, edited by Michael W. Helfield, 45–67. Peabody, MT: Hendrickson, 2009.

———. "Pharisees in the Narratives of Josephus." In *Josephus, Judea and Christian Origins: Methods and Categories*, edited by Michael W. Helfield, 185–215. Peabody, MT: Hendrickson, 2009.

Mattila, Talvikki. "Naming the Nameless: Gender and Discipleship in Matthew's Passion Narrative." In *Characterization in the Gospels: Reconceiving Narrative Criticism*, edited by David Rhoads and Kari Syreeni, 153–79. JSNT Supplement Series 184. Sheffield, UK: Sheffield Academic, 1999.

May, Gerald G. *Addiction & Grace: Love and Spirituality in the Healing of Addictions*. San Francisco: HarperSanFrancisco, 1988.

Mays, James L. *Amos*. Old Testament Library. London: SCM, 1969.

Mazar, B. "The Military Élite of King David." *Vetus Testamentum* 13 (1963) 310–20.

McCabe, David R. "How to Kill Things with Words: Ananias and Sapphira Under the Apostolic-Prophetic Speech-Act of Divine Judgment (Acts 4:32–5:11)." PhD diss., the University of Edinburgh, 2008.

McCormack, Bruce. "Grace and Being: The Role of God's Gracious Election in Karl Barth's Theological Ontology." In *The Cambridge Companion to Karl Barth*, edited by John Webster, 92–110. Cambridge: Cambridge University Press, 2000.

McDowell, John, ed. *Philosophy and The Burden of Theological Honesty: A Donald MacKinnon Reader*. T & T Clark Theology. London: T & T Clark International, 2011.

McGarry, Eugene P. "The Ambidextrous Angel (Daniel 12:7 and Deuteronomy 32:40) Inner-Biblical Exegesis and Textual Criticism in Counterpoint." *Journal of Biblical Literature* 124 (2005) 211–28.

McGinnis, Claire Mathews, and Patricia K. Tull, eds. *As Those Who Are Taught: The Interpretation of Isaiah from the LXX to the SBL*. Society of Biblical Literature Symposium Series 27. Atlanta: Society of Biblical Literature, 2006.

McKnight, Scot. "A Generation Who Knew Not Streeter: The Case for Markan Priority." In *Rethinking the Synoptic Problem*, edited by David Black and David Beck, 65–95. Grand Rapids: Baker Academic, 2001.

McKnight, Scot, and Joseph B. Modica, eds. *Who Do My Opponents Say That I Am? An Investigation of the Accusations against the Historical Jesus*. The Library of New Testament Studies 327. London: T & T Clark, 2008.

Meier, John P. "The Circle of the Twelve: Did It Exist during Jesus' Public Ministry?" *Journal of Biblical Literature* 116 (1997) 635–72.

Merenlahti, Petri. "Characters in the Making: Individuality and Ideology in the Gospels." In *Characterization in the Gospels: Reconceiving Narrative Criticism*, edited by David Rhoads and Kari Syreeni, 49-72. JSNT Supplement Series 184. Sheffield: Sheffield Academic, 1999.

Merenlahti, Petri, and Raimo Hakola. "Reconceiving Narrative Criticism." In *Characterization in the Gospels: Reconceiving Narrative Criticism*, edited by David Rhoads and Kari Syreeni, 13-48. JSNT Supplement Series 184. Sheffield: Sheffield Academic, 1999.

Metzger, Bruce M. *A Textual Commentary on the Greek New Testament*. Princeton, NJ: UBS, 1971.

Metzger, Marcel, ed. *Les Constitutions Apostoliques*. Sources Chrétiennes 320. 3 vols. Paris: Cerf, 1985-1987.

Meyers, Carol L. "Was Ancient Israel a Patriarchal Society?" *Journal of Biblical Literature* 133 (2014) 8-27.

Michaels, J. Ramsey. *1 Peter*. WORD 49. Dallas: Word, 1988.

Miller, James E. "A Critical Response to Karin Adams's Reinterpretation of Hosea 4:13-14." *Journal of Biblical Literature* 128 (2009) 503-6.

Miller, M. "Greek Kinship Terminology." *The Journal of Hellenic Studies* 73 (1953) 46-52

Miller, Patrick D. "Deuteronomy and Psalms: Evoking a Biblical Conversation." *Journal of Biblical Literature* 118 (1999) 3-18.

Miller, Stuart S. "Josephus on the Cities of Galilee: Factions, Rivalries and Alliances in the First Jewish Revolt." *Historia: Zeitschrift für Alte Geschichte* 50 (2001) 453-67.

Miller, Susan. "Exegetical Notes on John 12:1-8: The Anointing of Jesus." *The Expository Times* 118 (2007) 240-41.

Minear, Paul S. "Far as the Curse Is Found: The Point of Revelation 12:15-16." *Novum Testamentum* 33 (1991) 71-77.

———. "Jesus' Audiences, According to Luke." *Novum Testamentum* 16 (1974) 81-109.

Mitchell, Alan C. "The Social Function of Friendship in Acts 2:44-47 and 4:32-37." *Journal of Biblical Literature* 111 (1992) 255-72.

Moberly, R. W. L. "Did the Serpent Get it Right?" *Journal of Theological Studies* 39 (1988) 1-27.

———. "Does God Lie to His Prophets? The Story of Micaiah ben Imlah as a Test Case." *The Harvard Theological Review* 96 (2003) 1-23.

Moessner, David P. "'Eyewitnesses,' 'Informed Contemporaries,' and 'Unknowing Inquirers': Josephus' Criteria for Authentic Historiography and the Meaning of παρακολουθέω." *Novum Testamentum* 38 (1996) 105-22.

———. "Luke 9:1-50: Luke's Preview of the Journey of the Prophet like Moses of Deuteronomy." *Journal of Biblical Literature* 102 (983) 575-605.

Moloney, Francis J. *Glory Not Dishonor: Reading John 13-21*. Minneapolis: Fortress, 1998.

———. *The Gospel of John*. Sacra Pagina. Edited by D. J. Harrington. Collegeville, MN: Liturgical, 1998.

———. *Love in the Gospel of John*. Grand Rapids: Baker, 2013.

Monro, Harold. *Judas*. Cranleigh, UK: Samurai, 1907.

Moore, George Foot. *A Critical and Exegetical Commentary on Judges*. International Critical Commentary. Edited by Samuel Driver, Alfred Plummer, and Charles Briggs. Edinburgh, UK: T & T Clark, 1966.

Morris, Leon. *The Epistle to the Romans*. Grand Rapids: Eerdmans, 1988.

———. *The Gospel According to John*. The New International Commentary on the New Testament. Grand Rapids: Eerdmans, 1984.

———. *Revelation*. Tyndale New Testament Commentaries. Rev. ed. Grand Rapids: Eerdmans, 1987.

Morriston, Wesley. "God's Answer to Job." *Religious Studies* 32 (1996) 339–56.

Mounce, Robert H. *The Book of Revelation*. The New International Commentary on the New Testament. Grand Rapids: Eerdmans, 1977.

Mounce, William D. *Pastoral Epistles*. WORD 46. Dallas: Word, 2000.

Mowery, Robert L. " Subtle Differences: The Matthean 'Son of God' References." *Novum Testamentum* 32 (1990) 193–200.

Moyer, Clinton J. "Who Is the Prophet, and Who the Ass? Role-Reversing Interludes and the Unity of the Balaam Narrative (Numbers 22–24)." *Journal for the Study of the Old Testament* 37 (2012) 167–83.

Mullen, E. Theodore, Jr. *The Divine Council in Canaanite and Early Hebrew Literature*. Harvard Semitic Monographs 24. Cambridge, MA: Scholars, 1980.

Muller, Jac J. *The Epistle of Paul to the Philippians*. The New International Commentary on the New Testament. Grand Rapids: Eerdmans, 1984.

Müller, Mogens. "The Reception of the Old Testament in Matthew and Luke–Acts: From Interpretation to Proof from Scripture." *Novum Testamentum* 43 (2001) 315–30.

Munro, Winsome. "Women Disciples: Light from Secret Mark." *Journal of Feminist Studies in Religion* 8 (1992) 47–64.

Murphy, Roland E. *Proverbs*. WORD 22. Dallas: Word, 1998.

Myers, Bryant L. *Walking with the Poor: Principles and Practices of Transformational Development*. Rev. ed. Maryknoll: Orbis, 2011.

Myers, Ched. *Binding the Strong Man: A Political Reading of Mark's Story of Jesus*. Maryknoll: Orbis, 2012.

Nasrallah, Laura. "The Acts of the Apostles, Greek Cities, and Hadrian's Panhellenion." *Journal of Biblical Literature* 127 (2008) 533–66.

Neer, Richard. "Delphi, Olympia, and the Art of Politics." In *The Cambridge Companion to Archaic Greece*, edited by H. Alan Shapiro, 225–64. Cambridge: Cambridge University Press, 2007.

Neill, Stephen, and Tom Wright. *The Interpretation of the New Testament: 1861–1986*. Oxford: Oxford University Press, 1988.

Neirynck, F. *Duality in Mark: Contributions to the Study of the Markan Redaction*. Bibliotheca Ephemeridum Theologicarum Lovaniensium. Leuven, Belgium: Leuven University Press, 1972.

Newman, Barclay M., Jr. "A Concise Greek-English Dictionary of the New Testament: Reflections and Ruminations." In *Biblical Greek Language and Lexicography: Essays in Honor of Frederick W. Danker*, edited by Bernard Taylor et al., 91–93. Grand Rapids: Eerdmans, 2004.

Newsom, Carol A. "A Maker of Metaphors—Ezekiel's Oracles Against Tyre." *Interpretation* 38 (1984) 151–64.

Nickelsburg, George W. E. "The Genre and Function of the Markan Passion Narrative." *The Harvard Theological Review* 73. Dedicated to the Centennial of the Society of Biblical Literature (1980) 153–84.

Niditch, Susan. "Eroticism and Death in the Tale of Jael." In *Gender and Difference in Ancient Israel*, edited by Peggy L. Day, 43–57. Minneapolis: Fortress, 1989.

———. *Judges: A Commentary*. The Old Testament Library. Louisville: Westminster John Knox, 2008.

———. *War in the Hebrew Bible: A Study in the Ethics of Violence.* Oxford: Oxford University Press, 1993.
Noble, Paul R. "Esau, Tamar, and Joseph: Criteria for Identifying Inner-Biblical Allusions." *Vetus Testamentum* 52 (2002) 219–52.
Nolland, John. *Luke 1—9:20.* WORD 35a. Dallas: Word, 1993.
———. *Luke 9:21—18:34.* WORD 35b. Dallas: Word, 1993.
———. *Luke 18:35—24:53.* WORD 35c. Dallas: Word, 1993.
Nugent, John C. "The Politics of YHWH: John Howard Yoder's Old Testament Narration and Its Implications for Social Ethics." *Journal of Religious Ethics* 39 (2011) 71–99.
Nürnberger, Klaus. *The Living Dead and the Living God: Christ and the Ancestors in Changing Africa.* Pietermaritzburg, South Africa: Cluster, 2007.
O'Brien, Peter T. *Colossians, Philemon.* WORD 44. Dallas: Word, 1987.
———. *The Letter to the Ephesians.* The Pillar New Testament Commentary. Grand Rapids: Eerdmans, 1999.
Olyan, Saul M. "The Israelites Debate Their Options at the Sea of Reeds: LAB 10:3, Its Parallels, and Pseudo-Philo's Ideology and Background." *Journal of Biblical Literature* 110 (1991) 75–91.
Oropeza, B. J. *In the Footsteps of Judas and Other Defectors: The Gospels, Acts and Johannine Letters.* 3 vols. Eugene, OR: Cascade, 2011.
Osborn, Eric. *Irenaeus of Lyons.* Cambridge: Cambridge University Press, 2001.
———. *Tertullian, First Theologian of the West.* Cambridge: Cambridge University Press, 1997.
Osborne, Grant R. "Response." In *Rethinking the Synoptic Problem,* edited by David Black and David Beck, 137–51. Grand Rapids: Baker Academic, 2001.
Paffenroth, Kim. *Judas: Images of the Lost Disciple.* Louisville: Westminster John Knox, 2001.
Page, Sydney H. T. *Powers of Evil: A Biblical Study of Satan and Demons.* Grand Rapids: Baker, 1995.
Pagels, Elaine. *Adam, Eve and the Serpent.* London: Weidenfeld and Nicholson, 1988.
———. *The Origin of Satan.* London: Penguin, 1995.
———. "The Social History of Satan, the 'Intimate Enemy': A Preliminary Sketch." *The Harvard Theological Review* 84 (1991) 105–28.
———. "The Social History of Satan, Part II: Satan in the New Testament Gospels." *Journal of the American Academy of Religion* 62.1 (1994) 17–58.
———. "The Social History of Satan, Part Three: John of Patmos and Ignatius of Antioch: Contrasting Visions of 'God's People.'" *The Harvard Theological Review* 99.4 (2006) 487–505.
Pao, David W. *Acts and the Isaianic New Exodus.* Grand Rapids: Baker Academic, 2000.
Pao, David W., and Eckhard J. Schnabel. "Luke." In *Commentary on the New Testament Use of the Old Testament,* edited by Gregory Beale and Don Carson, 351–404. Grand Rapids: Baker Academic, 2007.
Papias. "Fragments of Papias." http://www.ccel.org/ccel/schaff/anf01.vii.ii.html.
Park, Eugene-Chun. "Rachel's Cry for Her Children: Matthew's Treatment of the Infanticide by Herod." *The Catholic Biblical Quarterly* 75 (2013) 473–84.
Parker, Simon B. "Divine Intercession in Judah?" *Vetus Testamentum* 56 (2006) 76–91.
———. "Ugaritic Literature and the Bible." *Near Eastern Archaeology* 63.4 (2000) 228–31.

Parsenios, George L. *Rhetoric and Drama in the Johannine Lawsuit Motif.* Wissenschaftliche Untersuchungen zum Neuen Testament 258. Tübingen, Germany: Mohr, 2010.

Parsons, Mikeal C. *Acts.* Paideia Commentaries on the New Testament. Grand Rapids: Baker Academic, 2008.

———. "The Character of the Lame Man in Acts 3–4." *Journal of Biblical Literature* 124 (2005) 295–312.

———. *Luke.* Paideia Commentaries on the New Testament. Grand Rapids: Baker Academic, 2015.

Pataki, Andras D. "A Non-Combat Myth in Revelation 12." *New Testament Studies* 57 (2011) 258–72.

Patmore, Hector M. "Did the Masoretes Get it Wrong? The Vocalization and Accentuation of Ezekiel XXVIII 12–19." *Vetus Testamentum* 58 (2008) 245–57.

Patrick, Dale. "The First Commandment in the Structure of the Pentateuch." *Vetus Testamentum* 45 (1995) 107–18.

Patterson, Stephen. *The Gospel of Thomas and Jesus.* Foundations & Facets Reference Series. Sonoma, CA: Polebridge, 1993.

Pausanias. "Pausaniae Graeciae Descriptio." http://www.perseus.tufts.edu/hopper/text?doc=Perseus%3Atext%3A1999.01.0159%3Abook%3D1%3Achapter%3D2%3Asection%3D1.

Pearson, B. W. R. "Idolatry, Jewish Conception of." In *Dictionary of New Testament Background: a Compendium of Contemporary Biblical Scholarship*, edited by Craig Evans and Stanley Porter, 526–29. Downers Grove: InterVarsity, 2000.

Pelham, Abigail. "Job's Crisis of Language: Power and Powerlessness in Job's Oaths." *Journal for the Study of the Old Testament* 36 (2012) 333–54.

Pelling, Christopher. "The Urine and the Vine: Astyages' Dreams at Herodotus 1.107–8." *The Classical Quarterly* New Series 46 (1996) 68–77.

Petersen, Norman R. "The Composition of Mark 4:1—8:26." *The Harvard Theological Review* 73 (1980) 185–217.

Pierce, Madison N. "War: Fighting the Enemies of God, Not Man." *Biblical Theology Bulletin* 43 (2013) 81–87.

Pilgrim, Walter E. *Good News to the Poor: Wealth and Poverty in Luke–Acts.* Minneapolis: Augsburg, 1981.

Plato. *Laws.* Edited by T. E. Page. Loeb Classical Library. Vols 1–2. Cambridge, MA: Harvard University Press, 1961.

Porter, Barbara N. *What Is a God? Anthropomorphic and Non-Anthropomorphic Aspects of Deity in Ancient Mesopotamia.* Vol. 2 of Casco Bay Assyriological Institute. Winona Lake, IN: Eisenbrauns, 2009.

Powell, M. A. *What is Narrative Criticism?* Guides to Biblical Scholarship. Minneapolis: Fortress, 1990.

Pressler, Carolyn. *Joshua, Judges and Ruth.* Louisville: Westminster John Knox, 2002.

Price, Jonathan J. "The Enigma of Philip Ben Jakimos." *Historia: Zeitschrift für Alte Geschichte* 40 (1991) 77–94.

Raabe, Paul R. "Deliberate Ambiguity in the Psalter." *Journal of Biblical Literature* 110 (1991) 213–27.

Rainbow, P. A. "Idolatry." In *Dictionary of the Later New Testament and Its Developments.* Edited by Ralph Martin and Peter Davids, 527–29. Downers Grove: InterVarsity, 1997.

Redding, Jonathan. "Revelation 12 as Combat-Creation Myth." Essay. 2011.
Reece, Gregory. *Irony and Religious Belief.* Religion in Philosophy and Theology 5. Tübingen, Germany: Mohr, 2002.
Rendsburg, G. A. "David and His Circle in Genesis XXXVIII." *Vetus Testamentum* 36 (1986) 438–46.
Rengstorf, Karl H. *A Complete Concordance to Flavius Josephus.* Leiden, Netherlands: Brill, 1973.
Resseguie, James L. *Narrative Criticism of the New Testament: An Introduction.* Grand Rapids: Baker Academic, 2005.
———. "Reader-Response Criticism and the Synoptic Gospels." *Journal of the American Academy of Religion* 52 (1984) 307–24.
———. *The Revelation of John: A Narrative Commentary.* Grand Rapids: Baker Academic, 2009.
Ridderbos, Herman. *The Gospel of John: A Theological Commentary.* Translated by John Vriend. Grand Rapids: Eerdmans, 1997.
Roberts, Alexander, and James Donaldson. "The Ante-Nicene Fathers." http://www.ccel.org/ccel/schaff/anfo1.i.html.
Roberts, Terry. "A Review of BDAG." In *Biblical Greek Language and Lexicography: Essays in Honor of Frederick W. Danker*, edited by Bernard A. Taylor et al., 53–65. Grand Rapids: Eerdmans, 2004.
Robertson, A. R. *Word Pictures in the New Testament.* Nashville: Broadman, 1933.
Robertson, Martin. Review of *Amazons in Greek Art*, by Dietrich von Bothmer. *The Burlington Magazine* 100 (1958) 329.
Robinson, James M. *The Secrets of Judas: The Story of the Misunderstood Disciple and His Lost Gospel.* San Francisco: Harper SanFrancisco, 1989.
Rodd, Cyril S. *Glimpses of a Strange Land.* Old Testament Studies. Edited by David J. Reimer. Edinburgh, UK: T & T Clark, 2001.
Rogerson, John. *Theory and Practice in Old Testament Ethics.* Edited by M. Daniel Carroll. JSOT Supplement Series 405. London: T. & T. Clark International, 2004.
Rosner, Brian S. "No Other Gods." In *One God, One Lord. Christianity in a World of Religious Pluralism*, edited by Andrew D. Clarke and Bruce W. Winter, 149–59. Grand Rapids: Baker, 1992.
———. "Temple Prostitution in 1 Corinthians 6:12–20." *Novum Testamentum* 40 (1998) 336–51.
Rousseau, Adelin, and Louis Doutreleau. *Irénée de Lyon: Contre Les Hérésies.* Sources Chrétiennes 263. 3 vols. Paris: Cerf, 1979–1982.
Rudman, Dominic. "Creation and Fall in Jeremiah X 12–16." *Vetus Testamentum* 48 (1998) 63–73.
Ruprecht, Louis A., Jr. "Mark's Tragic Vision: Gethsemane." *Religion & Literature* 24 (1992) 1–25.
Ryken, Leland, et al., eds. "Idol, Idolatry." In *Dictionary of Biblical Imagery*, 415–18. Downers Grove: InterVarsity, 2000.
Sandiyagu, Virginia R. "ΕΤΕΡΟΣ and ΑΛΛΟΣ in Luke." *Novum Testamentum* 48 (2006) 105–30.
Sandoval, Timothy J. "Revisiting the Prologue of Proverbs." *Journal of Biblical Literature* 126 (2007) 455–73.

Schiffman, Lawrence H. "The King, His Guard, and the Royal Council in the Temple Scroll." *Proceedings of the American Academy for Jewish Research* 54 (1987) 237-59.

Schipper, Jeremy. "'Why Do You Still Speak of Your Affairs?' Polyphony in Mephibosheth's Exchanges with David in 2 Samuel." *Vetus Testamentum* 54 (2004) 344-51.

Schmidt, T. E. "Riches and Poverty." In *Dictionary of Paul and His Letters*, edited by Gerald Hawthorne, Ralph Martin, and David Reid, 826-27. Downers Grove: InterVarsity, 1993.

Schnackenburg, Rudolf. *The Gospel According to St. John*. Translated from German by Kevin Smith. 3 vols. London: Burns and Oates, 1968-1982.

Schneider, Stanley, and Morton Seelenfreund. "Kotnot or (Genesis 3:21): Skin, Leather, Light, or Blind?" *Jewish Bible Quarterly* 40 (2012) 116-24.

Schultz, Brian. "Jesus as Archelaus in the Parable of the Pounds (Luke. 19:11-27)." *Novum Testamentum* 49 (2007) 105-27.

Schultz, Samuel. *Leviticus*. Everyman's Bible Commentary. Chicago: Moody, 1983.

Schwartz, Seth. *Josephus and Judean Politics*. Vol. 18 of Columbia Studies in the Classical Tradition. New York: Brill, 1990.

Seifrid, Mark A. "Romans." In *Commentary on the New Testament Use of the Old Testament*, edited by Gregory Beale and Don Carson, 607-94. Grand Rapids: Baker Academic, 2007.

Sellew, Philip. "Interior Monologue as a Narrative Device in the Parables of Luke." *Journal of Biblical Literature* 111 (1992) 239-53.

Setzer, Claudia. "Excellent Women: Female Witness to the Resurrection." *Journal of Biblical Literature* 116 (1997) 259-72.

Seward, Desmond. *Josephus, Masada and the Fall of Judea*. Philadelphia: Da Capo, 2009.

Sharp, Carolyn J. *Irony and Meaning in the Hebrew Bible*. Bloomington: Indiana University Press: 2008.

Shepkaru, Shmuel. "From After Death to Afterlife: Martyrdom and Its Recompense." *Australian Jewish Studies Review* 24 (1999) 1-44.

Sherlock, Charles. *God on the Inside: Trinitarian Spirituality*. Wanniassa, Australia: Acorn, 1991.

———. *The God Who Fights: The War Tradition in Holy Scripture*. Vol. 6 of Rutherford Studies in Contemporary Theology. Lewiston, NY: Edwin Mellen, 1993.

———. *The Overcoming of Satan*. Grove Spirituality 7. Bramcote, UK: Grove, 1986.

Sherwin, Simon J. "In Search of Trees: Isaiah XLIV 14 and Its Implications." *Vetus Testamentum* 53 (2003) 514-29.

Shurr, William H. "Society and Gender in the Gospel of St. Luke." *Soundings: An Interdisciplinary Journal* 84 (2001) 181-99.

Sibinga, Smit. "The Composition of 1 Cor. 9 and Its Context." *Novum Testamentum* 40 (1998) 136-63.

———. "Zur Kompositionstechnik des Lukas in Lk. 15:11-32." In *Tradition and Re-Interpretation in Jewish and Early Christian Literature: Essays in Honour of Jürgen C. H. Lebram*, edited by J. W. van Henten, 97-113. Leiden, Netherlands: Brill, 1986.

Sievers, Joseph. "The Role of Women in the Hasmonean Dynasty." In *Josephus, the Bible and History*, edited by Louis Feldman and Gohei Hata, 132-46. Leiden, Netherlands: Brill, 1989.

Siew, Antoninus K. W. *The War Between the Two Beasts and the Two Witnesses.* Library of New Testament Studies 283. Edited by Mark Goodacre. London: T & T Clark, 2005.
Siker, Jeffrey S. "'First to the Gentiles': A Literary Analysis of Luke 4:16–30." *Journal of Biblical Literature* 111 (1992) 73–90.
Silva, Moisés. *Biblical Words & Their Meaning. An Introduction to Lexical Semantics.* Grand Rapids: Zondervan, 1983.
Sim, David Campbell. "There Will be Weeping and Gnashing of Teeth: Apocalyptic Eschatology in the Gospel of Matthew." PhD diss., King's College, London, 1993.
Siquans, Agnethe. "Foreignness and Poverty in the Book of Ruth: A Legal Way for a Poor Foreign Woman to Be Integrated into Israel." *Journal of Biblical Literature* 128 (2009) 443–52.
Smit, J. "'Do Not Be Idolaters': Paul's Rhetoric in First Corinthians 10:1–22." *Novum Testamentum* 39 (1997) 40–53.
Smith, Christopher R. "The Structure of the Book of Revelation in Light of Apocalyptic Literary Conventions." *Novum Testamentum* 36 (1994) 373–93.
Smith, David R. *Hand This Man Over to Satan.* London: T & T Clark, 2008.
Smith, Dennis E. "Table Fellowship as a Literary Motif in the Gospel of Luke." *Journal of Biblical Literature* 106 (1987) 613–38.
Smith, Mark D. "Of Jesus and Quirinius." *The Catholic Biblical Quarterly* 62 (2000) 278–93.
Smith, Mark S. "The Heart and Innards in Israelite Emotional Expressions: Notes From Anthropology and Psychobiology." *Journal of Biblical Literature* 117 (1998) 427–36.
Smith, Ralph L. *Micah–Malachi.* WORD 32. Dallas: Word, 1984.
Snow, Deborah, and Jonathan Pearlman. "Fitzgibbon Promises To 'Deal' With Judases." *Sydney Morning Herald*, June 6, 2009.
Soggin, J. Alberto. *Judges: A Commentary.* Old Testament Library. Translated by J. Bowden. London: SCM, 1981.
Soller, Mohe, "A Latch and Clasp Connecting Deuteronomy 33:27–29 with Genesis 3:22–24: A Proposed Interpretation." *Jewish Bible Quarterly* 34 (2006) 12–15.
Soulen, Richard N., and R. Kendall Soulen. *Handbook of Biblical Criticism.* 3rd ed. Louisville: Westminster John Knox, 2001.
Sowers, Sidney. "The Circumstances and Recollection of the Pella Flight." *Theologische Zeitschrift* 26 (1970) 305–20.
Spät, Eszter. "The 'Teachers' of Mani in the 'Acta Archelai' and Simon Magus." *Vigiliae Christianae* 58 (2004) 1–23.
Spencer R. A., ed. *Orientation by Disorientation: Studies in Literary Criticism & Biblical Literary Criticism.* Pittsburgh, PN: Pickwick, 1980.
Stagakis, G. J. "ETA(I)RIZW in Homer, as Testimony for the Establishment of an 'Hetairos' Relation." *Historia: Zeitschrift für Alte Geschichte* 20 (1971) 524–33.
Stahn, Hermann. *Die Simsonage.* Goettingen, Germany: Vandenhoeek and Ruprecht, 1908.
Stassen, Glen H. "The Fourteen Triads of the Sermon on the Mount (Matthew 5:21 7:12)." *Journal of Biblical Literature* 122 (2003) 267–308.
Steenberg, M. C. "The Role of Mary as Co-Recapitulator in St Irenaeus of Lyons." *Vigiliae Christianae* 58 (2004) 117–37.
Stein, Robert H. *The Synoptic Problem: An Introduction.* Leicester: InterVarsity, 1987.

Steinmann, Andrew E. "The Structure and Message of the Book of Job." *Vetus Testamentum* 46 (1996) 85–100.

Sterling, Gregory E. "'Athletes of Virtue': An Analysis of the Summaries in Acts (2:41–47; 4:32–35; 5:12–16)." *Journal of Biblical Literature* 113 (1994) 679–96.

Still, E. Coye, III. "Paul's Aims Regarding εἰδωλόθυται: A New Proposal for Interpreting 1 Corinthians 8:1—11:1." *Novum Testamentum* 44 (2002) 333–43.

Stokes, Ryan E. "The Devil Made David Do It . . . or 'Did' He? The Nature, Identity, and Literary Origins of the 'Satan' in 1 Chronicles 21:1." *Journal of Biblical Literature* 128 (2009) 91–106.

———. "Satan, Yhwh's Executioner." *Journal of Biblical Literature* 133 (2014) 251–70.

Strong, John T. "Tyre's Isolationist Policies in the Early Sixth Century BCE: Evidence from the Prophets." *Vetus Testamentum* 47 (1997) 207–19.

Stuart, Douglas. *Hosea–Jonah*. WORD 31. Dallas: Word, 1987.

Sweeney, Marvin A. "The Critique of Solomon in the Josianic Edition of the Deuteronomistic History." *Journal of Biblical Literature* 114 (1995) 607–22.

Talbert, Charles H. *Matthew*. Paideia Commentaries on the New Testament. Grand Rapids: Baker Academic, 2010.

Talbott, Thomas. "Freedom, Damnation, and the Power to Sin with Impunity." *Religious Studies* 37 (2001) 417–34.

Tasker, R. V. G. *Matthew*. Tyndale New Testament Commentaries. Leicester, UK: InterVarsity, 1961.

Tate, Marvin E. *Psalms 51–100*. WORD 20. Dallas: Word, 1990.

Tavo, Felise. *Woman, Mother and Bride: An Exegetical Investigation Into the "Ecclesial" Notions of the Apocalypse*. Leuven, Belgium: Peeters, 2007.

Taylor, Bernard A., et al., eds. *Biblical Greek Language and Lexicography: Essays in Honor of Frederick W. Danker*. Grand Rapids: Eerdmans, 2004.

———. "Hebrew to Greek: A Semantic Study of σπεύδω for the New English Translation of the Septuagint." In *Biblical Greek Language and Lexicography: Essays in Honor of Frederick W. Danker*, edited by Bernard A. Taylor et al., 136–48. Grand Rapids: Eerdmans, 2004.

Tertullian. "The Five Books Against Marcion." http://www.ccel.org/ccel/schaff/anf03.v.iv.i.html.

Thiselton, Anthony C. *Language: Liturgy and Meaning*. Bramcote, UK: Grove, 1975.

———. *New Horizons in Hermeneutics*. Grand Rapids: Zondervan, 1992.

Thoma, Clemens. "The High Priesthood in the Judgment of Josephus." In *Josephus, the Bible and History*. Edited by Louis Feldman and Gohei Hata. Leiden, Netherlands: Brill, 1989.

Thompson, John. *The Book of Jeremiah*. The New International Commentary on the Old Testament. Grand Rapids: Eerdmans, 1980.

Timayenis, Telemachus. *The Original Mr. Jacobs: A Startling Expose*. https://ia801407.us.archive.org/9/items/originalmrjacobootimgoog/originalmrjacobootimgoog.pdf.

Tonstad, Sigve K. *Saving God's Reputation: The Theological Function of Pistis Iesou in the Canonical Narratives of Revelation*. Library of New Testament Studies 337. Edited by Mark Goodacre. London: T & T Clark, 2006.

Torrey, Charles C. "The Foundry of the Second Temple at Jerusalem." *Journal of Biblical Literature* 55 (1936) 247–60.

Tran, Quang D. "Yahweh, the Bad Shepherd? Defamiliarization and Pastoral Symbolism in Zechariah 11:7–17." *The Expository Times* 126 (2015) 530–39.

Tritle, Lawrence. "Warfare in Herodotus." In *The Cambridge Companion to Herodotus*, edited by Carolyn Dewald and John Marincola, 209–23. Cambridge: Cambridge University Press, 2006.

Trivedi, Bijal P. "The Death of Herod Agrippa (New Research Reveals His Horrific Desease)." https://www.documentingreality.com/forum/f149/death-herod-agrippa-new-research-reveals-his-horrific.

Twelftree, Graeme. "Blasphemy." In *Dictionary of Jesus and the Gospels*, edited by Joel B. Green et al., 74–77. Downers Grove: InterVarsity, 1992.

Udoh, Fabian. "The Tale of an Unrighteous Slave (Luke 16:1–8[13])." *Journal of Biblical Literature* 128 (2009) 311–35.

Ukpong, Justin S. "The Parable of the Shrewd Manager (Luke 16:1–13): An Essay in Inculturation Biblical Hermeneutic." *Semeia* 73 (1996) 189–210.

Utley, Bob. *Luke the Historian: The Gospel of Luke*. Study Guide Commentary Series New Testament 3A. Marshall, TX: Bible Lessons International, 2004.

Vaggione, Richard P. "Over All Asia? The Extent of the Scythian Domination in Herodotus." *Journal of Biblical Literature* 92 (1973) 523–30.

van der Horst, Pieter W. "Silent Prayer in Antiquity." *Numen* 41 (1994) 1–25.

van der Veen, J. E. "A Minute's Mirth . . . Syloson and His Cloak in Herodotus." *Mnemosyne Fourth Series* 48 (1995) 129–45.

Van Henten, Jan Willem, "Dragon Myth and Imperial Ideology in Revelation 12–13." In *The Reality of Apocalypse. Rhetoric and Politics in the Book of Revelation*, edited by David L. Barr, 181–203. SBL Symposium Series 39. Atlanta: Society of Biblical Literature, 2006.

Van Holten, Wilko. "Hell and the Goodness of God." *Religious Studies* 35 (1999) 37–55.

Van Til, Kent A. "Three Anointings and One Offering: The Sinful Woman in Luke 7.36–50." *Journal of Pentecostal Theology* 15 (2006) 73–82.

Van Wees, Hans. *Greek Warfare: Myths and Realities*. Duckworth: London, 2004.

Van Wolde, Ellen. "Does 'innâ' Denote Rape? A Semantic Analysis of a Controversial Word." *Vetus Testamentum* 52 (2002) 528–44.

———. "A Text-Semantic Study of the Hebrew Bible, Illustrated with Noah and Job." *Journal of Biblical Literature* 113 (1994) 19–35.

Vanstiphout, Herman. "How and Why Did the Sumerians Create Their Gods?" In *What is a God? Anthropomorphic and Non-Anthropomorphic Aspects of Deity in Ancient Mesopotamia*, edited by Barbara Porter, 15–40. Casco Bay Assyriological Institute Vol 2. Winona Lake, IN: Eisenbrauns, 2009.

Vargon, Shmuel. "The Blind and the Lame." *Vetus Testamentum* 46 (1996) 498–514.

Vermes, Geza. *The Dead Sea Scrolls in English*. 4th ed. Sheffield, UK: Sheffield Academic, 1995.

Via, Dan O. "Ethical Responsibility and Human Wholeness in Matthew 25:31–46." *The Harvard Theological Review* 80 (1987) 79–100.

Voelz, James W. "The Greek of Codex Vaticanus in the Second Gospel and Marcan Greek." *Novum Testamentum* 47 (2005) 209–49.

Vogel, Dan. "Eve—The First Feminist: John Milton's Midrash on Genesis 3:6." *Jewish Bible Quarterly* 40 (2012) 19–24.

Von Seters, John, "Love and Death in the Court History of David." In *Love and Death in the Ancient Near East: Essays in Honour of Marvin H. Pope*, edited by John Marks and Robert Good, 121–24. Guildford, CT: Four Quarters, 1987.

Wagner, J. Ross. "Moses and Isaiah in Concert: Paul's Reading of Isaiah and Deuteronomy in the letter to the Romans." In *As Those Who Are Taught: The Interpretation of Isaiah from the LXX to the SBL*, edited by Claire Mathews McGinnis and Patricia K. Tull, 87–105. Society of Biblical Literature Symposium Series 27. Atlanta: Society of Biblical Literature, 2006.

Walker, Christopher, and Michael Dick. "The Mesopotamian Mīs Pî Ritual." In *The Induction of the Cult Image in Ancient Mesopotamia: The Mesopotamian Mīs Pî Ritual*, edited by Christopher Walker and Michael Dick, 1–31. Vol. 1 of State Archives of Assyria Ritual. Helsinki, Finland: The Neo-Assyrian Text Corpus Project, 2001.

Walsh, Jerome T. "Summons to Judgement: A Close Reading of Isaiah XLI 1–20." *Vetus Testamentum* 43 (1993) 351–71.

Walters, Kerry S. "Hell, This Isn't Necessary After All." *International Journal for Philosophy of Religion* 29 (1991) 175–86.

Watts, J. D. W. *Isaiah 1–33*. WORD 24. Dallas: Word, 1985.

——— . *Isaiah 34–66*. WORD 25. Dallas: Word, 1987.

Watts, Rikk E. "Mark." In *Commentary on the New Testament Use of the Old Testament*, edited by Gregory Beale and Don Carson, 111–249. Grand Rapids: Baker Academic, 2007.

Weaver, Darlene F. "Taking Sin Seriously." *The Journal of Religious Ethics* 31 (2003) 45–74.

Webster, John. "Introduction." In *The Cambridge Companion to Karl Barth*, edited by John Webster, 1–16. Cambridge: Cambridge University Press, 2000.

Weeden, Theodore. *Mark: Traditions in Conflict*. Philadelphia: Fortress, 1971.

Weima, Jeffrey A. D. "1–2 Thessalonians." In *Commentary on the New Testament Use of the Old Testament*, edited by Gregory Beale and Don Carson, 871–89. Grand Rapids: Baker Academic, 2007.

Weitzman, Steven. "David's Lament and the Poetics of Grief in 2 Samuel." *The Jewish Quarterly Review New Series* 85 (1995) 341–60.

——— . "Lessons from the Dying: The Role of Deuteronomy 32 in Its Narrative Setting." *The Harvard Theological Review* 87 (1994) 377–93.

Wenham, David and A. D. A. Moses. "'There Are Some Standing Here....': Did They Become the 'Reputed Pillars' of the Jerusalem Church? Some Reflections on Mark 9:1, Galatians 2:9 and the Transfiguration." *Novum Testamentum* 36 (1994) 146–63.

Wenham, Gordon J. *Genesis 1–15*. WORD 1. Dallas: Word, 1987.

——— . *Genesis 16–50*. WORD 2. Dallas: Word, 1994.

Wesselius, Jan-Wim. "Joab's Death and the Central Theme of the Succession Narrative (2 Samuel IX–1 Kings II)." *Vetus Testamentum* 40 (1990) 336–51.

Whitlark, Jason A., and Mikael C. Parsons. "The 'Seven' Last Words: A Numerical Motivation for the Insertion of Luke 23.34a." *New Testament Studies* 52 (2006) 188–204.

Wiersbe, Warren W. *Classic Sermons on Judas Iscariot*. Kregel Classic Sermons. Grand Rapids: Kregel, 1995.

Wierzbicka, Anna. *What Did Jesus Mean?* Oxford: Oxford University Press, 2001.

Wilcock, Michael. *The Message of Chronicles*. The Bible Speaks Today: Old Testament. Edited by J. A. Motyer. Leicester, UK: InterVarsity, 1987.

Wilhite, David E. *Tertullian the African: An Anthropological Reading of Tertullian's Context and Identities*. Millennium Studies 14. Edited by Wolfram Brandes et al. Berlin: Walter de Gruyter, 2007.

Williams, Anthony J. "The Mythological Background of Ezekiel 28:12–19?" *Biblical Theology Bulletin: A Journal of Bible and Theology* 6 (1976) 49–61.

Williams, David J. *Acts*. New International Biblical Commentary 6. Peabody, MA: Hendrickson, 1995.

Willis, Wendell Lee. *Idol Meat in Corinth: The Pauline Argument in 1 Corinthians 8 and 10*. Society of Biblical Literature Dissertation Series 68. Chico, CA: Scholars, 1985.

Wilson, Robert R. "The Death of the King of Tyre: The Editorial History of Ezekiel 28." In *Love and Death in the Ancient Near East: Essays in Honour of Marvin H. Pope*, edited by John Marks and Robert Good, 211–18. Guildford, CT: Four Quarters, 1987.

Winiarski, Catherine E. "Adultery, Idolatry, and the Subject of Monotheism." *Religion & Literature* 38 (2006) 41–63.

Wink, Walter. *Naming the Powers: The Language of Power in the New Testament*. Vol. 1 of The Powers. Philadelphia: Fortress, 1984.

———. *Unmasking the Powers: The Invisible Powers that Determine Human Existence*. Vol. 2 of The Powers. Philadelphia: Fortress, 1986.

Wright, Christopher J. H. "The Righteous Rich in the Old Testament." *Evangelical Review of Theology* 35 (2011) 255–64.

Wright, David P. "Ritual Analogy in Psalm 109." *Journal of Biblical Literature* 113 (1994) 385–404.

Wright, Jacob L. "Warfare and Wanton Destruction: A Reexamination of Deuteronomy 20:19–20 in Relation to Ancient Siegecraft." *Journal of Biblical Literature* 127 (2008) 423–58.

Wright, John W. "The Founding Father: The Structure of the Chronicler's David Narrative." *Journal of Biblical Literature* 117 (1998) 45–59.

Wright, Nigel T. *Judas and the Gospel of Jesus: Have We Missed the Truth About Christianity?* Grand Rapids: Baker, 2006.

———. *The Last Word: Beyond the Bible Wars to a New Understanding of the Authority of Scripture*. New York: HarperCollins, 2005.

Wright, Stephen. "Debtors, Laborers and Virgins: The Voice of Jesus and the Voice of Matthew in Three Parables." In *Jesus and Paul: Global Perspectives in Honor of James D. G. Dunn for his 70th Birthday*. Edited by B. J. Oropeza et al., 13–23. Library of New Testament Studies 414. London: T & T Clark, 2009.

Xavier, Aloysius. "Judas Iscariot in the Fourth Gospel: A Paradigm of Lost Discipleship." *Indian Theological Studies* 32 (1995) 250–58.

Xenophon. *Institutio Cyri*. Edited by L. Dindorfius. Leipzig, Germany: Teubner, 1880.

———. *Opera Omnia*. Vols 1–2 of Scriptorum Classicorum Bibliotheca Oxoniensis. Edited by E. C. Marchant. Oxford: Oxford University Press, 1900.

Yadin, Azzan. "Goliath's Armor and Israelite Collective Memory." *Vetus Testamentum* 54 (2004) 373–95.

———. "קוֹל as Hypostasis in the Hebrew Bible." *Journal of Biblical Literature* 122 (2003) 601–26.

———. "Samson's ḥîdâ." *Vetus Testamentum* 52 (2002) 407–26.

Yamasaki, Gary. "Point of View in a Gospel Story: What Difference Does It Make? Luke 19:1–10 as a Test Case." *Journal of Biblical Literature* 125 (2006) 89–105.

Young, F. W. "Wealth." In *The Interpreter's Dictionary of the Bible* 4, edited by George A. Buttrick, 818–19. Nashville: Abingdon, 1962.

Young, Ian M. "Israelite Literacy: Interpreting the Evidence: Part I." *Vetus Testamentum* 48 (1998) 239–53.

Zehnder, Christopher. "What Does It Mean to 'Serve Mammon'?" *New Oxford Review* (2012) 34–37.

Zwiep, Arie W. "Judas and the Choice of Matthias: A Study on the Context and Concern of Acts 1:15–26." PhD diss., Wissenschaftliche Untersuchungen zum Neuen Testament 187. Tübingen, Germany: Mohr, 2004.

———. "Judas and the Jews: Anti-Semitic Interpretation of Judas Iscariot, Past and Present." In *Jesus and Paul: Global Perspectives in Honor of James D. G. Dunn for his 70th Birthday.* Edited by B. J. Oropeza et al., 72–82. Library of New Testament Studies 414. London: T & T Clark, 2009.

Index of Authors

Abramson, G., 58.
Ackerman, J., 60.
Ackerman, S., 49, 53.
Adams, K., 99, 100.
Aghiorgoussis, M., 118.
Ahearne-Kroll, S., 102, 103, 158.
Aimers, G., 33, 111, 112, 113.
Aland, K et al., 199, 210.
Allen, L., 33, 35, 76, 99, 139, 140, 212, 226.
Allison, D., 9, 146, 156.
Anderson, A., 53, 54, 55, 56, 58, 60, 108, 134, 215.
Anderson, G., 73, 77.
Anderson, P., 174.
Arbel, D., 74.
Arnal, W., 143, 149.
Asheri, D.; Lloyd, A. and Corcella, A., 24, 25.
Aune, D., 87, 115, 118, 119, 142.
Aus, R., 83, 84.
Avioz, M., 52, 54, 60.

Baker, D., 31, 32, 34, 35, 60, 130, 131, 133, 134, 208.
Balla, P., 94, 141.
Bammel, E. and Hauck, F., 134, 141, 143, 144, 145.
Baragwanath, E., 24.
Barclay, J.M.G., 37.
Barker, M., 71, 109, 111, 114, 117.
Barnett, P . . . 118, 119, 187.
Barr, J., 22, 73, 74, 75, 77.
Barrett, A., 62.
Barrett, C. K., 136.
Barth, K., 1, 5, 6, 7, 12, 14, 16, 17, 18.

Bartlett, J., 27.
Barton, S., 39, 134, 143, 144, 149, 183, 190.
Baruchi-Unna, A., 32.
Bauckham, R., 2, 145, 162, 192.
Baxter, W., 205.
Beale, G. K., 69.
Beale, G. K. and McDonough, S.M., 118.
Beasley-Murray, G., 117, 118, 119, 142, 193, 195, 208, 209, 213, 214.
Beavis, M., 39, 41, 144, 149, 150, 151, 155, 158, 159, 172, 202, 207.
Bellemore, J., 26, 28.
Ben-Dov, J., 134, 140.
Bertoluci, J., 74, 78.
Best, E., 40.
Biddle, M., 57.
Biguzzi, G., 117.
Blenkinsopp, J., 53, 55, 58.
Blevins, J., 117, 118.
Bligh, P., 189.
Blomberg, C., 169, 188, 189, 211, 212.
Bock, D.L., 40, 74, 101, 102, 142, 155, 157, 166, 185, 193, 207.
Boden, P., 88, 90, 221.
Bodner, K., 114.
Bolt, P., 144, 184, 185.
Bond, H., 41, 97, 169, 185, 203, 209.
Bovell, C., 71.
Bovon, F., 41, 168, 176, 191, 201, 206.
Boyd-Taylor, C., 36.
Branden, R., 40, 104, 109, 122, 176.
Brant, J., 107, 183, 192, 206, 209, 210, 229.
Braun, R., 108, 109, 131.

Brenk, F., 97.
Breyer, C., 144.
Brondos, D., 17.
Brown, D., 85, 107.
Brown, M., 141.
Brown, R. E., 40, 196, 229.
Bruce, FF., 80, 81, 83, 84, 145.
Brueggemann, W., 139.
Budd, P., 93.
Bultmann, R., 85.
Bunta, S., 77.
Busch, A., 103, 158.

Caird, GB., 117, 124.
Calhoun, G., 24.
Cane, A., 1, 5, 14, 15, 16, 17, 18, 231.
Capper, B., 141, 146, 150, 167.
Carasik, M., 60.
Carlson, S., 155.
Carr, D., 76.
Carson, D.A., 16, 33, 113, 147, 195, 196, 228, 229.
Casey, M., 8.
Charlesworth, J., 72, 73, 101, 187.
Childs, B., 36, 68, 69, 89.
Christensen, D., 29, 30, 92, 99, 132, 133, 196.
Clines. D.J.A., 110, 111, 112.
Cohen, E., 44, 45.
Collins, A., 115, 117, 119, 121, 122, 203, 205.
Collins, R.F., 202.
Comfort, P.W., 90, 95.
Cooper, L., 76.
Corner, S., 44.
Cosgrove, C., 82.
Craigie, P., 76, 92, 132, 138, 139, 140, 196.
Craigie, P.; Kelley, P. and Drinkard, J., 139.
Cranfield, C.E.B., 142.
Cripps, K., 179.
Cross, F. M., 126.
Crossan, J.D., 8.

D'Angelo, M., 136.
Daube, D., 53, 54, 58, 59, 210, 215.
Davids, P., 142, 147.
Davies, W.D., 179.

Davies, W.D. and Allison, D.C., 41, 42, 104, 116, 146, 161, 165, 172, 179, 180, 188, 199, 206, 212.
Day, P., 107, 109.
Delamarter, S., 132, 138.
Derrett, J. D., 174.
De Voragine, J., 24.
DeVries, S., 59, 114.
Dewald, C., 24.
Dick, M., 86, 87, 88, 89.
Dickerson, P., 79, 80.
Dillard, R., 138, 139.
Dindorfius, L., 9.
Dixon, E., 203.
Domeris, W., 132, 139, 140, 141, 212.
Donahue, J., 174, 178, 184, 189, 203.
Dowd, S. & Malbon, E. S., 214.
Downs, D., 142, 143.
Duke, P., 195.
Duling, D., 82.
Dunn, J D. G., 37, 145.
Durham, J., 92, 140.

Eberts, Jr., H W., 136.
Edwards, J., 53, 187, 189, 193, 194, 234.
Ellingworth, P., 141, 145, 147, 157.
Elliott, J. H., 179.
Emerton, J. A., 52.
Eslinger, L., 71.
Evans, C., 171, 172, 178, 184, 185, 198, 204.
Eynikel, E. and Hauspie, K., 72.

Farmer, W., 156.
Fee, Gordon D., 101.
Fekkes, J., 115, 116, 121.
Feldman, L., 93.
Ferda, T., 226.
Fernando, A., 79, 80, 81, 83, 135, 136, 138, 171.
Ferreiro, A., 80.
Fidler, R., 130.
Fitzgerald, J. T., 173.
Fitzmyer, J.A., 40, 41, 115, 134, 162, 180, 191, 201, 210.
Fleming, D., 110.
Flint, V. et al., 97.
Fossum, J.E., 79.
Foster, P., 156.

INDEX OF AUTHORS

Foster, R., 140, 212, 214.
Fotopoulos, J., 95, 96, 98, 227.
France, R.T., 40, 102, 103, 104, 120, 141, 144, 155, 157, 158, 159, 164, 167, 168, 170, 174, 175, 178, 183, 184, 185, 187, 188, 198, 200, 209, 230.
Franke, C., 69, 89.
Frankel, D., 33.
Freedman, D. N., 57.
Friesen, G., 117.
Furnish, V.P., 37, 38, 142, 143.
Furstenberg, Y., 94.
Fusco, V., 185.

Gagnon, R., 80, 136.
Galpaz-Feller, P., 46, 47, 50, 51, 52.
Garrett, S. R., 39, 41, 74, 76, 79, 80, 81, 82, 84, 135, 137, 155, 209.
Gaston, L., 102.
Georgia, A., 192.
Gerhardsson, B., 156.
Gilbert, G., 61.
Glancy, J., 39, 42, 180.
Gockel, M., 7.
Goddard, C., 22.
Goering, G., 74, 75.
Goldingay, J., 35, 80, 83.
Goldingay, J. E. and Wright, C. J. H., 92, 94.
Good, D., 159.
Goodacre, M., 155, 156, 161, 171.
Goulder, M., 70, 89, 160.
Grabiner, S., 76, 110, 112, 115, 117, 123.
Grassi, J., 183.
Gray, P., 69, 70.
Greenberg, G., 1, 5, 6, 8, 9, 17, 18, 21, 22, 218.
Greenspahn, F., 86, 90.
Grindheim, S., 179, 188, 189.
Grossman, A., 45.
Grudem, W., 16.
Gruen, E., 92, 93.
Gruenwald, I., 92.
Grundmann, W., 19, 79.
Guelich, R., 102, 103, 120, 155, 157, 158, 161, 162, 164, 167, 168, 170, 184, 185, 203.
Guillaume, P., 111.

Gujarro, S. and Rodríguez, A., 192, 193.
Gunn, D., 47.
Gunton, C., 6.

Habel, N., 110, 133.
Hagner, D., 42, 104, 127, 141, 144, 146, 148, 149, 161, 165, 169, 170, 171, 172, 179, 180, 188, 189, 190, 205, 209, 213.
Hahn, S and Bergsma, J., 93, 99.
Harb, G., 175.
Hartley, J., 47.
Hauck, F., 140, 141.
Havrelock, R., 76, 77.
Hawkin, D., 157, 164, 165.
Hawthorne, G.F., 39.
Hays, C., 143.
Hendriksen, W., 179, 212, 213.
Hepner, G., 54.
Hertzberg, H.W., 59, 131, 139.
Hill, A., 132.
Hobbs, T.R., 140.
Holst, R., 192, 193.
Holter, K., 68, 69, 88, 89, 220.
Homsher, R., 76, 122, 123.
Hood, J., 143, 148, 186, 188.
Hoppe, L., 130, 131, 132, 133, 134, 139, 140, 141, 142, 143, 144, 146, 147, 148.
Horsley, R., 101, 102, 114, 133, 140, 144, 145, 148, 151, 160, 180.
Huggins, R., 156, 175.
Hughes, P.E., 38.
Humphrey, E., 118, 126.
Hunsinger, G., 7.
Hunt, P., 25.
Hurtado, L.W., 37.

Ilan, T. and Price, J., 62.

Jacobsen, T., 86.
Janowitz, N., 86.
Janzen, D., 59.
Janzen, W., 56, 112, 215.
Japhet, S., 109.
Jebb, R. 24.
Johnson, L.T., 37, 41, 43, 70, 80, 82, 135, 136, 143, 162, 187.
Johnson, W., 22.

Jones, A. H., 62.
Joosten, J., 98.

Kalimi, I., 57.
Kamell, M., 142,147.
Kaye, B. N., 83.
Kazen, T., 136.
Keener, C., 37, 39, 40, 105, 116, 148, 149, 160, 165, 168, 171, 172, 176, 179, 180, 186, 188, 189, 190, 195, 196, 200, 202, 209, 212, 213, 214, 216, 219, 230, 235.
Kelhoffer, J., 47.
Kelly, H.A., 72, 84, 104, 107, 108, 109, 110, 112, 115, 135.
Kelly, JND., 16.
Kelley, N., 28, 63.
Kennedy, J. 86.
Kent, G., 191, 192.
Keown, G. L.; Scalise, P. J. and Smothers, T. G., 34.
Kerkeslager, A., 83.
Kidner, D., 130.
King, F., 16, 28, 43, 44, 65, 115, 137, 195, 198, 207, 210, 229.
Kingsbury, J., 188.
Kittel, G. and Friedrich, G., 22, 141.
Klassen, W., 1, 5, 9, 10, 11, 17, 18, 21, 22, 25, 26, 28, 44, 66, 83, 112, 163, 169, 178, 197, 198, 199, 200, 211, 212, 213, 214, 218.
Klauck, H-J., 1, 5, 11, 12, 13, 14, 17, 18.
Klawans, J., 99.
Klein, R., 31, 87.
Kleist, J.A., 3.
Knoppers, G., 132.
Konstan, D., 45.
Kostenberger., 37, 195.
Kovacs, J., 124, 229.
Kraemer, R., 81, 158.
Kruse, C., 37, 38, 144.
Kuecker, A., 40.

Laato, A., 69.
Lachs, S., 179.
Lacocque, A., 111.
Ladd, G.E., 95, 117, 118, 119, 124, 127.
Lamarche, P., 214.
Lane, W., 144, 147, 158.

Landry, D. and May, B., 150, 151.
Launderville, D., 73, 78.
Lee, G., 45.
Lee, J. A. L., 23, 37, 41, 188.
Leech, G., 22.
Leeming, D., 50.
Leloup, J-Y., 1, 17.
Lemos, T., 52.
Levine, N., 73.
Levinson, B., 93.
Lewis, T., 99.
Liddell, H.G. and Scott, R., 21, 23, 44.
Lindsay, M., 6, 7.
Ling, T., 110.
Linnemann, E., 155.
Loftus, F., 26.
Longenecker, R.N., 38, 95, 145, 212.
Lorton, D., 88.
Louw, J. and Nida, E., 19, 23.
Lowery, R., 87, 132.
Luck, G., 34, 97, 102.
Lynch, C., 146.

Macaskill, G., 87.
Maccoby, H., 1, 5, 6, 7, 12, 16, 17, 18, 44.
MacKinnon, D.M., 14, 17, 209.
Malbon, E., 160, 164.
Malina, B., 110.
Mann, C.S., 150.
Marcus, J., 187.
Maritz, P., 1, 2, 44, 84, 183, 193, 208.
Marshall, I.H., 70, 79, 81, 134, 136, 151, 162, 176, 187, 188, 190, 224.
Martin, M., 157, 196.
Martin, R., 37, 38, 39, 84, 142, 147.
Mason, S., 91, 96, 97, 98.
May, G., 70, 71, 73, 77. 78.
Mays, J., 140.
Mazar, B., 215.
McCabe, D., 79, 80, 135, 137.
McCormack, B., 6.
McGarry, E., 212, 214.
McKnight, S., 155.
McKnight S. and Modica, J., 207.
Meier, John P., 12, 153, 156, 167, 229.
Merenlahti, P., 169.
Metzger, M., 4.
Michaels, J. R., 16.

Miller, J., 100.
Miller, M., 45.
Miller, P., 99.
Miller, Stuart., 28.
Minear, P., 117, 119, 120, 157, 173.
Mitchell, A., 136.
Moberly, R. W. L., 71, 73.
Moessner, D., 167, 173.
Moloney, F., 172, 197.
Monro, H., 1, 17.
Moore, G.F., 27, 31, 32, 47, 48, 49, 50.
Morris, L., 117, 118, 119, 123, 124, 142, 195, 196.
Morriston, W., 111.
Mounce, R., 117, 118.
Mounce, W., 141, 142, 143.
Mowery, R., 205.
Moyer, C., 34.
Muller, Jac. J., 142.
Müller, M., 155.
Munro, W., 191, 192, 193.
Murphy, R., 34, 139.
Myers, B., 140,
Myers, C., 102, 144, 145, 155, 157, 159, 160, 167, 168, 171, 175, 177.

Nasrallah, L., 70, 82.
Neer, R., 24.
Newman, B., 29.
Newsom, C., 76, 77.
Nickelsburg, G., 192, 193.
Niditch, S., 29, 30, 31, 33, 34, 43, 46, 47, 48, 50, 51, 56, 58, 125.
Noble, Paul R., 46.
Nolland, J., 105, 115, 130, 134, 141, 142, 143, 146, 150, 151, 161, 162, 166, 168, 170, 171, 173, 176, 190, 200, 209, 210, 224, 230.
Nugent, J., 132.
Nürnberger, K., 86.

O'Brien, P., 142, 145.
Olyan, S. M., 64.
Oropeza, B.J., 15, 135, 158, 168, 169, 179, 186, 198, 201, 208, 209, 229, 230.
Osborn, E., 3.
Osborne, G., 156.

Paffenroth, K., 5.
Page, S., 72, 73, 78, 96, 98, 99, 102, 103, 105, 108, 109, 110, 113, 114, 120, 187, 191, 227, 234.
Pagels, E., 72, 85, 86, 87, 109, 117, 187, 189, 191, 195, 209, 231.
Pao, D.W., 18, 19, 67, 68, 69, 70, 80, 83, 201, 220, 235.
Pao, D.W. and Schnabel, E.J., 115, 134, 143, 151.
Park, E-C., 116, 122.
Parsenios, G., 183.
Parsons, M., 79, 80, 82, 83, 134, 150, 166, 191, 210.
Pataki, A., 117, 122.
Patmore, H., 73, 77, 78.
Patrick, D., 69, 92.
Patterson, S., 143.
Pelham, A., 111.
Pelling, C., 25.
Petersen, N., 164.
Pierce, M., 30, 125, 131.
Pilgrim, W., 135, 144, 150.
Porter, B., 90.
Pressler, C., 46, 47, 48, 50, 52.
Price, J., 62.

Raabe, P., 100.
Redding, J., 123.
Reece, G., 97.
Rendsburg, G.A., 46.
Resseguie, J.L., 117, 124, 142, 144, 158, 161, 162, 167, 171, 174, 183, 193, 234.
Ridderbos, H., 187, 195, 196, 214, 228, 229.
Roberts, T., 22.
Rodd, C., 111, 113, 132, 211.
Rogerson, J., 32, 33, 36, 113.
Rosner, B., 70, 89, 92, 100.
Rousseau, A. and Doutreleau, L., 3.
Rudman, D., 68, 69.

Sandiyagu, V., 19, 91.
Schiffman, L., 28.
Schipper, J., 55, 56.
Schmidt, T.E., 142, 143.
Schneider, S. and Seelenfreund, M., 70.
Schultz, B., 156, 187, 210.

Schwartz, S., 26, 27.
Seifrid, M., 37.
Sellew, P., 131, 150, 191, 192.
Seward, D., 26, 27, 28.
Shepkaru, S., 64.
Sherlock, C., 110, 112, 113, 114, 120, 124, 125, 126, 127, 128.
Sherwin, S., 89.
Sievers, J., 26.
Siew, A., 116, 117, 118, 120, 121, 122.
Siker, J., 199.
Silva, M., 22.
Sim, D., 42, 116, 122, 128, 147, 188, 189, 205.
Smit, J., 95, 96, 227.
Smith, David., 35, 112, 135, 136, 141, 200.
Smith, Dennis., 134, 173, 176, 192.
Smith, Mark D., 116.
Smith, R., 32, 110, 112, 113, 118, 212, 214.
Snow, D. and Pearlman, J., 1.
Soggin, J. A., 27, 31, 32, 47, 48, 49.
Sowers, S., 117.
Spät, E., 80.
Stagakis, G., 44.
Stassen, G., 148, 149.
Steinmann, A., 112.
Sterling, G., 135, 136.
Still, E. C., 96.
Stokes, R., 108, 109, 110, 111.
Stuart, D., 75, 99, 140.
Sweeney, M., 54, 132, 133.

Talbert, C., 212.
Talbott, T., 189, 190.
Tan, P., 121.
Tasker, RVG., 179.
Tate, M., 141.
Tavo, F., 116, 117, 119, 126.
Taylor, B., 34, 45.
Thoma, C., 25.
Thompson, J.A., 140.
Timayenis, T.T., 1, 17.
Tonstad, S., 75, 76, 119, 124, 128.
Torrey, C. C., 212.
Tran, Q., 213.
Tritle, L., 24.
Trivedi, B., 82.

Twelftree, G., 158, 208.

Udoh, F., 150.
Ukpong, J., 150.

Vaggione, R., 24.
Van der Horst, P., 63.
Van der Veen, J. E., 24.
Van Til, K., 191, 192.
Van Wees, Hans., 25.
Van Wolde, E., 54.
Vanstiphout, H., 90.
Vargon, S., 56.
Via, D., 186, 189.
Vermes, G., 89.
Von Seters, J., 57, 58.

Walker, C. and Dick, M., 87, 88, 89.
Walsh, J., 69.
Walters, K., 190.
Watts, J., 68, 69, 99, 116, 139, 197.
Watts, R., 40, 41, 104, 165, 230.
Weima, J., 83.
Weitzman, S., 34, 57, 58, 93, 99, 131.
Wenham, G., 71, 130, 131.
Wesselius, J. W., 53, 54, 57, 58, 59, 60.
Whitlark, J. & M. Parsons, 209.
Wilcock, M., 138.
Williams, A., 73, 76.
Williams, D., 69, 70, 80, 81, 82, 134, 135, 136, 137, 230.
Willis, W.L., 96, 98, 99, 227.
Wilson, RR., 74, 75, 76.
Winiarski, C., 92, 93.
Wink, W., 79, 95, 96, 108, 110, 112, 113, 124, 146.
Wright, C., 130.
Wright, Jacob L, 30.
Wright, S., 42, 179, 189.

Xavier, A.,196.

Yadin, A., 47.
Young, F. W., 130, 133, 134.

Zehnder, C., 134, 141, 143, 146, 147.
Zwiep, A., 7, 13, 60, 149, 204, 215, 217, 229, 230, 231.

Index of Major Passages

OLD TESTAMENT

Genesis
1	70, 71, 84
2-3	73, 76, 77
3	70, 71, 72, 84, 117

Exodus
20	91, 92

Numbers
22-23	33, 109
25	92, 93, 99,

Deuteronomy
1	31, 73
2	30
5	17, 91, 93
17	132, 133
19	30, 43
20	29
22	54
24	92, 140, 147, 196, 223
32	89, 95, 98, 99, 106, 152, 226

Judges
6	10, 32
13	48, 50
14	47, 48, 51, 52
15	27, 43, 46, 47, 48, 50, 51, 52
16	35, 46, 49, 50, 51, 52

2 Samuel
2	58
3	58
9	56
12	53, 60
13	53, 54, 55
15	55, 60
16	45, 55, 56, 59
17	56
24	108, 109

1 Kings
2	55, 58, 59, 61, 108
11	91, 131, 132, 133
22	108, 113, 114, 115

1 Chronicles
21	108, 109, 110, 122, 126

2 Chronicles
32	30, 139

Job
1	40, 108, 111, 112, 115, 126, 128, 133
2	35, 109, 111, 112, 115, 126
42	110, 133

Isaiah

14	76, 82, 116
26	118, 122
40	19, 68
41	69, 201
42	68, 70, 201
44	68, 69, 86, 88, 89
45	32, 69
46	89
65	99
66	116, 117, 122

Jeremiah

19	212

Ezekiel

28	73-83, 84, 221

Zechariah

3	84, 107, 108, 109, 110, 112, 113, 115, 126, 128
11	140, 211-214, 236

NEW TESTAMENT

Matthew

2	115, 116, 122, 129, 222, 229
5	143, 148, 223
6	95, 127, 146, 147, 148, 149, 152, 223, 224
10: 1-4	160-161
10: 5-10	167-170
12:22-37	104-105, 106, 119, 224
13: 10-23	119, 141, 165
14: 13-21	170-172
18: 1-6	175-176
20: 17-19	178-180
23	187, 188, 199, 214
25	22, 23, 39, 65, 187-190
26-27	39, 207-208
26: 3-5	186-190
26: 6-13	191-193, 194
26: 17-30	197, 198-200, 219
26: 47-56	44, 205-206, 208-211, 220, 222
27: 1-10	211-214

Mark

1	202
3: 13-19	157-160,
3:20-30	102-104
4: 10-33	164-165
6: 6b-13	167-170
6: 30-44	170-172
9: 33-37	174-175
10: 32-34	177-178
12	183
14: 1-2	182-186
14: 3-9	191-193
14: 12-26	197-198
14: 43-50	202-204, 208-211

Luke

6: 12-16	161-163
7: 36-50	191-192, 216
8: 9-15	166
9: 1-6	167-170
9: 10-17	173
9: 46-48	176-177
11:14-26	105
16	149-151
18: 31-33	180
22: 1-6	190-191
22: 7-23	197, 200-201
22: 47-53	206, 208-211

John

12: 1-8	191-193, 194-197

Acts

1: 15-26	215-216
5	135-138
8	79-81
12	81-83

1 Corinthians
8	94-96
10	94-96

2 Thessalonians
2	83-84

James
5	147, 152, 231

1 Peter
3	16

Revelation
2	94, 95
12	115-124
20	124-128

NON-BIBLICAL REFERENCES

Herodotus	24, 25, 90, 97, 212, 225
Xenophon	9, 24, 25, 96, 97, 101, 225
Josephus	25-28, 61-65, 91, 97-98,
Irenaeus	3, 5
Tertullian	4, 5